Rocking with the Reaper

An Unplanned Journey
into Mindfulness

JAYNE PIGFORD

with poems by Arthur Downs

Some of the proceeds from the sale of this book
will go to renal charities

Published by Goldcrest Books International Ltd
www.goldcrestbooks.com
publish@goldcrestbooks.com

ISBN: 978-1-911505-94-5
eISBN: 978-1-911505-95-2

For William and Betty,
my amazing, resilient parents

Chapter One
The Princess Is Cast Into Hell

"Change your life today. Don't gamble on the future, act now, without delay."

Simone de Beauvoir

People who've heard about my twenty years of health nightmares but don't know me well often greet me with a furrowed brow as they ask, "How *are* you?" When I reply, "I'm good, thanks," with a beaming smile, their doubtful faces make me wonder whether I'm in denial about my precarious situation or quite possibly as mad as a badger. Just like when I thought *that was the best* (as well as the worst) *thing that ever happened to me* when I came out of a bloody, seven-month wrestle with death in hospital. Or when I was given some heavy duty medication which could "either kill or cure" me, then sat in my big, green hospital chair feeling like a Cheshire cat with salmon *and* cream. Don't get me wrong, I have my storm cloud moments when death's thunderous bellows and electric fury lash me to my knees but, so far, despite everything I've been, and am still going through, the frenzied clouds keep passing and I find myself whistling again. My dance (rock) with the terrifying Reaper has taught me just how phenomenal our human spirit is and how to feel alive! It's also convinced me that we're not worthless sinners, but creatures with heart – and great potential...

My life fell apart in 1998. I was thirty-one and a lively, attractive (not that I really knew that) and energetic woman living in Nottingham in the UK's Midlands. I had good friends, my own home, (well it would be when I'd paid the bank £128,000 for my £42,000 mortgage), a sweet tabby cat who had appeared on my sofa one morning and a lovely new bloke. My passions were dancing, playing tennis and bounding round a basketball court with work colleagues on Tuesday evenings; being sporty was a big part of my life and identity. In my work as a child protection social worker I enjoyed the camaraderie of my colleagues and the challenge of my role; I was a superhero, flying from crisis to crisis in a bid to save wounded children at risk of harm and neglect! Needless to say, the job was also very stressful; I had a massive caseload and lived in constant fear of a child being seriously injured or killed. I'd also just finished the second of a four year, part-time MSc in Gestalt psychotherapy, another huge pressure and emotional rollercoaster. I knew that I was burning my candle at both ends and had asked if I could reduce my working week to four days but I was refused and so in the spirit of my family's stoic and uncomplaining manner, just got on with it and gave little further thought to my fried nerves and weary body. In the habit of being a 'good,' driven perfectionist, I continued to give my all and rarely had time off work so when I developed a burning bellyache, it felt indulgent to be flopped on my sofa for a week, snoozing and watching daytime TV. A locum GP had diagnosed a bladder infection and given me antibiotics but when I was becoming ever more exhausted, a second doctor sent me to the hospital. After preliminary blood tests and a lot of waiting, I was directed into a six-bedded ward and told to get undressed. The self-important, hyperactive princess in me was not impressed.

"Is this bloody thing supposed to gape open at the back and show everyone my backside?" I snarled as I was swallowed whole by a tent-sized cotton 'gown'.

"Don't worry," replied the cheery, pony-tailed nurse, "You need to get into bed anyway."

"You must be joking, I've got a case conference report to write!"

"To be honest, you look a bit pale and like you need some rest."

"I'm fine! Anyway I haven't time to rest 'cause this report has to be in for Monday."

"Well here's a side table; it goes across your bed."

"I've just got belly-ache, I don't need to lie in blooming bed!"

"Come on now, it's doctor's orders. That's just the way it is." I gave her a vicious prod with my evil eye and ranted "Yes and look at the state of the world because of 'that's just the way it is' attitudes!" As she looked at me as if I were insane and possibly dangerous, I shoved my flat brown boots, boot-cut jeans and muted pink 'hoody' into the wooden bedside cabinet. Trying to breathe deeply I climbed onto the hard mattress and she 'left me to rest' but my feeble attempt to relax lasted about a minute; as I wrestled with the baffling complexities of my bed's electronic mechanisms, which lifted and lowered both my head and feet, my fear and shock again erupted in anger: "You bloody stupid pile of mechanical shite..." The bed calmly retaliated by sloping me distinctly head-downwards. Little did I know how grateful I would soon be for that electrical assistance in sitting up.

Once I'd slid myself down over the infantilizing crinkles of a plastic sheet and my belly pain had eased off a bit, my nose became aware of the overpowering stench. Thick, nauseating waves of urine, faeces, vomit and throat-stinging sterile fluid; the grotesque aromas of sickness and death. Then my brain registered the noise. It was unbelievable. This was a place where sick people were supposed to be healing but there were machines and call buttons beeping and buzzing all over the place, *the dring, dringing* of phones, doors slamming, tea, medicine and equipment trolleys clattering, bins banging, heels clopping, taps gushing, patients moaning and a confusing buzz of layer upon layer of chattering voices. And this was before visiting time, when the booming assault got even worse.

When a nurse whisked back the curtain around my bed, visual chaos was added to the mix; a host of different people were scuttling up and down the ward. I presumed those with ties and stethoscopes round their necks were doctors and that the different shades of blue and beige uniforms symbolized a hierarchy of nurses. The chaos suddenly turned into a haunting, tunnelled silence as my attention locked onto the gaunt, older woman in the opposite bed who was crumpled into a pile of pillows with a bloody dressing stuck to her bony neck. As I took in her stark vulnerability, all I felt was lip-curling disgust and when she opened her eyes and caught me staring, I just looked away, no doubt making her feel crap. Not wanting to engage with any more sickness, I gritted my teeth against my pain and wriggled from the bed to pull back round the brown, flowered curtain (designed to disguise any blood stains, I would later learn from a mischievously macabre nurse). I felt relief as I blanked out the woman's frightened eyes and the fleeting image I'd glimpsed of a hooded Death sitting cross-legged in the big green chair beside her. It also felt good to have the curtain between me and the ward's four other fragile older women, who, in my tense, 'armoured' state, I found frightening and slightly repulsive; I was young, athletic and independent, they were wrinkled, sick and nothing like me!

Back in my curtained cocoon, I didn't understand that fear of my own vulnerability and inevitable ageing (and my arrogance) was getting in the way of my compassion, and my brain slipped into its default position of guilt and self-criticism.

Oh God, I'm such a bitch! So much for being a right-on social worker! Mmm, maybe the chapel's pastor's right and I am just a cold, heinous sinner who was born bad to the core, maybe I...Oh shit!

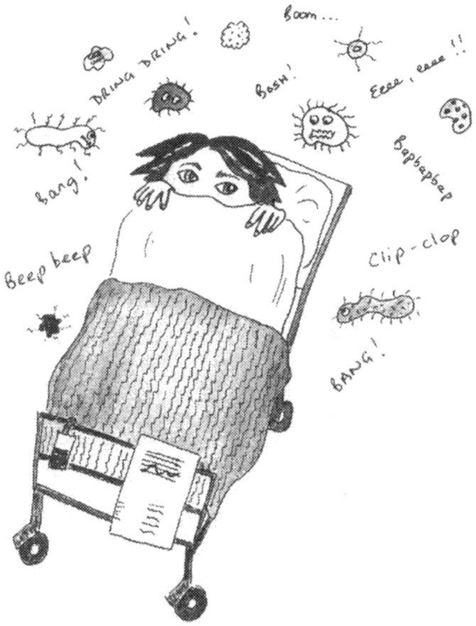

I sucked in my breath and pulled my sheet up over my face as I was hit by the shocking thought that a vast array of nasty bugs and viruses were probably circulating through my airways, including MRSA, a killer bug which the news had recently reported to be annihilating vulnerable hospital patients the length of Britain. It turned out, however, that trying to suck air through a thick, starched sheet was a slightly suffocating experience and, reasoning that a sheet probably wouldn't save me anyway, I attempted to counteract my anxiety by grabbing my work bag and dragging my paperwork out onto the side table. *Come on, Jaynie, concentrate, concentrate* – but the pages were a shaky blur. Feeling parched, I decided instead to go in search of a drink but as my crooked figure emerged through the curtains I was hit with a scary "No!" from a frowning, medium-blue clad nurse. "You have to stay in bed!"

"Blooming heck, I just want a drink; I'm fine! My GP was happy for me to come here on the bus..."

"You wouldn't be here if you were fine."

I was raging with indignation at being told what to do but "Tut," was all the argument I could muster as a hot poker seared my belly and a cold sweat broke out all over my body. "I'll fetch you some water."

"Thank you. Could I have some painkillers too please? I can see you're busy but it is over an hour since I asked for some."

"I'll speak to the doctor."

I tugged my curtain back on, slid my damp body into the bed and curled around my screaming belly. *I'll speak to the effing doctor! How can you be in hospital in 1998 and be in this amount of bloody agony? What the...* My internal rant was interrupted by my curtain being whipped back again, this time revealing a neatly-bobbed woman in a taut, white uniform pushing a trolley rattling with three-inch, colour-topped glass vials. My heart constricted; I knew from experience what this meant before her cool announcement of "I need some blood from you." I slowly uncurled myself to present my arm and tried to smile appreciatively but my fearful 'reptile brain' (the early, cave-dwelling part of our brain and nervous system with its quick-fire, sabre-toothed-tiger-spotting, 'fight, flight or freeze' response) had taken control of my face muscles and produced a vicious scowl instead; my fear still had me gripped in aggressive fight mode. Thankfully my rational frontal cortex (the logical, analytic, compassionate part of our brains which has developed more recently but generally reacts slower than the reptilian alert centre) managed to come on board in time to stop me giving the phlebotomist a swift left hook as her vicious needle pierced my arm.

I felt completely at the mercy of these strange, uniformed people. Would someone poison me with penicillin as they had my mum when she was a little girl of six and in hospital for three months with a mysterious hole in her neck which had to be cauterized – as four nurses pinned her down — with some sort of burning hot tar? Would a nurse spill scalding water on me like one had my little Mama?

My hostile mood wasn't helped when the '*Mid-blue Ice Queen*' plonked a cup of lukewarm water onto my bedside table and it tasted of the scratched plastic cup it came in. Again modelling the honed technique of my hard-core, female Yorkshire lineage, I seethed, "Please can you draw my curtains now?"

"They need to be open."

"I want them closed! They're *my* curtains!"

"Well actually they're not and we need to be able to keep an eye on you." In my defensive brain state, I misunderstood her desire to care for me and snapped, "What do you think I'm going to do? Set the place on fire? I hate being gawped at!"

"I'm sorry but that's..."

"Please don't say that's just the way it is or I might strangle you."

"I'd really prefer it if you didn't."

"I'm sorry, that was a really stupid thing to say." My tears welled up but I ground my jaw until my teeth nearly cracked and managed to ask, "Have you any idea when the doctor's coming? I need to get home. I feel like a prisoner."

"She should be here soon." *Oh okay, a female doctor at least.*

"People have been saying that for ages."

"Your blood results obviously aren't back yet but it shouldn't be long..."

"And meanwhile we patients have nothing better to do eh?" *I've got to see little Danny at his foster carer's tomorrow; he was looking so crushed last week when his mum didn't turn up for his contact visit...*

"Try and relax, eh?"

"Relax! Look, I'm sorry, I know it's not your fault but this isn't exactly the best place to relax in is it?"

"Not really. It shouldn't be long though. Do try your best to calm down. I appreciate it's not easy." I softened as my reality was acknowledged and a tear escaped down my cheek.

"Thanks," I mumbled, looking away so my 'weakness' couldn't be seen.

Focus on your report! Focus, focus, screamed my brain but as the nurse whisked away I was smashed with a tsunami of wayward flashbacks which I'd managed to keep frozen in a dark recess of my brain for over a decade. University education wasn't a part of my family's working class world but having visited my then boyfriend at Wolverhampton Polytechnic and been inspired to copy his loving, open-minded, bohemian mum, Judi (who showed me that life didn't have to be rigid or hard), I'd decided that moving south to party and study social work would be a great alternative to full-time work! I was busily revising for my A-levels when I developed a severe pain in my leg. I recalled the jovial, red-nosed GP telling me that I'd just pulled a muscle when I'd known that the pain was much worse than that. I'd given the doctor a very clear account of having had numbness in my buttock as I sat on a desk at school which then, over a week, turned into a throbbing pain, worked its way down my right leg and then lodged like a burning coal in my swollen calf. The doctor stuck to his guns and insisted on only prescribing Paracetamol despite my leg looking like a tree trunk. I then remembered, with a waft of contempt, the slow, patronizing shaking of the bearded, spectacled head of a second GP who, several days later, also dismissed my lucid account of the symptoms and my suggestion (which came from the older, female half of my Saturday job employers in the town's veg market) that I "may have a blood clot or something." The doctor gave me a drug to try and reduce the swelling; it did nothing. I have a vivid memory of my young, desperate self, lying in the bath, trying to run my leg under the tap in a vain attempt to ease the feeling that it was about to explode and choking back my sobs so I didn't upset Mum and Dad. Unused to crying (which was seen as 'mardy' and 'soft' in my family and often met by "Come here while I give you something to cry for") I was both amazed and ashamed at the waterfall of tears flowing down my face.

A DVT, or deep-vein thrombosis, was eventually diagnosed by a hospital 'Accident and Emergency' doctor over the Easter holiday. I was prescribed Warfarin, an anti-coagulant drug which would "thin" my blood and "hopefully" disperse the blood clot, and sent home with a pair of cumbersome crutches. They only had low dose Warfarin tablets at my village's chemist shop and I gagged on about twenty of the small, chalky brown pills. Nobody seemed to worry about the clot potentially moving to my heart, brain or lungs and there was no investigation of potential causes; it was put down to having just gone on the contraceptive pill. I toyed with the dark, swirling thought that God was punishing me for having sex before marriage, one of the most heinous sins both at home and within the Strict Baptist chapel where, following Sunday school, I was dragged by my mum for two long, excruciating services every week. On reflection I wonder if there was some deep self-sabotage involved in my DVT; I was over the moon at the thought of leaving home to do a degree but my mum was devastated and I was going well outside my family's norm; would I still belong? Maybe it was just the amount of the stress hormone 'cortisol' going round my body; I hated exams and had nightmares about exams looming but not having revised for years afterwards.

I'm glad to say that I had my first lucky escape; the clot didn't dislodge to give me a heart attack, stroke or a 'PE' (a pulmonary embolism, or clot on my lung). It did irreparable damage to my right leg though, leaving it permanently swollen, with a blue ankle where the blood, which can't get through my damaged major vein, leaks from the over-pressurized smaller veins and capillaries. For years I hated the fact that my legs were uneven and that my damaged leg hurt and swelled even more when I danced or walked a long way. In my vanity I used to wear a cut-off sock under my leggings to try and balance my legs out. Interestingly, it never entered my head to complain about my GPs' appalling misdiagnosis; that's not what you did in the 1970's as the daughter of a shop cleaner and woollen mill spinner.

Neither did I imagine for a second that being unheard by doctors would become a terrifying bane of my life.

Chapter 2
Bliss and Trauma in Paradise

"The pain I feel now is the happiness I had before. That's the deal."

C.S. Lewis

Lying in my hospital bed thinking w*hat if this blooming lot don't believe how much my belly's hurting?* was stressful but my anxiety went off the scale as my memory dredged up, in vibrant shards, my deeply suppressed three-weeks in hospital in Austria when I'd had a second DVT. This time it was in my left leg. I was twenty-one and holidaying with my Austrian boyfriend, Gerhard, on a beautiful, isolated beach in Crete.

I'd met 'Gerly' whilst 'Inter-railing' for a month round Western Europe at the end of my first year at polytechnic. I'd never been abroad before and our awesome trip, funded by twelve-hour shifts in a pork-pie factory, is another story; 'Six daft girlies survive Europe on eighty quid and fifty wet-wipes'. We'd exhausted ourselves trying to sleep on filthy train corridors (where a quarter of one of super-organised Tina's wet-wipes was an absolute luxury) and trudging for miles, loaded with huge rucksacks, around Paris, Rome, Naples and Athens. We were then annihilated by a gut infection on a campsite in Corfu and decided to head for the middle of nowhere in Austria, with visions of clean, healing air and freshly-baked bread on a village green. Getting off the train at a tiny, random station we headed for the nearest bar-café and met a bunch of friendly, long-haired Austrians, like us, in their early twenties. Our German was rudimentary and their English wasn't great but we managed to laugh a lot and understood enough to accept beaming, limping Rudi's invitation to stay at his new pad in the country (he'd lost a foot in a motorbike accident, just as most of the gang had suffered one bike injury or another, as we lot had on mopeds in Greece; another of my lucky escapes was Gilly and I just missing a head-on collision with a tourist bus!) Rudi's wallpaper was a bit flaky but we were very grateful for the quiet floor space and excited at the prospect of a party which was happening the next night.

My first sight of Gerly was him standing in front of the cooker in his baby-blue t-shirt, holding up a lump of burnt bread. Tall, lean, with a thick, muscular neck, big blue eyes, dark stubble and tousled curly hair, he looked like Michael Landon, the kind father from the sentimental TV series *Little House on the Prairie* and appeared to have his gentle temperament – also like my dad. It would take four years' psychotherapy training a decade later for me to understand the notion of 'transference' where we unconsciously attribute imagined characteristics to somebody based on their similarity to a previous person in our life and feel an automatic attraction (or aversion) to them. Neither did I yet know about 'repetition-compulsion' where we're unconsciously attracted to people similar to our parents or carers in the hope of getting what we didn't get enough of as children. This time we *will* get the love, affection, praise or positivity we so craved from this familiar person and it will be *heavenly*! Even if we don't get what we need, we unconsciously sense that we'll at least be able to take some control by mastering those awful, archaic feelings which haunt us — like the physically abused child who marries a violent partner, the rape victim who becomes a prostitute or the Vietnam veteran who gets into fights...Anyway, I'm going off on one (a blooming interesting subject though); for now let's just say my 'love at first sight' with Gerly was simply pure bee to dahlia attraction.

Gerly and I only had two days, a dance and a few quiet conversations but I cried as the girls dragged me onto a train for our next sweaty, flea-ridden adventure. When we got home and Gerly had sent me the bronze bangle he'd been wearing, I ran up and down the stairs for five minutes, whooping for joy. Next came a recorded cassette. As he'd said he liked them, I expected to hear Genesis or Talking Heads but it was him chatting to me with his deep, gentle voice; this and his occasional, hilarious, Austro-English pronunciations warmed the depths of my soul. Following several dreamy visits to one another, Gerly decided to resign from his job in a pharmaceutical lab and move into my shared student house in England. The following summer we planned a holiday in Greece, via Austria. It was an arduous journey through the then Yugoslavia to our sunny paradise; two packed trains, a dusty bus which felt like being crammed into a slow-cooker and then a leg-frazzling hike over a small mountain in forty degrees — but all had gone to plan. Pre mobile phones, we managed to meet up with Gerly's friends and were soon having a ball frolicking in the white sand and warm, turquoise sea. We played cards and board games in the bamboo-clad tavern at the end of the beach where the wizened, almost toothless owner, his chuckling, pudding-shaped wife and a posse of beige cats welcomed us with beaming smiles, priceless purrs and the rich aroma of barbequed fish. We slept in caves and tents under a sky so packed with stars that just a glance was enough to blow my mind. My soul was free!

A young German family had made it to our peaceful Heaven

in their dusty campervan. They were my dream; a stubbly, dark-haired dad and pretty blonde mum (I was bottle blonde at the time) who were a bit hippy and seemingly close, with an energetic, curly-topped boy of about six and a sweet, saucer-eyed girl who was three of four. I secretly watched them as they played on the beach and sat laughing over dinner, imagining Gerly and me, with our children, being like them in a few years' time. Life couldn't have been better.

Then came a familiar pain in my left thigh. I tried to persuade myself that I'd just pulled a muscle but when it came to the point that I couldn't walk and had to drag myself along in the sea to get to the tavern, I knew that I was in serious trouble and no way could I walk back over the mountain. Luckily, a young, smiley Greek man who was making a delivery to the tavern stuck us in the open back of his battered red van and returned us, albeit bumpily and dustily, back to civilization. Afraid of dislodging my suspected blood clot by flying, we had a torturous overland journey back to Austria. I remember placid Gerly shouting at a woman on a train who'd accidentally banged into my leg and nearly knocked me unconscious with the pain. *Oh shit, this has got to be another blood clot; maybe whacky author Louise Hayes was right in her belief that clots are a way of stopping the flow of joy...have I sabotaged myself again just as I was having a brilliant but naughty time? God and my mum wouldn't have been impressed by my holidaying on a nudist beach...*

In the Salzburg '*Krankenhaus*' (what a great word for hospital) I got the *most* welcome painkillers and was then sped round on a trolley-bed, including past a duck pond, I recall, to undergo various excruciating, leg-squeezing procedures for which I had pigeon English explanations at best. Finally, with Death smirking a sickening grin over the shoulder of a tall, bearded doctor, it was confirmed that I did have another DVT and that "I was lucky" that it hadn't killed me. I realized at this point how appalling my care had been in Yorkshire with my first DVT and that I was in a pretty vulnerable state. *Oh my God I'm going to bloody die here,* shrieked my brain's manically alarming amygdala.

Oh don't be stupid, you're in hospital, they won't let you die, reasoned my front cortex.

But people die in hospitals all the time!

Oh you don't want to think about that...

Actually I do; it's my job to look for danger!

Look you're being very negative...I'm young and fit, of course I'll be okay...

My parents' fragile self-esteem came from our relatively good looks (my mum won a village beauty contest at seventeen, my lean, muscular dad had a chiselled face and a great quiff and I won a teddy in a bonny toddler competition) so I'd always been aware of the *surface* of my body. My Gestalt therapy training expanded on this with its emphasis on body language and looking at the close relationship between poor mental and physical health, but apart from noticing my banging heart and burning lungs during hockey games and cross country runs at school, I'd never given much thought to the *inside* of my body. Now I realised, in a bit of an exploding 'Acme' cartoon bomb kind of way that I was living in a miracle! I had a constantly beating, electrically-charged heart circulating blood around an estimated *sixty thousand* miles of veins, arteries and capillaries, a cricket-pitch length of intestines cleverly processing my food and huge lungs oxygenating my blood, muscles, brain and organs so that I could move, think, repair and build new tissue. My liver and kidneys kept me toxin-free with thousands of enzyme and filtering reactions per minute and I had incredible senses which allowed me to see, hear, smell, taste and feel my environment. In my skull was the most complex, mind-blowing object on earth, with a hundred billion neurons making *millions* of unique connections and giving me the super-power of conscious thought. With just this basic knowledge of my body I was blown away. *Mmm...hello, amazing little body!* I didn't realise that this glimmer of bodily awareness would be the start of a fascinating journey which would massively enhance, and possibly even save, both my life and my sanity.

I spent three weeks in the Austrian hospital, trying desperately to get my head round the guttural sounds of those around me. Not being able to understand what people, including my doctors, were saying was terrifying and my 'fight-flight' system whirred, often manifesting as defensive criticism and paranoia; *What's that bloody idiot looking at me like that for? Does that condescending cow think I'm stupid?* I was equally hard on myself. At mealtimes I felt awkward having food delivered to my bedside; *Get you, being like the lady of the manor* and when the nurses came to change my sheets I told myself I was being *a lazy bitch* just sitting back and watching them; I felt compelled to try and help, despite the terrible burning in my leg. I'd no idea that I was acting out patterns of stoic self-sufficiency and nervous compliance which had begun with my great-grandmother, Sarah-Ann, nearly a century earlier, when she lost her mother at eight and was tied to the kitchen stove by a washing line so that she couldn't play out but instead had to cook for her father and two drunken adult uncles. Sarah-Ann's brutal treatment developed in her a vicious inner self-critic which, in turn, berated my grandma, my mum and myself for being anything less than permanently hard-working and perfectly helpful.

My ancestors passed down some vanity too though, thinking about it, possibly not from straight-talking Sarah-Ann who cut off her long, beautiful hair to honour a bet and rarely wore her false teeth, or my great-grandfather, a tough colour sergeant major who never went to a dentist but pulled out his teeth with cat-gut and a slammed door. Being confined to hospital, with my perfectly straight teeth, I felt terribly disappointed that my plans for going out looking great with my best ever tan had been ruined! As usual though, because fear and sadness weren't part of my outward repertoire, I covered them with cheery smiles when Gerly and his family and friends came to see me, stacked with cuddly, wobbly-eyed caterpillars and bars of soft Swiss chocolate, just as I did when there was a resounding "No" from the doctors every time I begged to be discharged. Despite my façade, my spirits sank as the long, lonely days and anxious, sleepless nights went by. A terribly ill, stick-boned older woman in the next bed was snoring into my brain like a pneumatic drill every night, driving me to such frustration that I resorted to banging my head on the bottom of my bed. When images of Death appeared, stalking around our ward in slow, arrogant steps, I shamefully thought, *take her...go on, please put her out of her misery! She's old, she's suffering...* This was only a fleeting thought that I didn't really mean but still, not many positive points there on my karmic balance sheet!

As was my familiar pattern from being about five, I'd tried to protect my easily-stressed parents from worry by not telling them where I was but as my return home became overdue Gerly finally called them. Because they'd never been abroad (other than my dad doing National Service and going on a work trip from his mill to check out wool-spinning machines in Paris and Hamburg) and money was tight, I don't think it occurred to any of us that they could've jumped on a plane to join me. My mum recollects Gerly's brief, pigeon-English call to her, saying that I'd "ring when I could" as one of the worst times of her life – I wasn't allowed to get out of bed for three days and when I did eventually call her we both broke our stoic pattern; neither of us could speak for crying.

When a tall, kind, round-spectacled doctor told me – in English – that I could finally leave hospital, I wanted to kiss him. Then he gave me his parting diagnosis; "It seems that you have 'Lupus' or SLE, that is, Systematic Lupus Eurythmatosis."

"Systematic what?" I asked.

"It's an auto-immune disorder. We" (or to be more precise, 'Ve') "are not sure why it happens but it seems to be a sort of self-destruct process where your own antibodies attack your healthy red blood cells. This gives you a high risk of your blood clotting."

"Oh" mouthed my slightly frozen face.

"Don't worry, we'll put you on an anticoagulant medication which will keep your blood thin and should stop you from clotting anymore."

"Oh. Well that's good then."

"It is. But you may get a little tired. There's a chance of pains and swellings of an arthritic type too and in extreme cases damage to the organs – but we seems to have caught this early..."

"Organ damage! My God, which organs?"

"Sometimes the kidneys, sometimes the liver or the heart. It in many ways can manifest. It's a strange and complicated illness which comes in random flares, possibly with some relationship to stress."

"So can you sort it out? Is there a cure?"

"Well, not exactly..."

"Not exactly?"

"Well no, I have to say that there is not a cure. But all the time we're finding out more about it and in England you have some very good doctors..."

I stared into space for a while. "Is there anything else that I need to know?"

"Well...you may get a type of butterfly-looking rash on your face; Lupus is named after the Red Wolf...and you should stay out of the sunshine as you may get a rash on your body..."

"What? Stay out of the sunshine? But that's my favourite thing!" *Oh crap!*

"Well, you can wear a powerful sunscreen and a hat and this should be okay."

"Oh, okay." *Yeah, right.*

"Oh another important thing, which I am guessing, knowing you are a student, may be bad news..." *Oh God...* "You should avoid alcohol because it can interact with the anticoagulant medication and make your blood too thin." *OH SHIT!*

"What do you mean too thin?"

"Well you could have bleeding problems." As I stared at the doctor the bottom fell out of my world; 'snakebite and black' (lager, cider and black-current cordial) was part of my staple diet and the alcoholic fuel that got me dancing and talking to blokes.

"And there's just one more thing I wish I had not to tell you, but I must."

"Are you sure? Maybe I could wait a while for that bit, eh?"

"I'm sorry. You do need to know this. There is a chance of getting blood clots in the placenta during pregnancy; it is our experience that it can be a little difficult for Lupus patients to have children. A pregnancy could be very dangerous for you and the baby – but it's not impossible. You would have to come off the anti-coagulant drugs should you ever want to become pregnant because it can damage the foetus..." At this point my memory of the conversation shrivelled up. So did my self-esteem. *Oh my God. Well I might as well chuck myself under a bus! Gerly's gonna do a runner for sure. Shit. Lupus? Fucking wolf woman! Phwww...Mmm; I wonder if my overenthusiastic antibodies could somehow be used for the treatment of cancer or AIDS or something?...God, imagine if I miscarried just as I was bonding with an amazing new life...or died in childbirth leaving my baby motherless...oh my God...*

I have no memory of coming out of hospital though I do recall suggesting to Gerly, in floods of hysterical tears, that we should end things there and then but he reassured me that he loved me and, despite my suggestion that he took some time to think about it, flew back to England with me. It was only when we landed at Heathrow that we discovered that Gerly wasn't allowed back into the UK. The immigration officer got a spectacular ear-battering from me but to no avail; in order for us to be together, Gerly had to return to Austria and sign paperwork in Vienna declaring that we would get married within the next six months. Gutted though I was as I waved him off, I reflected that at least now he'd have the space to think about things. I didn't really expect him to return.

After a few days with my parents where, in my distraught state, I went to my mum for the first hug since being about five, I hobbled to my local hospital with my Austrian paperwork. Luckily for me, I live near a big teaching hospital. I was told that I needed to go to the 'Anticoagulant Clinic' every few weeks to have my 'INR' (International Normalization Ratio) or the thick-ness of my blood checked. I'd then get instructions from a doctor about how much anticoagulant (Warfarin) to take. I had to keep my INR between a range of two and four; less than two and I could have more blood clots, higher than four and I could have internal bleeding problems. Warfarin wasn't particularly good for veins, it could "fluff them up" but the doctor was clear that clotting risks outweighed the risk of 'fluff.' Years later I find that slightly debatable but I suppose it was a no-brainer at the time.

I continued to have the odd outpatient appointment with a Lupus doctor but remained pretty well. I was tired at times but the only obvious signs of this weird, multi-symptomatic, wolfish disorder (which was apparently most prevalent amongst women, often women of colour, of child-bearing age) was the occasional red spotty sun rash on my arms and throat, and my fingers and toes going blue and a bit scaly on occasions – 'Raynaud's Syndrome'. I was prescribed 'Hydroxychloroquine' for this; it's actually an anti-malarial drug, but it seemed to sort out my hands and feet. The doctors I saw were pleasant enough and they weren't too negative about the prospect of my miscarrying or dying in childbirth. Thankfully my powers of denial slowly strengthened and if the horrendous thought that I might never be a mother poked its way through my defences, I comforted myself with the idea that I'd spend my life doing VSO (Voluntary Service Overseas) and helping hundreds of children. Then I'd adopt a needy orphan who was desperate for a mum. The worst case scenario was being a foster mum; I knew from social work how many devastated kids needed a loving home.

Thank God I didn't have a crystal ball.

When my friend Mary bought me the book *Lupus for Women*, I looked at the first page about 'sticky blood' and then tucked it away in my bookshelf and got on with living my manic student life. I danced, partied, replaced alcohol with pot, played basketball and tennis with gusto (despite my swollen leg) and, studying politics, social policy, sociology, economics, psychology and philosophy, immersed myself in distracting facts about injustice and oppression. What was a bit of Lupus compared to being one of the seven hundred and eighty-five *million* people in the world living without clean water or the *third* of the people on our planet without access to a decent toilet?[1] What was Lupus compared to the many people

1. *These figures are actually from a Water Aid pamphlet in 2020.*

experiencing domestic violence or child abuse on a daily basis in the UK? I felt lucky that I was the first person in my extended family – and one of few working-class youths back then – to make it to poly and hoped that if I ate well I wouldn't be one of the working-class northerners who I learnt in a lecture were likely to die about seven years before our southern, middle-class counterparts. The government's current Department of Health website still clearly identifies higher death rates in the more deprived areas of England and Wales such as the North of England and the Welsh Valleys. Their map of regional deaths is quite stark, with London, the south and more affluent areas clearly having lower death rates.[2] I also felt fortunate that I was white in terms of being about ten times less likely to be stopped and searched and having much less chance of being imprisoned, sectioned, brought up in poverty or suffering the daily horrors of institutionalised racism as my contemporaries of colour[3] and I wasn't being targeted with hatred or condescension for being gay or obviously disabled. Pah…Lupus poopus…

As well as being brought up 'hardy' and reminded of God's blessings every Sunday, I'd grown up with my parents watching the daily TV news and, seeing so much suffering, recognised how lucky I was. My mum has a massive heart and was forever donating money to charities and my grandad, Arthur, who'd survived the Second World War, also taught me about gratitude; his shabby book of poems, which he'd dreamed of having published and which my mum got out frequently after his death (and always cried her way through reading them) included this one:

---

2. See www.gov.uk/government/organisation/department-of-health/about/statistics

3. See the shocking statistics on the government website – https://www.ethnicity-facts-figures.service.gov.uk

Count Your Blessings

Do you ever count your blessings
when the clouds seem dark and grey,
when evil things start falling
and you feel you must obey?

Do you count them when the birds sing
and spring starts to unfold,
when a sunbeam from the dawning sun
bathes your cheek with purest gold?

For however dark and grey
the clouds may seem to you,
if you'll only count your blessings,
you'll find there's lots of blue.

Arthur Downs

Chapter 3
A Shocking Diagnosis

"I'm the one that's got to die when it's time for me to die, so let me live my life the way I want to."

Jimi Hendrix

Back in my sweaty, English hospital bed waiting for my mysterious female consultant to arrive, it struck me that I wasn't quite as hard-core as I'd liked to believe. Because my sensitive parents' early years were imbued with a lot of swallowed down terror, they weren't good at empathising with mine. If I was frightened they'd often laugh, take the mickey or get annoyed, desperately defending against the lingering fear hidden deep within themselves; if they'd felt my pain, they'd also have been overwhelmed by their own. So they tried not to feel. And so did I. Hence here I was, hardly breathing, tensing every muscle and telling myself that I was overreacting and being a big baby but my pounding heart and manic brain ran amok. *Lupus, bloody lupus; maybe this pain's some mad organ damage...maybe my cells are being eaten alive and I'm disintegrating...what if it's another blood clot? Oh shit, I really need to get out of here; I can't miss Donna's case conference on*

Monday – what if they won't let me out of here for three weeks like in Austria? Oh my God, my belly really hurts! What if…

"Hello. I have your blood results." Feeling my face flush like a cherry, I looked up at my haematology consultant, a Dr H., I furtively logged from the identity card pinned to her baby blue blouse. She was in her forties, smiling (*there's a good sign*) with wayward, shoulder-length hair and no inkling of a plummy accent or tweed which made me, in my class-based 'us and them' programmed brain, conclude *okay, she might be alright.* I swallowed hard. "Okay, sock it to me. Am I disintegrating?" Looking puzzled she calmly replied, "No. But it does appear that you may have internal bleeding in your abdomen."

"What?" I mumbled as my brain screamed *what's she talking about? Internal bleeding! Bleeding I can't do a thing to stop but which could kill me?* "Um. But why would I be bleeding? I haven't banged myself or swallowed anything sharp."

"We don't know."

"Bleeding from where?"

"I'm sorry, we don't know yet."

"Oh...so can you do anything to stop the bleeding?" I finally managed to ask.

"We'll know more when you've had a scan. In the meantime we'll give you some blood" she said simply, without her initial smile, I noted.

"So could I bleed to death here?"

"Hopefully the bleeding will stop." After a moment of staring into space, my brain kicked back online and I asked, "Did you just say that you were giving me blood?"

"Yes. It will make you feel much better."

"Oh..." My mum was a regular blood donor (bless her kind heart, she's given one short of fifty pints) and I'd seen people being given blood on TV dramas but I couldn't believe this was going to happen to me. I shook my head a few times which brought up the question, "How thin's my blood? What's my INR?"

"It's a bit high...just over seven."

"Oh my God!"

"Don't worry, it's probably just that the antibiotics the GP gave you interacted with your warfarin. Hopefully we'll get it under control..."

'Hopefully' lodged in my brain in huge neon letters but I daren't ask any more; I knew that with an INR of eight, irrespective of any random internal bleeding, it can kill you. *Oh my God I need to get out of here,* was all I could think as Dr H. walked away and my brain pictured Death whirling like a demented dervish at the bottom of *my* bed. I was relieved by the distraction of a young, bushy-browed 'registrar' skidding up to me with a plastic tray. "I just need to put you a cannula in."

"Will it hurt?"

"Not really." The "just a sharp scratch" was actually a vicious needle being painfully embedded into the back of my hand. The cannula was attached to a narrow rubber tube which, in turn, was connected to a thick plastic pouch full of dark, sickening *blood* which was hung up on a metal stand to drip thick, purple-red globules silently into my body. I panicked as I contemplated the source of the blood; was my donor a man, woman, a smoker or a speed freak? Somebody infected with a horrendous disease? Little did I know at this time that my biggest worry should have been the fact that I was being given somebody else's collection of antibodies.

My contemplations about my blood donor were suddenly interrupted by a flurry of white coats and clipboards which moved in to surround my bed. I stared at the six or so strangers, each of them looking back at me with a blank face or awkward smile. A 'ward round.' "Hello, you must be our new patient" said a beak-nosed man as he thrust his pale, bony hand towards me. "I'm Dr Phillips. I see we've got your blood up. Super."

"Hi." As I poked my limp hand out from beneath my sheet he turned away to address a rather handsome, strapping man about my age – another registrar, said his badge – who was fumbling with a heavy file. Presumably *my* file which I suspected, rightly, that he wasn't going to share with me. "HB?" snapped Dr Phillips.

"6.7"

"Platelets?"

"92"

"WBC?"

"Um...2.9"

"Lovely. Lovely. Two units, U's and E's, LFT's. Temperature?

"37.5"

"Okay. Lovely, lovely." I stared round the blank wall of faces talking this bizarre language and waited for somebody to translate. Nobody did. "And how are you feeling?" asked the doctor, finally addressing me. "I'm okay, I...I mean what..."

"Oh you should be getting a scan this afternoon and we'll have to give you a bit more blood, I'm afraid; just top you up a bit."

"Oh, I, um...what, um...oh, okay."

"Right then. Lovely. We'll see you anon" chirped the doctor as he turned to move along, drawing his minions behind him like a pale, mumbling cloud. I wanted to shout after the floating posse "What the hell was that about?" but just stared after them in shock. Despite not understanding the medics' language, I had twigged enough to make very real the fact that I was totally powerless and completely dependent on a load of strangers who didn't seem particularly interested in me as a human being. My self-important princess had no power here.

My ability to trust in others wasn't exactly well developed in the first place. I guess the roots of this could've started when my great-grandmother was tied to the oven, once watching one of her drunken uncle's urine drip through the upstairs floorboards onto the kitchen table and her day's baking. I imagine some of my great-grandfather, Colour Sergeant Ben-John's trust in humanity would have been obliterated when he was following distant politicians' ruthless orders and possibly herding women and children into disease-ridden concentration camps in the Boer War and then dodging machine-gun fire and being splattered by his peers' blood and brains in the First World War's insane trench warfare. Once home, like many traumatised ex-troops, he (as instructed at the end of the war (!) and no doubt because of the unbelievable horror) never talked about his war-time experiences and he rarely left the safety of his home, other than to place the odd bet on the horses and, with shiny boots and a chest-full of medals, to collect funds for ex-servicemen during the town's annual 'Poppy Parade.'

My grandad Arthur's trust would have been blown during the Second World War when, trying to piece together young sailors and soldiers as a qualifying nurse on his Navy rescue ships, he listened to his screaming peers being dragged into the bloody depths by sharks or minced up in the propeller of his *own* ships when they also came under fire and had to leave quickly.

I doubt my dad's trust in the world was developed much

by living in poverty alongside ten siblings who lived on 'jam bread' and had to listen to their mother's screams as she died of cancer when he was fourteen, followed by the death of his strong Geordie, quarryman father a year later. Going straight into a forty-four-hour week in the local textile mill at fifteen and becoming a virtual slave to his older sister and her work-shy husband who 'took him and his younger siblings in,' no doubt added to his trauma. Patient and gentle though my dad is, he was often serious, distant and unable to express much affection or instigate play with us as children. His buried shame and learning from his own parents – and virtually mute, supercool actors like Clint Eastwood – meant that he found it much easier to be 'tough,' which translated as critical and distant, rather than 'soft,' that is, complimentary and affectionate.My dad's trauma, and his associated fearful nervous system, had tried to protect him by closing him down (the parasympathetic part of our nervous system can calm us too much if its feeling threatened or helpless, making us uncommunicative, insular or depressed.)

My mum's trust was annihilated when her dad abandoned her to go to war when she was three and couldn't soothe and protect her as the bomb sirens pierced the air and she was pushed under the kitchen table. I'll bet her dad couldn't always soothe her when he came back from the war three years later, with his thick, brown, curly hair reduced to wispy grey straggles and no doubt carrying a good dose of rage-fuelling Post-Traumatic Stress Disorder. As my mum puts it, though he was generally loving, "he could be sharp sometimes." The damp outside toilet, shared by two other families, frazzled my young mum's nerves further as she lived in constant terror of a rat getting past the 'tipping plate' and biting her. She found filling the tin bath (with a 'pigging can') from the kitchen stove and helping her mum wash with a 'Dolly tub' and wooden mangle, hard and scary work. Her unbelievable pain and terror as a six--year-old in hospital for three months, having only weekend visits from her parents, was the traumatic lid on the pressure cooker. So whilst my mum could be very loving, made clothes for all my teddies as well as me and my 'Tiny Tears' doll and played for hours with my older brother (by two years) and me, her trauma – and the helplessness that came with it – made her crave control and she could become easily angered, cutting and unpredictable; home was not always a safe or happy place. To provide for us, my dad ran for the seven-o-clock bus every workday morning (including Saturdays), my mum would go without food to give it to us and we had some great birthday and Christmas presents (including roller skates, a typewriter and an orange Raleigh bike) but I learned pretty early that my emotional needs weren't that important; my feeling weren't on the agenda. God, duties at 'The Chapel' and her overwhelming feelings often came first with my mum, just as football, cricket and later, fishing and crown-green bowling, were priorities to my dad. I often accompanied my mum on her boring 'ministerings for the Lord' and sat through many a Saturday game of my dad's but neither of them ever came to watch my brother or me playing our sports; we mostly just 'fitted in' like many of our young contemporaries in 1970's Yorkshire.

Seeing few demonstrations of closeness between my parents and having learned within my family – and from my peers – that vulnerability was scorned instead of soothed, emotional distance was reflected in my own intimate relationships where I tended to choose men with whom I couldn't really get close – or develop trust. My first great love (well second maybe; I did like rugby-playing Darren in 'fifth form') who got me to poly, had been a blond heart-throb in the year above me when I started my A-levels. I adored him and slept with him in the hope that I'd marry him one day but he wounded me deeply when he was unfaithful within the year; the foundations of my defensive wall - in addition to what had been passed down from my family-were established. Following a few short relationships in which I was totally unable to communicate (that would have meant being vulnerable) I met my third serious love – after Gerly – at a party in London where he'd spellbound me with his travelling tales (especially of swimming with dolphins!) He was lithe, funny, kind, adventurous, creative, wise and encouraged me to reflect on and share my feelings as he talked about such deep things as needing to love yourself before you could properly love anybody else. He was also a little unstable. Before we got together he'd told me about a spell in psychiatric care following a failed attempt to sort out the Gulf War from his sister's home in Israel and then burning his clothes in the airport - but that was nothing like actually seeing him get ill. Whilst still living in London he'd unexpectedly turned up at my door at midnight as an unshaven, wild-eyed somebody else, stolen my car and, when I finally caught up with him via the police, was lying on the floor of a grim Victorian psychiatric hospital with his penis hanging out of his jeans, laughing hysterically and being completely 'unreachable.' It was traumatising to say the least and it required him sleeping with his landlady to persuade me to let him move in with me. This relationship did however get me into therapy; my initial six sessions (before I got hooked on the fascinating process) were meant to help me establish whether or not I could stay with a man who periodically thought that he could fly and handed out money on the street. I decided I couldn't risk him being the father of my possible children.

As for Gerly, I messed that up completely. Gerly had obtained his paperwork in Vienna to say that we would be married within six months and returned to England – but I bottled it. Because I couldn't tell whether Gerly's apparent arrogance was German accent related, he wasn't sure he wanted to stay in England (and I could never have mustered the courage or devastated my parents by leaving the country) and I didn't know if I'd be able to bear him the children he might want, the uncertainty freaked me out and the thought of maybe needing to divorce one day was too scary for me to contemplate; I imagined it would've annihilated my God-fearing mum. With her traumatised core and tears that were even more powerful than her rage, I'd learned very early to tune into her needs and emotional states rather than my own and this was now a deeply ingrained habit. So, breaking both my own and Gerly's hearts, I put my mum's feelings first and packed Gerly back off to Austria. (As I'm sitting here editing in 2020 wondering if it's right to blame my mum, I need to add 'I was just too scared.')

Interestingly, the universe gave me more chances to make amends with Gerly, like a few years later when I bumped into him five minutes after arriving amidst the *hundred thousand* people at the Glastonbury Festival. I remember him placing one of his big hands on the bottom of my back as we stood watching a band and feeling like I'd come home. When I went travelling, aged twenty-nine, I'd written to Gerly to tell him that I was going to Asia and Australia for six months and he phoned me forty-five *minutes* before I left the house to fly to New Delhi. He was leaving for Amsterdam the next day – to get a flight to New Delhi! I wish I'd just called the travel agent and postponed my flight to Kathmandu planned for the day after I arrived in New Delhi. But I didn't; I was quaking at the thought of getting on a plane to Asia on my own anyway and because it had been a real challenge to get a seat on the Kathmandu flight and I had a tight schedule of flights to follow over the next six months, I didn't dare cancel it. I don't know what was going on in the murky depths of my subconscious alongside being struck down by God or my mum if I divorced; an intuitive knowledge that Gerly wasn't the prince I'd made him into? A fear of getting married and finding out sooner rather than later that I couldn't have children? A fear of intimacy, of being rejected, of change – or even of being happy? Who knows? Gerly said he'd try to meet me at the guest-house I was heading for in Kathmandu but this was still pre-mobile phones and the universe had given up on us. Our phone call was the last time I would have contact with him for the next fifteen years. You won't believe it when I tell you about my eventual marriage...

And so to bed...I think I need my teddy! I feel sad thinking about my family's pain and my disastrous love-life but at least I've managed to avoid writing more about my hospital nightmare for a couple of pages...*crafty, Jaynie, very crafty...*

Chapter 4 Learning About Fear

"Our attitude, in the face of life's challenges determines our suffering or our freedom."

Tara Brach

As I watched another bag of blood drip its thick globules into my body, I felt shocked to my core. *How can I possibly be this ill? God, is this my punishment for refusing to submit to you and repent for my sins? I finally meet a lovely man and then you do this? Don't I deserve to be happy?*

A week before my admittance to hospital I'd spent a beautiful weekend floating down the beach at Robin Hood's Bay, staring into the blue eyes of my new, pony-tailed love. I'd only been seeing 'Matthew' for six weeks, though I'd known him vaguely for a few years as he lodged up the road and I'd recently been his eager student at yoga and self-defence classes. We were basking in the bliss of a new relationship, thinking we'd found the 'perfect other.' I'd been alone for the previous two years, immersed in my mind-bending psychotherapy training and the required therapy and I thought I was finally 'sorted' enough for a healthy relationship and had found a kind, sane, deep, bright, sensitive, compassionate, musical and trustworthy man to possibly settle down and have children with– and if my dad struggled to cope with his long hair and my mum his untidiness, that was tough.

When Matthew arrived at evening visiting time, all beautifully windswept from his cycle-ride and looking muscular and lean in his usual shorts and blue cotton vest, my heart leapt – but I felt myself shrink in shame. I was a sickly wreck in a hideous hospital gown and I had *internal bleeding*. When he hugged me and asked how I was, I ground back my tears and slipped on my familiar 'I'm fine' mask. "Oh a bit of bleeding apparently, but the doctor thinks it'll stop on its own. Probably has already."

"Bleeding from where?"

"Oh they're not sure yet."

"What do you mean they're not sure!"

"I know."

"Not a bladder infection then?"

"Seems not."

"How's the pain?"

"Oh not so bad…I've had some pain-killers, I'm okay…I should be home soon. Are you okay?"

"I miss you already."

"You too." By now I was sticking my nails into my palms to stop myself crying. "What you been up to?"

"A couple of yoga classes but I couldn't really concentrate."

"Did your students behave?"

"I think so; it's all a bit of a blur. I don't like this. I don't like it at all."

"It'll be over soon. Don't worry."

"But I am worried!"

"Give over and give me a hug. Excuse the fact that I stink though..."

Hoping that Dr H. would pop along any minute and tell me that I could go home with Matthew, I was gutted when a goatee-bearded nurse and the Ice Queen turned up with yet another grotesque bag of blood and began the serious business of checking various serial numbers before attaching it to my body. "How long will that take to go through? Can I go home when it has?" The nurses gave each other a quick, knowing look. "I'm sorry but it looks like you'll be staying with us tonight," said the man.

"But I've got a cat at home who needs me!"

"I'm sure your chappie here can feed him." When Matthew nodded I cast him a poisonous princess glance. "I'm sure he'll be fine 'till tomorrow" soothed the Ice Queen. "Imagine how pleased he'll be to see you! Like my Alan is after a night shift."

"Mmm." Feeling a glimmer of respect for her excellent cat-naming, I rechristened the Ice Queen 'Mid-Blue Alan' and tried to get my head round the idea of staying overnight in the dismal room of death. It took a while to accept that I *couldn't* go home, that I *had to* stay in hospital. On my own. Knowing nobody. With internal bleeding. I roughly wiped at the tears which popped out as I asked Matthew to give Morty-cat a big cuddle and not tell my parents what was going on. As he tentatively hugged me, kissed my forehead and waved me goodbye, even his wild, corkscrew curls looked deflated. I felt guilt for causing him such worry and I panicked that he'd want to run a mile; *mmm, maybe I should just end things with him now...*

When the ward lights went out and the chaos lessened, I came to know the meaning of lonely. Whilst travelling alone in Asia I'd suffered the occasional moment of isolation between hooking up with fellow backpackers but that was nothing compared to this. This was vulnerable, in pain and scared-out-of-my-wits-with-no-distractions lonely and my heart was banging far too wildly for any sleep. My frightened autonomous nervous system was revved up and in action-ready 'sympathetic' mode and the 'parasympathetic' part of it, the soother which calms you down after a spell of 'being on it,' didn't stand a chance. I spent the night tossing and turning on my sweaty plastic bed, fuming about the continuing noise; bleeping machines, piercing phones and the totally unbelievable full-volume chattering, heel-clomping and door-banging of some of the night staff. My inner princess noted that none of the nurses spent a minute trying to comfort me or anybody else (I'd no conception of how busy they were) and I had moments of not knowing whether I was awake or dreaming as my mind wrestled with the reality of being confined in this dingy hell-hole. A particularly surreal hour had me being whisked by tattooed porters down draughty, eerily quiet corridors for my ultrasound scan. As cold jelly was squirted onto my burning belly and a computer-mouse-like scanner dragged over my pain, I tried to blank out the pictures of the happy mums-to-be plastered all over the walls.

Despite being exhausted and in a lot of pain, at nine the next morning I asked that the ward's trolley-based pay-phone be brought to my bedside so I could let my manager know that I, Ms Indispensable Princess, couldn't make it to work but would hopefully be there for my case conference on Monday. My next memory is of Dr H. appearing again. My insides gave her an ungrateful scowl whilst I forced a feeble smile to my face; still in fight-flight mode, my nervous system and reptile brain continued to regard her as the enemy I had to escape from. "We have your scan results," she calmly announced.

"Ugh. Go on..." I managed, wondering if my banging heart could actually explode.

"It seems that your ovary's bleeding."

"Oh." *What are you talking about! How can my ovary be bleeding? The Lupus doctors never mentioned my ovaries! Oh my God, just when I thought I'd found a potential father for my children...*She gently added, "And we need to operate pretty quickly..."*An operation? Having my belly cut open with a long silver blade so a bunch of strange men can stick their hands* inside *my half-naked body?*

I can't remember the rest of our conversation; maybe the hippocampus in my brain had frozen (as it appears to do during trauma, stopping the normal processing of memories into a coherent timeline, hence the seemingly real flashbacks that can come with Post-Traumatic Stress Disorder.) Maybe it was on this occasion that I cleverly deflected my brain onto Dr H.'s impressively crumpled blouse, wondering if she was just a woman after my own heart who avoided ironing wherever possible or simply had too many home responsibilities on top of her massive job. I like to think that I smiled appreciatively at Dr H. and chirped, "Right then, let's do it," but it's equally possible that I went green and swore. Death again entered my peripheral vision, sitting on the windowsill swinging his bony legs; I tried to convince myself that he was watching the older women on my ward, not the tennis-ball-whacking me!

Knowing the surgeons would have to thicken my blood for the operation, I was scared that I may clot to death, and psyched myself up to phone my mum. "Hiya. Y'alright, Mama?"

"Yes, love, we've just been t' supermarket. It's blooming cold here. Is it there?"

"I'm pretty warm at the moment actually. Are you sitting down?"

"Well I'm perched on the settee arm, the cat's sitting here too. She's so funny, she..."

"Mum..."

"...came in this morning with the dirtiest nose, I..."

"Mum..."

"...told your dad I..."

"MUM!"

"What, love?"

"I'm okay but I'm in hospital."

"Oh no! What's wrong?"

"I'm fine, don't worry but I thought I'd better tell you."

"Have you got another blood clot?"

"No. The opposite. A bit of a bleed from my ovary apparently but they're operating to sort it out, it's okay. I've got a good doctor."

"They'd better look after you! Have you got your toothpaste and pyjamas?"

"Yes, Mum, I'm fine, I've got everything I need, don't worry."

"Well phone us and let us know how you get on. You'll be okay....won't you?"

"Mum, I'm fine. Matthew's been and he's told Maria, Kazza and Jez so I'll bet they'll come later. Really, I'm alright."

"Yes, that's what you said when you were in that Austrian hospital."

"This doctor says they'll sort it out and she doesn't seem worried."

"Oh well, you just rest. God will look after you."

"Yes, Mum. Look, I'd better go. I'll ring you tomorrow."

"Don't forget!"

"I won't."

"I love you."

"I love you too, Mama. Don't worry! I'm alright. And love to Dad."

"I'll tell him. Bye, love."

"Bye, Mum." And then I cried until the excruciating shaking of my belly held me still, just as my mum was no doubt quietly bawling too.

I had to have a plethora of blood tests to check whether my

blood was 'thick' enough for the operation; being on warfarin complicated things significantly. At lunchtime, as my trolley bed was finally wheeled towards the operating theatres, the grim reality of my condition was starkly reflected back to me in the frightened, sideways glances of hospital visitors. *Oh God, please stop this pain and get me out of here...*

After the operation I was woozy and sore but a smiling Dr H. reassured me that all had gone well. She explained that underneath the padded dressing on my belly was a four-inch cut just above my pubic bone but the surgeons had managed a neat job which should heal soon and wouldn't be visible when my shaved hair regrew. As Dr H. told me I'd be home soon, my nervous system calmed a little and I was able to return from my fear-based reptile brain back into my rational and empathic front cortex, becoming a less grumpy, self-focused princess and more sociable. I started to chat with my fellow patients who, of course, all had a unique and interesting story to tell and I began to see that the uniformed staff on Ward E17 were warm and friendly people. They seemed professionally distant whilst hanging 'meds' on my drip-stand or taking my blood but as I opened up and started chatting, they flowered into real people. Jovial Jo had a spaniel called Sid, David Essex look-a-like Gary had an energetic teenage daughter who 'bled his wallet dry', giant-brained Paul was studying for exams, Tina's daughter was a "princess" and Gentle Claire, who had a very overweight cat called Lucy, was looking for a fella. In turn, a less spikey me seemed to become more real to them; they asked me how I felt, empathized with my physical pain and fear and apologized for having to stick needles in me. I felt gutted when Dr H. came to announce that my blood seemed stable now, so I was being transferred to a gynaecology ward.

My new ward was only divided from two more by a thin, partial partition and so was particularly hectic. The stale, stuffy stench wasn't pleasant and the harsh fluorescent lights made everything slightly hazy but this was nothing compared to the assault of the constant *noise;* it was like being in a goldfish bowl in the middle of a building site; a loud, mind-piercing racket slightly muffled somehow by the sheer force of all the other sounds. I know I'm banging on (so to speak) about the noise but even as I sit here writing I've just noticed how tense I am. Even my portable CD player's headphones at full volume didn't drown out the hellish sound and I was *desperate* to run round in circles screaming, "SHUT UP! SHUT UP!" Actually I wanted to swear venomously and run a mile but when I tried to stand up my legs just crumpled. I was becoming sleep deprived and increasingly angry again as the noise and fear tore at my brain; I began to worry that I was heading towards madness.

My anxiety wasn't helped by the fact that I had to press my buzzer to ask for a drink or painkillers; 'being demanding,' despite a part of me being a self-important princess, pushed me into another inner part (let's call her Little Miss Humiliation) who had a conditioned response of feeling shame after being frequently humiliated for asking for things or being 'needy' as a child. Whenever I wanted to ask for help as an adult, in came an automatic feeling of shame. I also felt shame that my athletic self was having to ask for bedpans; hard plastic bowls which I struggled to heave myself on to. My belly remained bloated but the rest of me was disintegrating at an incredible rate; my muscular arms and legs were becoming bony sticks and my previously taut backside, a sagging bag of skin. My ego (princess self) freaked. *Oh my God, look at the state of me; what will Matthew think? Oh my God, I must look disgusting...* In a pattern copied from my mum and perfected by about the age of about ten, there was little self-compassion but plenty of anger towards myself; I hadn't even got the strength to sit up in bed, yet all the other women on the ward were able to walk to the loo and the shower. I was being *pathetic* just lying there; a *stinking weakling.* I returned to my unsociable 'poisonous princess' mode, hating anybody looking vulnerable (in therapy spiel, 'projecting' my own hidden fear and vulnerability onto them and then hating them for it, just as my parents couldn't tolerate it in me.) I begged for the curtains around my bed to be drawn at every opportunity in a bid for some privacy but sometimes I wasn't allowed and I had to just lie there, simmering with rage as the constant flow of staff and visitors looked at me in my pyjamas. I pressed my morphine pump as often as it would allow, in a bid to space myself out as well as ease the physical pain, but the cold frozen vegetables remained disgusting and the clattering tea trolley at six o'clock in the morning, followed by nurses keen to force tablets down my throat and drag me out of bed to change my sheets, remained shocking. I felt something like my grandad when he was away at war but, sadly, lacked his sensory imagination.

In a Foreign Land

Now I long for the song of the soaring lark
for the scent of new-mown hay,
to see the blush of a rose new born
unfolding her dress so gay.
Yet though my soul be so weary
I see them all and more,
for all are enshrined in my innermost heart
that I reach through memory's door.

I hear the song of a soaring lark,
smell the scent of new mown hay,
I see a rose just newly born
and my skies are no longer grey
I hear the song of a mountain stream
tis a song that will never cease
and as I see the swirl of a speckled trout
to my soul at last has come peace.

Arthur Downs

My soul was nowhere near peaceful and I was desperate to get out of hospital, not just because I hated it but so I could cuddle up with Matthew and Morty-cat, start my third year's psychotherapy training and be there for 'my' work children. I was still ringing the office and asking visiting colleagues how the children were; I felt so guilty about my sudden abandonment of them when they'd been let down, one way or another, so much already. My colleagues were keen to tell me all about my clients; anything to avoid talking about the reasons for my pale, sickly face. At first I'd looked forward to visiting times but as I got weaker, my friends no longer aired their everyday problems, feeling that anything sounded trivial next to the state I was in and I began to feel lost. I was comfortable listening, offering advice and being, in the words of Eric Berne, the founder of the psychotherapy model TA (Transactional Analysis) a 'rescuer.' A rescuer seeks security within relationships (and jobs like social work) by being a care-taker, being needed. I'd been well-trained in this role by trying to defend my dad against my mum's frequent criticisms and listening to her woes as a teenager. A rescuer often links up with a 'victim,' somebody who tries to guarantee some security within relationships by acting a bit helpless and needy. The idea of being a victim in any way made me cringe in shame (though I can play that role at times) so being a helpless patient was excruciating.

Chapter 5
On Hospital Dynamics

"The way we talk to our children becomes their inner voice."

Peggy O'Mara

As another week went by, my searing belly pain continued and I began to look about six months pregnant. I presumed it was just post-operative niggles. I also thought it was only routine for my gynaecologist, giant-sized, kind-eyed Mr Mascarenhas, to come to my bedside every morning in his slick, three-piece suit to beam a grin at me and stick his stethoscope to my belly. As the days passed though, his easy smile began to tighten and my nerves prickled in response. They frazzled like Frankenstein's when 'Mr Masc' solemnly announced, "The operation didn't work, Jayne."

"What?"

"It appears you're still bleeding." *Oh my God, I really am gonna die!*

"Oh."

"Which means we'll have to operate again."

"Oh no!" *Oh shit, oh shit.*

"I know, I'm sorry."

"Well, you tried your best."

"It may be a bit more complicated than last time but we'll go into the same cut if we can."

"Complicated?"

"Well you have no bowel sounds. I think all the blood in your abdomen has stuck your bowels together."

"Oh my God." *Oh shit, are they going to have to cut some of my bowels out?*

"Don't worry. We have a team of very good surgeons, including a fabulous bowel surgeon and we should be able to sort this out."

"What and save everything in my belly?" *Oh please, please...*

"We will do our very best." He smiled. I clenched my teeth but tears slipped down my shame-red cheeks. He passed me a tissue; "It's okay to be upset." He touched my hand. I felt soothed and strengthened by his genuine care and managed a weak smile. "Right then..."

On the second Sunday of my hospital stay I said my usual cheery "See you in a bit" to a silent and panda-eyed Matthew and my spaced-out parents who, despite my protestations that I was okay, had driven from Yorkshire to check for themselves (my gutsy mum had learned to drive when I threw her the challenge at fifty-three.) My dad, in his usual quiet, ghost-like style, hardly said a word during visiting times and even my mum, who usually talks non-stop, quietly munched her way through bags of crisps, looking very young and lost. I presumed the familiar environment was regressing her back to being an isolated, screaming six-year-old having her neck cauterised. I wondered if my dad was regressing to his teenage self and reliving the agonizing deaths of his parents. It was gutting to be causing the people I loved so much pain.

Despite my compassion for my mum and dad, I also felt moments of anger and despair as I realized that they both appeared to be intimidated by the men and women in uniforms.

"Please can you ask them for my pain-killers Mum? They're over an hour overdue now."

"Oh they'll come in a minute."

"I'm really struggling ..."

"They'll come soon. They're busy, love."

"I know"*...and meanwhile I feel like I've got a slice of glass circulating round my pelvis!*

"Dad, can you ask how long it'll be?"

"Mmm. In a minute..." I wanted them to be my advocates, to fight for me! Fortunately I also understood that they'd grown up with the 'scientific paradigm' (and the notion that science can conquer all) and the old 'medical model' which held the position that the person in the white coat was all-knowing and should be totally deferred to, especially when he or she was middle class and articulate and, the most scary aspect of all, the person who could save your daughter's life – or not. I'm sure they feared that if they argued or rocked the boat I might get worse care. I understood their worry because I shared it. The weirdest thing about being in hospital is probably the fear of causing a stir and upsetting the people your life depends on, no matter how they treat you. The feeling of powerlessness is beyond words.

Because I was still taking anticoagulants, I had to wait on a 'trolley' outside an operating theatre for my blood to thicken enough for the surgery. I felt sick as I looked at the big, peeling doors and I found it hard to blank out images of Death pacing up and down the corridor, whistling a slightly jubilant tune. I felt like I was in a dream and I'd wake up to a lovely Sunday dinner with friends or family at any minute and, another part of me was very clear-headed. I probably only managed to stay sane because I had such faith in our medical system and my Gentle Giant. His smile seemed genuine, he asked how I was emotionally as well as physically, talked just enough about himself to be a 'real' person, was sensitive about sticking his stethoscope down my pyjamas, took time to explain things to me and looked into my eyes when he spoke to me. Despite my faith, however, my whole body was trembling as I was finally sucked into the sterile-stinking theatre and ordered to count backwards into my gentle whoosh of anaesthetic oblivion...

When I came round from the operation I was mortified to see a centimetre-wide tube poking out of a bloodstained dressing on my belly; it was delivering grotesque strands of clotted blood into a plastic pouch hanging over the side of my bed. The olive-skinned giant explained that that this was "just a drain" I'd need for a few days – but my bleeding had been stopped. I cried with relief as Mr Mascarenhas told me that my bowels were intact and even now, as I write, I can still feel the immense gratitude toward him and the other theatre staff who missed their Sunday dinners that evening to perform my long and complicated operation. I wasn't particularly grateful, however, when Mr Mascarenhas broke the news that I'd lost an ovary in the process. My latent nightmare that I may not be able to have children seemed to be materializing and I became haunted with visions of my ovary, a full fifty percent of my potential, beautiful babies, being mercilessly incinerated or flushed down a drain by a person with an uncaring blank face. It was a hard time and I felt very alone. My family, Matthew and friends, all happy that I was alive, couldn't really share my pain; I still had one good ovary, after all. Of course there was no privacy to grieve. There was no privacy for anything in the crazy chaos and having to stiffen my upper lip drenched me with the sad hormones and chemicals which a good sob would have released. My head span. The whirring wasn't helped by the fact that nobody knew why I'd started bleeding in the first place; there was a question of whether a cyst on my ovary had burst but nobody really knew why. Neither did the doctors know why, as my fellow patients were gradually discharged to the safety of their homes, my bloated body had a fever and a weakness which continued to pin me to my bed.

A week later I was upset to miss the first weekend of my therapy training but the next one was six weeks away so I was pretty confident that the doctors would have sorted me out by then. In the meantime I resolved to just try and go with the flow of the hospital routine. Woken at six, the first tablets and drip medications were administered, followed by a few bites of cold, chewy toast at about eight. Next was an embarrassing bed-bath – I couldn't believe that I needed help to wash – and then being hiked into my bedside chair so my sheets could be changed (the washing bills in hospitals must be huge!) I'd then watch for the dreaded blood-sucking phlebotomist and the intimidating ward-round posse. If I was lucky a short snooze ensued, followed by a spot of lunch if I could stomach it – usually not; I was still really bloated and being frequently sick as my bowels were still out of action. After lunch came round two of my tablets. I'd then wait for Matthew and sometimes other kind visitors. Usually I loved this break from my isolation though I could feel very distant from the real world and too exhausted and depressed to talk much. Normally an avid reader, I felt books were too heavy to hold up, and chatting with fellow patients in beds and bedside chairs ten feet away was physically hard, so I spent much of my non-visiting time just quietly observing. It was actually a trainee psychotherapist's dream being surrounded by a whole cross-section of people – patients, staff and visitors – from almost all walks of life (many of the wealthy were no doubt in their private hospitals.)

It struck me that here was a microcosm of our wider society, with its clear hierarchical structures. Just as most powerful politicians, company bosses, judges and priests are white, often privately educated men, here they were the senior consultants and surgeons. At polytechnic, in my quest to understand human development, I'd learned that alongside poverty, poorer schools and diets, institutionalised racism, etc the 'Self-fulfilling Prophesy' was a big player; the notion that we become what's expected of us by our parents, carers, teachers, the media and class or cultural norms and biases. Hence working-class and kids of Afro-Caribbean descent often *expecting* and then getting poor exam results and menial, low paid jobs (if they're lucky; as I edit here in 2016, I've just heard on BBC Radio 4 that about a quarter of young people in the UK are unemployed). Conversely, more middle-class and privately educated young people fully expect to do well; mostly white public school boys make up about seven percent of male pupils in the UK yet secure about half of the highest paid, most prestigious jobs[4] (despite them, of course, not always being the brightest folks). In one lecture at poly I'd been taught about an ethically dubious psychological experiment where Robert Rosenthal and colleagues went into a school, did tests on the children and then told the teachers which children would progress over the coming year. Sure enough, in retests at the end of the experiment, the identified children had come on the most. It was then revealed that these children had been picked at *random* and that it was only the expectations of the teachers that had led to their advancement; 'The Pygmalion Effect'. Label a child clever and tell him that he's expected to achieve great things and he's likely to. Tell her she's going nowhere and she may well believe it, and unconsciously create a life which reflects her belief about herself.

I never cease to be amazed in my work with therapy clients, at just how much people's deep beliefs determine their self-image and subsequent behaviour. I've had clients who, having been called greedy and put on diets as children, still think they're fat when they're *tiny*, or end up morbidly obese, eating for comfort and because they *can*. I see highly intelligent people who were criticized, developed slowly, weren't good at essays

4. *See the interesting Guardian article https://www.theguardian.com/education/2016/feb/24/privately-educated-elite-continues-to-take-top-jobs-finds-survey.*

and exams or were put into low streams at school and think they're daft, and there are many kind, warm and beautiful people who were treated badly and think they're horrible and ugly. I no longer presume that someone who looks like they 'have it all' on the outside feels like that on the inside, or vice versa. What seems to count is not the outer circumstances of our lives so much as our inner 'programming' in childhood (much of which can be picked up in our neighbourhoods, of course); it's this which determines the way we think about ourselves and our circumstances as adults. Thank God for 'neuroplasticity' (the brain's capacity for rewiring and growth) and our ability to change our programming and restructure our brains throughout our lifespan!

As I observed from my hospital bed I wondered how many people had concluded as children that they were bad or unworthy. Some of the working-class porters were very witty and clearly as bright as buttons; would things have been different for them if they'd been told by an Eton professor how clever and deserving they were? Would the doctors have made it if they hadn't grown up with their parents' and teachers' expectations and encouragement? How many more people of colour would be doctors if it wasn't for racism and massive inequality of opportunity?

I'd been fascinated by the nature of humanity since being a child when I first questioned my mum's Christian view that we're born sinful so my ears pricked up when we started looking at the 'nature versus nurture' debate at poly – was it mostly our genes or our circumstances which moulded us? My brain positively hoovered up lectures on 'Attachment Theory' (generally attributed to John Bowlby[5] in the 1950s and 60s, though much of the leg-work was apparently done by his typically invisible female colleague, Mary Ainsworth). They

5. *See Dr John Bowlby, bibliography p. 432*

devised experiments to observe the 'attachment patterns' or bonding of babies with their mothers, with the mums going out of a room for a little while and then observing how the babies reacted. Babies with a good, secure attachment tended to get upset when their mums left but were easily comforted and soothed on her return; they'd learned that their mum was their place of safety. 'Secure attachments' tend to happen with 'tuned in' mothers who delight in their babies, can respond to their physical and emotional needs, provide consistent, soothing care and help them to express and understand their different emotions. "Oh, sweetie; are you feeling sad? Do you want a cuddle? ...Ooh...look at that frown, you look very cross, what's the matter?" Attachment researchers (many have followed Bowlby and Ainsworth) have found that 'securely attached' children tend to grow up with clarity about their emotions, a belief that they are inherently lovable, that relationships are a source of love and comfort and the world a safe and exciting place. They tend to be happy and empathic. When bad things happen to them as adults, these individuals often cope well as they've 'internalised' their parents' calm, soothing voices, "Come on, flower, it'll be okay..." and are able to comfort and reassure themselves, remaining connected to their rational, grounded, empathic front cortex.

Research has also shown that if parents or carers are inconsistent, absent a lot (leaving the baby with people she or he doesn't have a strong attachment to) don't express delight in their child (from a fear of losing their baby for example, or being ill, drunk, drugged, traumatised, stressed out, depressed or very narcissistic) and are often unable to 'mirror' or explain their children's feelings back to them and soothe their emotional needs, then secure attachments are not easily established. In the Bowlby experiments, these babies were not particularly comforted when their mums returned to the room and sometimes positively ignored them, having learnt, very early, only to rely on themselves emotionally. Poor attachments often lead to low levels of self-confidence and self-esteem in adulthood and a limited ability to self-soothe when stressed or upset, hence often flipping out in aggressive, self-protective, instinctive 'reptile brain' modes or turning to drugs, alcohol, self-harm, overwork, over- or under-eating, compulsive sex, sleep, shopping, gambling, computer gaming, constant TV or a variety of other distractions to cope with overwhelming, confusing feelings. These adults didn't learn that others delighted in them, so struggle to feel delightful or secure in relationships; they sometimes lack empathy and have a strong tendency to put others down so they don't feel so bad about themselves.

If our attachment patterns are really bad and we experience parents or carers, teachers and other significant people in our lives often ignoring, shouting, scowling at, hitting or abusing us, we often grow up believing that the world and other people are unsafe. If our emotional needs are experienced as 'bad' or unsafe ("Now be quiet and be a big boy"... "Don't you scowl at me like that or I'll knock it off your face!") these feelings have to be suppressed and eventually this blanking out of 'unacceptable' feelings can become so habitual that we lose our ability to contact and express our feelings, know what we want or how to ask for it. We can then grow up with a fear that we'll be emotionally abandoned or made to feel ashamed in our hour of need if we ask for something or show our vulnerability – or feel ashamed, crazy or wrong when we contact these 'unacceptable' emotions. A glimmer of fear or sadness and *whoosh* – in comes an automatic feeling of shame! (And can't I relate to that! I used to drive a friend mad with my self-berating every time I expressed an emotion... "Jayne, you just feel what you feel and that's okay!" he'd cry in exasperation.) Poorly bonded, insecure children tend also to be less able to establish good boundaries, concentrate and learn; they often have poor connections between their reptile brain and their soothing, grounding, rational front cortex, hence often being anxious, confused, depressed and unassertive or defensive, agitated and aggressive (and a pain to teachers because they simply *can't* sit at a desk and concentrate.)

Well, yup, this insecure attachment business sounds a bit familiar; my mum was my loving place of safety, yet her trauma, which came out in her out-of-control shouting — and sometimes, as with many parents in 1970's Yorkshire, hitting – also meant that she was often the one scaring me. My dad was my protector, yet his trauma and macho, 1940-50s working-class upbringing often kept him in his distant bubble with little understanding of my internal world and then came all the reinforcement of my lack of worth from my philandering boyfriends...Ouch, no wonder I have a mashed up attachment system, a huge fear of criticism and rejection and little faith that others can comfort – or love – me. Mmm...

As a social worker I saw insecure attachments in abundance and worked with hundreds of so-called 'dysfunctional families.' The 'cycles of deprivation' clearly revealed how insecure attachments (often exacerbated by the stresses of poverty) led to the same poor attachments in the next generation, with history – and abuse, violence, helplessness and criticism – often being repeated. As I observed politicians shrieking at each other like children in the House of Commons, I also wondered about the attachment trauma in families where children often have nannies and are sent away to boarding schools at a young age. Did these poor or broken attachments explain some of our leaders' intense drive to achieve power but express low levels of empathy and compassion? Thinking about it, our feelings-adverse, dog-eat-dog paradigm is the perfect breeding ground for psychopaths and sociopaths who've had poor attachments and lack empathy but need to be in control and I guess the more we reward ruthless competitiveness and let good morals slip and the less we challenge the 'cut-throat neo-liberalism norm,' the more these people will succeed...

Recent advances in epigenetics have shown that our genes are turned on and off in relation to our experiences, so our attachment patterns can affect us right down to a genetic level. Neuroscience, with its brain scans, electrical imaging and blood tests, is showing that when we're cooing at and cuddling babies, that's when they release chemicals which physically *grow* their brains and bodies.[6] Studies of unloved children in Romanian orphanages[7] have shown them to be severely disturbed with actual 'holes' in their brains, and abused children are often identified by social workers, health visitors and GPs because of their 'failure to thrive,' that is, not growing and developing well. (It was awful to see scrawny, blank-faced babies in my work.) Love and security equals good growth in both the body and brain; abuse and isolation often equals less growth and poor connections to 'grounded' and empathic brain areas. This calls into question our punishment of, essentially, often brain-damaged people and I would argue that our prisons should be healing people, not hurting and humiliating them and making their issues worse, just as homeless people who've had awful pasts should be helped and nurtured, not scorned. *Maybe the Beatles were right – "All you need is love!"*

Don't worry if you didn't get much love; read on for some methods to make up for poor attachments and how to rebalance your brain! And of course there are no hard and fast rules, we're all unique individuals with fluctuating capacities for connecting with others and many people who grew up in tense or scary environments are often the most perceptive amongst us because they had to grow long 'antennae' in order to suss out whether or not they were safe, and people who have suffered can be the most empathic and ready to give to others.

After a decade's social work I was pretty convinced that

---

6. *A great book about this is 'Why Love Matters' by Sue Gerhardt*
7. *Nathan A Fox – www.researchconnections.org/.../Fox_Nathan_StressMtg2012.pdf*

we're definitely not born sinful. I'd met no sinful babies but saw, again and again, how difficult circumstances slowly sucked the joy out of children and brought out depression and aggression in them – as children and adults. Now I believed that though we may be born with certain genetic potentials, it's mostly our experiences which make us who we are; what's said to and happens to us becomes the way we think about ourselves; if we're being hurt or ignored all the time, we conclude that it *must* mean we're bad and unlovable and our critical internal voice becomes vicious. We may then begin to act 'bad,' covering up our vulnerability and broken hearts with defensiveness and aggression.

My psychotherapy training reinforced my positive view of humanity; the Gestalt model of the human being, borrowing from Buddhism, maintains that we are born with loving kindness at our core (again you only have to spend time with happy children to see how geared up they are for connection and wanting to be helpful despite being pretty self-focused up to about seven) but we sometimes have our inner goodness covered by our hurt or 'baggage'. I was over the moon when I read in 'I Heart Me, The Science of Self-Love' by David R. Hamilton that Charles Darwin's 'survival of the fittest' notion had been misinterpreted[8] (by a Herbert Spencer). Apparently Darwin actually said that the most sociable and *cooperative* creatures – and humans – survived the best and that 'sympathy' for others is the strongest gene and force in we humans (stronger than the 'selfish' survival gene) and the main reason for our successful parenting and survival. Apparently in his book *The Descent of Man* Darwin only mentioned survival of the fittest a few times but love many times, stating, "We are because we belong." It seems that the 'survival of the fittest' notion was

---

8. A good, succinct article about this can be found in the 'New Scientist' at https//www.newscientist.com/article/dn13671-evolution-myths-survival-of-the-fittest-justifies-everyone-for-themselves/.)

used by some white males at the time to justify the Industrial Revolution's inequality, competition and greedy individualism (and later, fascism) and, sadly, it indoctrinated us with the view that we're aggressive, selfish beings by nature and that the accumulation of wealth and possessions – and power – over others is inevitable. Finding joy in cooperative, empathic living and the mystery and awe of our miraculous world began to be lost in the Western world as the powerful Protestant work ethic and profit-led 'doing' and *competing* took root and we became identified with our possessions, our roles and *me* and what *I* own, how *I* look, what *I* believe and how much better *I* am than you/him/her. We began to lose 'we' – unless our 'us' was seen to be better than another group or race of 'them'.

So, it seems that we're relational beings who can't grow, develop or stay sane in isolation and therefore we develop deep relational habits as children in an attempt to maximise our levels of attachment or connection to others and continue these familiar patterns of relating into adulthood. As I watched from my hospital bed, it was fairly clear which patients (and staff) like myself, had been told as children that they shouldn't be 'soft' and cry for attention. They'd become stoic, having learned that they had to be 'fine' in order to stay in their parents' good books and remain emotionally attached to them. Like young, teddy-hugging Jenny who'd just miscarried for the second time and looked devastated in the quiet moments but forced a beaming smile whenever she was approached.

Then there were people who could be 'victimy' and had learned to get care and attention by pretending to be helpless or making their pain and needs hugely obvious in order to be noticed. "Nurse, nurse, help me please, I need some painkillers, I think I'm dying!" wailed Margaret in her pink, frilly nightie. I wanted to slap her, just as my demands had annoyed my stressed parents; my programming that asking for help and attention equals being very bad indeed was deeply ingrained.

Some patients were jovial jokers – like Celia in her cat-paw pyjamas who, whatever the pain levels from her hysterectomy, kept up a constant stream of puns and knock-knock jokes. I'd put money on the fact that she'd had to adopt a comedienne role in her youth in order to try and guarantee relationships, attention and a sense of belonging within her family or peer group. She wouldn't have had much success in my family where 'being silly' wasn't appreciated at *all.*

Some patients were chatterers (like my mum) who couldn't stand a quiet moment with their feelings. Then there were the angry complainers (princesses like me) whose aggression and criticising covered up our fear and vulnerability. Others, like me once I'd 'defrosted' enough, were 'rescuers,' having learned to focus on and look after others in order to feel a sense of security and safety. Many doctors and nurses were classic 'rescuers' who nearly killed themselves running around being heroic; "Oh I should have had the day off today with this cold but I came in anyway…oh I'm so busy but I'll get you some pills…" They clearly got a great sense of satisfaction and personal identity from being such martyrs but made me as a patient feel guilty for existing. Similarly, apparently caring "Oh, darling, how are you?" comments without a real hearing of my answer said to me 'I'm feeling great being a self-important and oh so caring nurse but I don't *really* see you and empathise with you; I just pity you and feel a little bit superior, not recognising that, deep down, I have the potential to be just as vulnerable as you are…' Despite being treated like a child, I soon learned to show gratitude to such types; responding with a sarcastic "Yes I'm fine, darling" one miserable, feverish day meant that I had to wait even longer for my painkillers. *Jaynie, you should know by now not to challenge a rescuer's yummy self-image; and come on, be compassionate, remember you don't like to have your positive view of yourself challenged either…*

Then there were the more genuinely compassionate staff

who, despite being overworked, were still in touch with their feelings, not just their 'I'm good' self-image. They didn't hide their emotions behind their stethoscopes but met their patients as fully fledged, suffering human beings and allowed themselves to be impacted. They quietly soothed our distress without a great show – the use of your name, a warm smile, an acknowledgement of the pain, a gentle touch; person-to-person relating. This human contact made me feel safe, reduced the anxiety-fuelling cortisol which was whacking my body and instead allowed me to release oxytocin and other 'happy hormones' like dopamine and serotonin. As well as making us feel great, oxytocin has been found to be just what patients need; it aids digestion, boosts the immune system (fighting off everything from infections to cancer) and reduces inflammation which is linked to a host of illnesses including auto-immune diseases such as ME, Fibromyalgia and *Lupus*. Oxytocin has also been shown to reduce ageing; more human contact may yet replace Botox! Oxytocin's known as the happy and the 'compassion hormone' because it makes us more open and loving; people in love are pumping out the stuff. When we do something kind we release a dose of oxytocin. If a person responds to our kindness with a smile, we release even more oxytocin and by now our nervous system's calmer and the chilled, safe, pro-social part of our brain's lighting up like a blooming supernova – which makes us smile at the next person we meet; they smile back, get *their* oxytocin boost and it's turning into a very good day for everybody![9]

A not so good time was had by the little creatures in Harry Harlow's famous 1958 rhesus monkey experiments which really impacted me in a psychology lecture at poly (partly because of the results and partly because the experiments were so cruel[10]).

---

9. David R Hamilton explains all this oxytocin stuff brilliantly in his book 'I Heart Me'

10. A good reference is www.simplypsychology.org/attachment.html.

Baby monkeys kept in isolation (from three months up to a year) and then put with other monkeys became strange, withdrawn, aggressive and unable to socialise and communicate (like the Romanian orphans.) They indulged in self-mutilation, tearing out hair, scratching and biting. In another experiment, baby monkeys were put in a cage with two pretend 'parents,' one made of steel and offering food and the other covered in fur. Most often the babies clung to the fur parent rather than the one with food, starkly illustrating our powerful mammalian need for comfort and connection. Similarly a 1970s study of rats, 'Rat Park,'[11] gave them the choice of water or water laced with heroin. Sole rats generally went for the heroin, often eventually overdosing and dying in the process. Rats in social groups mostly stuck with the water and few became addicted to the heroin. Mammals freak out on their own, as we know from our dastardly use of solitary confinement as a severe punishment. Heart disease and the incidence of strokes has been found to be about three times worse amongst socially isolated people[12] and studies have shown that loneliness is a significant predictor of unhappiness, mental instability,[13] illness[14] and even early death.[15] From all I've read over the years, the majority of serial killers and psychopaths had lonely or abusive childhoods.

Talking of disturbed people, I was relieved to conclude that there only seemed to be a few of these amongst the staff team of the gynie ward but they did stand out; they seemed to have

11. *Lloyd I Sederer MD's 2019 article– www.psychiatrictimes.com/substance-use-disorder/what-does-rat-pack-teach-us-about-addiction*
12. *see the British Medical Journal's study review at https://heart.bmj.com/content/102/13/1009*
13. *https://www.mind.org.uk/information-support/tips-for-everyday-living/loneliness/about-loneliness*
14. *See this interesting article by Dr Sanjay Gupta: https://www.everydayhealth.com/news/loneliness-can-really-hurt-you/*
15. *This article suggests that loneliness may increase the chances of dying by up to 30 percent! https://www.nhs.uk/news/mental-health/loneliness-increases-risk-of-premature-death/*

little respect for colleagues or patients, and rarely listened. As I watched the goings on around me, I reflected on our world and the games that we play with our hierarchies, power imbalances and role-plays; a stethoscope often gave an air of assurance whilst a mop could bring rounded shoulders. Many at the top of the tree clearly considered themselves superior and expected deference from those below. It made me sad or cross (depending on my mood) when I heard curt orders, patronizing comments or simple indifference being passed downwards. It made me livid when the insensitivity and bullying was passed right down to us totally dependent patients at the bottom of the pile. "What's wrong with you?" a large, po-faced nurse asked timid, blue-rinsed Brenda. "You had some painkillers an hour ago."

"Well they didn't work."

"Come now, stop being a baby...I've got better things to do than sit and hold your hand all day!"

Was the nurse in pain herself? Was she stressed out or unhappy? Had she had poor attachments or early trauma and was bullying as she'd been bullied? Had some old pain associated with a nasty parent or teacher just being triggered because Brenda reminded her of them? Was she afraid of her own vulnerability, her own ageing? Hadn't she been trained in self-awareness and compassion?

Many nurses were of course like blooming angels, *so* kind and sensitive, as were many doctors who didn't look down on those less qualified. When I heard them being humble, polite, respectful and inclusive, it made my heart sing – and sometimes joyful tears of hope for humanity pricked my eyes. Here was a system with obvious hierarchies yet these people, from *all* social backgrounds, and indeed, many cultures and countries, *could* work as a team, all trying their best, together, to heal their fellow human beings. What gave the good doctors and the kind nurses their open hearts and warmth? What made them more able to stay with their feelings? Had they had strong,

loving attachments with their parents? Were they being well-supported by their seniors and peers and feeling safe and valued enough to stay calm and grounded? Had they looked at themselves and developed more self-awareness? Had they had compassion training? I asked various nurses and doctors how much training they got in 'how people tick,' how to develop a good bedside manner and get support so that they could carry on authentically and warmly in the midst of such intense pain and pressure; the sad answer was always "Not a lot" or "None." I was gutted to hear this; they were expected to face massive trauma – and death – on a daily basis without relevant training or emotional support. *Unbelievable! No wonder so many nurses and doctors drink a lot, resign or commit suicide!*

Despite my attempt to focus on others, my hospital bed provided too much time and space to avoid also viewing myself – and my own levels of empathy. I'd have an encounter with a doctor or nurse and then lie for two or three hours, just drifting in and out of feverish sleep and reflecting on that exchange. I saw that I could be chatty and appreciative, forming relationships quite easily. I also saw that I could think cruel thoughts and be snappy, sarcastic and cut off from my empathy. It was interesting to see that my 'poisonous princess' appeared mostly when I was in pain or scared. The more small, vulnerable and powerless I felt, the bigger and more powerful I tried to see myself or act. Sometimes I saw myself going through the different stages of the fight-flight-freeze process; one minute I'd be like a wild dog, swearing and 'playing hell', as my mum would say (fight), the next I'd be telling myself that I just had to call a taxi and get out of hospital, whether I died or not (flight) and then I'd see myself like a head-bowed child, frozen to the spot. Oh how I was reflecting on our human condition! Actually my reflections probably started when I was about four and listening to my Grandad if the following poem of his is anything to go by...

Life's Picture

God gives us all a canvas, with brushes large and small

For we've got to paint a picture that will hang upon life's wall.

Some use gold and silver paints, make pictures bright and gay

Yet others show great courage for their paints are dark and grey.

Pictures of failure, courage and fame all hang upon life's wall,

The work of a lifetime hung there when the painter receives his call

And when the master sees them at some he'll smile with pride

Then find fault with others that golden paints won't hide.

And when yours comes to hang there the master will judge that too

For the picture your brushes have painted will be a picture of you.

Arthur Downs

Chapter 6
On Being Kissed by Death

"Quantum theory…reveals a basic oneness of the universe. It shows that we cannot decompose the world into independently existing smallest units. …nature doesn't show us any isolated building blocks but rather appears as a complicated web of relations between the various parts of the whole."

Fritjof Capra

A fortnight later and absolutely desperate to get home, on with my new relationship and back to work, my bowels were still not working. The Gentle Giant reassured me that they were just "a bit shocked." I was terrified that they wouldn't come out of shock and attempted to maintain some semblance of control by being 'on the ball,' which must've been a right pain for the busy staff, especially those who liked patients to be seen but not heard. "What's this medication do? Please can I see my scan results? What's happening with my blood? Where's this fever coming from?" I soon realised, however, that the doctors' long, convoluted answers to many of my questions were basically saying, "We don't know." My spark and princess-self waned. My spark was dimmed more with each staff member who whacked in needles or poked about with a stethoscope with no introduction or conversation, as if I were an inanimate object, a job to get through. It made me feel like hospital property. A body but no-one in it. As the pain, fevers and vomiting continued, my body waned too and I increasingly lay back with defeated acceptance.

Then I began to cough. It was a sore, raspy cough and when it seemed to be becoming difficult for me to breathe, doctors from all over the hospital began to flock to my bedside; was this a renal, cardiology, gynaecological, haematological or purely illogical situation? The medics began to question me about where I'd travelled and whether I'd ever taken any weird drugs or medication. I flashed back to the mind-blowing joints which I'd smoked in local charmer George's mud hut in Kenya but I didn't think they would count. I told them about the centimetre-wide infected spot I'd had on my face in Laos and a nasty coral cut in Thailand which swelled up my whole foot and forced me to go to an Accident and Emergency department in Malaysia – but the doctors didn't think they were relevant. Despite the sombre shaking of many medical heads, I told myself that I'd just caught a cold from a snotty nurse and silently vented my anger towards her for coming to work with such a nasty bug. (I didn't realise what 'back to work' disciplinary crap she may've had to face had she had taken time off!)

Part of general, at least twice daily 'obs' (routine observations of heart rate, blood pressure and temperature) was 'SATS' or saturation levels of the oxygen in your blood, tested by an ingenious, painless plastic clip slipped onto the end of your finger. As my breathing became more laboured, my connection to the SATS machine became permanent and I watched with saucer eyes as the 98 to a 100 percent oxygen ideal on the monitor screen dropped from 97 to 92 whilst my heart rate sped up... *Bloody hell, I'm breathing quickly...sit up, Jaynie... that's better...oh no it isn't...oh shit, my chest feels really* *tight…I don't believe this…oh God, I can't breathe…I'm just panicking, calm down, Jaynie, calm down…*I realized with a shock what an immense gift – simply breathing – I'd taken for granted.

My panic spiralled when a pan-faced nurse strapped an oxygen mask to my face and I got a glimpse of Death's dark eye sockets looking like infinite black holes, but as I took deep breaths of about twenty percent pure oxygen my breathing improved and Death faded from my mind again. With an oxygen tank in tow, I was then wheeled back to my initial ward of E17, the haematology ward, because my blood had begun to do "weird things;" my clotting patterns seemed "irregular," possibly due to the blood-thinning heparin that I'd been given after my operations. There seemed to be evidence of both clotting and bleeding but nobody really knew what was going on or what to do about it. It was later confirmed that I did have 'HIT' – Heparin Induced Thrombocytopenia – which was gutting; the medication intended to help me had made me much worse.

I was grateful to be met by the familiar, warm and friendly staff team of E17 and when I was reconnected to a SATS machine my oxygen levels had gone up to 95. *See, you were just panicking…you're going to be okay,* I told myself, smiling reassuringly at Matthew from behind my hissing plastic mask and squeezing his slightly damp hand. We sat in silence for a while, keeping tabs on the steady 94 and 95 but then suddenly the avalanche let out an echoing creak and up pinged 91. 90. I snatched away my oxygen mask to croak a request to Matthew that he count out loud to try and help me regulate my increasingly erratic breathing. When his slightly choked voice began its steady flow of numbers I dived into the depths of his blue eyes, desperately grasping for an antidote to my exploding fear. His eyes were wild and scared though and when the nurse came in, looked at the monitor and turned up my oxygen supply, I knew that Matthew's wide pools of blue couldn't be my solace. I'd now been put in a side room on my own, so neither could I project my vulnerability onto other sick people and avoid seeing it in myself; my terror was raw and my skin wet through. *Go away, Death, please, please go away...*

I gulped down the increased oxygen supply and for a while my heart stopped pounding quite so madly and '93' pinged onto the screen. *Okay, and breathe in...and relax, Jaynie... phew, and out...in...ah, you'll be okay now. Come on see, stop being a drama queen, it's not so bad.* I then saw Matthew's pupils dilate as they flicked to the monitor again and his quiet counting faltered; 89. *Oh God, oh God...* 87. 82. *Oh God, please don't let this be happening. Oh God, this is surreal...* 81. My head was getting woozier and my whole body pounding.77. *Bloody hell, I'm in serious trouble here...*As the avalanche let out a thunderous crack and began its menacing slide down the mountainside, I was engulfed in a chilling, numbing reality; I wasn't a danger-flaunting, hard-core, professional princess but a completely vulnerable human being.

As I began to fade away, Dr H. sped to my bedside to tell me that I was being taken to the 'High Dependency Unit.' I just stared at her. "You have pneumonia - and they'll be able to take better care of you there." My gaunt face remained frozen. "And you'll be back soon" she added as her eyes flitted around the room. I was devastated; I didn't want to become just a bed number again and have to suss out a whole new staff team, and 'high dependency' didn't sound good. On the way to my new home, the blessed porters tried their best to reassure me that it was a good ward but as the doors of 'HDU' swung open I felt like I was being wheeled into the bowels of Hell. The security door clinked firmly behind me. This was the room of death that you saw on TV... *It can't be real,* I thought; *I can't be so ill that I need to be in here!* 'Eerie' doesn't come close to describing the atmosphere; 'horrific' feels closer but that somehow belies the clinical stillness which filled the darkened room. At one end was a nurses' station with a desk-full of files, telephones and monitor screens and down the room six beds were lined up in rows of three. Some were surrounded by the brown-flowered curtains. The visible patients were attached to a complicated array of tubes, drips and monitors with flashing luminous numbers and dancing graphs. Bap...bap...bap...bap...bap... bap...bap; an electronic voice signalled to the world that these fragile bodies were barely alive.

Unable to even stand up now, I was rolled from my 'trolley' onto a six-foot plastic board (a 'slide') and then deposited, feeling like a chunk of meat, onto a bed next to the nurses' station. Despite my lack of mobility, immobile bowels, choking chest pain, frequent sickness, burning fever, total exhaustion and being fixed up so that I was beeping wildly alongside my peers, I just couldn't take in that I was one of those desperate people. I remember staring into Matthew's saucer-wide eyes and simply shaking my head. Less than a month ago we'd opened our hearts on a moonlit beach. Now here we were in the middle of a real-life nightmare with me trying to cough up disgusting green gunk. How could life be so crazy?

I was assigned on HDU to beefy Nurse Brian whose warmth and chatter initially calmed me but with each view of my decreasing oxygen levels, his joking patter slowed down and my panic grew. When I no longer had a scrap of energy left to try and cough up the thick, infected phlegm that was suffocating me, and sweat was pouring down Brian's pink face, he brought me a new oxygen mask. It was a hefty, plastic affair with a big, thick rim which cut into my cheeks and, as it blew air into my lungs, almost choked me. I spluttered and gagged for a while in a sheath of ice cold sweat but finally got into a rhythm and began to breathe again; my oxygen levels rose. Tears rolled down my cheeks as I tried to persuade Matthew with a weak nod that I was okay. I tried to convince myself too; *Jaynie, stop being dramatic, of course you're not dying...*

You're not out of the water yet though, are you?

Oh will you stop being so negative, you drama-crazed amygdala![16]

Look, maybe there is a God and if you're gonna die you'd better get repenting quick...

I'm not gonna die! And surely I've not been bad enough for Hell!

Well you've hardly been godly.

I haven't killed anybody and I do try and be nice to people!

Yes but you haven't repented one little bit, have you?

Okay, okay! God, I'm sorry. I'm sorry I'm a worthless sinner and please don't let this be happening. Please don't take me now, just as I've met Matthew, please, please...oh God, I can't breathe...what's all that beeping? Oh shit...oh shit...

As my oxygen monitor screamed its final warning and Brian ran to call the crash team from the Intensive Care Unit (ICU) Death was doing cartwheels. *Bloody hell, this is unreal...I'm dying...Oh my God, my mum and dad are gonna be destroyed! What about my brother losing his little sister? And poor Matthew! And Maria, oh my God, she'll be devastated – so will Carol and Trisha, Gilly, Doreen, Julie and Jeanette...oh and Frankie, she lost her dad; this will do her head in! And my children at work will be traumatized all over again... and Morty! What about little Morty-cat? Oh my God...*

16. *Our brain's 'red alert' centre*

And then something really strange happened. Despite my totally conscious grief for my loved ones, I was suddenly struck by the fact that, for me, I felt completely at ease, peaceful and totally fine with what was happening. *Well, this is weird! I like being Jaynie, I love my life so why am I not upset? I should be upset, I'm bloody dying! Hey, this is bizarre… amazing… but then I'm not really dying, am I? My individual body may be dying but it doesn't really matter because I'm connected to everything else, after all.* I had a vision of the solar system and some deep feeling that I was 'the whole' as well as a tiny part of it. I sensed that despite losing my life, it wasn't really being lost because I was *absolutely* connected to everything else – other people, animals, trees, the earth and the stars. We were made from the same energy and space dust, the same atoms and very similar DNA; I was an integral and essential part of a life-force which was *everything*. The wave of little me was crashing but the sea was still dancing. I also felt that my journey wasn't over, that I was carrying on; my body was being lost but my energy or consciousness or form was just changing. It was a beautiful feeling which I can't quite describe in words. It was like I was a stream of consciousness or spirit, about to be released into the freedom of the cosmos, into peace, into the next experience… As I continued to think *my God, this is whacky! I'm dying… yet it's so beautiful…* the crash team arrived and whisked me to the Intensive Care Unit where they knocked me out and put me on a respirator. A machine breathed for me through my thirty-second birthday.

I was woken up about a week later, sad that I'm missed the cake that the kind HDU staff had bought for me but overjoyed that I no longer felt the fear of the wrathful God of my childhood; there'd been no sign of Lucifer as I'd looked over the edge! I remember weakly smiling at my wonderful revelation. *So, still alive then! Great…actually; weird…* I'd opened my eyes to a beam near the ceiling dancing with pretty strands of the purples, blues and greens of washing up liquid bubbles. It took me a while to stop being transfixed by the flowing rainbows and look around the sterile white room where white-uniformed staff were watching me watching them. It was like being in a specimen jar. But I was a very grateful specimen and my inner princess was quiet. I'd forgotten this but it's a vivid memory for my brother and makes us smile; apparently the first thing I said to him on being brought back into consciousness was, "Fuck me, where's my toothbrush? I feel like I've eaten a slug!" Ah, Jaynie, such a lady. I wasn't aware of this either but whilst I was unconscious, Nurse Lesley, a lively red-haired Scot about my age, had been clearing my lungs, plaiting my hair, washing me and tending my body's every need with great compassion, sensitivity and expertise. I would be introduced to Lesley by Matthew in Asda several months later – which was a very strange experience. It was lovely to be able to thank her, but very odd to be known so intimately by a person I didn't recall at all.

When I was moved out of Intensive Care and back onto the High Dependency Unit it was the middle of the night and because this time I wasn't so intensely focused on trying to breathe, it felt even scarier than I remembered. Not only were the bleeping machines pulsing out the fragility of life, this time strangled, tragic voices groaned weakly for help and one young woman kept screaming. I thought that was bad until she stopped. It was like being deposited in the sea with a twenty-foot shark cruising around, deciding who to eat next. For once I put aside any concerns about being too demanding a patient and begged a clearly-glad-to-see-me-alive Nurse Brian to find me a television. I stared at it, wide-eyed, right through the night. I remember watching a documentary about the plains of Kenya. It was horrendously gory watching a lion rip into the neck of a helpless gazelle but somehow the sickening scene felt appropriate for this room of death. A few weeks later I would empathise more deeply with the fragile gazelle. My arms were horrendously bruised and it was getting increasingly difficult to take my blood for the at *least* once daily testing, so the medics decided to insert a 'line' into my neck from which to take blood and administer medication. I was given a local anaesthetic in the side of my neck and then a silent, grey-haired man stood behind my bed and cut a hole in me. He then pushed a (six-inch long?) plastic tube down a big vein towards my heart. My recollection is that I could hear the tube squeaking as he pushed it in. Gross. And surreal. And the start of a line-related nightmare which wouldn't reveal itself for another fourteen years.

Having a line put in wasn't quite as surreal as, whilst in the ICU, seeing a man in the opposite bed who I presumed had been in a crash or something because his head looked like it was being held together by a scaffolding of different wooden sticks. I couldn't understand why they'd used such a mish-mash of shabby wood. When I expressed my outrage to Nurse Karen she laughed heartily and told me that I was bonkers. Apparently, the man never existed; I'd lost it. Nurse Karen, now there's another great women and hilarious, blonde, buxom tomboy, who I was lucky enough to have as my main carer. By this point most of my visitors looking at me in my blood-soaked, bloated horror could only answer "fine" when I weakly asked how they were, again making me feel like the only person in the world with any problems....apart from Karen. She would sit with me in the middle of the night, when the beeping was drilling into my brain, and she'd talk, about her life and her difficulties with her boyfriend, as if I were a fully-fledged, intelligent, responsive human being. She'd also make me roar – well croak - with laughter. Thank you, Karen. You were probably going against hospital protocol which says that staff shouldn't share personal information with patients, but in your open human-ness you were an absolute gift.

That's not to say I wasn't *extremely* grateful for the visits of family, friends and work colleagues at this time despite their "I'm fine" responses. I felt guilty about them visiting (finding a parking space was a nightmare, never mind facing the horror) but I also appreciated that they kept coming, with the help of Matthew's 'visitor's rota.' A friendly face meant the world to me – as did the fact that Matthew didn't do a runner. Still sharing the intense shock, he visited me every day for long periods, giving me *much* appreciated back massages; lying in bed for weeks on end isn't as comfy as you'd imagine! Without Matthew's care and my hope for our future together, I wonder if I'd still be here; we spent hours talking about opening a therapy cum yoga centre when I got home and getting married in a wood. I sketched the strappy, flowing, baby blue dress I'd make; he planned to wear his shorts. Sharing such a mind-blowing drama, and Matthew being my ears and voice on occasions when I was asleep or too weak to talk, brought us close very soon (once I'd got over my guilt at not 'releasing' him.) I have wonderful memories of seeing him walking into my room with his shy smile, love and concern beaming at me. My heart was so grateful, open and full of love.

My parents were also around a lot; after my pneumonia shock they came down every weekend. It must have been completely exhausting. I felt so guilty for putting them through so much but I was also aware of a rebellious, childish joy that my mum was putting me before her chapel and my dad before his bowling for the first time in my life. Naturally Mum and Dad were totally blown away by the whole situation; Northern working-class culture is not good preparation for communicating with middle-class doctors speaking in gobbledegook. Neither is English culture in general very helpful when we hide the sick away in hospitals and neurotically try to ignore the subject of death, accusing anybody who mentions it of being morbid. It doesn't equip a very sick woman for speaking to her parents or help devastated parents speak to their only daughter who is disappearing before their eyes. Maybe that's why I don't remember many conversations with Matthew or my family, though I was talking as best I could from behind my oxygen mask and between snoozes. Maybe it's too painful to remember their pain – and my terror – or maybe we just maintained a chirpy conspiracy of silence for the first few months. I'm kind of proud of us; considering our Yorkshire tendency to look on the grim side of things (we've not had an easy history Up North; even William the Conqueror tried to wipe us out) we all managed, mostly, to hang on to the hope that I'd be okay. Or maybe it was just huge denial. My mum read an early draft of my first chapter a while ago and said, "I'd no idea you were so frightened."

It wasn't always easy to put on a brave face, mind you. I remember feeling *very* uneasy, if rather important and unique, when doctors from all over the hospital – renal, coronary, gynaecology, haematology, hepatobiliary (liver) – huddled together in the middle of HDU to discuss the different parts of my failing body. Despite their giant brains they still hadn't a clue what was going on but my heart appeared to be failing, my liver doing poorly, kidneys barely crawling along and my blood acting weirdly again. The insensitive doctors peered at my notes, talked shop with colleagues around my bed without including me and sent my stress, rage and cortisol through the roof. The good doctors looked into my eyes, asked me how I felt and explained as much as they could. They seemed to care about me as a fellow human being and even though they still didn't know what was going on, their words matched their expressions and this made a *massive* difference to my terror.

Chapter 7
Previous Acquaintances with Death

"There are those who forget that death comes to everyone. For those who remember, all quarrels come to an end."

The Buddha

I was introduced to death the day before my fifth birthday when my grandad, Arthur, died. He'd just spent the years with me that he'd missed with my young mum when he was sent to war and, according to my mum, we adored each other. I trusted him enough to jump off the local pool's diving board when I was two and am grateful that he encouraged the risk-taking my mum would've been too scared of. When he died I apparently asked who would give me my sixpence spending money now (the shame!) but I guess I was really asking who would love and cuddle me like he had? My grief came out in alopecia; I hated it when the wind blew and showed my bald patches.

I suppose death remained a quiet but constant presence throughout my childhood as my mum's grief at the loss of her father turned her to God and gave her a frequent desire to 'cast off these mortal shackles' and meet Him – and her dad – in

Heaven. Death was also around in my constant vigilance about being 'good' enough to avoid a God-angered thunderbolt. Then, at twenty one, I had a spiritual moment which offered a different perspective to the vengeful God bellowed about at my mum's chapel. I was on holiday in Cyprus with my friend, Nik, whose height and mass of strawberry blonde curls matched her vivacity. We were lying on the edge of a quiet harbour looking up at a massive sky of stars when I suddenly proclaimed, "I think I've got it!"

"Got what? You made me jump then and I nearly fell in!"

"Oh sorry. What it's all about."

"Oh, right."

"I reckon we just learn and experience all we can while we're here then take it all back to the whole, whatever that is."

"What, like telling everybody in Heaven about your life?"

"No, more like our little bit of learning from life adding a bit to total consciousness or God or whatever...maybe contributing somehow to human evolution...what do you think?"

"I think I need a beer."

"Mmm...but then again, maybe we need to try and contribute towards human evolution whilst we're still alive!"

"Yeah. I think you should..." We carried on watching the thousands of glittering diamonds above us until my brain came up with another notion. "Maybe this theory explains suffering." This was an issue that I'd struggled with since being a child; I just couldn't accept that an all-powerful God would allow so much pain and devastation across the world. "What do you mean?" asked Nik.

"Well maybe a terrible life is consciousness or God or whatever just having another *different* type of experience, a challenging one – and one that makes everybody else blooming grateful!"

"Bit tight though."

"Mmm. But not as tight as a crap life being seen as some

sort of punishment for being sinful…" I'd of course got no idea at this point that so much joy, growth, wisdom and kindness could come from suffering.

A few years later my interest in 'the bigger picture' was sparked again when I read about Eastern spirituality and found theories of 'god' which seemed to vaguely resemble my own. The Hindu tradition maintains that we have an individual 'soul' consciousness, 'Atman,' which is part of the wider 'Brahman' consciousness, the all-knowing collective whole. Buddhism, a route to happiness rather than a god-centred religion, has a similar notion with 'The Mind' behind the mind; a peaceful, happy and loving awareness or wisdom behind the chattering, conditioned ego with all its warped perceptions, insecurities and suffering. Taoism also speaks of an eternal, all-encompassing, indescribable 'Tao' or 'The Way'. Even Western psychoanalyst Carl Jung claimed that there is a 'collective consciousness,' a consciousness we all share with 'archetypes' or characteristics with which we're all familiar.

Writers like Jiddu Krishnamurti and Thich Naht Hanh offered me ways to access the 'Mind' behind my self-obsessed mind and to change the world by changing myself. Techniques like meditation and yoga could enhance my awareness and help me find a connection to the compassionate, happy state behind my self-centred ego and its desperate attempts to 'big me up' at every opportunity. I liked my ego though – my view of myself with my 'bonny face' and my academic, athletic and creative capabilities – and the thought of trying to tame my ego disturbed me. My whole sense of self came from my external attributes and I had little notion of my 'internal life' and the absolute joy that can come from the body's amazing senses and just 'being' (rather than doing) in our amazing world. Besides, I felt incapable of sitting still long enough to meditate or do much yoga and told myself that the answer to the world's problems was not sitting meditating but going on more demonstrations;

we needed collective action! Throughout my twenties I worked, danced and demonstrated my way (anti Poll Tax and anti-Apartheid rallies mostly) straight over the practices suggested by these strange Eastern men and any further thoughts about death (other the constant underlying fear of an abused child being killed at work) floated from my mind.

I was twenty-eight and on my six-month backpacking trip in Asia and Australia before I consciously thought about death again; my travels actually turned out to be a series of brief flamencos with Death. Before I set off I'd practiced my passionate dance with both my Lupus consultant and GP who both advised me against my trip. "But I play tennis regularly and basketball every Tuesday," I told the GP. "And I haven't had a day off sick for years!"

"Well yes but you have Lupus."

"And?"

"And you could have a blood clot or other complications. You're at great risk of infection too."

"Well I won't eat any meat or salad washed in tap water."

"And how will you get your blood tested? You need to keep taking warfarin, especially when you're flying."

"It's Asia, not the moon! They have Western clinics and hospitals, even in Nepal."

"Jayne, it's really not a good idea, what if..."

"Look, I'm going; if I don't have a break from social work I'll probably end up dead anyway."

"Can't you go to Europe at least..."

"My flights are booked. I'm going next week! Please sign my form!"

"I don't think..."

"I'm going. It's up to you whether I go with or without insurance..." He reluctantly signed his illegible squiggle. I didn't read the small print of my insurance documents.

I was sick with anxiety at Gatwick Airport where I was

being waved off by a jittery, pale-faced Kazza and a hysterically giggling Karen (who, gratefully, I trusted, along with my other conscientious lodger and friend, Carol, to take good care of my home.) It made for a great photo; my eyes are the size of dinner plates! On the plane to New Delhi I tried to block out my doctors' concerns by chatting with the gentle, velvet-voiced Irishman sitting next to me. As we shared our fears over a glass of wine – mine were not being able to get my blood tested, losing my medication, being eaten by a shark or being forgotten by my friends back home – I managed to resist an impulse to curl up like a koala and cling on to the man's arm.

On arrival I spent twelve hours sitting on my rucksack in Delhi airport, waiting for my connection to Kathmandu and watching groups of families. Many had several adults and the children in their midst tended to move between them for their attention. Nobody was shrieking at their children like we Brits can do; I wondered about our pressurized, isolated nuclear families in the West and our so-called 'progress.'

I was completely exhausted on reaching the dinky Kathmandu airport, but, as my taxi wound through the filthy streets, my disbelieving eyes were *wide* open. The rusty, corrugated shacks, with dirt-stained washing draped over dusty bushes, were people's *homes*. The rickety tables on the side of the road covered in pigs' heads, trotters and a million flies were butchers' shops. I couldn't believe it when I realized that the shapes moving between the scavenging cows and pigs on a steaming, stinking rubbish tip which spread out on the banks of a wide, brown river, were human beings. I'd seen this sort of thing on the TV but witnessing it live hit me at a much deeper level. I realized that I lived like a queen.

In a degree of shock I arrived at the smart-looking, three-story 'Kathmandu Guest House,' with its clean outside café area, confident in well-travelled Ged and Jules' recommendation, but to my horror it was full; I had no Plan B and how would

Gerly find me if he made it to Kathmandu? Luckily for me, my crumpled look was enough for the kind, chiselled-cheeked receptionist to offer me a weird basement room with a dingy light and grey, peeling walls. I perched on the grimy bed and suddenly felt desperately lonely and afraid; what on earth had I done? I'd left my friends, family and everything I knew half a world away, and here I was in a strange, dishevelled country where I might not manage to get my blood tested! I could die out here – alone.

As I sat staring at the patterns on the filthy window, with my temperature and blood pressure mounting, I saw a beautiful brown mouse scuttling up the curtain. Normally I would have been horrified but a part of me was glad of a living companion! Having said that, I didn't sleep much. The next day I began to chat to fellow backpackers in the guest house café and to my relief I'd soon arranged to share a lovely clean room with Rita, a wiry, humble American with a few weeks' informative experience of Nepal. As with my Irish plane friend, our mutual isolation quickly brought us close and, having formed a little group with other travellers, within a few days we were relaxing on huge cushions set around low, candlelit restaurant tables, eating tasty lentil dahls and laughing happily at stories from all over the world. I'd left a big note on a backpacker noticeboard telling Gerly which room I was in.

By this time I'd been out exploring chaotic Kathmandu with its narrow streets where colourfully decorated, rickety trucks blasted their horns and music, electric rickshaws zipped about beeping like crazy and sacred cows roamed lazily in the midst. The smog was so thick that it left your eyes and throat stinging after two hours but I'd managed to find a clean, private clinic with English-speaking doctors who could test my blood. The doctors needed a 'control' sample of blood which Rita offered without a moment's hesitation – and again weighted my belief on the side of people being innately kind. When I was given my blood results I heard Death quietly chuckling; the numbers meant nothing! Luckily, after a few manic phone calls and fax exchanges with my panicked friend Maria and medics back home, I had my blood results in an INR format and knew how much warfarin to take.

I could now relax and bask in my surroundings. As I watched the Nepalese people greet each other with praying hands, a bow of the head and "Namaste," which translates along the lines of 'The god in me greets the god in you,' I remembered my old excitement at the idea that we're all a small part of 'god.' At every turn in Kathmandu was a Buddhist monk clad in orange robes, a spindly, sarong-clad, white-faced Hindi Sadhu (holy man) with stripes painted on his face and dreadlocks hanging to the floor, an ancient Hindu temple adorned with explicit sexual images (sex is seen as a way of connecting with The Divine) or a Buddhist 'stupa' (a pointed temple made up of concentric circles) adorned with hundreds of prayer flags flapping their messages out on the wind. Spiritual souvenirs like singing bowls, Tibetan bells and embroidered Third Eyes filled the gift shops.

It was fascinating to think that the Nepalese people surrounding me were basically the same as me, with the same senses, intuition, feelings and needs but yet their 'programming,' what they'd hoovered up from their culture, was so different to my Pagan-Christian-scientific-colonial-capitalist one. It made me really reflect on what had seeped into my brain throughout my lifetime and inspired me to paint myself naked, desperately pulling a reel of cassette tape out of my brain.

Death, like spirituality, is also very present in Nepal. Just outside Kathmandu I visited the funeral site of Pashupatinath which hosts Nepal's most sacred Hindu shrine. On the banks of the Bagmati River I was amazed to see big log fires built on square, stone bases or ghats with bodies, wrapped in shrouds, being placed on top of the pyres by their families and slowly burnt. Worshippers were wading in the river where the ashes were being brushed, cleansing themselves in the holy water. Happy children were splashing away. I've since learned it's disrespectful to watch the funerals but I was mesmerised as the corpse of an elderly woman, in a purple shroud, was placed on a pyre and incinerated. There was something disturbing and yet natural and moving about seeing death being dealt with so openly.

Given their Hindi and Buddhist traditions, I guess that many Nepalese people believe that the dead are reincarnated; perhaps this brought a calmness about death that we've no conception of in the West where we have no notion of 'coming back' or, for many of us, even carrying on. I can remember wondering whether the Nepali's open and perhaps more accepting attitude towards death had something to do with their seemingly soft, warm natures, and friendly, sparkling eyes – despite their shoeless children and stinking piles of rubbish. Even the men seemed gentle and loving as they walked down the street with their arms around each other. *Mmm.* I observed, *macho bullshit and defensive coolness is not necessarily 'the way it is'. Mmm... are we missing out on our aliveness by hiding death away so carefully?*

I certainly felt alive the first time I danced closely with death in Nepal. I was on a five-day white-water rafting trip, being thrown up in the air, smashed with a clawing ton of icy water and nearly plunged into the murderous, crashing torrent of the Kali Gandaki. This immense river has cut rock like butter and formed miles of stunning gorges where rickety wooden footbridges swing high above the swirling current. As I was thrashed and soaked, I laughed in Death's (slightly green) face but a year later, when I heard on BBC Radio 4 that a British woman had just drowned on a similar rafting trip down that awesome river, I was quietly humbled.

My second quickstep with Death came on the second day of a three-day jaunt in the Himalayan lowlands. I'd planned to go trekking with a chatty Geordie who I'd met on the rafting trip but she'd lost her passport; well, she said she had but maybe she just had more sense than me. Alone or not, there was no way I could be in Nepal and not see the Himalayas! It was bad enough that I couldn't go to high altitudes because I was on warfarin and so vulnerable to random bleeding. I was also desperate to find a solitary place in the mountains where I could scream my head off and release the sadness, tension and horror which I was carrying from social work, the scary bits of my childhood and possibly the genetically transferred trauma of two World Wars and my parents' childhood horrors! The field of epigenetics is now suggesting that trauma appears to be passed on generationally, possibly genetically.[17]

My trek had begun on slightly rocky, open terrain with air so fresh I was almost high and stunning views of immense, snow-capped peaks but now I was strolling through the rich, green scent of a sunlit wood. Suddenly I froze at the sound of a loud chattering noise. I held my breath, staring around wildly. All

---

17. A light article can be found at https://www.dailymail.co.uk/health/article-6283585/The-vicious-cycle-trauma-Suffering-passed-generations-study-reveals.html

was quiet. I resumed my walk, speaking words of comfort to myself and I'd just begun to notice the magical shafts of dancing sunlight again when there was a loud rustle about twenty feet to my left and the bushes parted to reveal two furry monkeys staring at me through large, brown eyes. The curious pair were closely followed by several more, some of which were about three feet tall and fairly broad, but I buried my apprehension and just took in the absolute magic of being with beautiful wild monkeys! They looked so wise and aware. I marvelled at our mutual study session until they quietly returned to their private world. I resumed my journey with a *huge* grin on my face. Until I reached the next tiny village and shared my excitement with a waiter who explained to me in very concerned, broken English that those cute monkeys can be, "Dangerous...very dangerous..."

If you take my two DVT's at eighteen and twenty-one to be my lucky escapes numbers one and two and the insane rafting number three, then maybe my monkey magic was number four. Escapes five and six came a day later. I'd been walking without seeing a soul since the beautiful, piercing blue dawn and at one point had reached a fork in the spindly, grass path. I hadn't a clue which way to go, so stopped, sat down and took a beaming selfie (yes, ahead of the game with selfies!) just in case this was to be the last photo that my parents had of me. I then asked my deceased grandad to show me the right way and something led me down the right path. By late afternoon I'd reached the dusty hamlet I'd been aiming for. I was offered a cup of tea and told by the actions and a few words of a water-carrying young woman wearing a long, dusty dress and smiling the stunning, olive face of a goddess, that the journey to my day's final destination, the village of Ghorepani was, "Steep, big steep."

I mustered my courage as I left the wonky, wooden hamlet, trying to forget about the sign that I'd passed warning tourists against trekking alone because of the 'violent robberies' that had occurred in the area. *Probably not the best place for my mega scream then.* As a grey mist entered the already dim wood I was passing through, I tried to focus on the beauty of it swirling through the trees and took 'arty' photos but in the back of my mind, my anxiety was spiralling. I'd been walking *downhill* along stony paths for over two hours; could 'big steep' mean downhill? I suddenly felt *very* alone and possibly a touch foolhardy (!) – I was wandering round on my own, totally lost in the stunning, but completely wild Himalayas.

Eventually I emerged from the creepy wood into a clearing. The mist was quite thick by now but I could make out a big pile of stones – 'gratitude stones' apparently; another contributor to the Nepalese sparkly eye phenomenon perhaps. Leaning against the rocks, casually folding his arms, was a man. He looked Nepalese but was dressed in trainers and a purple shell-suit, an outfit well beyond the means of many Nepalese. *Oh no! Here's a violent robber! Should I strike a martial arts pose and shriek wildly, just give him my rucksack, try to hit him round the head with it, or attempt to run past him?* There was no way round; behind the rocks was a steep incline and in front of it, a vertical drop. In the end, I took a deep breath and, with wobbly legs and my heart nearly bouncing out of my chest, I inched stiffly towards him. He just looked at me with a blank face. *Oh God, how silly I've been...who in their right mind would have done this...what if he throws me down the cliff...oh SHIT!* In the end, ignoring Death (who was jumping up and down with glee on the top of the rock pile) I beamed a huge smile, bowed my head, squeaked the most cheerful "Namaste" that I could muster and, once past him, ran like the wind (ruck-sack and all – those were the days!) When I reached the beautiful, flickering lights of rickety Ghorepani, it looked like Heaven.

With sweet relief bursting from every pore, I checked myself into a rustic, wooden hotel where a sagging bed and a battered table were the luxuries and it was *freezing*. I sat around the creaking wood-burning stove that evening with Swiss helicopter pilot, Christian and his Nepalese trekking guide, Hom. Even before Hom told me about the frequent disappearances of people in the mountains, I knew on one level that I'd just had my sixth lucky escape. Yet I didn't *really* take in the fact that I'd just had an afternoon in the close presence of Death. Or maybe I did and that's why I felt great – and *alive*. I wonder if dangerous sports are so popular because, as well as bringing you right into the 'aliveness of the moment,' they give you the buzz of *mastering* potential death. I once met a surfer-biker in Portugal who took the craziest risks surfing over rocks and "smashing it" round motorbike circuits and he'd had a traumatic introduction to death by losing most of his family as a boy.

My seventh close call came when I was in Thailand a few weeks later. I'd just travelled from hectic, smelly Bangkok with its huge, Western-style shopping centres flanked by street vendors flooding the pavements with their delectable, colourful food, and I'd landed, via a small motor boat, on the gorgeous, dirt-tracked island of Koh Samui (this was 1996; now, sadly, there are tarmac roads and a mass of hotels, I hear.) Lugging my rucksack and crumpling in the intense heat as I checked out the rentable wooden beach-huts, I saw a towel hanging on a short washing line. I was sure it was the very same towel that I'd given to Jason, an ex-Marine from Lancashire, who'd been my rafting instructor on the Kali Gandaki and had hung out with a group of us when we'd got back to Kathmandu. I eagerly called his name. His big, beaming "Ey-up lass" as he stuck his shaggy head out of the door was beautiful. Here was another of those amazing coincidences just when I was feeling lonely; it's moments like that when I really do wonder whether everything is more connected than we have a clue about. Jason and I hired a moped and, with our hair blowing in the wind, went on a tour of the beautiful, temple-strewn island, marvelling at twenty-foot, golden statues of the Buddha and stopping off to eat fresh rice and noodles, and banana porridge, in clifftop and beachside cafés. Then we stopped to climb up the side of a beautiful stream cum waterfall which cut through some tropical forest growing on a hill-side. We laughed heartily as we dragged ourselves up through the shining greenery, with Jason, who was as fit as a fiddle, egging me on and me begging for mercy but really loving the exhilaration of sweating more than I'd ever done in my life; I felt incredibly alive and free. Not so five minutes later when we were crossing the stream and I slipped and fell straight down onto a big, pointed bolder, coccyx first. I thought for moment that I'd paralysed myself, but then excruciating pain shot up my back, at which point I wondered if I'd broken my spine or hips. Thankfully I got away with a ten-inch lumpy bruise which was pretty sore but brought the bliss of being nurtured in a lovely wooden beach hut just next to a turquoise ocean by a kind northern lad who, like me, loved cuddling and playing chess.

New Year's Eve brought my eighth near-miss when I was having the time of my life, getting into techno rhythms at a wonderful, partly open-air night-club where cooling sea breezes wafted the pounding dance floor. Probably as a result of drinking the pop-like local whisky, I fell off the stage and was just about to hit my face on the wooden floor when a passing knight in shining armour deftly whisked me from the air! A complete stranger, who I can't picture at all, had come into my life, probably saved me from death, a life with a mashed up face or a broken neck and then a minute later was gone. I somehow sustained another bruise, this time from the back of my knee up to my bum, but again I didn't really take in how close a shave it had been or how lucky or blessed I was. It's only on reflection that I feel *immense* gratitude. I'd love to thank that man.

Mmm...and now I'm wondering about survivor guilt, something my grandfathers would no doubt have felt in abundance when they returned from the wars having seen so many peers die so horribly. Grandad lived in a small, damp, dark house cut into a hillside for years when he didn't need to and Sergeant Ben-John, who rarely socialised or had fun, only ever sat on a hard wooden chair. Was I, in the depths of my subconscious, not allowed to be happy and so threw myself down the waterfall and off the stage when I felt gloriously happy? Would being happy exclude me from the depressed family norm and my feeling of belonging? Could I be happy when I was a sinner, my parents had never travelled, my brother was stuck five days a week in a dirty engineering works and children were starving all over the world?

Anyway…Australia brought another few close shaves which weren't self-sabotage; the first thing I saw as I stuck my head under the water on the exquisite, mind-blowing Great Barrier Reef (so amazing because I couldn't name, conceptualise and therefore take away the wonder of what I saw) was a five-foot, fin-topped, black and white sea-snake which nearly made me swallow my snorkel. Then there was the abseiling in the Blue Mountains near Sydney (which really do look blue as a result of the eucalyptus trees' oil mixing with dust particles, water vapour and a blast of sunshine.) Following about ten minutes' instruction from a chilled, dreadlocked youth, we were cheerily encouraged to walk backwards over a cliff overhang and after about six paces were met by a two hundred feet vertical drop through pure air. I had a *massive* jolt of adrenalin (and a brief glimmer of Death swinging merrily beside me in his skull-decorated parachute) as I momentarily forgot which angle I had to hold the rope in order to slow down and stop!

My last dance with Death in Australia came whilst sea kayaking. We'd been out in the waves having a fantastic muscle-wrenching, wave-bouncing scream and were slowly making our way back towards the shore. As we passed an anchored fishing boat, creaking with the suspense of a Hollywood classic, I saw a fin; a triangular fin and a six foot shadow under the water. "Oh, oh...we've got company" I managed to squeak, pulling my oars into my kayak and desperately trying to persuade myself that it was just a friendly dolphin – which it may well have been. I didn't convince myself very well; I was being zapped with sickening flashbacks from 'Jaws' the entire ten minutes of my shaky, wave-assisted float back to shore. Again though, it never *really* registered in my brain that maybe I'd been close to death, just as it didn't when I was throwing myself out of a plane tied to an Australian giant called Animal and diving through the sky at god knows how many miles an hour with my face flapping in the wind! Death was something that happened to other people, not young, attractive, invincible women like myself. It makes me smile now, picturing my daft self with a big, inane grin on my face, totally oblivious to Death manically shoving wild monkeys at me, hooting with laughter as I fall off the dance-floor and begging my finned friend in Australia to bite my kayak in two.

If only I'd taken the time to turn round and really look at Death and the massive gifts he has to offer.

I never got my mega scream by the way; in the Himalayas I kept thinking about it but would then meet a herd of brightly decorated and bell-clanging goats being skipped down the mountain by a toothless, leather-faced old man and a couple of shoe-less children. Then there were the men carrying tables, packages or, in one case, an elderly man in a basket, and the random wooden houses perched on the mountain-sides with glittering nets of sweetcorn hanging outside. Deep in the rainforest of Lombok (an island next to Bali) when I'd hooked up in Singapore airport with a fascinating, earthy Czech musician, Jana, I thought it was looking good for a howl until I noticed smoke swirling through the trees and again, didn't want to freak anybody out. I did manage a few underwater screams in Thailand but was always afraid of attracting a killer shark who can apparently hear from blooming miles away. In the end, I got what I really needed beneath my scream. Limping through Kuala Lumpur with a massively swollen foot from the coral cut in Thailand, I was lost, hot, in agony and desperate to find a park to lie down in. After a lot of manic tree-like arm waving at puzzled Malaysians, I finally found a big, leafy park. I lay down under a tree and started to cry. Then I continued crying. And then I cried some more as I let my mind just drift through traumatic memories; frightened, lonely L. being sexually abused by his dad, T.'s mother choosing her husband over her teenage daughter and letting her go into care when he'd been having sex with her from the age of seven, D. sitting crumpled and alone on the floor of a dirty children's home, baby C. crying and choking in a roomful of thick cigarette smoke, his skinny little body failing to thrive...

I then cried for another couple of hours for little Jaynie as I had flashbacks of my mum shouting and lashing out (instead of crying) and my dad sitting silently behind his paper when I was desperate for him to ask me how my netball game had gone and give me a hug. I cried for my brother with his fear of change and the arthritis in his foot and hips which stopped him playing football when he'd finally stood up to Mum and told her he *was*, after years of sadness and held in rage, going to play football with the local team on Sundays. I cried for Sarah-Ann tied to the oven as her friends played outside, for Ben-John sitting on his hard chair with his pipe and Whist tobacco, spitting onto the front of the iron stove (with Sarah-Ann calling him a 'dirty bugger') as he tried not to remember the brain-blasting bombs and sobbing, bloody men sitting amongst the rats and fleas in the trenches. I cried for Arthur as he wept for humanity over his book of poems, for Grandma Annie as she cut off her needs, feelings and imagination in an attempt to be a 'good girl' and avoid the wrath of her traumatised and grief-stricken parents (on top of everything else they lost two sons in one year), for my mum screaming in agony as she was having her neck burned and my dad cowering in shame at school when the teacher asked him why he'd come to school wearing pumps with holes in when there was a foot of snow.

It was the most healing day of my life.

I don't know what beliefs my Grandad had about death; some of his poems refer to God but this one's about a ghost and gives you a bit of light humour (if you can decipher the Yorkshire dialect) after all my talking about death!

Jooa – a – Flaar Bills

A saw a gooast t'other neet, as plain as plain can be
– run a cou'nt, a wo glued bi't feet when it said "Let's talk ter thee.
Ave just come daahn here ta look araand and just for a bit of a talk
– am stalled a liggin wi' mi 'ead tet grand, so a thought ad come for a walk.

A lived 'ere when a wor a lad – 'appen tha's 'eard 'bart me?
Nah don't bi flayed, am not ser bad, tha's ner need ta knock at knee!
As ter ivver 'eard a Jooa-a Flaar Bills? 'Im at stopped Taahn 'all clock?
Thi 'unted mi all over t'ills cus ad donned owd Lord Mayor's smock.

Wot's ta say, tha's nivver 'eard o' me? Whor the 'eck wor ta born?
The wor a reet do when a came ta dee- it lasted well inter morn".

Bi naah a wor nooan as flayed – a knew 'e meant mi no 'arm
A di'n't care haah long 'e stayed, a wo just feeling sooa calm.

"As ter getten aaht a thi oil?" I said "Waint sumdy miss thee up theer?"
'E grinned and said "If tha uses thi 'ead tha gets a day off ter come 'ere".
Sky wo leettening, it wer a'must dawn when 'e said "Ad better make tracks,
if arm not theer when 'e blows 'is 'orn as ter spend a day on th'aase acks."

Then off 'e went affoor a could blink, straight through bedroom wall
sky wor already shewing pink and a wonder if 'e missed 'is call.
Sooa if a gooast yer 'appen ter see and 'e says 'is name is Jooa,
'E'll bi art on a gooasts' little spree – nah don't meck a dorve fert dooa.

Arthur Downs

Chapter 8
Grandma Goes Instead of Me

"Dying seems less sad than having lived too little."

Gloria Steinem

For all my obliviousness to Death when I was dancing with him in Asia and Australia, he smacked me right between the eyes one sunny morning in hospital when I was out of the High Dependence Unit and back on Ward E17. It appeared that I was on the mend; after many hours of sitting on a commode squashing my belly, my beautiful, clever bowels were back in action, a fact noisily celebrated by the delighted staff on the HDU! I was now on a small, cosy E17 ward with three other friendly women and feeling relatively sociable. Thelma was in the bed next to me; a bubbly, gold-decked woman of about fifty who'd had problems with her heart but was feeling well. I was happily going along with the morning bustle and had managed to chew a little toast, sip my stewed tea and respond to Thelma's chat (in between sucking at my still present oxygen mask) when the porters arrived to take her for a scan. "See you in a bit," she chirped – but she didn't leave the room; at the door the porters shouted for help and a huge commotion ensued with all the medics on the ward dashing to help…but it was too late. Thelma had gone. Her body was brought back to her bed, surrounded by her curtains and left, lying ten feet away from me, until her distraught relatives arrived. Nobody talked about what had happened and I was jittery for days, seriously wondering if Death would cut me down so shockingly next. The sensitive staff must have seen my trauma as they kindly moved me to the next available side room.

I'm reminded of another of my grandad's poems, written again with some Yorkshire dialect and one of my favourites. It's not really relevant to Thelma but it is something I've always borne in mind through my life!

Death's Reaper

When death's reaper crooks his finger
an' says "Come on – ah thee
aah iver 'igh an' mighty,
tha torm 'as come ta dee."

Some bid 'im welcome wi' a smile,
to them 'e comes a friend,
but others look wi' fear and dread
– thi waint believe it's th'end.

Oll bet old Stalin didn't grin
when 'e gate 'is last call;
'e thought 'e wo' that mighty
'e'd nivver 'ave ter fall.

'e med 'is puppets sing and dance
all along life's stage
and thaasands shivered in thi' shoes
win 'e gate in a rage.

But nah 'is liggin stiff an' cowd,
a tryrant at's 'ad 'is day
and wheeriver 'e's goan 'e's tain wot 'e owes
an' bi sure 'e'll 'ave ter pay.

Soa naah yah tin-pot tyrants 'at think
yer God Almighty
yer niver know when t'reaper's due
so be wise an' tread more lightly.

Just remember life tis virry short
and it's a long time yer'll bi dead
– it's far, far better to be owing nowt
and when tha's gone revered.

Arthur Downs

Eventually, after more gruesome weeks of terrible pain and fevers, the doctors figured that I'd got blood clots all over my body, which explained why my kidneys were failing, my liver struggling and my heart grinding to a halt. I became even more concerned that I might be following Thelma. I'm sitting here trying to remember how I related to my loved ones at this time. I have some mental snapshots; my brother's huge pupils in his warm blue eyes, my mum's semi-hysterical comfort-eating and incessant cleaning of my room, my dad's sickening hunch as he slowly dragged himself around and Matthew's sad, silent face buried in his newspapers. I no doubt put on my usual brave face and pretended that I was okay; they probably put on brave faces and pretended that they were okay. But there was *so* much pain. I must have looked terrible. I was slipping into sleep a lot, had burning bed-sores on my back and heel, and after two months in bed my body had completely disintegrated. I realised how much I'd taken for granted my relatively fit and pain-free body. Despite the flow of morphine, the searing pain in my belly, lungs and kidneys was almost unbearable; a jump from the fourth floor window crossed my mind.

I also had 'procedures' to grind my teeth at. One day an unknown doctor arrived with an enormous, silver syringe; just the needle was about six inches long. He'd brought a support team of nurses who, after giving me an extra dose of morphine, lifted me out of bed and supported my floppy body to sit on the edge of it. I finally saw the advantage to having a tent-like gown which gaped open; it created the space for the doctor to pierce my screaming back with his monster syringe and draw some of the suffocating fluid from my lungs. Apparently I had pleurisy as well as pneumonia.

Another horrific memory is having a rubber pipe stuck up my nose and then having to swallow it as it hit the back of my throat in an excruciating, gagging nightmare; the idea was to fit it to a plastic pouch which could collect the horrendous green bile which I was constantly throwing up. The pouch came off once while I was asleep and covered me in the foul green stench. It wasn't easy to change my gown or pyjamas by this point as I still had a line hanging from my neck and drains trying to catch fluid and blood coming out of my chest and belly; I've got scars all over, some I can't even remember getting. I also had daily x-rays. As I was still unable to get out of bed, a tall, white x-ray machine was wheeled to the ward and I was dragged upright by two nurses who pushed my back against a slab of cold, hard lead. Whilst everybody else got the hell out of there to avoid the radioactivity, I had to submit to the toxic zapping, angrily wondering why they couldn't just *ask* me how my lungs were feeling compared to the day before.

I was distraught that I'd missed my second therapy training session by this point and was facing the reality that I'd have to lose my lovely, trusted training group and join a new one the following year. If I was still alive. The future was becoming a bit hazy; did I have one? I'd sailed through school, poly and job interviews; all had gone to plan. This was not in my life's plan and it was *shocking*. And yet sometimes I felt almost chilled. For the first time in years I wasn't feeling the huge responsibility and worry of work, had stopped caring what I looked like and I couldn't make plans. Now my days had narrowed into psyching myself up to reach for the water on my bedside table and swallow the never-ending flow of tablets, many of which were still sitting in their inch-high paper cup when the nurses brought the next lot. Then there was the mustering of energy and more pain, on strict physiotherapy instructions, to try and cough up gunk from my lungs or breathe more than just a tiny wisp. I noticed that being 'anchored in the moment,' with my focus on just breathing, was kind of peaceful.

I'm happy to tell you that in my more relaxed state, having grown to trust the E17 staff, my fear was no longer being expressed as princess arrogance or detached disgust for my fellow patients. Now I knew what pain was and that I was as vulnerable and fragile as the next person, I didn't need to defend against that fear and felt more open-hearted. Back on a ward (my side room was needed for a dying patient) I cringed for old Winifred, wincing in pain as her swollen body was turned over by the nurses, my heart wept for young, nail-varnished, hair-straightened Christy as she cried at the latest bad news about her failing heart and I made a huge effort to wave and smile at sombre, dishevelled Alice whose thinning hair stuck out from her pale scalp like a frightened scarecrow's. I also felt great warmth for the nurses and doctors as they flew about like road-runners for twelve hours at a time, putting their backaches and migraines aside as they dished out smiles and compassion. I was being painted a very lovely picture of we humans.

As my condition deteriorated I was moved back to a side room. It was a bit lonely but also sweet relief from the general clatter and chaos. In my little room, my retreat, I met with a further degree of stillness and, as I had in the Austrian hospital, I met with my body. I'd experienced some body-awareness whilst travelling in Asia; for once not pushed for time, I'd sat in musky stone temples and practised deep 'belly' breathing (when your belly gets pushed out by your diaphragm on the in-breath and calms your nervous system) or touched my toes and stretched my Achilles heels out on kerbs or rocks as I waited for buses, planes and trains. I did a bit of yoga, allowed my body to be pampered by a Thai masseur on the beach and spent time relaxing in warm oceans (when I wasn't worrying about Great Whites or monster jellyfish.) In Asia and in books over the years I'd come across the notion of 'chi' or 'universal energy' but had never given it serious thought. Now, in my desperation, I tried to visualize chi coming down through the crown of my head and into my lungs; bright golden, green, sky-blue or white luminous energy whirling round and soaking up the thick, gunky fluid. I pictured glistening waterfalls washing away the blood clots in my organs. And for the first time in my life, I began to be gentle with myself; instead of the usual *for goodness sake, what's wrong with you*? I was now thinking, *Come on, little body, it's okay, you can get through this...and I promise I'll look after you better if you do...*

When I wasn't in my little mind-body bubbles I did yearn terribly for 'life outside.' I was desperate to breathe fresh, chemical- and bug-free air, walk through autumn leaves and crunch warm toffee apples. Being imprisoned on Bonfire Night, one of my favourite evenings, was hard; I could see the silent flurry of rockets through the windows but felt separate to that world. I had my memories though, my favourite being aged about ten and guarding the bonfire at the end of our street with my brother and our friends and raiding bonfires on 'The Estate;' oh the fear, excitement and pure exhilaration! Apart from when I fell backwards off a four-foot fence (more sabotage?) Bonfire Night also brought immense joy courtesy of the *sack* of fireworks supplied by my grandma's next door neighbour who worked at Standard Fireworks. I wasn't used to abundance.

Eventually, when horror and wrestling with basic bodily functions had become my everyday norm, one clever liver doctor suggested giving me a massive dose of steroids. Amazingly, my fevers ceased, my pain eased and, rocket-fuelled by the steroids, I was finally able to get out of bed and hobble to the loo and shower – and my God, that was brilliant; I'd forgotten the simple joy of feeling warm water caressing my body. When a smiley Dr H. came to tell me that I could leave hospital just before Christmas 1998 I was still very wobbly on my feet, had a bloated, waxen face and a body like a stick but I was over the moon to be alive and going home. I was able to limp from Matthew's car into a shop to buy a few Christmas presents and finally curl up with him and his warm, soft skin.

Christmas turned out to be a disaster, not only because it was shocking returning to the world with a body which felt about eighty, but because my giggling grandmother, Annie, died. She was ninety-three and fed up with her arthritic and hardened artery pain and I'm sure her worry for me didn't help despite my mum's attempts to protect her from the full picture. I felt like I'd contributed to her death. I'm so glad that I was out of hospital before she died and got to lie on her bed with her. "Hi, Grandma. Thank you so much for all your love…" I wonder if she and my grandad are together, and looking out for us; what a lovely thought. I wish I believed it.

For the 'driven me' there was some tragedy in my grandma's death as she'd never read a book, travelled beyond Blackpool or done anything but work as a simple 'winder' in the mill, clean, shop, hang out with family and scrub her neighbour's steps – yet she'd regarded her life as happy. The real calamity was her funeral, which was like something out of a Monty Python sketch. My brother almost burnt out his car trying to keep up with the hearse as it flew from the chapel of rest to the crematorium with Grandma's flowers sliding all over the place. A lot of strict Baptist dogma about going to hell without repentance was spoken by the pastor at the Chapel of Rest, basically condemning my grandma to hell. I expected her life and personality to be talked about during the crematorium service; her great Victoria Sandwich cakes and shin-beef stew, her Thursday cupboard-cleaning, daily cross-wording, immense patience, mischievous humour and loving arms. When the pastor continued to harp on about damnation I whispered a plea to my mum to let me stand up and speak about Grandma, but being easily shamed and fearing any sort of confrontation (especially with the male head of the chapel) she said no. When the maroon curtains slowly closed behind Grandma's coffin I was appalled, devastated and so angry that, when my mum asked me what I'd thought about the service as we were leaving the main hall of the crematorium, I snapped, "It was the biggest load of crap I've ever heard in my life!" My croaky remark reverberated sickeningly in the silent place. I was so aware that this might've been my funeral as well as being gutted and ashamed for my grandma. My mum wasn't impressed either to be fair and I regret making the day even harder for her.

I was later to go on a great journey of self-exploration by thinking about my funeral. What would I want? How would I want to be remembered? It made me really reflect on who I am. I've written an 'I'm Dead' document on my computer now, with a request of how I'd like my funeral to be. That feels good (control freak to the end!) I'd like a party for my wake; a gathering where people try and open their hearts to one another in a genuine way and remember me for being a woman who, despite my flaws, tried to be 'real', honest and compassionate and live life to the full. Funny stories about when I didn't manage that are also welcome! The tunes I want include The Hothouse Flowers' 'One Tongue' (about universal understanding, connection and compassion), John Lennon's 'Imagine' (about us living in peace) and the hymn 'Make me a Channel of Your Peace.' Also 'Born Free' on departure! I'd like a reading of one of my favourite poems, *The Invitation* by Oriah Mountain Dreamer; my beautiful friend Maria doesn't like public speaking and I don't like to picture her crumpled face trying to read it at my funeral but I bet she'd give it a go, bless her lovely heart and rich Cumbrian lilt. My favourite bit of the poem is:

"It doesn't interest me what you do for a living; I want to know what you ache for and if you dare to dream of meeting your heart's longing....I want to know if you can be with joy, mine or your own, if you can dance with wildness and let the ecstasy fill you to the tips of your fingers and toes...I want to know if you can live with failure, yours and mine and still stand on the edge of the lake and shout to the silver of the full moon, "*Yes.*"...I want to know if you will stand in the centre of the fire with me and not shrink back..."

Oh but please, don't let my funeral be yet! So much for thinking I felt strong enough to write about my hospital memories today; this is really hard and I'm starting to feel irritable, tired and rigid with tension... Bloody crap. I need to go for a walk...

Chapter 9
Back in the Hell-Hole but Learning and Learning

"Happiness is your nature. It is not wrong to desire it. What is wrong is seeking it outside when it is inside."

Ramana Maharshi

Okay, my lovely walk on the park, imagining my stress sinking down through my feet and into the ground has revived me; onward and upward and all that...By January 1999 I could hobble pretty well again, my bowels and lungs were feeling much better, my scars were healing, muscles strengthening and my blood results improving. I'd still got one ovary and things with Matthew were good; we were both over the moon that I was alive and after my initial grief at feeling so wrecked, I believed I'd get better and my, wasn't I going to *live*!

So much for that. In the middle of January a familiar pain hit my belly and I was rushed back into hospital. Now my left ovary had burst! Luckily, a few bags of blood and some intravenous medication seemed to sort me out and I was home in just over a week. A month later I'd just about got over the shock and was starting to make plans again when the same pelvis-ripping pain grabbed me. On the way to the hospital

Matthew and I were both silent; neither of us could bear to speak of the potential catastrophe we could picture. I was sick to the stomach and literally shaking with the thought of more needles, pain, powerlessness and imprisonment and sure enough, I'd got another internal bleed which was quickly followed by more stinking vomit and a burning fever, this time from septicaemia. Again, I watched with a mixture of horror and gratitude as more strangers' blood dripped into my body along with gallons of steroids, antibiotics, anti-inflammatories, diuretics and gooey, orange platelets...but still I kept going downhill. There were familiar ward-round murmurs of, "White cell deterioration...auto-immune activity...irregular clotting...non-identifiable infection." My lungs were filling up with fluid again, my kidneys were failing, my liver struggling and my heart losing power at a massive rate. Again, as the weeks went by, it wasn't obvious to the medics what to do, though Dr H. fought for me like a warrior. She escorted me in my bed down corridors and demanded urgent scans, phoned the ward or came in to see me on her days off and was still in her office until midnight sometimes. I'm now sobbing with gratitude towards her.

I cried a lot back in hospital too, partly because of the pain and desire to be at home and partly because my brother's second beautiful son was born as I was dancing with death again and I had catapulted my family into sickening trauma – and frequent, long car journeys – instead of celebration, joy and my brother being at home with his partner and sons. I tried to persuade my family to visit less but they'd have none of it. I was back on E17 with amazing Dr H., Doctor D., the quiet, dry-humoured Scot and his beautiful, compassionate, female registrars, curly-mopped brunette Dr S. and gentle, slender, blonde Dr G. (they reminded me of the women from Abba) – both were good, conscientious and empathic women who talked to me as if I were their equal. As did the wonderful nursing staff team; strict but kind Sister Denise, who would tell Matthew off for not cleaning up my room, grounded, patient Paul, cool, laid-back Gary, my 'adopted mum,' warm, child-less Margaret, Jo the giggler with her whacky mass of butterfly clips and wild, auburn tufts, dark-bobbed, warm-hearted Tina and beautiful, softly spoken and deeply compassionate Claire (who would later settle down with my friend Jez; he spotted her on a visit and all it needed was a match-making word or two from me...I was half dead but it's one of the best things I've ever done!)

One day when Nurse Claire was on shift, I was having more trouble than usual breathing. Then I started hyperventilating and, unable to breathe, I started to panic but Claire took my hands in hers, looked deeply into my eyes, and with soothing, reassuring words patiently calmed me down; a terrifying yet beautiful encounter. Tender moments also came with the auxiliary nurses, Carol, Del, Kelly and Bev who would joke, reassure and chat as they wheeled me, like a rag doll, over to my side-room's bathroom and helped me onto a plastic chair where they'd shower me and wash and brush my hair. I didn't feel comfortable being naked and so helpless in front of them but incredibly I found that it got easier; it's amazing what we can get used to! I was learning such a *massively* important lesson in receiving help from a place of vulnerability; my needs weren't bad or too much for people after all. I was also learning how to not give a monkeys about how I looked; having no boobs was now irrelevant!

As I observed from behind my oxygen mask, I was again struck by the open-hearted magic at work on E17; feelings and emotional care were integral to the workings of the ward, right from the top down. There was a recognition that dealing with death and horror all day (from doctors to reception and admin. staff) required support. "How you doing? Are you okay? Do you need some help here?" were regular phrases. I didn't hear anybody say "I'm not doing that because it's not my job" – the team worked *together*, being connected by mutual concern. Hence the staff team were more able to remain in the calm, compassionate parts of their brains and nervous systems and pass on their calm warmth to us patients. It wasn't a village like in this poem by my grandad but it was my safe place.

The Village of My Dreams

Just come along, bide with me
and picture if you can,
a little village by the sea
as yet unspoiled by man.
A friendly spirit greets you,
you find no evil way –
in this village I'll show you,
there's room for all to stay.

So come along, don't hold back,
just come along with me
where people's hearts are never closed
where souls are sweet and free.
I know it well this little place,
know every house and street
I know each happy, smiling face
that in my visits meet.

Come along, lose those fears,
you'll find it well worthwhile –
look around, you'll see no tears
only joy and happy smiles.
No tramp of armies' marching feet
e're disturbs its calm,
nor yet voices raised in heat,
only hearts are warm.

I long to come here every day
but alas it cannot be

I begrudge each moment I'm away
for here I'm always free.
Could I but put the world there,
besides its moorlands streams,
we'd do away with all dull care
in this village of my dreams.

Arthur Downs

Later, as I healed enough to sit up, I secretly observed the little details of the E17 staff's uniforms – belts, badges, tunic or trousers – their hairstyles, eye colour and aspects of their lives and drew a cartoon picture of them all; it wasn't a lot but they loved it, framed it and put it on the wall. It felt so good being able to give at least a little something back.

I timed my cartoon drawing right; a week or two later I lost my capacity to draw when my limbs swelled into branches of puffy fluid because my organs were failing so badly. I had another ton of blood clots throughout my body. I did my best to swallow the never-ending tablets and sip nutritional drinks held to my mouth but I threw most of them back up. I hated having to have paracetamol stuck up my bottom to try and ease my pain. Again I tried to help myself by doing visualisations, like imagining healing energy entering my body as I breathed in and toxicity and stress leaving on my out-breaths. Who knows what impact this had. Certainly, just like placebos (sugar pills which one believes to be medication) have been shown to boost everything from antibodies to natural opiates (painkillers) and serotonin (a 'happy hormone'), visualising positive healing is being found to have a massive impact on our bodies, possibly right down to the genetic level.[18] I also remain curious about the impact of Matthew's gentle, long, white-haired friend Mick who,

---

18. Easy read at https://www.medicalnewstoday.com/articles/306437#what-is-the-placebo-effect or more thorough read in David Hamilton's book 'I Heart Me' Interesting videos by Joe Dispenza on YouTube, e.g. at https://youtu.be/DBC3HZpWKAM or https://Heal your body with your mind.

to the puzzlement or ridicule of many staff members, brought me healing crystals and gave me Reiki[19] (the transmission of 'healing universal energy.') Again research is now looking at the exchange of electrical heart energy between people and finding it to be a very powerful force.[20] One day Mick had just given me a Reiki treatment and said he'd imagined a lovely field of daffodils. Five minutes later my friend Frankie arrived with a *massive* bunch of daffodils.

Despite the intense pain and my total helplessness, I *still* struggled to believe that I was so ill. I had a tape recorder in hospital, already knowing that it would be a monumental memory and I have a recording (or *had* a recording, it's interesting that I seem to have lost the tape) of my weak, croaky voice saying. "They say my heart's knackered. Only working on twenty-five percent. Can I believe that? No I can't." Bloated like a balloon, I was soon returned to the High Dependency Unit where I was kindly received but became a virtually paralysed body on a bed. Unable to bend my swollen limbs, I had to ask for *everything* which brought a whole new level of vulnerability; I had to disturb the busy staff to ask for a cup to be held to my lips or my lumpy body moved to a more comfortable position by a team of four nurses tugging me up the bed, "after three," on my bottom sheet. I felt like a complete burden. My dad had taken unpaid leave from work by now, leaving him and mum with no income and living full-time in my house; they were crumpling before my eyes. Matthew had also given up his work as a yoga teacher and was becoming exhausted with his daily life at the hospital. I tried desperately to remain as cheerful and

19. A modern book giving a whole overview of Reiki is The Reiki Sourcebook by Bronwen and Frans Stiene and there are hundreds of books about the healing qualities of crystals.

20. An interesting article is at //www.healingheartpower.com/power-heart.html. The author refers to the Heartmath Institute (www.heartmath.org) which is central to energetic heart research and has a good reference library.

positive as I could; I remember trying to persuade my mum that the blood red catheter bag that was collecting my urine was a result of drinking too much Ribena.

I didn't always manage to be cheerful of course – I've managed to conveniently block this out but my mum tells me I could be cross and tetchy sometimes; "You were just so frustrated." Luckily my rage was tempered by Matthew's calm presence and wonderful back massages; being in my body was a living nightmare but his tender touch again helped to keep me sane. The guilt I felt for putting him through the horror (and not being able to massage him in return) was assuaged a little by the fact that his dad began to visit him at the hospital and their previously problematic relationship began to heal; I was so thrilled by this beam of positivity.

I was also chuffed when, one random day, I made an interesting discovery about pain. I absolutely *detested* needles by this point but as a young registrar (junior doctor) arrived to take a second lot of blood one day, I thought *just observe this.* And so I simply watched with curiosity as the needle pierced my arm and I tried to describe the feeling – *Oh yes that hurts like hell… mmm… burning... stinging …ooh …intense heat …* and 'standing back' and observing the pain somehow made it more bearable. I've since learned that Buddhists talk about 'secondary suffering' or the second dagger (or arrow) which can be applied to both physical and emotional pain. The first dagger or, in my case, needle, is the pain; that's real and it can be terrible. The second dagger, which can make it worse, is the *thoughts* about the pain; *oh my God, that needle's the size of a nail! I hate that phlebotomist! Oh God, this is never going to end…oh this is so unbearable…* or, with emotional pain; *Oh this is awful, I'm never going to stop crying, oh I feel so unhappy, oh this is so unfair, my life's ruined! Oh why me?* As I began to just *observe* my fear and sadness and let myself cry, or shake if I needed to, without labelling my feelings a disaster (or myself an over-reacting, mardy baby) I noticed that the emotion would generally pass. Research – and one of my heroines, Buddhist speaker and writer, Pema Chödrön suggests that intense emotions generally last about ninety seconds[21] and this is what I was discovering. I also realised, if I adopted 'curious observation,' (a classic mindfulness term I'd come to learn about) that my pain wasn't as constant as I'd thought; there were moments and blocks of time when my fear and sadness or the pain in my body wasn't so bad or even a problem – like everything in our universe, the pain changed from moment to moment. I was in a total state and yet my mind and how I chose to think about the situation could ease – or worsen – my pain! Going with the feelings from my body 'in the moment' was grim but not half as bad as when I thought about the future and added catastrophic stories.

Having discovered how to manage my pain better, I soon discovered a similar thing about the horrendous, brain-bending noise; if I just lay back and relaxed, letting the sounds just come and go, rather than ranting like a maniac in my head about how terrible it was and being livid with the people making the noise or leaving my door open, it wasn't so bad. I'd later learn about the 'mindfulness' of pain and sound and viewing pain and sounds like clouds passing by instead of creating secondary suffering by whipping things up into a frenzy with panicking thoughts. More learning and liberation!

Talking of thoughts, I'm told that most of the time my mind remained lucid but one night on the High Dependency Unit I can remember being concerned about the fact that I had a roaring fever which was bringing hot and then icy flushes, and I was unable to pull my bedding up or down according to my temperature because my arms were so bloated. I then got into

21. *See www.elephantjournal.com/2015/10/the-life-changing-90-second-secret/*

my head the idea that the nursing staff were allowed to pull my blankets up for me four times during the night but began to panic that four times wouldn't be enough, I'd be freezing! Eventually I figured that I'd be okay because the other woman in my bed would also have her quota of four, so throughout the night we'd have eight blanket pull-ups and we'd be okay. I guess my psyche had totally split by this point; 'I' was probably fine whilst the imagined 'other woman' was perhaps the one whose body was broken. It's amazing what our minds can do in order to cope; sometimes short-term 'madness' is actually a fabulous coping mechanism which can retain long-term sanity and this was certainly 'creative adjustment to mad circumstances' (the Gestalt psychotherapy notion of mental ill-health) at its best.

As well as learning that I had the capacity for 'madness' (or clever creative adjustment) I began to learn another precious insight; amidst the horror there were still beautiful moments of appreciation and joy. A kind word, a beaming smile, a bouquet from friends in Australia or, when my fluid retention started to ease off, wriggling up the bed on my own. One long night (I rarely slept well) I called Nurse Taj over to tell him how excited I was that I could bend my arm enough to pick my nose! Pulling two inch, gooey blood clots which felt like they were being sucked out of my brain wasn't exactly pleasant but it was brilliant being able to breathe through my nose for the first time in weeks.

Talking of blood, one day my good friends Carol and Kazza had come to visit. I'd been back in hospital for about a month, was on E17 and relatively stable. We were merrily chatting (as much as I could from behind my whirring oxygen mask) when a doctor came in to fit another 'line' in my neck and told my friends he'd "Just be half an hour if you want to wait outside." On their return, after a terrifying thirty minutes with another strange man cutting a hole in my neck and pushing a long foreign object into my subclavian vein, we resumed our chat.

Until Kazza stopped speaking mid-sentence and Carol turned a weird shade of green. I craned my line-burdened neck round to follow their eyes and saw a fine spurt of deep red blood squirting across the room and running down the white wall. Nurse Gary (aka David Essex) was bleeped by Carol as soon as her shocked body would move, and he came to my rescue with a huge cotton pad. We smiled again as the bleeding stopped... until I suddenly started being violently sick and Carol and Kazza were ushered out of the room and replaced by a frantic 'crash team' of doctors and nurses. As they worked together on my body, prodding, squeezing, attaching and injecting, I realized that I was actually being sick from my lungs, not my stomach, and then I registered that I was drowning...I was surrounded by all these medics but was unable to tell them that I couldn't breathe in between the torrid bursts of yellow, gooey liquid which were splashing all over me and blocking up my oxygen mask. Luckily my front cortex kicked in and reasoned *your lungs can only hold a certain amount of fluid, they'll be empty soon...just hang on Jaynie, be calm, it's OK*...I saw disappointment take over the excitement on Death's face as the fluid finally stopped pouring and I was able to suck in some beautiful, life-giving air. (Oooh...I'm covered in goose-pimples as I write.) When the crash team left, Kazza and Carol crept back into the room. I was too shocked and exhausted to explain what had just happened. They were too freaked out to tell me that my heart had just stopped. But we sat together. And when they rose to leave but saw the panic in my eyes, they sat with me a bit longer. I'm sobbing as I remember their loving tenderness and attempts to clean the blood from my favourite yellow and white strappy pyjamas.

Having such a deep-seated belief in my being a worthless sinner who shouldn't ask for anything, again my experience of being cared for at this time was *incredibly* healing. I have lovely memories of my mum tenderly feeding me yoghurt and crushed ice from a teaspoon and stroking my sweaty head.

(She'd followed her health visitor's advice and fed me by the clock rather than my bodily needs as a baby – and I can still struggle to identify when I'm hungry.) I also recall with tender joy my dad and brother rubbing my toes when I was in so much pain that they were the only part of me I could bear being touched and then later, letting me push my feet against their hands in an attempt to strengthen my sticky legs. It was the first time I could remember my dad ever touching me and having non-violent contact with my brother. I revelled too in finally being able to really feel my friends' love when I saw it so clearly in their expressions, tears and continuing visits as the months went by. My self-worth was also boosted by visits from staff on wards that I'd passed through, such as chatty Karen and Scottish Lesley from the ICU and stuttering, handsome Nurse David from HDU, who had appreciated my suffering and gently washed my hair one day as he took the mickey out of, and offered to shave, my wildly hairy legs. *Well, maybe I am an okay person.* At one point my workplace heard the false news that I'd died and selfishly, it was kind of fabulous to hear that my office had people crying all over the place; even though I knew it wasn't just about me I did think *Ah; maybe people really do like me!* Another absolutely mind-bending, heart-changing revelation came when my friend Jez, who'd been adopted and was in the process of trying to track down his birth mother, made a pact with God that if I lived he'd give up on meeting her. I was mortified that he'd made such a deal and tried to persuade him to undo it – but on another level appreciated that this was one of the most beautiful things that anybody had ever done for me. Learning that I was lovable without needing to be helpful, pretty, clever, hard-working, funny, sexy, sporty, tidy, and self-sacrificing was amazing. I guess this, and the fact that I'd got nothing to lose (or do) were probably partly why, despite the state of me, I often felt great. My internal voice was now being kind to me instead of constantly critical. I realised that, despite having had my ego blown to shit and losing my identity as an attractive, athletic, professional woman, I was still *me;* I was still a human life-force with incredible senses, thoughts and feelings and the capacity to smile my appreciation. I felt loving and open in my just *being*. Being in my body, 'in the moment' and *alive*.

Interestingly, I most clearly remember visiting times when friends cried with me. Mainstream culture tells us that we should pretend to be jolly when we visit people who are suffering in an attempt to cheer them up but actually the opposite helped me more. I was a mess and nothing was going to change that but when friends – like the bubbly comedienne Trish and cool, hard-core Abi – broke down and cried with me I was relieved from my isolation. Sitting with me in my pain without trying to 'hide or fade or fix it' (going back to *The Invitation* poem) showed me how much they cared and that cheered me up much more than light-hearted tales or jokes. I'm sure it made me fight harder to live too; I didn't want them to be gutted.

An opposite and very disturbing time came when I listened to a situation involving a total lack of emotion and connection. There was an older woman in the bed next to me and when she was having her consultation with a doctor behind her curtain (supposedly in private) I could hear every word. She was told that she was dying and there was nothing else they could do. Then she was left alone. My eyes streamed along with hers as I listened to her quiet sobs. When her sister-in-law arrived at afternoon visiting time their conversation went something like this: "Ooh gosh, it's cold outside. Luckily I didn't have to wait long for the bus. Well you're looking brighter than you did on Friday."

"Am I?"

"Yes, why don't you feel well?"

"No. Not at all."

"Oh we all have bad days, don't we?"

"I'm afraid I've got some bad news."

"Oh."

"I'm afraid I'm done for."

"Oh don't be silly now, let's have no more talk like that; you're just feeling a bit rubbish today."

"No really, the doctor said..."

"Oh you don't have to believe what the doctors say! It's like when they told Peter Ellis that he needed his leg off; well I only saw him the other day walking through the village. Now, we'll have no more morbid talk like that. Shall I get you a coffee from the machine? I know you like them."

"Thank you," said the lady, sighing heavily. When her husband came to visit in the evening the conversation followed the same course. He actually told her to stop being silly when she tried to tell him that she was dying. Later, when her curtain was pulled back I turned to her and told her that I couldn't help overhearing what had been said and that I was sorry she was in such a difficult place. I told her about my experience of nearly dying, how peaceful and wonderful it was. Her tearful smile met mine and we had a moment of beautiful connection. She thanked me. I was mortified when she died the next day, alone, no doubt worrying about her affairs not being in order and not having said her proper goodbyes because her loved ones, indoctrinated into our death-ignoring, spirituality rejecting 'scientific paradigm,' were too fearful to meet her. I just hope she wasn't eager to die because I'd told her how great it was!

Two months in and again I was *so* grateful for the sensitive staff of E17. They knocked on my side-room door before entering and respected my occasional written plea, stuck on the door, to be left to rest before I went mad with sleep deprivation. Other less empathic doctors, nurses, phlebotomists, physiotherapists, cleaners, water-testers, tea-ladies and the myriad of other busy staff burst into my room as a job to get through. Don't get me wrong, I was grateful for their input but having been woken up for about the tenth time one day and being left – again – with my door wide open and the ear-bashing chaos from the corridor whacking me full-on, I threw a plum across the room; the gooey splat against the wall was superb.

On the days when I saw a lot of staff who didn't 'see' me, the feeling of invisibility made me feel like I was alone on the moon. The fact that nobody really knew what was wrong with me didn't help. One random day Dr H. came to tell me that "The Lupus doctor doesn't think you have Lupus after all."

"Oh. Is that good then?"

"Well, it seems you may have something called Antiphospholipid Syndrome."

"Anti what?"

"Antiphospholipid; it's a very rare sort of 'sticky blood' disorder which explains your tendency for clotting."

"Is this better or worse than Lupus? Can you do owt about it?"

"We'll just keep doing what we're doing. There's no cure as such. Also, um, it appears...um..."

"What!"

"I'm afraid you have MRSA."

"Oh shit! Oh sorry...I mean oh no; is that gonna finish me off then?"

"We'll do all we can. Be prepared that your nurses and visitors will have to wear protective clothing for a while..." My feeling of separateness was intensified greatly when family, friends and medical staff came into my room wearing plastic aprons and gloves; another barrier between me and the normal world. I was no longer just a scary sick person with an illness nobody had heard of, I was a menacing, *contagious* person with a killer bug.

Then came some amazing news. A nurse told me that there was a woman called Sophie in the next room with this rare Antiphospholipid Syndrome. I was desperate to go and see her but the MRSA was keeping me in 'isolation' (an apt term). My desire to connect with this mysterious Sophie had me writing her a letter at three in the morning, just introducing myself and saying hi. When she replied the next day I was over the moon; I was no longer alone in the world! Somebody else was living with the fear of clotting to death and having a life stuck to hospital and needles; the mutual understanding – she wrote about how scared and "pissed off" she was – felt great. Over the next few days we exchanged several letters and I felt bereft when she was moved to another ward. I bumped into spirited Sophie several times in the hospital over the following year; it was great to actually see her and I got to hear a bit about her party lifestyle and the secret morphine stash wedged into the top of her walking stick. Though we seemed very different people and I hardly knew her, when I was told about her death a few years later it whacked me.

Shortly after Sophie's move from the ward, my spirits took another beating when I had what was possibly the most traumatic experience of my hospital stay. At half-past twelve one night an on-call doctor who I didn't know came to my room with an injection. I'm so lucky that I happen to be a control freak and asked what it was. "Just heparin."

"Oh blimey, I can't have that; my first clotting episode was possibly a result of Heparin Induced Thrombocytopenia."

"You need it."

"I'm allergic to it!"

"No you're not."

"What do you mean, no I'm not? Have you read my notes?"

"Yes, I've seen your file."

"What, all seven of them?"

"Look, I know what I'm doing!"

"Well I don't think you do! I've had possible HIT!"

"No you haven't, that wasn't on the file."

"Why on earth would I make that up?"

"Look it's just a small injection."

"I don't care how small it is, it might kill me and I'm not having it!"

"You have to have it!"

"I am *not* having it!"

"Well on your head be it then!" he snarled, crashing out of my room and leaving me in a huge panic that I might clot to death without the injection.

It was another long, fretful and sleepless night but when Dr D. came the next morning and confirmed my position I was so thankful for being on the ball and strong enough to stand up for myself. That's the 'medical model' to the max! If you're a medic or nurse reading this, PLEASE, for goodness sake, make sure you *listen* to your patients! They might just know more about their medical history than you do. I heard on BBC Radio 4 that deaths from medical errors in the UK are estimated at forty thousand people a year, many due to poor communication. I'll bet many could be avoided if doctors would check things out with their patients! To put things into perspective, this forty thousand is of course only a fraction of the millions of patients treated successfully every year, so on the whole medics do an *amazing* job. As another random aside, did you know that our NHS is the fourth largest institution in the world, behind the Chinese People's Liberation Army, the Indian Railways and Walmart?

I spent a long time reflecting on the heparin-wielding doctor and wondering why he couldn't hear me. Was he afraid of not following orders or so overworked and stressed out that he couldn't think straight or connect with his compassion? I remember asking a kind junior doctor what emotional support they get during their eighty-hour working weeks. "We don't get any; I just talk to a couple of other trainees but you have to be careful who you talk to."

"What do you mean?"

"Well let's just say, weakness is rather frowned upon."

"What, you mean having normal human feelings in the face of massive suffering and death?"

"Well, yes."

"Do you have a counselling service you can access?"

"Oh no. There's not much chance of a consultancy post if you've been for counselling."

"What? Oh my God! You mean you have to become a robot?"

"Well I suppose so. There are studies which show that newly qualified doctors have a lot of empathy but three years in we tend to have become pretty hard-core."

"Oh, please try and hang on to your heart! You're so kind and lovely. I know it must be so hard though without support and being encouraged to cry out and process the trauma you feel. What an insane system."

"Yup."

How typical of our culture, which encourages us to ignore our feelings and pop antidepressants to cover them up (that's currently up to one in six Brits)[22] and neck literally tons of painkillers to keep us at work and profits up. I guess our denial of feelings is why the biggest killer of our twenty to thirty-four year-old men in the UK is suicide; it accounts for a *quarter* of young men's deaths.[23] I was gutted when I heard that, as I was when I heard that more soldiers from the Afghanistan conflict have killed themselves than were killed by the Taliban.[24] Being conditioned from an early age to 'be strong' and 'just get on with it,' it seems men – especially soldiers who are trained to be emotionless killing machines – simply get overwhelmed by their feelings instead of crying and talking them out. Whilst our young men kill themselves, our young women are using self-harm on a massive scale[25] to deal with their overwhelming and unexpressed feelings coming from exam pressures, trying to be cool and popular on social media, look like air-brushed models and keep up with the latest clothes and gadgets. According to a recent Radio 4 report about half of all British girls aged seven to twenty-one have mental health issues at some point! Studies have also revealed that about a third of adult Brits experience anxiety-based sleep disorders[26] and many of us are so stressed out with trying to keep up with work targets, the latest phone, decking and 'look' that we can't think straight and easily get angry, argumentative, defensive, blaming, distrustful, controlling, stressed, depressed – and ill. In our exhaustion and low mood we try to soothe ourselves with drink, drugs, shopping, screens and manic activity – and on the miserable cycle goes.

My myriad of clients who come via a wide spectrum of workplace counselling schemes used to talk about personal

22. *www.bbc.co.uk/news/uk-23553897*
23. *www.dailymail.co.uk/home/you/article-2047921/Silent-taboo-suicide-young-men-UK.html.*
24. *www.bbc.co.uk/news/uk-23259865.*
25. *www.nhs.uk/news/mental-health/worrying-rise-reports-self-harm-among-teenage-girls-uk/*
26. *https://www.nhs.uk/conditions/insomnia/*

issues such as bereavement or relationship difficulties but in recent years most have dragged themselves into my therapy room with depression and anxiety, having crashed and burned under the pressure of increasingly insane work targets – whilst knowing that their CEO is earning millions. Bank cashiers are having to harass people to buy stuff they don't need, managers' brains are smoking under the pressure of making ever increasing profits, engineers and mechanics are being forced to sell products as they try to fix potentially explosive boilers and broken vehicles, experienced, dedicated employees are feeling crushed by being rated after every job, and public service workers, with ever shrinking resources, are having to follow so many rules and fill in so many papers about targets and outcomes that they're going insane. And most of these clients come to me blaming themselves for being 'weak' and feeling ashamed for carrying the label of being anxious or depressed rather than realising that they're having a perfectly *normal* reaction to our crazy, year-on-year profit-increasing system! Where did the insane idea of increasing profits every year come from? Why can't we be satisfied with and celebrate just a good (or often *huge*) profit? Aaaggghhh! And breathe, Jaynie...

Okay, I'm calm again. I don't remember the sequence of events in hospital from this time; I was in and out of the High Dependency Unit (with its gentle, amazingly clever and brave staff team) on a fairly regular basis, becoming even friendlier with the joking porters. The porters; now there's a group of non-arrogant, widely tattooed, mostly middle-aged or older men who deserve another mention. There are nearly thirty miles of corridors in 'my' hospital and the porters walk a bed and wheelchair-pushing average of about *fourteen miles per day* – for a relative pittance. Now that's dedication. Those porters were a godsend. They were so strong and yet gentle and throughout my hospital stay, whatever my condition, they continued to talk to me like a human being and made me laugh under the most dire circumstances. They also talked to and supported each other and I'd put money on there being less suicide amongst porters than self-reliant, emotionally cut-off doctors. Thank you for your humanity, Mr Porters, you're stars, I bet you give much more to your patients than you realize and you all deserve medals (as well as more pay!)

On balance I eventually reached the conclusion that, despite a lack of training in compassion, little formal support for the staff's emotional needs and the power-crazed arrogance of some individuals (often rooted in fear, no doubt), hospitals really are amazing places; I can remember thinking *the love in here must show up as a glowing, golden light from space.* There's so much talk of the NHS being in crisis but little's said or written about the incredible work that *is* being done. Few hospital employees work only the hours they're paid for (and often pay rates are appalling) and the amount of physical and emotional energy that they give during each shift is amazing. I spent hours revelling in the beauty of the humanity I witnessed from my bed and thought it would be a good idea for all young people to do a period of 'national voluntary service' in hospitals to learn about compassion and what's important in life – and to see the consequences of car crashes, stress, violence, drug use, crap diets, self-harm etc. We're making some serious cock-ups on this planet but we're also capable of such goodness! If only we could ease up on profit-driven targets and ego-driven competition and let our natural caring and cooperation shine through. If only we could all be encouraged and supported to get in touch with and deal with our feelings instead of blaming, raging, lording it over others or getting anxious and depressed... If only we'd acknowledge and come together to talk about – and cry away – our communal trauma, pain and guilt from our colonialism, wars and oppression. What a wonderful world it could be! Another of Arthur's poems springs to mind....

God's Garden

There's room in God's great garden,
room for one and all,
room for the high and mighty,
for the humble and the small.

'Tis a garden full of fragrance
where golden friendships bloom,
where a heart however weary
will always find there's room.

There's flowers in abundance
and each one plays its part,
forming restful bowers
inside sore, weary hearts.

This great garden is never full,
there's always room for more,
room for all and everyone,
through it's open door.

Arthur Downs

Well I guess it's debatable whether our hospitals do have the room for everybody; as I edit in 2019 I'm flashing back to a terribly depressing interview with a doctor who was on some TV news recently; he was saying how many thousands of people are dying as they wait outside hospitals in ambulances because no beds are available – but 'the flowers' are doing their very best given the resources available and we should be so grateful to them...

Chapter 10
Happiness at the Strangest Time

"Being here and now, with life simply as it is, is the paradise we have been seeking."

Suryacitta, The Happy Buddha

It wasn't long after the heart failure, being 'sick' from my lungs incident that the plastic, two feet square fluorescent light above my bed started to go strangely orange. Just the bottom edge at first, then a few days later a quarter of the flat surface was covered...then a half...three quarters...and then Dr H. had me whisked back to the Intensive Care Unit. I'd got a massive brain haemorrhage. I was put back on a life-support machine whilst my eyes, my mum tells me, were protruding "like two pieces of liver." It's probably good that I was unconscious... and I'm now bawling again as I think about how lucky I am to be here and so relatively well considering how *totally* mashed up I could have been. I've just been reading the amazing, life-grasping Kati Van der Hoeven's book *Living Underwater,* also published by Goldcrest Books. The author had a random brain bleed at twenty and woke up with 'Locked in Syndrome' and an inability to move anything but her eyes. That could so easily have been me.

I remained unconscious in ICU for nearly a week with one machine breathing for me and another dialysing my kidneys. After being brought out of sedation I was so racked with intense, raging pain all over my body that I ungraciously asked Dr H. to "Please put me down! If I were a horse or a dog you'd put me out of my misery!" She looked gutted. I swallowed. "I'm sorry; I didn't mean that...let's keep going eh?" I'm an advocate of closely regulated assisted dying but yet I'd possibly be dust by now if it had been an option for me at that point. In ICU I was back being cared for by lovely Lesley. She understood my fear and pain and encouraged me, in the grim hours of the night, just to scream. I could hardly mumble, never mind scream but somehow my flooded lungs managed to find the space to let out a croaky howl. I couldn't believe that the wretched animal sound was me, yet somewhere in that sound was a vote for life.

It wasn't looking good though. After a week in ICU, the kidney dialysis wasn't working, my heart was seriously struggling and my liver failing; the blood clots all over my body had led to 'complete organ failure.' An Intensive Care doctor took my distraught parents, brother and Matthew into the flowered counselling room to tell them that there was nothing else they could do. I was to be sent back to E17 for palliative care and it was estimated that I would be dead within ten hours. Again, as much as I believe in doctors being honest, I'm glad they decided not to tell me how grim things were, fearing I may give up my fight to live. (Oh the harsh dilemmas of the medical profession!) I wish my friends and family hadn't had to carry that awful ten-hour burden.

Apparently, I woke up the next morning telling Matthew "Well that was a bit of a rough night," and Maria was saying only last week (her big, beautiful eyes still looking slightly traumatised) how blown away she'd been when she came back to the hospital the next day to say another final goodbye and was greeted with my beaming grin. I don't remember much from this time but I do know that Dr H. hadn't given up on me, bless her amazing, courageous heart and once I'd come through my 'ten hours' kept doing what she could for me. No words – or these tears *again* choking me up as I write – can express my gratitude. I once read that a cardiologist involved in the transplantation of early heart pace-makers believed about eighty percent of a patient's recovery was due to their faith in their doctor, just as many individuals have died straight after the death of a spouse, a terminal diagnosis or following a curse by a 'witch doctor.' By this point I felt that Dr H. and I were working as a team. The power imbalance between us had been equalled a little after she'd mentioned bits about her own life, like caring for her sick parents (making her even more of a superhero to me.) She'd also talked about my important role in my health care; I was to try and breathe deeply, sip nutritional drinks (I'd not eaten for months again by now) swallow my pills and move my swollen body about as much as I could – and she'd sort out the rest. She'd secured my trust.

Taking of doctors, as I lay 'on the brink' on E17, a cardiologist came to see me to assess whether my heart was strong enough to withstand further kidney dialysis. All my test results were terrible and apparently he wasn't feeling hopeful but because, as had become my daily routine when I could manage it, I was sitting up in bed writing thank-you letters to people who had sent flowers or written to me (thank God for connection) he approved me for dialysis and I was whisked off by ambulance to another hospital. (Oooh…a very sad, animal-sounding whimper just emerged spontaneously from my mouth; my body's unconscious 'implicit memory' system obviously remembers this traumatic move.) I was received at my new home by a prim receptionist leaning over her desk and asking, "Who are you? We have no record of you coming." After I was finally wheeled into a stark, dark side-room, my scary welcome was followed by a doctor peering over his glasses and asking me why I was lying down! My terror went through the roof; my life was in the hands of a bunch of strangers who didn't seem to have a clue about me. I remember feeling increasingly depressed and withdrawn during my time there, writing no letters and talking very little. I was very close to asking Death to take me.

After more kidney dialysis, which I can only remember vaguely (being connected by my neck line to a big, whirring machine) I was eventually returned to my regular hospital and my beautiful, safe E17 where I was met by the bubbly receptionists Debbie and Catherine's whoops of delight. I cried with joy, no longer the stoic princess who would bite her lip rather than being seen shedding a tear. A few days later I cried again when Dr H. sat herself down next to my bed and, as usual, told me how it was. "Your white cells are going mad, your platelets (the blood's clotting agent) were on a count of one yesterday, your red blood cells are really low again and there's major inflammation ...we need to calm your auto-immune system down..."

"Go on..." I croaked.

"Chemotherapy. The honest truth is that it may cure you..." she looked into my eyes "Or it may kill you." I stared blankly as my brain froze into nothingness for a while but when it buzzed back to life I managed a weak, "Look if you think we should, let's do it."

And so the chemo began and my pathetically weak body strained even more under the vicious poison. I watched, heartbroken, as my long, thick, dark hair started to fall onto my pillow in sickening clumps.

Given how I was still in mega pain, constantly being sick and totally drained, you'd expect that this was my rock bottom time, but to my amazement, I had periods of feeling fantastic. I remember sitting propped up by pillows in my big, green bedside chair and feeling like my heart was *open*. I was bursting with love, gratitude and a *massive* appreciation of life. I'd looked out of my fourth floor window in awe at the grey clouds floating by and was acutely aware of how miraculous they were; their moisture had risen from the sea and lakes and would rain down to water tiny seeds which would grow into luscious crops. I thought about the farmers across the world getting up in the early hours and the crop-pickers bent double in the fields; the men drilling for oil on filthy, barren rigs, all the people building and driving transport ships, planes and lorries, the men and women preparing and packing food, wholesale and supermarket workers stacking and selling it, the hospital cooks beavering away in hot, sweaty kitchens and the auxiliary nurses dishing food onto my plate (when I could eat). I realised how lucky I was to be supported by an *amazing* planet and all these fellow people, just as I had thousands of people behind all my medication and machinery, my warm bed, soft pyjamas, the cards on my wall and even my grey, cardboard sick bowls. Aware that I'd probably be long dead by now in most countries in the world, I felt *incredibly* grateful. *Oh my God, have I gone mad? How can I possibly feel this good when I might be dead*

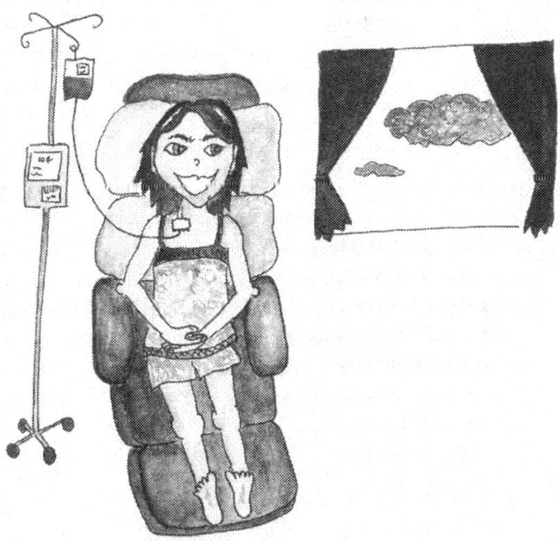

tomorrow? This is bizarre; what the…? But how amazing life is! God, I love everybody! And if I die, well thank God I've danced like nobody's watching, thank God I did a job which helped people, travelled, really saw the trees, loved deeply and had fun! Funnily enough I didn't reflect on how many handbags or shoes I'd had or how clean my house had been. *Still, surely I should be feeling crap at this point; I could be dead tomorrow and I really don't want to die…this is seriously weird…my god, life is amazing…*

Again so luckily, my self-destructive auto-immune reaction was slowly whacked into submission by the chemotherapy. With the help of my loving family, Matthew, friends, the kind nursing staff and even strangers (friends of my mum and some of my nurses and their connections were praying for me the length of the UK) I began to feel life slowly seeping back into my body. Interestingly, a shamanic perspective is that love's required to pull the soul back into somebody's body when they're really sick, and I felt very loved.

The chemo only cost me half of my hair. I was also lucky to keep most of my eyelashes and dark eyebrows and when my tufty locks grew back, they became the beautiful corkscrew curls I'd always wanted. Interestingly, my hair which didn't fall out had horizontal stripes; I presume the paler lines grew when my holistic body was saying "Forget colouring the hair! We need all the energy for the serious stuff!" I wasn't the only person who had a hair disaster at this time; my sensitive dad, who could only stay for ten minutes at a time when I was in Intensive Care, also lost clumps of his brown hair and had bald patches which eventually grew back pure white; for a while he looked like a badger. (Ouch.)

With my hair still thinning but very furry legs, I was eventually able to nibble food again and was transferred to the hospital's 'Nutrition Unit' to fatten me up; once Dr H. had got the fluid off my body I looked like a skeleton. I was immediately christened Shaun by a shiny-bobbed nurse who had unsubtly scanned me from top to bottom with a look of something close to disgust. She meant Shaun the sheep from the Wallace and Gromit films (which I love) on account of my knobble-kneed stick legs (which I didn't love.) My mum still rages about the "horrible way that nurse looked you up and down! I would've given her a mouthful if I'd not been scared of her treating you badly." I think I was about the nurse's age; had she been taught, like me, to be repulsed by vulnerability or was her fear of death whacking her round the head?

Despite the nurse, I immediately liked the small, cosy Nutrition Unit. I had a side room with pink, instead of standard white walls, a comfy bed and, joy of joys, it was calm and quiet. Then I was asked what I'd like to eat. Wondering if this was all too good to be true I suggested melon and ten minutes later my jaw nearly hit the floor as I was presented with a *glass* bowl (beautiful, clean, shiny glass instead of the usual worn, plastic crockery) full of melon balls with strawberry and kiwi pieces! It felt like a mirage. From then on I was away; I revelled in the privilege of choosing my dinners which Christine (a slightly dishevelled, worn-out looking woman, whose warmth came, I suspect, from an understanding of what suffering was) cooked just for me. Apart from fresh vegetables that is; I couldn't believe that even the specially designed nutrition unit only served the hideous frozen, orange squares of same-tasting root vegetables.

Looking back, having since learned about 'mindful eating,' I realise that I discovered this on the nutrition unit. Rather than just knocking back food as I focused on cutting up the next mouthful or thinking about the next thing I had to do, I was eating slowly (I didn't have the energy to go faster) and, because I'd not eaten for so long, I was really savouring each beautiful, rich morsel. I was so aware of how lucky I was to have this food, with so many in the world, including the UK, starving or hungry and I'd learned how blessed I was simply being able to eat and digest food. My sense of taste was such a gift!

I was soon eating small portions with gusto and my body began to rebuild. Three weeks on I could *finally* get out of bed, stand on my own wobbly legs and spend ever increasing minutes with Matthew supporting me so I could transfer weight from leg to leg on the spot. It was again beautiful feeling the length of Matthew's strong, solid body but I was conscious of mine being both bony (my limbs, back and bottom) and bloated (my face and belly; I actually wonder if I had a 'malnutrition belly.') Eventually, with a Zimmer frame for support, I was able to hobble to the sink – and the mirror above it. *Oh my God! There's the blue of my eyes but why are the whites so yellow? My God, is this sick, bloated, grey face really me? And my eyebrows! Blooming heck, what was my mum thinking, letting me look like a werewolf? I need some tweezers…* My shock was interrupted by the brusque but kind-hearted sister bursting into my room with the cheery announcement, "Right, today's your lucky day; we're taking your catheter out!"

"You must be joking!"

"Nope!"

"There's no way I'll make it to the loo in time!"

"Don't worry, you're bound to have a few mishaps but that's okay; everything's covered in plastic and designed to be washable."

"Oh great! By the way, isn't there a rule about letting your patients to look like some weird Dennis Healey werewolf?"

Laughing, she said, "Ah, it's brilliant seeing you coming back to the land of the living. See you later!"

Despite my reluctance to pee randomly, bodily functions had actually taken on a slightly different perspective by this time; what would have humiliated me previously had become almost normal. I'd had weeks (when my bowels were working) where I'd had to lean my useless body face-down over my bed whilst family, friends and nursing staff, using a big spray can, foamed up my bottom and wiped it clean. I'd also had to be lifted out of bed by a hoist and plonked onto commodes next to my bed – with my bottom and boobs hanging out for all to see. And so, catheter removed, I was sitting in my green chair, discussing with my dad my latest interesting find from my *Encyclopaedia of World History*, when my bladder began to whimper. I tried to get up for the loo but my legs buckled and my bladder muscles were useless so I had no choice but to just sit and pee on my plastic-covered pillow! The gentle tenderness with which my dad just got on with cleaning me up was beautiful; I imagine it was a relief for him to finally, finally be able to do *something* to help his daughter.

I'd had my historic encyclopaedia for years but never looked at it. Now I was glued, piecing together humanity's evolution across the globe (or regression, I would argue, in the many places where the native people's understanding of ecology and living in tune *with* the natural world was obliterated by the West's murder and oppression of the people.) It made me smile to see what funny sheep we are by sticking to prescribed fashions, from big white ruffs and flea-bitten wigs to specific skirt and hair lengths but it gutted me to see that battles, wars and cruelty seemed to have been a part of life as far back as 'civilisation' began. It seemed so *silly* that years of sickening war often ended in negotiations which could've happened at the beginning! Yet things *had* improved; we no longer cheered at 'witches' being burnt or dunked, (about seventy-five thousand of them, a quarter male) rubbed our hands at gladiators being ripped apart by lions or packed into town squares to see people being decapitated or hung. Most of us no longer thought it acceptable to enslave people, view women as male property, lock up men for being gay or beat up black men in custody. We'd also progressed with our expanding awareness; with life on the farm a few centuries back we just cared for our families but as villages came together we related to other local people and spread our concern to them. With a move to the cities we began to identify (with our accents, work, local characteristics and sports teams etc) with our towns and cities and the people living with us and as we moved about more we developed more connection with the people in our counties and then (perhaps aided by the wars as well as the TV and even more movement), our country. Encompassing care for our peers in Europe became our next move in the UK (but's let's not go there, what with 'Brexit' and all...) and maybe, just maybe, we've now evolved enough to spread our compassion worldwide and identify with all human beings. For me that's real human maturity.

And so, my history study, on top of the compassion I'd experienced in hospital, fuelled my belief that we humans *are* evolving and that we have the capacity to move beyond war, boundaries, hierarchies and injustice – and I'd not yet read the latest optimistic research from 'Positive psychology' and neuroscience about us being physically wired to connect...

In time, my bladder regained some control and, joy of joys, my hissing – or on ICU and HDU, gurgling – oxygen mask was finally removed. My voice was weak and croaky but at least audible. Then it was time to have fun! Having finally got rid of the MRSA I was allowed out of isolation and Matthew took me on wheelchair trips to the small rooftop garden; this was usually reserved for staff but they knew how much I needed some air – and wasn't it fresh! The breeze and sun on my face felt like Heaven! Matthew also took me for meals to the hospital canteen and over pasty, beans and chips, as he talked about his extended family, I realized how little I knew about this man who I'd been on such a massive journey with. What was even weirder was wondering who he was getting to know; who was I now?

The other massive perk of getting rid of MRSA was being allowed to have a bath. I'm grinning as I recall myself in the deep, steaming water with a sublime smile on my face. My bony spine ground on the ceramic base but as the heat soaked my aching body, I was ecstatic. It was massively reassuring that my mashed up, broken body could, from the *inside*, still give me immense joy.

Well, despite the bath memory, I'm not feeling altogether cheery as I'm editing this chapter; I also remember how hard it was to get out of the bath on my sticky legs and the shame of Matthew seeing my hideous body. I can't believe I was so broken – and that I may be again. How are you with my story? Intrigued? Bored? Shocked? Relieved? Determined to take better care of yourself? I really hope the latter's the case.

Chapter 11
The Devastation on the Cake

"Deep down in the human spirit there is a reservoir of courage. It is always available, always wanting to be discovered."

Pema Chödrön

I had an interesting bit of encouragement back in 2009 when, towards the end of a week's planned 'writing holiday' I finally faced writing this chapter. I'd been avoiding it for most of the week (on top of several years) with cleaning, gardening, paper-pile sorting, e-mails, Facebook, piano playing and mindless TV. I then watched a random film, after which I grabbed my laptop and hammered out the following...

'What a film! *Amistad*, directed by Steven Spielberg, is about a group of African people who were violently enslaved. They bravely fought their captors as they were being transported across the Atlantic in the stinking belly of a ship but were recaptured and imprisoned in America whilst the legal system decided their fate. Did they belong to their captors, the Spaniards of Cuba, where it was alleged that they were born into 'legal' slavery or were they illegally enslaved in Africa and therefore should be freed? The film was devastating, but fantastic too; the suffering was so clearly painted. On the ships, if the anti-slavery authorities came by, there was sickness, rebellion or low provisions, the captors would tie a line of live people to a rope and then attach it to a sack of rocks – which were slid over the side. The scene of the men and women being dragged, naked and screaming into an inevitable, watery death was horrific and I'll never forget it – or stop appreciating the fact that I've been lucky to avoid such immense suffering. Needless to say, I sobbed my way through the film and, though it was so painful, I realised that I was glad that I'd learned what suffering is (though obviously nowhere near on the scale of being a slave.) I was glad that I could feel the pain of others because it made me feel alive. Human. Real. Fully here. My suffering was what made me pick up my laptop again just now and keep writing in order to try and do what little bit I can for our crazy world and connect with others who are suffering.

During the film, Anthony Hopkins is a lawyer who comes out of his retirement to represent the Africans in the Supreme Court. In a dramatic scene Hopkins had just made it clear to the main African character, a strapping, gorgeous and gentle man (Djimon Hounsou), just what they were up against – the political climate preceding the American Civil War when the South and those in the North, rich or poor enough to benefit, wanted slavery to continue. Hopkins asked him what he'd do. "Call on my ancestors" he said, at which point I spontaneously bawled my little heart out, feeling a deep connection to mine. So, then I had my swearing, Craven-A smoking, four needle sock-knitting great-grandmother, my fierce sergeant major great-grandad who used to silence his family with one wag of his finger when 'The Archers' came on the radio, my happy, dippy, patient grandma, my deep, poetic grandad and my amazingly resilient and loving parents behind me as I wrote this...'

I left the Nutrition Unit after about a month and was wheeled back to my lovely E17 where I was greeted by the staff's genuine hugs, grins and celebration; I was starting to look human again. I can't remember how many weeks later it was when Dr H. breezed into my room with a big smile on her face. "I have some good news for you."

"Blimey. What's happening?"

"Are you ready?"

"Go on..."

"You can go home!"

"What?"

"Really. You just need to heal now."

"Oh my God! And can I take an oxygen tank, just in case?"

"You don't need one, you'll be fine."

"Really? Just a little one maybe?"

"Really. Your lungs are clear now."

"Oh wow. Blimey. Home. The outside world. So will I be okay then?"

"I'm sorry, Jayne, I don't think you'll play tennis again but I don't see why you can't have a reasonable quality of life."

"Mmm. What does that mean?"

"Nobody knows; you're making amazing progress. It may take a while but with your spirit nothing would surprise me. Enjoy what you have. Oh and just eat little and often."

"I can't tell you how grateful I am for all you've done for me. There are just no words."

"Well, we made a good team, eh?"

"Yeah," I managed as I choked back my tears, of relief, gratitude, hope...and fear. I was over the moon at the thought of respite from needles, noise, six-o-clock wake-ups, cold diced carrot, my friends and family no longer having to suffer and finally being able to curl up with Matthew without drips and drains in the way – but I was also scared stiff. It was one thing being a physical and emotional wreck in a hospital surrounded by understanding people but another being out in the real world where I would be expected to re-join the busy capitalist machine and get on with 'doing' at ninety miles an hour whilst looking young, fit and gorgeous. And what if I had another brain haemorrhage or my heart stopped? I'd studied Goffman's notion of 'institutionalisation' at poly with interest; people being unable to cope on the 'outside' after years inside psychiatric hospital but I'd never imagined that I'd suffer from it! The cars in the hospital car park looked like something out of *Star Trek* as Matthew loaded me and my rickety wheelchair into his. I panicked at twenty miles an hour, clinging to the dashboard and begging Matthew to slow down. As we pulled up at my house, it looked crazy with its cheery yellow paintwork and I was slapped by the wild cacophony of colour and chaos inside; a sparse white hospital room was a million miles from this. My parents had cleaned it beautifully but I didn't recognize the owner of these wooden statues, candles and giant plants. I initially felt delighted as I shuffled through the patio doors into my garden but as I bent over to pull at a weed, I was hit by reality; it just laughed in my face.

NO!!! NO! Don't make me go there! I don't want to write anymore it's too painful…let me put the TV back on…who wants to read about all this bloody misery anyway?

It's okay, Jaynie; it's only a feeling; the worst thing that's going to happen is that you're going to feel a lot; just physical sensations…

I don't want to feel a lot; I've had years of feeling a lot!

Come on, flower, just a little bit more; maybe someone who can't bear the pain may come across your book and not feel so alone…maybe someone will think about a friend who's suffering and give him a ring…

Okay, okay…

I was a yellow, moon-faced, steroid-swollen woman, with deep, grey rings under my bloodshot eyes. I had knobbly sticks for arms and legs, ratty hair and a stooping, scrawny body; I looked pretty much like a wonky Belisha beacon. I couldn't get upstairs or do my 'resettling;' I had to just lie on the mattress which Matthew and my family had brought downstairs and allow them to take over my care. I wasn't strong enough to go out without a wheelchair for …mmm, a few weeks? I can't remember, it was so awful I've blocked out a lot. My relatively fit, attractive self who used to turn heads in the street was gone and had been replaced with an ugly, crumpled wreck. Much as I told myself it didn't matter how I looked, society's conditioning with its mass of beautiful, healthy people on TV and bill-boards ran deep and I felt ashamed and worthless.

I couldn't imagine feeling any worse but several months later I was asked to attend a multidisciplinary meeting of doctors to discuss my prospects of having children. It's actually a bit of a blur. All I remember is sitting at a big table in a windowless room with various doctors, including my Gentle Giant gynaecologist. It was unanimously agreed that it would be disastrous and probably fatal should I ever attempt to have a child, what with the risk of my ovary bleeding again (it seemed that my bleeds happened when I ovulated) and the strain on my body of carrying and delivering a baby. I could bleed – or clot – to death in childbirth and leave my baby motherless. When the Gentle Giant recommended that I adopt a child I just stared at him; I knew as a social worker that I'd never be approved for adoption with a body as knackered as mine.

My devastation was now complete. I might've risked damage to my body for the sake of having a child but no way could I ever risk leaving my baby motherless. Matthew wanted children and I couldn't imagine being with a man who didn't want to have a family. Having a painful wreck of a body was nothing compared to being told that I couldn't have children. I would turn on the TV and there were happy mothers and babies *every* time. There were pregnant women soaring down every street. I limped round supermarkets watching fit, healthy mothers beam at their babies. Alongside my brother having his second child, my best friend Maria had just had a beautiful baby girl and her motherhood was shortly followed by most of my friends. I felt like they'd grown up but I hadn't. They were part of womankind; motherhood was their connection to each other and to the women of the Himalayas and African plains, to Mother Earth, to the nurturing, loving archetypal woman – but I was alone and 'barren.' I imagined that they would feel loved and secure in their tight family units but I never would. They had meaning to their lives, I didn't. They were getting to witness the joy and wonder of a growing child and I never would – which was a *major* loss for a social worker and trainee psychotherapist so interested in human development.

I initially tried to cope with my health and baby traumas by appreciating the fact that I had survived against such odds and still had a lot in my life, including little Morty cat, who had hung about whilst I was incarcerated and eased my broken heart with his calm, furry presence. I had been welcomed home from hospital by my neighbours with a big banner strung from my garage and had offers of help at every turn, including from lovely Nurse Claire, who was now my friend and neighbour Jez's partner, and kind, bubbly Teresa, another experienced nurse who lived five doors away. However, as the weeks went by, I reverted to my old, familiar pattern of feeling like I was 'too much' and retreated into myself. I sometimes numbed myself out but also spent many hours curled up with Morty on my blue rug crying out my heart and soul to Pink Floyd's emotive *Division Bell* and *The Wall* albums. The imaginary wall between me and others had never been so huge. *What's the bloody point of being here if I can't have kids, play tennis, dance, do a meaningful job or travel far enough from a hospital to feel safe? Will I ever feel relaxed? And what's the point of kidding myself about Matthew? He's a black-belt and yoga teacher with a harem of fertile woman just dying to take full advantage of his muscular body, so why would he possibly want to be with me? I'm a fucking alien.* I sometimes felt the urge to scream out at the top of my voice, "Help me! Please, please, someone help me!" but more often than not I reasoned that nobody could really understand my devastation *or* make it better, so what was the point of even talking?

When I tried to 'pull myself together and get on with it' I inevitably covered my pain with frustration and rage. My anger was fuelled by a continuing regime of chemotherapy and steroids and also a hefty, personality-changing, monthly hormone injection, 'Zoladex,' which turned off my remaining ovary and sent me into a hot-flushed, premature menopause. I guess I also had Post-Traumatic Stress Disorder, flashing back to my peers dying, my lungs flooding and my blood squirting. I was having a lot of nightmares, felt like my nerves were connected to the National Grid and regularly wanted to kill myself or passing mothers. My mum stuck by me, bless her, and took my occasional rants at her with love and compassion but I gradually pushed Matthew away as my insecurity poured out as criticism – whilst at the same time he retreated and set up his own yoga centre without any reference to our joint dream and did things to push me away. Whilst on one of his residential yoga weekends, where my weak body depressed the hell out of me, I'd seen the way a woman, who looked a bit like a fit version of me, drooled over him and the sideways glances she gave to me. I knew (or my self-fulfilling prophesy did) that our relationship would soon be over – and it was. I actually spoke the words which confirmed our ending after a scary, almighty row (over him not responding to my desperate letter asking him to *please* just tell me how he felt.) I was devastated, as was he, he's since told me. The trauma was just too much for both of us. (Oh, where's my chocolate…) I'm pleased to tell you that Matthew and his yoga lady – after many years actually, so it wasn't easy for them – had two delightful children who are the joy of Matthew's life.

In the midst of my despair there was a strange but lovely moment which I shared with my grandad, despite the fact that he'd been dead for twenty-six years. I've been hearing my mum read my grandad's poems since I was little but I was shocked when, one miserable day, I got out his worn, maroon poetry book so I could copy and illustrate his poems for my brother's birthday and just happened to open it at this one, written for a local mum with her new baby.

New Born

Congratulations and a wish I send
That all your plans come true
And may you never lack a friend
In this world you'll find so new.

A dream come true is in your care
Bringing joys you've yet to meet
A jewel that you'll find so rare
As each new day you greet.

Yet there's many that are seeking
For the treasure you have found
The love you found when meeting
And hearing your babe's first sounds.

So just remember as you walk
Showing the world your treasure
Some will stop to look and talk
That God denies this pleasure.

Arthur Downs

I wept buckets as I read the end and a few more buckets in the hours and days afterwards; I no longer felt quite so alone. I wondered if the poem contained Grandad's grief at only having one child; apparently he wanted more but Grandma didn't; she felt too old by the time he'd returned from the war.

For months after my 'release' I was still going back to hospital regularly for chemotherapy, blood transfusions, scans, blood tests and appointments with my kidney, heart and liver doctors, my gynaecologist and haematologist. At first I enjoyed meeting fellow patients at the haematology outpatient clinic, again a random mix of people from all walks of life; cheery, wizened Italian M. who had a passion for knitting, lisping teenager, B, who played his latest nerve-twisting dance tunes for us, sombre, six-and-a half- foot, Caribbean W, who'd share his crosswords with us and D, a twenty-something bombshell with leopard-skin trousers, bottom-length blonde hair and a voice like a foghorn. My initial response to D. with my 'thou shalt not show off' programmed brain was intense dislike but I grew to love her party stories and wild refusal to give up on life. We all sat in rows in our green chairs being drip-fed medication, chatting, moaning, comparing pains and sometimes laughing. My quiet pleasure at being heard and understood by my fellow sufferers began to fade, however, as the months went by and, one by one, they were whisked away by greedy Death. It reached the point where I'd say a name and the receptionist would simply shake her head. When bubbly D. and her leopard-skin trousers disappeared the day after I went to visit and massage her as a pain-wracked in-patient, I kept myself to myself.

Another huge blow for me came three months after my release when Dr H. announced that she was moving away. I was gutted. And frightened. The metal statue of a dancing woman and a vase to say thank you to her didn't feel enough by a million miles. The funny thing about Dr H. was that she'd only arrived at my hospital three months before I was admitted. I look back at her unwavering, ass-kicking, giant-brained presence as a miracle. Thank you so, so much, once again, Dr H.

I didn't feel as confident in my care when Dr H. had gone and hated it when I kept having to be readmitted as an inpatient for more horrendous, bloodcurdling weeks of infections in my gut and various mini bleeds...more needles, more sickness, more death all around me, the vigilant battle to monitor my medication and the usual fights for release. I remember one time I'd processed my rage a bit by belting a punch-bag and got a bleed in my elbow but because I'd also got a bruise on my head (from a mirror which I'd propped up on my pillow and had fallen on me during the night) the doctors wouldn't believe that it wasn't a domestic violence issue and again I felt that awful, sinking feeling of powerlessness.

I can't remember how long it took me to get some strength back. It was probably only a month or so before I could hobble into the supermarket with the support of a trolley but it took many months to do much more than that. I remember, maybe six months on, trying to run on the local park but my legs felt like those of a wobbly, new-born foal. For months my bladder was still weak and caused me trouble on several occasions and one day I had to discard my knickers in Asda when I'd been unable to control my bowels. When you think about it, most of us have got so much to be thankful for on a daily basis and that's perhaps what kept me going. The days when I could walk, eat, make it to the loo and avoid needles were good days.

Seeing my despair on hospital days – I'd go into a degree of shock every time I went through the doors – my doctors offered me antidepressants but I didn't want to be in a permanent fuzz so I opted for more therapy. I remember gentle, stripy-socked, sand-booted Peter saying, "Well, you've danced with death, Jayne. Your challenge now is *living*."

"Well, yes, it was a lot easier dying. It felt so amazing when I was dying."

"Yes I know, you talk about that a lot."

"I miss that beautiful feeling, Peter. The pull of death's massive."

"I know."

"And I don't know how to live like this."

"You will."

"How on earth do you live with Death scaring the shit out of you constantly? If he doesn't come in the day he infiltrates my dreams."

"You'll find your way. We all have to."

Being able to sit with Peter, being totally real in my despair without worrying that he'd run away or think me crazy was such a gift. I do remember sticking my head under a blanket in shame as I sobbed at one point; sharing my pain still wasn't easy but, step by step, I cried my way back into life. Gestalt Therapy has a great piece of theory devised by Arnold Beisser

(1970)[27] who was wheelchair-bound and had presumably lived through a lot of pain; the 'Paradoxical Theory of Change.' The idea, borrowed from Buddhism, is that the more we face our hard feelings head-on (and, with therapy, share them) the quicker we process those feelings and move on – whilst, paradoxically, when we try to ignore our feelings, they have no way of transforming and so they keep biting us on the bottom and manifesting in rage, anxiety, depression and ill-health.

Mmm...Talking of hard feelings, this is seriously heavy shit and I'd rather be watching *EastEnders* and avoiding mine. I was just totally broken at this time and I feel so sorry for my younger self – and still scared it could all happen again. I need to go and have a good cry...

27. *He's on Google and see Gestalt Therapy in bibliography p. 435*

Chapter 12
Forging a New Life

"I choose to make the rest of my life the best of my life."

Louise Hay

About three months after my release from hospital I was out on my patio, gently swinging in my much adored, yellow, string hammock. I still felt wrecked, anxious, isolated and purposelessness. Lost in grim thoughts I wasn't noticing the warm sunshine on my face. Neither did I hear the crack of the brick pillar to which my hammock was strapped; I just felt myself moving forward then, in the moment that I landed heavily on the patio, I heard a crash of bricks and felt a terrifying weight of stone digging into my back! When I came out of shock I tentatively reached up my back to discover, with amazement, that there was only a tiny smear of blood. Slowly standing, I couldn't believe the mass of jagged bricks behind me which might have caved my head in if I'd leaned back another few inches or the front of the hammock hadn't dragged me so far forwards. I stood, sad at my shredded hammock which I'd carried all the way back from Guatemala, but agog at how lucky I'd been. Again! I stood up and stumbled round my patio looking up to the sky and asking *What, God? What do you want me to do? Okay, I get it, there's more going on than what we see through our microscopes and telescopes and my life's a total gift and I need to get on with it – but what? What shall I do?*

I decided that I'd try to write. I could still use a keyboard, I loved the creative process of writing and English had been my best and second favourite subject at school (after sport.) With poetic Grandad Arthur behind me, I enrolled on a ten-week cartoon course and began my 'writing career' with two illustrated books for, and based on, my nephews. The first, 'Brothers on Walkabout,' was about the boys meeting talking animal who were attempting to save the world from human destruction and the second, 'The Magic Mirror,' described their trip to another planet (via the mirror in next door's shed) where they were each taken in by the warring sides and ended up bringing peace and understanding to the planet by thinking magical 'good stuff' about the enemy and revealing both sides' false propaganda!

I loved moving in imaginary worlds but really saw the

cartoon course as a distraction rather than a road to a real income (that bloody crippling, perfectionist shame) and put more thought into how I was going pay my way. I was still off sick from work and just couldn't imagine getting up at seven-o-clock every morning and driving the twenty miles to work. I'd finished my chemotherapy but my gut was still getting blocked, anaemia was a constant problem, my coccyx still scraped on the bath and I spent half my time asleep. Yet my ego had been happy as a child protection social worker; I was being very good in my selflessness *and* I felt important. I chaired meetings, liaised with a myriad of professionals (making me feel less alien and indeed, sometimes powerful, in a middle-class world) and I had to regularly speed my Bat-mobile (well, Escort-mobile) to scenes of crisis in true superhero style! I loved being part of a close team and working with children. Now all I could envisage was either dropping dead with the stress or strangling someone who abused their child. I had regular fantasies about screaming at passing mothers at the best of times – "How come you can have children when I can't!" and I had to really rein myself in (and sometimes I didn't) when I came across stressed-out mothers giving their children a hard time. When I saw the work's doctor he had no hesitation in offering me the option of retirement on ill-health grounds with a lump sum and a small monthly pension. It was a hard decision but helped by my thought *I may be dead next year so whatever I decide, does it really matter?*

The following summer I threw my deeply ingrained frugality to the wind and, with a chunk of my retirement pension, bought my friend Frankie's soft-topped jeep. I wanted to feel the wind in my hair – and what was the point of money sitting in the bank when I might die soon? I also decided to apply to art school. I'd always loved drawing but never regarded myself as trendy or good enough to study art but what did I have to lose? I was on a week's stint in hospital (I've no idea what for, it all blurs into one) when I was invited for an interview for a part-time 'Art and Design' foundation course. I told my wide-eyed, baby duck-haired doctor that I needed to go. "I don't think so. You're attached to a drip."

"Yes and I'd really appreciate it if you'd un-attach me. It's only saline and I'm drinking again."

"You're in no fit state to go for an interview!"

"I'm in no fit state to miss this opportunity. I may not have time to mess about. Please, I've got to go!"

"You can't..."

"Look, I'll only be a couple of hours."

"But..."

"Please undo me. If I do it myself I might make a mess."

"Look..."

"I *have to* get on with my life."

"Tut. Two hours. And you'll have to sign yourself out."

"Fine. Thank you. I appreciate it."

I brushed my wild, part-tufty hair, managed to drag on some clothes and ordered a cab. As I gingerly lowered myself into my taxi the other back door sprang open and in jumped Peter who'd just come to visit me! I'd been seeing him for therapy about a year prior to the start of my nightmare and he'd been to see me a few times during my incarceration. Seeing him this day was simply beautiful. I'd done everything on my own my whole life pretty much and, despite my bravado, was nervous about how fragile I felt; he was like an angel appearing out of the ether. It wasn't a conventional therapeutic act to accompany me to my interview and wait to see how I got on, but it was a precious and massively healing one.

I think the cool, hairy, forty-something art college tutor who interviewed me was a little agog as I explained about my need to be brief so I could get back to hospital, and I must have looked terrible, but he seemed to like my argument that I had lots of inner turmoil to feed my art work! As I showed him some of my drawings (portraits mostly) he stroked his beard and frowned a bit but my enthusiasm seemed to sway him and finally he smiled and awarded me a place. I was over the moon. My life wasn't over; I was going to create!

I was so excited when, on day one of art school, we were given a big brush, had a huge sheet of paper taped to the wall and were told to just paint. It was like being at nursery school! Oh the freedom to express! Nietzsche apparently said, "We have art so we shall not be destroyed by the truth." I like that. Over the following months each brush stroke felt like an external expression and working through of my internal truth; the grey shadows, the hanging man, the bloody corpse, the isolated tower in the woods and the lino print of me shrieking which made Munch's 'Scream' look like he was having a laugh (actually it was nowhere near Munch's masterpiece but it felt good.) I guess I also wanted to make somebody understand how it was for me. Luckily my fellow student, chilled, chiselled-cheeked Jaq, who had been through trauma in her own life and wasn't afraid of pain, understood where I was coming from, swam with me in the depths and helped me to feel more connected to the world. Another of my classmates, a vicar's daughter who liked flowers and pretty colours, tended to look at me as if I were a threat to humankind. I guess I *was* a threat to her. I suppose I was to everyone; all my friends had to address the fact of their grim mortality every time they saw me, never mind when I talked about my fear of dying. I'm *so* grateful that most of my friends stuck with me.

I do wonder how sane I must have been as I look back now, what with my PTSD and all, but somehow I got through without any outrageous acts of violence or madness. Largely I think I stayed relatively okay because, despite all the pain, I had a vague awareness that what had happened to me was somehow positive; I couldn't explain or understand it, but I knew that I'd changed for the better and learned a lot. My mind kept saying, *don't be ridiculous, you're in denial, it was and is horrendous – end of story* but my deeper self knew different...

I was also helped at this time by coming across a national support group for people who couldn't have children; 'More to Life.' Meeting for meals sometimes involved a bit of a journey but it was worth it; being with other women who knew the devastating pain of childlessness helped to ease my terrible isolation and my feeling of being an alien creature. I saw that these women were still whole, delightful and purposeful despite not having children and I felt glimmers of hope that maybe there *was* more to life. Sadly though, I could still feel quite lonely in the group as I was the only one with major health issues and it was clear that some of the women, with their wide-eyed awkwardness, struggled to hear about my life. I gradually withdrew from the group – yet interacting with them occasionally on social media was and still is comforting.

Practically, a big help for me at this time was discovering a home-testing 'INR' machine. It cost me three hundred quid but meant I no longer had to drag myself to the anticoagulant clinic every month (or more) as I could test my blood from a finger-prick at home. I soon worked out how to calculate my doses of warfarin and the freedom felt wonderful. It also meant I could have a drink and not worry about it thinning my blood too much and killing me. I've been puzzled over the years as to why, having met many people on lifelong warfarin, more didn't have their own machine. I recently heard from an anti-coagulant nurse that I'm the only person with a machine in my area who doses herself. This smacks to me of a system which, in the spirit of the medical model, the doctors are seen as the experts and patients feel like idiots who haven't the sense to take care of themselves. For all the love and skill in hospitals, I think disempowerment's still a major problem.

My next healing step came about a year after my 'release' when I re-joined my old, four-weekly psychotherapy supervision group. I didn't have any clients to discuss but I valued the mental stimulation of listening about my peers' clients. I also loved the contact with 'Frank,' my safe, compassionate supervisor and my three co-supervisees, petite, giant-brained Jeanette, wiry, spiritual Neale and gentle, puppy-eyed Simon. Frank was a priest as well as a therapist and I went to talk to him about conducting my funeral, should I die. I hugely appreciated having on standby a trusted person who I knew would celebrate my life, say how great I was and not go on about hell and damnation! With the door to social work closed, I gradually began to imagine my life as a therapist and, two years on, I felt just about strong enough, physically and emotionally, to return to my training. It was a very challenging act walking into the room where my new group was gathering; I was terrified of being seen as an evil infiltrator of this established group. Funnily enough though, I'd met vibrant, chatty, fellow student Susie at a festival that summer and had been introduced to warm, fellow northerner, Dan, on a random visit to my friend Jez. Dan's reassurance that I was joining a friendly group and that he'd look out for me made it easier and as I plonked myself next to him and he beamed me a huge smile, my anxiety reduced.

I soon realized that I was a different person to the one who'd started psychotherapy training four years earlier. That had entailed me and seventeen other 'mature' students sitting round the edges of our training room on futons. All eager to learn about how our future clients 'ticked,' it was a shock to realise that a large part of the training was about sorting out our own heads so that we were less likely to bring our own 'stuff' into our work; distorted perceptions or expectations, interfering feelings, unconscious 'blind spots,' a lack of compassion, tendencies to criticize, judge, bully, shut down clients' feelings because we can't bear them etc. Thus the first hour and a half of each two or five-day training bonanza, began with 'group process.' Now, what are the words to describe it? A cringe-laden, paranoia-inducing nightmare from Hell? The idea was to sit quietly within the group and try to get in touch with your feelings then, when you felt like it and there was a natural space, share 'where you were at' with the group. "I'm feeling...I was just thinking...I'm aware of ..." Other group members would listen and then those who felt the urge would respond, "Ah, that's sad...I feel really impacted by..." and, when we really got going, "I felt angry when you said..." This may sound like an interesting little hoot to you but I was way, way out of my comfort zone and, being emotionally triggered by others' stories and tears, I spent most of the time thinking *Oh God, my heart's gonna burst! I feel like crying but that's ridiculous! What am I crying for? Come on, Jaynie, pull yourself together, you're just crying for attention! Oh God, if anybody comes near me to offer me a hug I'm gonna bloody scream!* I was pretty good at giving other people hugs and jumping in with empathic feedback at my peers' painful disclosures, but the potential shame of opening up and baring *my* innermost soul and vulnerability to a bunch of professional people who I imagined would think that I was a horrible, selfish, self-pitying and sinful Northern dimwit, was massive. My thoughts were such a classic example of projection and how we bring false beliefs from the past right into the present; my *parents* may have thought I was 'crying for attention' as a child but I doubt any of my co-trainees did.

I went home on day three of my first week's training, having finally spoken out in the group and, as I lay collapsed on my rug, my brain came up with an image of being in a court room with spooky, blank-faces (like the pink, featureless faces of the indoctrinated masses in Pink Floyd's *The Wall* video) slowly turning towards me in silent, critical judgement of my shame-ridden self.

One of the first things we discussed on the course was the notion of 'taking responsibility' for our feelings and actions, rather than being in the common habit of blaming somebody or something else for how we felt or acted. To practise this, our sentences had to begin with "I" so that rather than saying, for example "You upset me with that comment" we'd have to say "*I feel* upset by that comment" and then look at *why* we felt as we did. *Ah* I thought, *so I need to ask* why *I get annoyed if someone's showing off or* why *someone slightly letting me down makes me feel totally annihilated.* It was obvious, yet it felt like a revelation; *I* was responsible for my life and my feelings! Nobody had the power to make me react in certain ways; only I could choose how I reacted – and if I had a strong emotional response to something, it was generally linked to an old childhood wound being triggered. 'Show-offs' irritated me because I'd been told as a child that 'people don't like show-offs'; my peers who could ask for what they needed – like a hug or to sit next to a supportive person – annoyed me because I'd been humiliated (like my parents and their parents...) for having emotional needs. *Wow, I need to recognize what touches my buttons! Blimey, this is whacky!*

Going back into training, my feelings and vulnerability no longer terrified me quite so much, though I was never comfortable speaking in group process. I'd felt 'too much' in my first training group because my emotions had overwhelmed my sensitive parents but now I felt too much because I had a ton of heavy-shit existential grief! Incredibly though, it transpired that two other members of my new group had also had major life-threatening experiences and suddenly I was no longer alone with Death! One of these women was beautiful, gutsy, half-Italian, Wendy. Also new to the group, she was my age, single, had suffered traumatic belly operations and been advised against having children. Before long I'd made another good friend; a friend who really understood my situation. I had a lovely sense that the universe was looking out for me and felt so lucky that I was back in an environment in which emotions –

including my Post-Traumatic Stress Disorder – were a normal, acceptable part of reality. Happily, I could now sit close to my peers and allow myself to be hugged without feeling excruciating shame; I finally knew that I needed and deserved support. My training continued to be mind-blowing and scary at times - you couldn't help but relate to most of the clinical diagnoses you read about and touching our deepest pain was hard – but I absolutely appreciated how beautiful it was to share our raw humanity with each other. No matter what our powerful and professional façades, we were all vulnerable and wounded in different ways and to recognise this was such a gift. There's a great piece on the internet by an 'activist clown,' Wavy Gravy. He talks about how we often feel like we're on the 'bozo' bus and imagine all the cool, beautiful, 'sorted' people on another bus...but in reality there is no other bus and we're all just little scaredy-cat bozos trying to deal with the complexities and fears of being a human being.

As the months passed, I gradually got a swing back in my life; my tears and gruesome paintings still flowed at times but my tufty hair grew, my legs strengthened and by the second year of my therapy training I was able to do random Maori stomping round the coffee bar with funny, deep as the ocean, mother of four, Doreen and vibrant, earthy, Lancashire lass Susan and I was joined by all my peers in celebrating the return of my bum! There was still no tennis, death and childlessness remained my constant companions and I'd given up on the idea of having a loving partner but life was moving forward...

Chapter 13
Researching Death

"The more you open to life, the less death becomes the enemy. When you start using death as a means of focusing on life, then everything becomes just as it is, just this moment, an extraordinary opportunity to be really alive."

Stephen Levine

In my final year of my MSc therapy training I had to conduct a research project and write a dissertation. I mused for days on whether I should explore shame, anger, childlessness or the use of creativity in therapy but all the time it was obvious what I had to do. Death was the bane of my life and yet had motivated me to go to art school and was getting me out of bed no matter how rotten I felt; I just knew there was more to 'him' than I realised so I opened my laptop and Googled 'death and psychotherapy.' Mmm...given that psychotherapy is about living, and Gestalt therapy, in particular, about living in the moment, there wasn't a lot about death. I began to panic but then I came across the notion of 'death anxiety.' *Aha! Here we go...* Death anxiety, or a fear of death, was described by existential philosophers...*ah, existentialism! I remember being interested in that at poly* ... and some psychoanalytical psychotherapists as a condition which is at the quaking heart of every human being who is going to die. *Mmm, maybe there are exceptions; those who believe in reincarnation might not be so afraid and some people even welcome death as a release from suffering or as a path of martyrdom* – but I couldn't help agreeing that, generally, death was one pretty terrifying fact of life. Perhaps my thinking had been influenced by another of my Grandad's poems which had, along with his death in his sixties, warned me about the fragility of life as I was growing up...

Life's Thread

Life is but a slender thread,
passing through our span,
mocking at the efforts
and vaunted strength of man.

From the highest to the lowest,
to an army's marching tread,
all are in the balance
from this slender golden thread.

Man conquers space, builds his ships,
soaring like a bird,
whilst seeking inspiration
from the Master's spoken word.

From strength to strength we mortals,
yet life we cannot wed,
and the things we would accomplish
hang on this slender thread.

Arthur Downs

I shot to the library where my eyes tore at books which argued that death anxiety is so overwhelming, either consciously or unconsciously, that it may be a big factor in many avoidant or numbing behaviours, such as alcohol and drug-use. *Ah okay, maybe that's partly why so many of us are on antidepressants, drink or drugs!* The second defence against death anxiety was cited as being a workaholic. *Well that's nearly everybody in our mad Western world!* Sören Kierkegaard (1844).[28] suggested that death anxiety can make us 'Tranquilise ourselves in the trivial.' *My God, I wonder how much of our distractions – screens, shopping, lists of things to do and creating petty dramas is our attempt to block out the awareness of our mortality?* My giant-brained authors went on to suggest that magical thinking can be a big part of our defence structure against death; on some level many of us believe that if we're powerful, rich, good-looking, special, famous or even 'good' or loved enough, then we'll be so important that we can't possibly just die! *Oh my God, is that partly why we're often so materialistic and power-crazed? Fame, a big job, snazzy suit or designer handbag as a shield against death? Is this why some people are willing to sacrifice so much of their pleasure-time and energy to become a bigshot; do they want to feel too important to die, or at least be remembered by lots of people when they do?* I was reminded of eccentric Albert who lived next door and refused to allow his landlord (gorgeous, often kind Andrew, who makes me roar with laughter despite his nationalistic leanings and reminds me that people are always a mixture of things) to fit an indoor loo or hot water but who noted after his terminal lung cancer diagnosis that nobody would forget him. He was right; my neighbours and I still talk with affection about the wise, argumentative old scruff.

---

28. See bibliography p. 434

It was also suggested in my reading that 'social surrender' to cultural norms can be a defence against death anxiety; we generally don't want to stand out and be different from the crowd as that could attract hostility. *Bloody hell! Could suppressed terror be at the heart of our sheep-like, world-destroying lunacy?* The cheery existentialists went on to propose that, as if death anxiety weren't bad enough, another gut-wrenching aspect of being human is our inherent fear of being *alone;* all alone on a massive spinning globe in an infinite universe that has no obvious meaning. *Blimey, all the more reason then to try and fit in with the crowd and just agree with established social norms; that must be why those who challenges the status quo – or our own views – are generally regarded with hostility. I wonder if that's why people sometimes get angry when Dynamo, the amazing 'street' magician, has challenged their view of what's possible. So…we glue ourselves to social norms and fashions but then we compare ourselves to others and can easily feel we're not good enough; our car and house are too small, our bodies not thin or muscular enough – and then we try and fill the insecurity with material things, booze, drugs, food, Botox, manic activity etc… Apparently the happiest societies aren't the richest but the most egalitarian – with less comparisons.*[29]

Talking of crazy activity, as far back as I remember I've despaired about why we humans seem to go to war so readily (usually to feed the pockets, power or lunacy of the powers that be, I've since discovered) so I was struck by Otto Rank's suggestion[30] that 'the killing of the other' can be a deluded way of trying to avoid the overwhelming, unconscious fear of death because whilst the *other* person or people are dying, you're not. I gasped as I thought *Oh my God; the news every single day, violent computer games, gruesome films and TV*

---

29. See for e.g.' The Spirit Level' by Wilkinson & Pickett in the bibliography p. 436
30. See bibliography p. 434

programmes about death – police dramas, hospital dramas, murder mysteries, natural and man-made catastrophes! Every other programme is about 'the other' dying! I recently read in a newspaper (which doesn't, of course, mean that it's true) that in Brazil, a precarious mountain road which vehicles frequently fall off has become the country's number one tourist destination. It's like crashes on the motorway when we slow down to gawp...

And so I was hooked! It made sense to me that a fear of death could be as influential on our lives as our fears – and dodgy attachments – from the past. (I guess poor attachments are linked to a fear of death anyway as we're so dependent on our parents to keep us alive.) I'd always seen self-sabotage as being linked to unconscious beliefs about not deserving good things or us sticking to familiar patterns of misery and habitual, self-destructive behaviour (I see constantly in my therapy work that we humans don't half love to stick with what's familiar, no matter how miserable or unhealthy it makes us.) Now, however, I could see that fearing the loss of a very happy life could also be a reason for many of us keeping ourselves just this side of misery; there's not so much to lose if we die!

As if a fear of death *and* being alone wasn't enough, the existentialists went on to talk about the hefty weight of personal choice. Because we have imagination and know there are many life options open to us (in the affluent and unoppressive bits of the world at least) we can get overwhelmed. What if I make the wrong decision? I'll look like a fool and I might waste my precious, finite life on the wrong choices! My brain buzzed; my life's quest for understanding humanity's crazy side was coming to fruition. So...all I needed to do was face death, my fear of being alone and my dread of messing up my life, and I could get rid of my almost constant state of anxiety and relax into life, being *myself* and doing what made *me* happy, not just trying to copy societal norms and constantly feeding my insecure ego.

Hmm. How did I know that wasn't going to be easy?

As I read on, many writers suggested that the only way to fully face death was by having a deep sense of connection with a 'bigger reality' than the individual self, be this God or some other deep, preferably eternal connection. *Oh shit! I've got no connection to a spiritual being! I've got no blooming earthly connections to a husband or children, never-mind spiritual ones!* For weeks I panicked about what I could do to cope with my death anxiety but then came across the notion of the 'Near-death Experience' (NDE) a term coined by a Dr Raymond Moody in 1975[31] when, as a spiritually cynical cardiologist, he couldn't fail to notice that many patients who had come close to death talked about similar experiences. They spoke of a great sense of love and peace, a feeling of connectedness to everything and sometimes a white light, a tunnel, a crossroads, spiritual beings, life reviews and a feeling of coming back to Earth to 'spread the love.' Having strongly resonated with the sense of peace and connectedness that hundreds of NDE accounts talked about, I stopped answering my phone and whipped through book after book of similar experiences reported by both children and adults. There were even accounts of people having 'out of body experiences,' recalling events which occurred whilst they were unconscious and describing such things as objects on high shelves in their operating theatres; even blind people described what they'd *seen* happen during their operations.[32]

---

31. See bibliography p. 433 for 'Life After Life'
32. See Michael Sabom in bibliography p. 433

My own MSc research involved interviewing people who had diced with death; 'Bridget' who'd had a huge brain haemorrhage at twenty-five following a car accident, 'Gabrielle' aged thirty-three when she entered a coma with a heavy-duty virus, 'Nick' who went into a diabetic coma at nineteen and Wendy, my co-trainee, also nineteen when she had major belly surgery. They reported great fear, pain and panic as they became ill but, during unconsciousness or post operations, described similar experiences to those recorded in the literature; travelling weightlessly or feeling pulled towards a bright 'loving' light, feeling an exquisite sense of peace, love and determination to try and make a positive difference. I remember a tearful and beautiful experience with Wendy; as she talked about having felt like a spirit living a human experience, I knew, only in that moment, *exactly* what she meant.

I went on to read research about the apparent transformative effects of NDE's; people often talked about feeling more intuitive, energetic, 'alive' and connected to nature and other people. They talked about wanting to connect on a 'deeper' level and feeling more loving and inspired to 'do their bit' for the world, whilst also liking more time alone just 'being' rather than 'doing' and having a keener sense of the present moment. They became less materialistic and ambitious whilst having more of a thirst for knowledge and they felt more self-accepting and satisfied with life – and generally less afraid of death. My interviewees also reflected these changes and there were more beautiful moments during the taped interviews as we shared our common experiences. I was over the moon. *Hey! That's it! That's exactly it! Oh my God, I'm really not going crazy!* I knew *being in hospital was the best as well as the worst thing that's ever happened to me;* I knew *I'd changed for the better. Oh my God, I'm not going mad! Oh connections! Oh thank you, universe! Thank you Death for teaching me what's important.* Following a random conversation with my microbiologist friend, Matt about the fact that, historically, we were about thirty years overdue a mass pandemic, I wondered if that's what we needed; a global brush with Death to wake us up to what's important and save ourselves and our planet... (and on that story goes in my final chapter!)

I feel *so* lucky that I wasn't working as I researched and wrote my dissertation and had the time to laugh, cry and process the deep feelings that came with doing it. It also allowed the previously manic me to rest and heal; I was still a sore-gutted, anaemic, spindly-legged nervous wreck, having rib-banging palpitations at unexpected noises. I missed my job, being part of a buzzing office and lots of people's lives and I still wasn't sure what I had become now I wasn't a social worker, an athletic or sexy woman, a girlfriend or a potential mother. What a great time for an existential crisis! Thank you for your time, brave interviewees and thank you, wonderful authors, for slogging over your books and offering me the hope of finding myself again! And thank you, Morty-cat, for sitting quietly next to me as I read. Ouch... I still miss that solid, timid tabby who'd appeared on my sofa one morning and decided to stay. He never got over his obvious attachment issues and couldn't cope with being cuddled much but he gave a great head-to-head nuzzle!

I also need to thank Frankie, my wild, scarf- and long-cardigan-swirling, horse-mad friend and co-trainee who was doing her dissertation on why therapists choose the role. I offered to do a bit of background reading for her given that I had time and she's dyslexic and I came across a reference to shamans, the classic 'wounded healers.' When I read that the shaman has to dance with death in order to be able to heal others I smiled wanly. His dreams about flying made me sit up; *Oh wow...that mad, powerful dream that I had in hospital about flying over that shining blue harbour with the old galleons and then diving into the sea and it being oily and horrible...then that really vivid one when I was zooming like a speedboat just above the surface of the sea.* Learning next that shamans are said to talk with the dead actually felt a bit spooky; *Oh my God...that dream where I was talking with gorgeous Jason in the sports centre...I remember that so clearly too!* (That's lovely Jason Holmes, the gentle, blond and drop-dead gorgeous son of my mum's friend, Pat. I played with him as a child and he was in my year at school. He tragically died on his motorbike in his early twenties.) Reading that the final defining characteristic of a shaman is that he is generally regarded as barking crazy by a lot of people gave me a resigned smile. *Well then, there I am! A classic 'shamaness!' Yeah, I can cope with that; gone through loads of crap to get deeper, wiser, more in tune with nature and able to heal others...and I'm already regarded as bonkers for 'thinking too much' so there you go...*

As I read on it just got more and more interesting and my self-worth began to grow. Researchers such as Kenneth Ring[33] were comparing NDE's to other sorts of 'mystical' and 'mind-enhancing' phenomena including Abraham Maslow's 'Peak Experiences'[34] (mind-blowing moments which can precede huge changes in perception, beliefs and value systems), challenging 'rites of passage' rituals, the classic hero's dangerous journey, sixteenth century's St John of the Cross's *Dark Night of The Soul*, Jesus's forty days of wanderings in the desert and Buddhist 'awakenings.' Each tradition held the notion that intense suffering can reap amazing rewards, from the hero's beautiful princess to wisdom, maturity, deep understanding, peace and happiness. When I read in Richard Lawrence's *Little Book of Yin and Yang*'[35] that the Chinese word for 'crisis' also means 'opportunity' my heart smiled, as it did when I read Kenneth Ring's suggestion that 'mystical' experiences are 'growth

33. See bibliography p. 433 for 'Life at Death'
34. See bibliography p. 438 for 'The Farthest Reaches of Human Nature'
35. See bibliography p. 437

spurts' pushed for by the soul; a movement from one state of consciousness to another, a kind of human evolution. *Yehey! I'm just evolving! All these tears are just part of a beautiful transformation! I may be a confused wreck of a grub but maybe one day I'll soar like a butterfly...*

It was acknowledged in the literature that no-one in their right mind would choose the suffering inherent in such a transformation and that often extreme circumstances – brushes with death and the like – were required to be a catalyst for such change. I've since discovered that mindfulness, facing your vulnerability, being accepting and grateful can all help, but that comes later. At the time I just kept debating with myself whether my positive spin was a defensive strategy, a justification for my nightmare or whether I really had, as my instinct felt, changed for the better. I was sure I felt more peaceful inside and could now just quietly 'be' without immersing myself in non-stop thinking and manic activity in order to avoid my feelings and strive to be what society expected. I'd always appreciated nature but now it completely blew me away; I could stand for ages looking at the shades of green – and brown and yellow and orange – on a tree. I'd always had a degree of compassion but now I felt my heart open on a totally different level; I wanted to give to others because it felt right, rather than doing it to be seen as 'good.' Little did I know that universities across the world had started researching kindness and were showing that being kind causes chemical reactions in the body and brain which do indeed enhance happiness – and energy, confidence and self-esteem, health, social relationships and work satisfaction. It was being shown that kindness, like volunteering and caring for people, animals or plants, can even make you live longer.[36] Perhaps, as a species, that's all we need to know!

---

36. See for e.g. this article at https://www.quietrev.com/6-science-backed-ways-being-kind-is-good-for-your-health/

The final piece of reading which helped to rebuild the broken me was by a man who would become a bit of a hero, the physicist Fritjof Capra.[37] As I poured over The Tao of Physics, I came to understand that, like Eastern mysticism, quantum physics, the forefront of modern science, was challenging the fundamentals of the traditional scientific paradigm with its revelation that, despite our massive desire for clarity and control, there is actually no 'objective reality' and everything – including ourselves – is in a constant state of flux or change. On a quantum level, matter is constantly popping in and out of existence; nothing's solid (a table is just a load of dancing sub-atomic particles) and we can't measure anything without being a part of that observation – if we look at light one way, for example, it's a particle but looking with different equipment makes it a wave. Even we aren't solid; every day (or was it every week?) we're apparently exchanging about an arm's worth of particles with other living things, we renew our bodies about every seven to nine years and breathe air that's often just blown over from the other side of the world. Each day we take in and eliminate 'the earth' (food), water and heat from the sun; we are not separate! We're built from the same pool of atoms that made the dinosaurs; our bodies may have atoms which once belonged to a woolly mammoth, Joan of Arc or Martin Luther King. And every time we interact with something else, we're psychologically changed. There is no stable 'me'. There's nothing real! There's nothing solid and permanent that we can hang on to! *Oh shit!*

Luckily Fritjof's book *The Web of Life* offered me solace. It supported David Attenborough's conclusion to all his years of research and observations of nature; nothing is independent and every one of the ten million or so species on this planet is reliant on connections with other life-forms to survive. This

37. See bibliography p. 435

includes our total reliance on the myriad bacteria in our bodies which (get this if you don't know it) out-number our cells by *ten to one* and weigh about a kilogram in our gut alone! Ex-NASA scientist, James Lovelock's *Gaia Hypothesis*[38] suggests that our earth is a living organism and all the parts of it are like the cells on a body, all interacting and contributing to the whole living system. Apparently, every process going on around and inside us is a collection of incredibly complex interactions, right down to our gene expression. We're not just machines set at birth; our bodies and brains are constantly changing. Quantum physics' final whacky revelation for the new Shamaness-Jaynie was that when two electrons have interacted, then separated, they continue to respond to one another; if one spins so does the other, indicating some sort on 'non-local connection' deep in our world. *Yippee!* whooped my post Capra brain; c*onnections! I'm part of nature, my body's the same stuff that makes up every bird, dog, tree and cloud! My atoms are bouncing off my skin and making dust; the sun's rays are bouncing into me and making vitamin D! I'm breathing in oxygen from the trees and breathing out carbon dioxide back to them!* I was over the moon at my scientifically verified feeling of connectedness. *I'm not alone! I'm connected!*

My sense of connectedness didn't stop there. I continued reading, revisiting the major spiritual traditions which all spoke about a 'bigger picture' which we're all part of – the Buddhist Mind, 'cosmic intelligence,' Hindu's Brahman, The Eternal Tao... For all their diversity, they centred on the idea that happiness is to be found in love, peace and helping others. *Mmm...were my feelings of bliss in my big green chair in hospital, mid chemotherapy, me touching the loving, still 'Mind behind the mind' which is at the heart of humanity? Was my ego quiet because there was nothing she could do to big herself*

---

38. See bibliography p. 435

up? Threatened with extinction, was I finally recognizing the awesomeness and interconnectedness of life? And that I was an integral part of it. A part of consciousness, of Namaste's 'greeting the god in you'. I remember a very nice Jehovah's Witness coming to my door one day, trying to pass on her version of reality. I said I appreciated her attempts to save my soul but that I was coming to my own understanding of God. "Oh what's that, dear?" she asked, smiling. "I believe I am God," I smiled back. She stopped smiling. As she scuttled down the street I did shout "I believe you're God too…" but I haven't had a visit since. I really like the idea that 'God' is within our hearts and not 'out there' condemning and controlling us. If we are god – or consciousness - that makes us pretty responsible for our own actions, but hey, how lovely to think that we're all God, all the totality of life, with the same characteristics, feelings, strengths and weaknesses – no matter what our blooming roots, skin colour, shape or even species.

My therapist, Peter, once told me that in an ancient language (Aramaic possibly) Heaven and Hell are regarded as internal states and 'sin' is regarded as the psychological issues (our 'baggage') which stop us being happy (in Heaven.) A thousand quotes from my grim childhood Sundays sprang from my memory banks and I sat looking up Bible quotes on the internet until two in the morning…'The kingdom of Heaven lies within'… 'Know thyself'…'Blessed are the pure in heart for they shall see God'…'Except a man be born again, he cannot see the kingdom of God'…'As a man thinks in his heart, so he is'…'The truth shall make you free'…*Bloody hell. The Bible's a psychotherapy manual!* I felt relief; if I dropped dead when this book was finished (a nagging fear) I'd got the small job of the Bible to analyse!

Talking of books, I was telling you about my dissertation reading…where was I? Oh yes, researchers like Kenneth Ring suggested that NDE's and other mystical experiences were an indication of humanity evolving towards a more loving way of being...but could be pretty weird happenings. In their book *Spiritual Emergency* Stanislav and Christina Grof[39] listed such reactions as intense emotions, visual and sensory changes, tremors, panic, increased psychic and intuitive awareness and even unusual thoughts, such as believing oneself to have received 'messianic messages.' The Grofs pointed out that this state of affairs could easily be perceived as an 'emergency' (with people being given heavy-duty psychiatric medication) but with understanding and loving support, a person may instead experience an 'emergence' to a more profound state of wellbeing. A state where the self-obsessed ego makes way for a more soulful way of being, with more focus on bodily feelings and connections than often inaccurate, 'programmed' thoughts.

I reflected on the fact that this transformation sounded very familiar to the psychotherapy process; the death of the old, blinkered self as the painful realization of being fully human (selfish and controlling as well as kind, courageous and vulnerable) came flooding in, giving way to a more self-accepting, compassionate self which can *feel* its way through life. In my clinical work as a therapist this process of transformation normally happens over a period of time but I've had several clients who've been really self-critical and pretty hard-core (very critical of others) and then gone through a dramatic physical and emotional experience. It was as if they took off their defensive armour (Gestalt theory, from Wilhelm Reich, actually talks in terms of supressed emotions being held as 'body armour' in the muscles) and came out the other side much more self-compassionate, less judgemental and a whole lot more relaxed and happy. One guy, who'd had heart operations as a child and somehow felt responsible for the deaths of other

---

39. See bibliography p. 433

young patients, sat in my therapy room shaking like a leaf for half an hour then announced, "I've been carrying guilt for five decades but of *course* it wasn't my fault that my little friends in hospital died!" A female client, post a huge body-convulsing, sobbing weekend, said, "I'm even nice to my dog now and he seems to like me; he used to cower outside the back door but now he sits on my lap."

Writing up my dissertation was a challenge to say the least; I condensed my notes from about sixty books and journals several times but still had a thick wad of paper and realised that I was going to have to rely on my brain to bring together the different strands and ideas. And doing that was an amazing process. My brain just *did* it; I thought about something and then suddenly, hours or days later as I was making a cup of tea or hanging out my washing, something I'd read would spring into my mind and magically slot into place. Now how do our brains *do* that? My dissertation was a fantastic exercise in just taking things one small step at a time and letting the process, with its inevitable frustrations, just flow; Zen and the art of writing...what amazing creatures we are!

Chapter 14
Ignoring my Intuition

"Intuition is the highest form of intelligence, transcending all individual abilities and skills."

Sylvia Clare

For all my so-called evolution through nearly dropping dead, it turned out that my ego was still going strong and, as I neared the end of my psychotherapy training in 2002, got me into a right mess. I was still convinced that I was heading for a lonely life 'on the shelf' when the universe whacked me with a stonker. Frank, my trainer (of four years), supervisor and dissertation mentor, had been reading my research and, in my penultimate supervision, asked me to stay behind for a word. *Oh no! I knew my dissertation was crap. He must think I'm a right idiot...oh my God, what if I fail...*

"Jayne, this is a bit difficult. I um..."

Oh God, it really is bad!

"I've read your dissertation..."

Oh shit! I knew it!

"And it's fantastic."

"Oh...really?"

"Really. The depth of it's wonderful."

"Oh."

"But this isn't about your dissertation, well not really, though reading it made me realize something that I knew already…" *Oh God he thinks I'm crazy* "…Look, I just need to say this. I realize that I have deep feelings for you which I'd like to explore when you finish your training." *Oh my God, oh my God, oh my God!* I stared at him, open-mouthed. About five minutes later I managed a puzzled, "Oh."

"Oh good, you hadn't noticed then? I was worried that how I felt was obvious."

"No."

"I realize of course that you need time to think about it."

"Yes."

"Take as long as you like. I just had to let you know."

"Okay. Thanks. Yes, urm…I think I may be in shock."

"Maybe we could keep this between us for now – well, you can tell your therapist in confidence, of course."

"Yes okay."

He beamed his bright, dimpled grin. My face wouldn't smile back because it was too busy frowning in confusion. I arrived home in a daze and literally walked round in circles on my rug as I tried to take in what had just happened. *Me and Frank? Little damaged me and Mr Sorted? Mr adored by everybody? With me? Bloody hell, I didn't want to lose him from my life when my training finished but go out with him?! What would people think? And anyway, I don't even fancy him! Well, I suppose he's pretty fit for his age and I could get used to his neat side parting and gold tooth…But I'm a wreck! Surely he can't be serious? He must be having a mid-life crisis…Oh just imagine being loved by him though, he'd be so thoughtful! We could meditate together and talk for hours! We could have conversations where he'd own his crap and I'd own mine and we'd both be big enough to apologise…it could be so simple and so beautiful! And I wouldn't have to worry about him wanting more children. He knows all about me but he still wants to be with me...possibly...oh my God I could feel so SAFE! How can I say no? And how could I possibly hurt him, everyone would hate me! Shit, he might fail my dissertation too. Oh my God this is so crazy...*

A week later Frank caught up with me and asked for a kiss. It felt weird. My body and intuition screamed *No, Jaynie! This doesn't feel right, he's old enough to be your dad!* But as we began to meet and talk I saw that underneath his sleek, middle-class exterior was a familiar working-class 'lad' who I could relate to. We were also both in the 'death zone' – he'd lost his lovely wife several years earlier and we were in deep and lonely places. I was also swayed, if I'm honest, when Frank whisked me off to see his fantastic new property with its acres of land and we talked about creating a therapeutic community where people could come and stay in pine cabins to de-stress, do courses, meditate, watch the stars and sing round campfires. The dream of the therapy centre that I'd lost with Matthew had just been re-presented – except ten times better! Still, I was hesitant and confused for weeks, querying whether there was some mad 'process' going on, like Frank trying to save me where he'd failed with his wife, me wanting to have my unmet paternal needs satisfied or us both being a bit death-overwhelmed crazy. A few weeks later, when, despite some continuing apprehension, I'd begun to consider the possibility that I was a very lucky woman, Frank agreed that I could share my news with a friend - and co-trainee. She was initially joyous and sent me flowers but then began to feel that the situation wasn't right and talked about it in her therapy group. Her therapist felt that this ethically dubious situation shouldn't be contained by confidentiality and before we knew it the word was out and it suddenly felt like Armageddon.

There are strict ethical guidelines which maintain that

psychotherapy supervisors and tutors shouldn't have relationships with their supervisees and students (such is the enormous power imbalance and idealisation by the student). I felt like I was suddenly under the spotlight of a whole training institute, in fact several nationally, and I was paranoid that I was being seen as the evil woman who had seduced a good man, a *priest* for goodness sake! I was equally paranoid that I was being viewed as a simpleton who was being taken advantage of. Even amongst my co-trainees who were close friends I felt on very wobbly ground; most of them were appalled or devastated, feeling that I was being taken advantage of and that their trusted hero had crossed an unacceptable line.

I think my eventual decision to give this unlikely relationship a go, indeed *marry* Frank, was when he, knowing how devastated I was at being unable to have children, talked about how we could adopt a child from abroad. "Jayne, I have connections all over Europe."

"You can't just buy a child!"

"There are thousands of children abandoned in orphanages."

"But...aren't you done with kids now?"

"Jayne, I'd love to bring up a child with you."

"Really?"

"Really. I can't think of anything more beautiful."

I can remember thinking that it wouldn't be fair to adopt a child when I didn't know what my future held and Frank was over fifty, but the feeling of joy I felt as I imagined the possibility took hold of me. I'd loved spending time with my young social work clients and one day maybe I could be a mum – or even a foster mum – to a child who'd had a bad time and really needed some love; they may present challenges but I'd have the help of this lovely, wise man! I couldn't believe that, out of nowhere, I was being offered my *entire* dream on a plate; a child, a therapeutic centre and a deeply compassionate man - he even had a beautiful sheepdog, another thing on my wish-list since childhood when I'd watched John Noakes with his fluffy Shep on *Blue Peter*. I felt that after all my pain, the universe was making it up to me and I just had to give the relationship a try! How could I walk away? I'd walked away from Gerly, regretted it and didn't want to repeat my mistake. I was also very aware of Frank's professional reputation; I felt that if I'd not told my friend about us, the ethical explosion, with Frank facing potential disciplinary proceedings, may not have happened. It felt like we had our backs against the wall together but if we got married his reputation wouldn't be so wrecked. His adult children had also said that they'd find our relationship more acceptable if it was serious enough for marriage.

If I'd listened to my intuition instead of guilt, confused thoughts and stupid ego (*Oh, of all the woman he could have and he wants little old me)* I might've walked away; I wasn't comfortable with the ethics either but I tried to ignore my gut. I also tried to ignore my disappointment when, under the immense stress of the ethical outcry, I started peeing blood and my new love went on holiday. Given other major warning signs, some from things he told me he'd done, I felt scared and anxious when Frank arranged for us to meet the local vicar to book our wedding but again I allowed my instinct to be overridden by his argument that the reason I felt so unsure about our relationship was because I was afraid of being loved so wonderfully. There was actually some truth in that; my protective wall still lingered and I doubt I had as much love for myself as I needed for a trusting, relaxed relationship, especially one with a demi-god. I certainly didn't have enough strength; I couldn't disagree with Frank in any way – even when it came to doing up *my* house for him to move into I let him walk all over my wishes – but Frank said we'd go for couple's counselling to sort out the power imbalance once we were married.

Sitting on my sofa one day I tried to turn off my *thoughts* about Frank and just feel my intuition. I pictured a big, scary,

hairy monster. I told myself that was the pain he'd said would hit me when I let him close, the pain of someone giving you what you've longed for all your life and you feeling the great loss of what you've missed – along with the general terror of being hurt which comes from being open and vulnerable. I shook the image of the monster away and tried again, desperately hoping to see a picture of bliss but instead I got an image of a head craning out from under a door, with the body locked in the room behind it. Interestingly, I read somewhere that Einstein called intuition a 'sacred gift' and science 'the servant' and a recent study by a Dr Peter Heinl of ninety-four Nobel Prize winners[40] found intuition to be acknowledged by over eighty percent of them; inspiration came in periods of rest, not manic thinking. And so, I chose to ignore my clever intuition and got stuck into designing my Celtic-style dress for our fairy tale wedding, swooning at Frank's lovely letters and red roses and sending back romantic, love-struck letters of my own. I so wanted us to be happily swishing along in a little rowing boat together.

---

40. See: www.confer.uk.com/biogs/biog_heinl.html

Granny

Let's gi thi some advice, lass, nah tha's gittin' wed
an' tha'll bi viry wise if tha keeps it in thi yed.
Thi sey marriage is a lottery when it's noowt o't' sooat,
it's like two tied together in a little rowing booat.
Hah yer pull when yer in, shews 'ow far tha'll goa
fer if yer pulls in diff'rent ways ya'll boath end up on t' flooar.
Naah dunt bother thi yed over things 'at dunt matter
and one thing abone all, dunt start ta natter,
let 'im think 'is boss, tha'll get thi own way,
not ta much chelpin', let 'im 'ave 'is say.
Ay, a know what tha's thinkin' but don't thi forget,
tha'll think o' these words aah, mony a time yet.
Tha's gotten tha yed filled wi' these modern ideas,
tha don't know yet about heartache and tears
tears that'll bend thi and temper thi steel,
aah, tears that'll meck thi get daahn an' kneel.
An' naah lass, am gooin', all t'best o' luck
A know tha'll be alreet cos tha's nooan 'baaht pluck.
Just pull steady, lass, then tha'll booath agree
in yer little rowin' booat, on larf's open sea.

Arthur Downs

On the way to my wedding I had a beautiful, magical moment when my dad told me, for the first time that I remember, that I looked lovely and I enjoyed his proud look as we walked down the aisle, accompanied by friends on djembe drums and a cello (my concession for us marrying in a church instead of in nature.)

Our wedding was beautiful and a lot of fun, with brave friends singing and reciting poems – once I'd managed to get up that is; my whole body was almost paralysed on waking and Maria had to literally drag me out of bed. *Oh that must be because I was bending over doing the church flowers yesterday* chirped my silly head. My body was still screaming "NO" by the time we got to church; I couldn't kneel at the altar. Still, I ignored myself, just as Frank was possibly ignoring *his* self (having rushed the marriage to try and save his reputation, I think) when he dropped my ring in the church. Looking into Frank's eyes as we made our vows I think I meant my words; I felt a bit anxious but also optimistic, happy, honoured and immensely grateful that this was my wedding and not my funeral. In keeping with my feeling of aliveness I had a beautifully profound 'spiritual moment' when, as we sang Frank's chosen hymn, the lovely 'Make me a Channel of Your Peace,' a shaft of sunlight lit me where I stood and clarified a simple aspiration for my life.

Hey ho. Married life wasn't as I'd pictured it. There were no cosy mornings cuddling up and chatting in bed as Frank was off to the gym at the crack of every dawn, no decorating our stark white house together or having relaxing picnics by the river as his recent 'semi-retirement' turned into him manically establishing a new business miles away and training more in Europe. Having put him on such a tall pedestal, I'd no idea how wounded Frank was and how much he had to achieve in order to feel worthy, especially following the criticism from his colleagues about his ethics. I'd no idea how defensive and cruel his wounds could make him either, as I'm sure mine made me, but he refused to go for our planned couples counselling and things soon descended into darkness.

The hurt and vengeful parts of me are dying to tell you the dramatic - and devastating - nitty gritty of what happened from our honeymoon on, but that doesn't feel like the right thing to do - and of course it wouldn't be a balanced account. Let's just say that it took me about eighteen months to properly get my confused head around the fact that Frank wasn't who I thought he was and if it hadn't been for some totally random conversations with people who knew him well - and confirmed my reality – I may well have become a passive pull-along dog (the head craning out from under the locked door). I'd been very close to believing that I was responsible for all our troubles and had almost been persuaded to move away from my home, friends and good medical care to support Frank in the (childless) life that he had planned. Thank god for connections!

Despite all the hurt, it was hard saying goodbye to Frank. I literally thrashed about on my bed in indecisive torment when, after we'd separated, he phoned to ask that we give it another go; his sensitive, deep, bright and inquisitive side was lovely. In the early months of our marriage we'd cried with joy as we made love; finally, being married, sex was totally acceptable to me and when we were both open-hearted it was beautiful. I clearly remember the crumpling pain that I felt at his last touch of my arm – not to mention the blistering shame of such a disastrous marriage. But I had to take care of myself. The stress of the ethical outcry, organising a shot-gun wedding, living in a dusty building site for months and the constant travelling, 'doing' and arguing with Frank had taken a massive toll on my body. Since my seven-month spell in hospital I'd only been able to eat 'small and often' but now my belly felt like concrete and I could hardly eat at all. My nerves were shot again and sleeplessness, inner shaking and a frazzled brain had become my norm. The vicious divorce, with, in a final crushing humiliation, Frank citing me as the unreasonable party, didn't help. I could've been a rich woman and my solicitor couldn't believe it when I said that revenge, though very tempting, wasn't the answer. My integrity was more important to me than Frank's money. My mum survived the divorce by the way; she hated Frank by then and felt that God would understand that it needed to happen!

So, my dream of feeling safe, secure and happy had been 'bazookad.' (I would come to learn, of course, that looking for happiness outside of myself wasn't going to work anyway…)

I feel embarrassed telling you about my marriage but I can also look back at the Jayne – and Frank – of that time with compassion. And I learned a lot. For one, that I can be very submissive! Two, I have clever intuition if only I'd listen to it. Three, I can, ultimately, dig deep and be strong enough to take care of myself and four, I am a grown adult. Meeting other leading therapists through Frank (some whose books I'd read) I saw that, like him, they were no more 'sorted' than myself. I saw that the people at the top of the pile are not necessarily the wisest amongst us. Maybe the most driven because of their wounded inner child's need to feel seen (like me writing this book probably) or feel powerful or in control but not always the most together. We're all human, eh? No matter what our façade, we're triggered into old wounds and defensive shame by intimate relationships, fear, vulnerability – and power. I feel that I now take a wiser look at people in positions of power and that my habit of passively deferring to those in authority has been somewhat smashed to pieces (yee ha!)

For all my learning, I still felt afraid of Frank for years afterwards, especially when I heard that he was explaining our split by telling people I was crazy. I was too embarrassed to attend local training courses for a while and kept a low profile in the 'therapy world.' But you know what they say; what doesn't break you makes you stronger. I do sometimes wonder how deep my 'Frank scars' go but I can also feel grateful to him for helping me to grow so much. Gosh, I'm tired and not enjoying this. It's been a huge dilemma what to write about this episode; Frank had an awful time too and I should never have married him – but I don't want to be silenced by shame. Or power. And I want to encourage you to listen to your intuition – to your wise body – and not your ego's crazy thoughts!

Mmm...where to now in the realms of my memory? It all feels a bit of a blur post Frank; that's trauma for you. Whilst with Frank I'd been given the shocking news that my kidneys, damaged during my major clotting episodes of 1998-9, were struggling and could pack up in five to ten years. I mostly managed to block out my fear of that in the daytime but the long, empty nights on my own could be seriously grim and I was back in a state of floating aimlessly without a sense of connection. I missed my training group and the sense of safety and belonging I'd got from the 'therapy world.' I missed Frank's dog. I felt damaged. How could I have judged things so badly? Was I totally incapable of having a healthy relationship?

Then along came an angel. Randomly going to a different supermarket, my mum had passed a farm advertising sheepdog puppies. I happened to be visiting my parents that weekend and went to look at them. One glance was all it took; little Alfie came running up to me with his mischievous brown eyes, expressive, Rottweiler-type eyebrows and soft, silky black, white and beige fur. I fell in love. I went to the library as soon as I got home and read a pile of information about my wee collie...'are highly intelligent and closely related to the wolf... programmed to nip sheep's bottoms...can get nervous which may lead to aggression.' Mmm. Two weeks later, when Alfie was ready to leave his cow-herding mother and my mum and nephew brought him to my house, I had a shock; his sweet, flat face and cute round ears had grown longer and pointier and into my house entered a baby wolf! Six weeks later, whilst all the other puppies at training classes sat looking sweet and adorable, Alfie jumped up and down in a frenzy, attempting to bite either them or me. When the trainer asked where I got him and I happily chirped "A farm in Yorkshire," she rolled her eyes and tutted, "Oh no! You should only get collies which have been pets for several generations."

"Oh."

"Was he shy when you met him?" She slowly shook her head as I explained how "he came running straight over, jumped on my knee and licked me."

"You've got yourself, I'm afraid to say, a very dominant dog."

"Oh."

"Yes, I'm afraid if you want a cuddly lapdog you're going to have to get yourself another dog."

"Oh."

Little Alf's favourite toy soon became the sweeping brush which he'd grab, brush end and fly towards me as if it were a lance. Most bits of furniture had the 'Mark of Alf' proudly gnarled into them (until I covered everything in Vicks Vapour Rub), he loved to chew holes in my socks and knickers and one evening whilst I was out destroyed *two* of my best pairs of shoes. I still miss my favourite ever bouncy trainers, one of which I'm sure Alfie must have buried because it's never turned up. Luckily he was extremely cute and I just about coped with him and his nippy play but then he got attacked by two massive-headed, foaming-mouthed Rottweilers when he was about ten months old. As they suddenly sprang from behind a bush he managed to run away but could only throw himself into the park's closed gate; the sickening clang of dog against iron still rings in my ears. With my heart in my throat I ran as fast as my Bambi legs could go and joined the barking frenzy by whacking the beasts with my plastic ball-thrower until the owner managed to drag them off. I'm eternally grateful that they didn't cause Alfie – or me – serious physical injury but after that Alf's cheeky sheepdog nipping turned into scary bites; he bit me and most of my friends over the next two years and became a complete liability. His eye-balling me as his teeth gripped and dug into my hand once was terrifying. I seriously wondered whether I should get rid of him – but he was too old and spoiled for a farm and what could I put in an advert? 'For sale: Very sweet, puppy-eyed sheepdog, GSOH but has the occasional tendency to mildly crush the bones in your hand.'

And so I kept my furry child and partner substitute and, years later, after a few tons of dog-treats and some sergeant-major discipline, I have the most adorable and helpful friend in the world. Just like 'neuroplasticity' can change our brains and gene expression over our life-span, so it can dogs' it would seem. Alf's still not to be trusted with strangers – or even me a hundred percent if I'm honest, not that he's bitten me for years – but he's generally a friendly, responsive, well-behaved, loyal companion. I'm actually glad he's a good guard dog; when he's on the back of the sofa and bares his teeth through the front window he looks positively evil. In the garden he looks like a puppy. I pass Alfie the weeds and he takes them to the compost heap then stomps and bites the pile down; I never have to touch it. Getting excited and waggy in the process, he shuts the living room door and brings me the remote control, my bag, slippers and boots. He beams an exuberant grin at me every morning, 'kisses' and hugs me on request, wraps his paws round my legs in affectionate 'cling- ons' (or from his perspective, no doubt, total domination) whenever I come through the door, gives me 'five,' rolls over if I circle my finger, jumps in the air if I flap my arms and 'heels' (for a minute) if I stomp my foot. His latest trick is to put his paw in the air when I ask him who 'the most beautiful dog in the world' is! He often delights random strangers from the passenger seat of my camper-van (bought when my old jeep's door fell off) when I get him to wave (lift his paw) at them at traffic lights. We have a dance routine to the tune of 'Moon River.' All he wants in return for all the hours of delight he gives me are walks (which I love too) some play-time (ditto) a bit of food, being brushed, stroked and talked to, his evening massage and new 'sniffy' areas to explore now and then. Not a bad deal, eh?

With Alf's love of life rubbing off on me, I got back to rebuilding mine. I felt a kind of liberation; whatever I did, what was potential failure compared to nearly dropping dead and going through such a devastating marriage? First I started a whacky therapeutic dance class, 'Dancing Into Life,' with my co-therapist and friend Susie, a super-fit, blonde mother of teenage boys with a wonderful zest for life that few people parallel. We opened the sessions with a 'talking circle' where people could say who and how they were if they wanted to. Next came a guided stretch and warm-up period, where we'd rave on about the amazing miracle of our bodies, followed by us whacking a compiled music tape into the 'boom-box' and we were off; there were no dance steps, just the total freedom to move our bodies how they felt like moving. From a gentle, reflective start we'd slowly build up the music to a frenzied, sweaty middle (Queen's "Don't Stop Me Now" was my favourite tune at this point) when we'd fly around wildly, singing (or shrieking) along if the desire grabbed us. We'd then 'come down' to a calm, gentle, relaxing end and regroup to eat fruit and chocolate over a 'check-out' circle, sharing, if we wanted to, something we'd experienced or discovered about ourselves. Much modern research about trauma[41] suggests that it's helpful to complete whatever your *body* needed to do during a stressful or traumatic episode (like screaming, hitting out, shaking or simply moving, if you were frozen in fear) completing the 'fight, flight, freeze or feint' response – like animals shaking for a while after being

41. See bibliography p. 430

attacked. Alfie and I were attacked by another Rottweiler recently; Alf shook for two minutes then was fine; I, with my calf's Rottweiler mouth-shaped bruise and repetitive monkey mind but no shaking, took days to calm my nervous system down. And so it was wonderful to see dancers putting their shame and inhibitions to one side and getting in touch with their *inner worlds.* Some people danced pretty traditionally whilst one young chap jumped about a lot pretending to do football headers, some spent time rolling on the floor, twirling round the room or stomping like warriors.

Obviously Susie and I had our eye on the class and assisted anybody struggling but, to give a bit of inspiration and encouragement – and because we loved it – we joined in. I spent a lot of time just walking. Forward. Straight-backed. Trying to muster the determination and courage to rebuild my life. In other moments I was just lost in the music and letting, in the words of the fantastic poet Mary Oliver, 'the soft animal of my body love what it loved'.[42] Despite not having the strength or energy that I used to, I can't tell you how good it felt to stomp out the anger and shake off the fear that I couldn't express when I was in hospital being pierced, sliced, poisoned and irradiated. At the start of most classes I felt tired and a bit resistant but by the end, energised and at peace, having faced my feelings to release them. I would later go on to get a government grant to run the class and facilitated the whacky wildness for several years. I still miss it. I call into question the notion of 'crazy.'

My next rebuilding step was enrolling for two terms in a creative writing class. I *loved* the process of starting with a blank page and then sitting back and letting random ideas burst out of my brain. When the classes ended I continued to meet up to share written pieces with three of my co-students, professional writer Raif and two amazing, dry-humoured women who'd had a ton of pain and so weren't scared of mine. Linda's mum

---

42. *From the poem Wild Geese – see bibliography p. 436*

had suffered with major depression and Jane had a history of going through the mental health system. The acceptance, mutual support and encouragement to write out our trauma was invaluable to me.

Whilst married I'd worked from a shared office with Frank but now I established my therapy room at home, meaning I could do housework, take Alfie out and have little snoozes in between seeing clients. I like inviting people into my home; it feels like offering some foundation of trust to help us establish a relationship, and with the hundreds of clients I've seen I've never felt threatened or had any problems. Much as I enjoyed my work though, I missed my social work colleagues and felt a bit isolated so I advertised confidence-building and stress-management workshops. As bits of work came in with various charities I discovered that I loved this work too and a year later was employed by a further education college to teach those subjects (alongside interview and job-seeking skills.) Working mostly with groups of women, I'd run six or ten week courses, looking at why we didn't feel the confidence and self-worth that we could. My goal was to help my students see that their poor self-image was not inherent but *learned*. Learned from insecure families, a racist and narcissistic culture in which we're constantly fed (mostly white) images of how we supposedly *should* be, an education system which 'scraps' us if we don't do well in exams and a patriarchal system in which (largely white) men hold most of the power – and wages – in the health, legal and education systems, business, policing, media and government. (I know men have it tough too, also feeling unworthy in the face of perfect media images and under great pressure to be macho, 'successful' and emotionally self-reliant.) As 'my' women courageously shared their personal stories in the groups, each realized that they weren't alone with their struggles and feelings and that it was normal to be a vulnerable, scared human being – and sometimes a confused and irritated partner or mother. As we looked at their skills and positive characteristics, the women blossomed and began to assert themselves and take on more challenges. Each group I facilitated deeply fed my soul and confidence; these bruised women and I were growing together. It was magical.

Teaching stress management, like 'Dancing Into Life,' was also exactly what I needed. It was shocking as my research revealed that stress – and overdoses of cortisol (a major stress hormone) – is literally a killer. In 'fight-flight' mode, our bodies get ready for action; our energy and blood's diverted from our digestive and reproduction systems, organs, skin and rational, empathic front cortex into our muscles and danger-ready, self-focused reptile brain. Our heart, blood pressure and breathing rates go up, our pupils dilate and even our blood thickens, just in case we get bitten by that dastardly sabre-tooth tiger. If we are under stress for prolonged periods, it can leave our reproduction and digestion systems in disarray – hence a difficulty conceiving sometimes and all the 'irritable bowels' in the modern world. Constantly raised blood pressure and cortisol can shred our veins and whack our organs and immune system, which is presumably why cardiovascular disease and cancer are the two big Western killers.[43] When our brain's stressed and busy looking for danger, we can't think straight, remember, concentrate or focus and are more likely to get anxious, irritated and defensive. Stress is no joke! The US Centre for Disease Control and Prevention estimated recently that ninety percent of doctor visits are triggered by stress. My stress investigations convinced me that a stressful, trauma-marred childhood and the insane demands of social work had nearly killed me, and I felt determined to listen to my body – which still needed a lot of rest and rebuilding – and take better care of myself!

---

43. *See Department of Health statistics at www.ons.gov.uk/healthandsocialcare/causesofdeath*

Chapter 15
On Being Nearly Chopped in Half

"Life is like a game of cards. The hand you are dealt is determinism; the way you play it is free will."

Jawaharlal Nehru

Despite my determination to take better care of myself, come 2005 it transpired that I was fighting something of a losing battle. My gut wasn't happy. Perhaps linked to my bowels 'freezing,' not eating for so long or being sick so much back in 1998/9, my bile duct had scarred and narrowed and every three or four months for the previous couple of years I'd had to have (as a 'day case') 'ERCP's (endoscopic retrograde cholangiopancreatography, just for the record.) The hideous ERCPs involved being 'gowned up' (oh joy), laying on a bed in a small surgical room and then surrounded by masked strangers. I was stabbed with a cannula, given a sedative and then a thick, gagging tube, carrying a camera and a type of 'balloon' was fed down my throat to my gut where the balloon blew up my bile duct, painfully ripping it apart and making space for a stent (a small hollow tube) to be inserted into it. The idea was for my bile duct to heal around the stent, creating a wider passageway. I sometimes came round during the procedure, feeling that I was choking and had a hot poker burning through my gut. The determined medics' latest plan was to get three stents into my bile duct in the hope that it would then have been extended enough to be left alone. Needless to say, much as I appreciated the amazing team's efforts, I *hated* those ERCPs and was in excruciating pain and hardly able to eat for a week afterwards. My coccyx was grinding on the bath again.

I'd just had my traumatic three-stent ERCP when Doctor Rider called me into his office. A big man in a well-ironed stripy shirt, he was very professional but looked me in the eye and explained things with empathy. "Hiya, come in, sit down...I have some rather bad news, I'm afraid."

"I presume this relates to the fact that I feel like I've got a badger stuck in my gut."

"Yes. I'm afraid we've found some pretty big gallstones around your bile duct and I'm afraid our three stent plan hasn't worked. Your stents are stuck."

"What?"

"There must be a lot of debris in there along with the stents and gallstones; it's all a bit of a mess Jayne."

"I presume that explains my annihilating wind."

"Absolutely."

"So can you get the stents out?"

"I can't I'm afraid. Your only option now is to have an operation."

"You're kidding me!" Dr Ryder just looked solemn. "You're not kidding me?"

"No. I know; there's the antiphospholipid problem."

"What, you mean I might clot to death?"

"Well of course we'll do our best to avoid that. But yes, it could be a big operation and with your complications, very dangerous. I've referred you to Mr Brooks, a liver surgeon. He's really good."

"My god, I hope so." I walked out of there like a zombie.

Following my November 2005 appointment with the surgeon I wrote 'I haven't written for ages. I guess I've been avoiding a ton of terror. My appointment with my surprisingly young, handsome and 'human' surgeon, Mr Adam Brooks, who also looked me in the eye and acknowledged my fear (what a result) confirmed that I needed an operation to sort out my bile duct (bad result.) He sensitively explained, with hand-drawn diagrams, that now the stents are stuck, the risk of massive infection possibly setting off another catastrophic, auto-immune blood-clotting event is considered to be greater than the risks involved in surgery, high as they are. I have a week and a day – a week and fourteen hours to be precise – until I go into hospital for my "major operation." Through a seven-inch cut in my belly, my gall-bladder's going to be chopped out, along with my bile duct and then Mr Brooks and his "very skilled" colleague Mr Beckingham will attempt to create a new bile duct from my small intestines. It could be that my faeces will get "a bit runny" after the operation because my bile will be dripping constantly into my guts rather than it being regulated by my gall-bladder in the normal response to fat intake. I think that's how it goes. I didn't ask too many questions; I was too busy trying not to melt onto the floor. As I shuffled out of the hospital I felt a desperate need to grab any random stranger and babble my situation at them. I didn't want to tell any of my family or friends, "Hey, I have to have an operation, I have to wait 'till there's an Intensive Care bed available just in case my blood starts to do weird shit again or my struggling kidneys fail completely – and even with an Intensive Care bed, I might still die."

So, Death's got that horrible knowing look on his face again when he appears in the early hours and it's making my irritability levels distinctly unpleasant. I'm barking at Alfie and, as my inside feelings again affect my outside world, shop cashiers suddenly seem positively rude and drivers churning out loud bass music are receiving my full range of expletives. In my doctor's surgery the other day I caught the eye of a sad-looking woman and dug a friendly smile right from the bottom of my weary heart. She responded with a silent, pan-faced scan up and down the length of my body at which point I flipped and asked her whether she was afraid of stretching her face! What can I say? I feel so frustrated that my life's 'on hold' again; normally I try to use every day to do something positive but all I feel fit for at the moment is staring at walls in a dizzy sort of haze.'

When my delightful therapist friend Janie suggested a blind date with a friend of her husband I initially declined. Her telling me that he perhaps looked older than his years because of his white hair really didn't sway me but as she described his kind heart and witty humour her exuberance rubbed off and I had to admit that even dinner with Santa had the potential for fun, growth or learning so I threw on some old clothes and limped along. As soon as I saw 'Sean's beaming smile (with no white beard but very white teeth) and intense grey eyes, I cringed; he wasn't particularly smart in his faded shirt but I wished I'd washed my hair at least! As Sean talked about his life with humility and cracked jokes which made me laugh, I realised that Father Christmas had promise and when he walked me back to my car and asked if I wanted to go for a drink the following week, I was a happy bunny. I did think I ought to put my cards on the table though and, adopting my usual, super-honest style, told him that I'd love to but only on the understanding that I might be dead in a few months' time! Fortunately Sean had drunk a few beers and didn't run away down the street. Amazingly, he didn't scarper after our second or third date either and before long I had myself a new fella. The irony that I'd met a lovely man just as I could die wasn't lost on me. Maybe I was able to open up to him *because* I had an excellent possible get-out clause.

Despite my newfound love, I remained generally overwhelmed by my pending operation; *I can't die yet! Oh shit, oh shit! AAAGGGHHH! Oh God, someone help me! Please help me!* I also, as I had in hospital, found that in the midst of my terror and feint-level gut pain there were moments of absolute clarity and joy. I wrote: 'Life suddenly feels very simple. It seems to me that it's about loving and taking risks, noticing the beauty and remembering you're a living, breathing miracle of nature, who's privileged in a million different ways. I feel really energized, not in my body, but in my spirit; between moments of anger and despair at humanity, I feel moments of real hope for us and a real zest for trying to 'do my bit'. I'm loving this creative process of writing and I feel so alive! I've nothing to hide and could be dead in a few weeks so what's the point of worrying and not taking life by the horns whilst I'm still here? My walk in the park with Alfie this morning was beautiful; the cool, refreshing breeze stroking my cheeks, the rich smell of the fertile earth, the beautiful trees and clouds dancing…I feel fantastic and very privileged to simply be alive.

Ah! It appears that you do indeed have huge gifts to offer us, Dr Death.'

Just before my op. I continued…'It's a day before I go into hospital and two days before I have my belly sliced open by a group of strangers, yet I feel relatively calm today. This stems partly from a complete miracle last week when I went to have some pre-operative tests. During an 'ECHO' or heart scan, I gingerly asked how my heart was doing and the female technician replied, "Normal." After maliciously thinking *great, I have a right spark here*, I asked her to look a little more closely at my left ventricle, which had been starved of oxygen by blood clots in 1999 and I'd been told would never repair. "Normal," was her definitive response as she turned her screen to show me my beautiful ventricle pumping away its merry beat and "normal" was the word which swam through my treacly brain for the next few days. It was a shock in a way, but a fantastic one; *My God, another miracle…wow, maybe I will play tennis and reach 50 after all…if I get through the op…'*

Despite taking in the lovely moments, the times when I seriously questioned whether I'd survive the operation and pictured the faces of my family and friends, were *grim*. When I tried to suppress these feelings rather than just crying, my body took the brunt of it and my chest and torso pounded as if I was being electrocuted. I guess that's what people mean by panic attacks, and our feelings-averse culture is the reason why I get so many therapy clients with anxiety and panic; it really does seem that if we don't express our feelings, our bodies scream.

My periods of intense fear and grief forced me to once again confront my default position of keeping my feelings to myself. Thankfully my family and most of my friends were complete stars; when I dared to say how I really felt (or something close to it) they listened and hugged me. They didn't try to silence me and pretend that everything was okay, thus leaving me alone with my fear and I didn't try to protect them by being totally upbeat and leaving *myself* alone in my fear. They just sat with me in my pain. I felt guilty but deeply moved when friends teared up as, 'just in case', I told them how much they enriched my life. It felt so important to let them know this. It also felt important for me to tell close friends which of my possessions I'd like them to have should I die; I didn't want my obsessively tidy dad throwing my treasured wooden carvings, carried all the way from Asia, Africa and Central America, into a skip! I wrote 'I guess I want to leave my friends with reminders of me. I don't want to be just forgotten. I have no unfinished business now. I've made a will, said what I needed to say – and it wasn't depressing, it was beautiful; our shared tears meant the world to me – so much so that I'm bawling my eyes out now as I write. Bawling at the richness of 'connecting' in a real and genuine way with such courageous friends. There are bright Christmas festivities going on all over town and I'd much rather be pottering around Christmas shopping or singing carols than thinking about being chopped in half, but at least today I believe that I'm going to make it. Yesterday I spent an hour going over the worst case scenarios with Sean (being left with the effects of a stroke or total kidney failure being worse than my fear of dying) and allowing myself another good cry. Now I'm feeling 'grounded' and more optimistic. Gestalt's 'Paradoxical Theory of Change' theory again; I went right into my fear and sadness, crying out the toxins, hormones and chemicals that were making me feel overwhelmed in order to leave space for some positivity!

In my darkest moments I've been trying to find answers to why I have to go through this terror. I sometimes feel like Job from the Bible whose suffering just went on and on...more needles, pain, powerless, humiliation and more feeling massively insecure (why would Sean want to be with someone who's causing him so much stress and pain?) But I know that there are no answers. Shit happens. It is as it is. And at this moment Sean's playing some Spanish guitar in my front room and my body's vibrating at a beautifully smooth rate as I listen to his quietly strummed passion. If I do die I will have lived a sometimes challenging but often beautiful, exciting, fulfilling and meaningful life (I'm so glad I was able to help some people along the way) surrounded by a lot of love. What more could a person ask for? But still, I really hope that I get chance to finish this book...'

Two days before my operation, just as I was at the hospital having my second steroid injection in preparation for it, Surgeon Brooks called to say that the operation had been cancelled because the Intensive Care ward was full. My op. was rescheduled for a month's time. Part of me was frustrated but mostly I was over the moon '*Yeah! I have a reprieve! I feel like I've just been taken off Death Row! Just in time for Christmas! Wheeee! La, la, la, la, la, la, la (the 'Banana Splits' theme tune). Oh life's good...oh what a relief. I'm alive! I may need an operation in four weeks' time but for now I'm alive!'*

I had a lovely Christmas Day with Sean and Alfie, starting with champagne and swapping lovely thoughtful presents (actually Alfie didn't make much effort) followed by a Boxing Day at my parents' (sadly Sean's lost his) and for once I didn't feel the awful, wrenching pain of childlessness. I felt happy. The next month was a rollercoaster of panic attacks and worry, joy, fun, appreciation and awe. Incredibly, given my gut pain, the month also involved my first ever skiing trip when Sean took me to join his friends at their plush chalet in the breath-taking French Alps. On our first day in the snowy mountains, there was blue sky, sunshine and magical, glitter-like ice crystals floating in the air. My skiing was less magical; I was like Bambi on skis for the first few days and it took me a lot of falling over before I got the hang of it but I finally managed to swish down a slope with the wind in my hair and a huge grin on my face. On our last day my grin was replaced by a scream as, with jellied inner thighs, I wobbled off-piste, and straight up a massive snowdrift; Sean tells me that my flight off the top of it and a head-first landing (thankfully into soft snow) were quite spectacular! That evening's soak in the warm Jacuzzi on our chalet's outside balcony surrounded by luminous snow and a mass of stars was like Heaven and I really didn't want to go home and face reality again.

'It's February the 15th 2006 and the day before my operation. I don't want to be alone and yet I've made sure I am. Really I want Sean to hug, kiss and hold me whilst I sob my heart out but in this almost catatonic place I've reverted back to my fear that he might not like me if I'm 'too much.' You'll be okay, don't worry; he loves you and tomorrow will be fine... AAAGGGHHH, AAAGGGHHH, AAAAAGGGGGHHHHH! Phew, okay, that's better. Thank you, dear readers, for listening to my terror. Take care of you, J. xxx'

Chapter 16
On Still Being Alive!

"There are only two ways to live your life. One as though nothing is a miracle. The other as though everything is."

Albert Einstein

Back in 2007 I wrote 'Wheeeeeee! It's now a year after my belly operation and I survived! There were no nasty clotting complications or kidney deterioration and I was out of hospital in two weeks despite my operation turning into a massive five-hour ordeal with a ten-inch cut. It turned out that I had a huge abscess on my liver which had to be chopped away (thankfully your liver can regenerate) alongside my gall-bladder (which can't.) I now have a new bile duct made from small intestine. What clever, clever surgeons! Thank you *so* much, Adam Brooks, Mr Beckingham and your amazing team. The NHS ROCKS!'

I'd intended to write throughout my experience in hospital but only managed a few handwritten scribbles; being nearly chopped in half is really quite exhausting. Maybe I've needed a year before I could write about the trauma but really I think I was just getting on happily with my life and lacking the motivation; I'm only writing now because good old Death is hot on my trail and motivating me again. The bottom line is that, unbelievably, I need *another* operation on my gut; in the words of Mr Brooks, "Possibly just minor and key-hole…but keyhole would be pretty difficult and to be honest we haven't done this before." It's a good job it was my sexy surgeon, who I now trust, who said that.

A year on and I can hardly remember my two weeks in hospital as they're already mingling with the memories from my other twenty-odd admissions. I do recall my shock (when my dressings were removed) at seeing my belly being held together with crude, metal staples and looking like something out of a butcher's shop. I also have a clear vision of limping down the ward lolled over a Zimmer frame with tears flooding down my face but noticing that my tears didn't have as much shame attached as they used to. I felt pleased when I could look at a fragile older woman in the bed opposite and feel no disgust but lots of compassion.

I remember too, with a tearful lump of appreciation in my throat, my heroic surgeon virtually shouting at a High Dependency Unit sister on my behalf because she was trying to move me out of the unit whilst he felt I still needed it. He arrived at my bedside early one morning saying that he'd lost sleep because my temperature had begun to soar and he popped by often. Believing that my surgeon genuinely cared about me was again a healing gift – and it meant that I didn't feel too ashamed when he popped by one day and caught me bouncing my teddy (a beautiful gift from Kirsty) on my knee! I also had daily visits from my brilliant haematologist Dr D. who'd calm my sparking nerves following ward rounds when I'd hear strange faces mumbling about my low HB and depleted platelets and be catapulted back in time with my whole body sucking in on itself and becoming a tight, pounding ball of panic. Without hearing Dr D's gently soothing Scottish tones, I might well have flipped out. I'm again *so* grateful to Mr Brooks and Dr D. for being such kind and sensitive men who understood my psychological as well as physical needs.

It was a dream having Sean's loving support every day too and again my friends and family rallied round to encourage me on. My lovely neighbours and friends, Kirsty, Matt, Jez, Claire and Kazza took their usual, *much* appreciated care of Alfie (I *hated* having to abandon him) and brought him to visit me a few times (which was wonderful.) I missed Alfie most in the bad moments, like one day when I had to crawl out of bed for the usual bed-changing and bowl-wash. The pain in my lower abdomen had begun searing, I had started sweating and I literally couldn't stand up from my chair to get back into bed twenty minutes later. As I explained this through clenched teeth to the nurse, speculating that I had an infection, she replied with, "Well you were walking about and eating fine yesterday."

"Yes, that was yesterday," I pointed out.

"Come on, see, and get into bed."

"Really, I can't get up."

"But you need to get back into bed!"

"How can I get into bed if I can't move?"

"Well you have to. Doctors' orders. That's the way…"

"No it isn't the way it is because I CAN'T MOVE!" Her self-righteous indignation almost burnt me. I was whipped back to HDU a few hours later when my temperature hit forty degrees. I wonder how much compassion and understanding that nurse had received as a child; I suspect that she had to just get on with it, no matter what.

When I stopped writing last year, my life was a lovely flow of dog walks, cuddles, singing with Sean and us planning a future together. This felt like the first time in seven years that I'd been given the all-clear to live and I was so happy! My whole perception of myself had changed. I wasn't a useless physical wreck with a dodgy heart on the verge of death, I was an invincible woman who had managed to ski with an infected liver and survived a massive operation which could've threatened even the strongest person. I was hopeful that, as I'd had no blood complications during the op, my days of mass clotting and auto-immune related self-destruction were over.

Once I'd got over my week of post-operative nightmares, screaming, sweating buckets and, according to Sean, kicking and thrashing about wildly in bed (there's trauma and 'implicit' or unconscious body memories for you) I was soon back into living my life, designing a website for my therapy business which Sean was going to make for me and securing more classes and some team-building work. I was still a bit anaemic, sore-gutted and tired at times but thought, on the whole, that I was getting better. It was therefore a shock to hear my surgeon telling me that my liver tests were getting worse. So, here I am again. Just less than a month to go and I'm back in hospital. Again I have to go straight to Intensive Care in case my blood goes haywire. Oh God, will this ever be over? I'm back to panic attacks and sickness and am having terrible dreams and night sweats; according to Sean "It's like sleeping with a cod." Please wish me luck! Xxx

'It's now the 19th of March 2007, post my second gut

operation and here I still am! Phew....oh thank you, God, the universe, life, whatever. Just thank you! Thank you that the operation was straightforward, successful and only a three-inch cut on my original belly scar. Oh thank you that I'm sitting here on my settee with beautiful Alfie curled up by my feet. Thank you that I can walk, talk, laugh, eat, see, hear, taste and feel! I can't find the words to express my gratitude to the surgeons for all their years of study, sweat and skill perfecting. Two weeks ago I was revising my will and signing an operation consent form with a list of possible catastrophes nearly as long as my arm – but now it's all over and I'm alive! Apparently my 'blood condition' could be contributing to the formation of stones in my gut and it could be that I will need further surgery in the future, but hey, for now I've won another round with Death and I feel fantastic. You see there's the thing about life-threatening crap; when you feel good you feel bloody brilliant!'

'June 12th 2007. I have some amazing news; I played tennis yesterday! Sean and I had booked a court for four o'clock but at three I was still sitting in the bath crying my heart out; Dr H.'s words, telling me back in 1999 that I'd probably never play tennis again were echoing in my ears and I was terrified of keeling over. With Sean's cajoling, however, I finally got ready, crept tentatively onto the court and began a little knock around. It only took five minutes before I was beaming and prancing; maybe not with as much gusto as in my 'previous life' but whacking that ball felt superb! Wheeeee! I'm alive!'

On my high of 2007 I decided to look for a job; the mostly solitary nature of my work was rewarding but not *fun*. One day the free, local newspaper came through my door and as I reached to put it into the recycling bin as usual, my little inner voice said *Have a look.*

There won't be owt in there! It's rubbish.

There could be the perfect job; just look!

Tut...it's just a load of crap advertising – and crap jobs. I need to look on the web...

Just look!

Tut.

Just LOOK!

As if by some magical force of fate, I looked and there was my perfect job! At the community centre where I'd run my dance class, five minutes' drive away, they were advertising for a 'Family Development Worker' for sixteen hours a week who would put on classes and workshops, run a toddler group and whatever else seemed appropriate for local, disadvantaged and culturally diverse families. I wasn't sure I could handle the toddler group without feeling thoroughly depressed but I hoped I could find some fulfilment in trying to help lots of children instead of my own. With the help of some encouragement from giant-brained Sally, a parent volunteer at the toddler group and board member, I got the job and began to get paid to organize badminton sessions, 'Jamming Evenings,' 'Family Fun Days,' trips to the seaside, all sorts of classes and even a whacky pantomime. I loved it! It was heart-breaking at times being surrounded by babies and toddlers; I could feel like 'the alien' again, just observing normal human life from the outside, but I was also reminded that having children wasn't all fun – in fact blooming hard work; I had an easy life!

I realised just how easy my life was when people who were refugees and asylum seekers told me their stories of such horrors as the slaughter of their families, being raped by soldiers, their homes being burned to the ground or their cities bombed. Their experiences made me *very* grateful – and very angry that the UK is the second largest exporter of arms in the world,[44] that we devastated Iraq and were complicit in annihilating Syria. I was relieved that I'd learned by this point in my life that simply listening to wounded people was often enough to bring some comfort to them.

The best bit of my new job was working alongside some lovely people; our small team of five staff plus big-hearted Sharon in the Church office (who'd had a kidney transplant) and brilliant reception and toddler group volunteers including efficient, streamlined, Supersonic Sally, arty, calm, pink-haired Ged (who is so amazing that she recently had her head shaved to raise funds for the charity she co-established – 'Open House'[45]- to support women with post-natal depression) and quiet, fit as a fiddle grandmother, Carol. I felt a new sense of connection. Life was looking up again.

---

44. See for e.g. this depressing article at https://www.theguardian.com/world/2019/jul/30/uk-reclaims-place-as-worlds-second-largest-arms-exporter

45. www.openhouse-notts.org

Chapter 17
Conquering Fear with Tears

"The deeper sorrow carves into your being, the more joy you can contain."

Kahlil Gibran

In March 2008 I wrote, 'Well so much for life looking up! I haven't written for months and this time I'm not being motivated by Death but by desperation! I feel absolutely shit. Sean ended our relationship in October last year. We'd been arguing for a while and had very different communication methods, mine being to get it all out and talk and, when I was particularly scared or fed up, shout, and his being to keep it all in and, when he was particularly miffed, finish with me. Things weren't helped when I found out that his lodger, ex and business partner had bought a flat a year earlier but still hadn't moved out; as usual I'd picked a man where there seemed no space for me. My shouting made him back off just as him ending things several times made me more insecure and hysterical, which made him withdraw more; the downhill spiral was awful.

The problem is, I just can't seem to get over Sean or pick myself up; I really believed that he loved me, but then I also believed he liked our weekend dog walks but it turned out he didn't see the point of going for a walk unless it was to reach a specific destination. I'm once again, as in my marriage, left wondering what was real. The positive, energetic part of me has been cajoling and supporting my wounded part for a long time, encouraging her forward, making her look at the bright side. But now she's tired too. Really tired. It doesn't help that I'm very anaemic as my damaged kidneys go downhill (our kidneys chemically 'tell' our bone marrow to produce red blood cells). My white blood cells are also depleted and I've had virus after virus, probably from the toddlers at work, but my lethargy goes deeper than that. It's called despair, I think; despair that my kidneys are only going to deteriorate further and that I'm never going to bounce out of bed, full of the vitality of life and feeling good about myself.

I went on a first aid training last week and as the trainer talked about blood spurting from arteries I began to wobble. By the end of the day my temperature had reached 39.5 degrees centigrade and I was shaking like a leaf. A few days later I came across an article about trauma. It was like looking in a mirror; the feelings of constant anxiety, hyper-vigilance, terror, rage, helplessness, isolation, self-destruction (I'd been smoking again), paranoia and seeing everything from a scared, negative place. So I'm feeling right sorry for myself and I hope you don't mind, but I thought I'd try and share my feelings with you and try to 'process' some of my angst. I feel crap, I feel crap, I feel totally, totally CRAP!! ...Okay, the Paradoxical Theory of Change seems to be working...I feel so crap I want to jump from a very high roof and hear myself splat onto the concrete! Now I pause and ask myself 'Is that really true?' and I hear myself answering 'No it isn't.' Going to the extreme has brought me back to the middle ground again. Right then. Better get on with life...'

'Well it's now July 2008 and sorry to keep moaning but it's

just gone from bad to worse. Yesterday morning I was cheerily told at my regular renal appointment that it would be advisable for me to have an operation to have a 'fistula' made. That is, having (in my case) a potentially dangerous operation to cut a vein and an artery in my forearm and fix them together to produce a big, pumped up vein into which the needles are stuck for kidney dialysis. My kidneys' filtration rate is now only 16 percent; dialysis generally starts at 15 or just below. If I don't have a fistula op. and my kidneys suddenly pack up – which they apparently could at any time – I'd have to have a 'line' put in my neck, chest or groin whilst the fistula gets its two or three month 'bedding in' period. If you remember, a line is a rubber tube rammed into one of the big veins in your neck; – in the case of dialysis it then pops out of your chest (!) and has two short connectors which screw onto the lines of the dialysis machine. Lines can significantly increase the risk of life-threatening infection. Apparently people sometimes die having lines fitted. If I have the fistula operation I may clot to death.

Blimey. This is for real. My kidneys are shot. I've blotted out my worsening renal blood tests for years and put off speaking about it in any depth to my medics, friends (or you) but yesterday I was persuaded to talk to the nurse specialist about dialysis. I'd always thought that if my kidneys did pack up I'd have 'peritoneal dialysis' (PD) which you can do at home. It involves having a tube surgically inserted into your belly and then attaching this to four bags of fluid per day which detoxify you via the torso's inner lining in a process of osmosis. I'd imagined that four times a day at half an hour each session would be sort of manageable, if a pain in the arse. To travel you'd need a big camper-van for all the bags of fluid but driving across Spain and the Rockies would still be a possibility.

When I pulled up my t-shirt and showed the nurse my ten inch scar she attempted to hide her wince but failed miserably; she really didn't need to add "You probably have too much scar tissue for P.D." The alternative, 'haemodialysis,' involves being strapped to a four-foot machine at the stinking, post-traumatic stress-inducing hospital (amidst millions of bugs) three times a week for four hours. In the best case scenario I'd be tied to the hospital until I had a transplant – and in the words of my doctor, "A transplant is not guaranteed and it is only a treatment, not a cure because it brings with it problems of its own; the anti-rejection drugs weaken your immune system and make you more open to infections and some cancers. Um…and of course with your clotting history and the large number of antibodies you've picked up from all your blood transfusions, it could prove to be very complicated finding a transplant match for you…" I've got the telly on in the background as we speak (a feeble attempt to distract me from my overwhelming feelings) and an African tribal woman's just talking about how it's normal for the men of the tribe to beat their wives if they haven't got the tea on the table in time; in this moment I don't feel *quite* so sorry for myself.

I noticed that I just wrote about us speaking and I do feel that I'm talking to you. It helps. Thank you. I'd never told my brother just how shot my kidneys were until now and he was gutted: "I didn't know, sis, I didn't know…" It's so shit upsetting people and I'm still so drawn to hide away but I think I'd crack up if I did – though I still try and put on a positive twist; "My kidneys aren't finished yet Bro. Maybe I was destined to write and now I'll have to sit down for twelve hours a week at least!" I can be more real writing to you, mister or missis reader, because I'm presuming I can't hurt you like I do the people who love me. I feel absolutely atrocious and have thought about necking my well-stocked tablet drawer several times in the past few days. I've been asking family and friends if they fancy a trip; I want to go the Grand Canyon and The Rockies before I'm strapped to a stupid f'ing machine but no joy yet…oh here we go; I can feel the scream coming on, the pressure of my whole being wanting to go high-pitched hysterical and then whimper like a beaten dog...and now I've squashed it down and it all feels a bit surreal again. The crazy thing is, I was feeling really well. Only last Friday I was cycling in the summer breeze, smiling at a lovely, dimple-cheeked companion who I call 'Yorkshire' (I'm still too scared of intimacy and rejection to call him by his proper name.) I met him, following a lot of cajoling from a friend, via an internet dating site. My body's lean, my belly scar is nearly flat again (after awkwardly sticking out in a ridge since my big operation) and I felt close to my old self again, if a bit more tired and achy. My post-Sean depression had also been alleviated by three events.

The first was a six-day CBP (cognitive behavioural psychotherapy) training course where one of my co-learners was an interesting, funny man who'd recently cycled through Italy. It wasn't until we were at lunch on the fourth day that he talked about having had major heart surgery. As we compared notes on medications and having drains and the like I realized that I felt no different towards him than before I knew about his heart problems; he was still the same lovely person and this got me thinking. *Maybe I'm not just a wreck of a body after all, maybe I'm still a whole person despite my health issues. Maybe I won't be alone for ever...*

The second 'spirit enhancer' came in the form of His Holiness the Dalai Lama, the exiled spiritual leader of Tibet; at a live event I listened to his thoughts about happiness and how to live a meaningful life. Not only did I feel that I identified completely with what he was saying, I was also thrilled by the fact that the huge arena was packed with people who clapped and whistled in what I felt to be all the 'right' places. Mr Gentle, Chuckly Wisdom talked about our need firstly, to look inside and sort out our own 'shit' (he didn't use those exact words) so we're not aggressive, uncompassionate, out of touch with reality (like believing we're separate beings who can control things) or acting like blind sheep just following the crowd. Secondly, help others along the way and thirdly, enjoy the wonders of life! I felt totally affirmed. If I was 'out there' in crazy land, then so was the Dalai Lama (who was able to stay compassionate even as he talked about the takeover of Tibet by China) and all the thousands of people who applauded him!

The third Jaynie-healing event came in the form of a whacky weekend in an isolated training centre in the middle of Derbyshire. It was 'An Introduction to Psychodramatic Bodywork,' facilitated by a wise Canadian trainer, Susan Aaron and her team of warm and lovely assistants, including calm yet sparkly, deep as the ocean Jenny, a friend who'd told me about the course. The general idea was to release anger, fear and sadness from our bodies with the aim of feeling lighter, happier and more together. And it worked! It was absolutely beautiful; about forty of us got straight into sharing deep, raw feelings and hugs without knowing a single thing about each other. Kids, jobs, neighbourhoods; none of that mattered. The only thing that mattered was whether you could *feel* for yourself and for others. I left there knowing that I was barking mad in the eyes of many people; a glimpse through the window would have shown us whacking punch bags with pink baseball bats, lying on mattresses and screaming and shaking and huddling together on a sea of cushions with half of us crying. But I didn't care. Again, if these forty people, with their compassion, laughter and courage were viewed as 'crazy,' then I was accepting of that label too even though I felt beautifully light, happy and very sane.

On a wave of positivity, I decided to have a party to celebrate still being here a decade on from being given ten hours to live. Despite the terror, I wasn't going to give up on living and concluded that I'd just have to keep 'turning towards' and 'processing' my fear and grief to stay on a level. I have a good film lined up for tonight to have a good cry to – *My Left Foot* with Daniel Day Lewis. I'll delve into the pit of imperfectness and isolation with Daniel, who plays a man with cerebral palsy, and cry out some sadness and stress.

Well, a few weeks on from my bad kidney news and I'm settling down again. I realized the other day as I walked round the park thinking about dialysis and feeling totally grim, that there's still one thing I *can* do; I can try to live my life with grace. I still have choices. I can listen to the birds and look at the beams of sunlight through the trees or I can ignore them. I can take out my frustration on others or I can beat my settee with a roll of cardboard. I can curl up and wither away in fear and self-pity or I can hold my head up and continue to *live*. The part of me that knows it's absolutely pointless trying to fight or resist my destiny feels very calm. I'm sleeping better, feeling less cut off from my friends and enjoying day four of my holiday. I've taken two weeks off all my work and am sorting out my piles of old paperwork, cleaning my house and tidying my garden; I *will* be in control of some aspects of my life!

I'm noticing again, despite my grief, that I'm still enjoying lovely moments of connection with nature, friends and random strangers, like the vibrant, dreadlocked woman I chatted with on the bus the other day; she was struggling too (financial and depressed son worries) but we parted with beaming smiles. And the moments of terror do appear to be manageable if I just 'sit with them' until they pass. Half an hour ago I was propped on my kitchen table sobbing my heart out as I listened to a CD compilation which Sean made for me in the early throes of our relationship. As I just cried, I could feel the stress build-up of the last few weeks seeping out of my body. What a great design...shed a few tears and it's all so much better! What a crying, crying shame (ooh, a pun) that we live in a world which is so crazy that crying – physically releasing stress and sadness hormones in our tears – is seen as a weakness and avoided at all costs. Oh thank God I am less judgemental these days about 'negative' feelings. Thank God I know that my times of despair are times that I clear out sadness, learn humility, compassion, what's important and what I need to change in my life. I also notice what it is to feel fabulous when the despair lifts! Sad is sad, happy is happy yet it seems that somehow, in our Western culture, we've all got into thinking that sadness equals failure whilst happiness equates with success. "Yes, I'm good, thanks," we all chortle whether we feel okay or not and generally post pictures on social media which portray a happy life. But isn't life just a series of moments? One minute bawling your eyes out, the next laughing your head off; yin, yang and all that, one state flowing into – and defining – another. You can't have happiness without sadness. We Gestalt therapists – again borrowing from Buddhism – talk about suffering coming from trying to fight the inevitable pain of life, rather than just accepting it and walking through it. The latter seems to be my experience at the moment.

Whilst Buddhists talk about 'the second dagger' or 'secondary suffering' (the 'stories' or catastrophizing thoughts which make painful situations worse) psychologists talk about us having a 'negative bias' to our thinking. When sabre-toothed tigers lurked we didn't have fast legs or big claws and teeth so our brains learned to quickly perceive danger and *think* us out of trouble. In the modern world the sabre-toothed tiger comes in the form of suspicious strangers, work targets, parenting stress, bills, trying to look good etc but with the same self-preserving mind whirring. We worry even more when we notice that our bodies feel stressed, try to figure out *why* we feel stressed and then tell ourselves big stories to explain it ("He said..." "She did x,y z..." "My life's a nightmare...") and then get more stressed, hence cyclical, spiralling mind *and* body whirring! Have you ever noticed all the dramatic stuff that your brain comes up with on an average day? I've heard it said that between fifty and ninety percent of our thinking is worrying about things that will never happen! In the midst of all this worry, we try to gain a sense of control and solidity by thinking rigidly and with 'black and white' clarity; 'This is what the world's like...this is what life's like...this is what this race or person's like...this is the right political view...this is what I'm like...' And then we have to defend our views to the hilt...and good things rarely come of that!

So, here I am trying to accept that I have absolutely no control or certainty in my life, just the intention of trying to live with grace - and the rock tune 'Eighteen till I die' is now playing on Sean's CD. I just heard the line "It sure feels good to be alive" and I'm smiling like a wide-mouthed frog. Oh la la, how sweet life is if I go with the flow...feel sad, feel great, feel somewhere in between and don't *label* the feeling as negative or give myself a hard time for feeling crap! I no longer tell myself I *should* be strong and positive all the time – and then feel exhausted with the effort. If I just make time for myself to be sad and cry a bit, I always feel so much more relaxed and happy soon afterwards.

Emotional pain's not always easy to face in order to

transform it though, is it? I was too scared of my feelings to watch Daniel the other night and didn't watch *My Left Foot* 'till yesterday when I'd had a few days to relax and make head space for falling apart. I can't believe how you parents and full time workers don't go crazy when you have so little time for yourselves to just feel your feelings and take stock. I guess that's partly why so many of us Westerners are on antidepressants, booze and drugs and dying in droves of stress-related diseases. Daniel was brilliant as a man with awful cerebral palsy – and he got married in the end...phew...I cried my socks off at that bit...

I still feel very vulnerable but hey; it's not killing me. 😊

Well, it's not all over yet. I had a letter from the renal unit yesterday saying my kidney filtration rate has eased back up to eighteen percent. I've also just spent two lovely days with 'my' sexy Yorkshire man; he's not deep but he's cuddly, tells good stories and makes me laugh. Just what I needed. And thank you Universe that I'm able to switch off my panic about the future enough to enjoy the present and appreciate what I have. 'Yorkshire' and I watched *Sicko*, a Michael Moore film-documentary about the American health system. It's appalling; apparently people with any pre-existing conditions aren't eligible for private health insurance so they're stuffed before they even start (as I would be) and those who have insurance often find it impossible to make claims because of ridiculous get-out clauses (I recently heard Barrack Obama talking about a boy who's insurance was invalidated because he hadn't declared that he had acne) or have to pay contributions which leave them destitute. Millions of people can't afford health insurance - or medication - and die. Phew...and America portrays itself as a beacon of civilized progress! Normally such a film would depress me and I did wake up thinking how sad it is that a country as rich as the USA can just let its people die but I was also hugely relieved that I'm English and have the use of our fantastic health care system. How wonderful that we pay our National Insurance for the good of everybody. I know that's easy for me to say when I've had much more than my fair share but I like to think I'd be pleased to pay for anyone to use the NHS rather than watch them die. Given our colonial history of pillaging and brutal oppression it's not very often I feel proud to be British, but today I do.

And so 2008 continued; I had moments of almost catatonic dread but life went on, organizing craft and self-development classes and an Autumn Fayre at work and seeing a few private therapy clients. By now I'd built up confidence in my therapy work and could wade into the dark depths of my clients' pain with them without flinching. It felt like such a privilege being with them in that hard place, trying to figure out together what they needed. As in my own experience, I saw that the more clients avoided their feelings, the worse they felt but if they allowed themselves to connect with their feelings and 'process' their pain with a good stomp, cry or a simple acknowledgement of their fear, pain or shame, they invariably felt much better.

I never got to the Grand Canyon or The Rockies as nobody could come with me, which was gutting. My brother invited me along on a family holiday to Turkey instead but I didn't appreciate the intense warmth and quality time with my bro, two lovely nephews, my brother's fiancée and her quiet, delightful 'Emo' daughter. I chose to wallow in self-pity instead. I'd been given looks, brains, artistic flair, an athletic body and a sociable nature but I'd just let my health and some lovely men slip through my fingers. Now I was the shame-ridden maiden aunt with no family or partner, inwardly screaming vicious obscenities at the families packed round the pool. *Have you any fucking idea how lucky you are to have nothing to think about other than filling your fat children with Coke whilst I'm sitting here being lashed with massive existential terror?* My inner pain being expressed in an evil desire to put down and rant at innocent people seems to be a classic example of the bane of humanity, eh? Avoiding our pain and shame by humiliating and blaming others and getting angry. Luckily, once I'd spent a few hours on my Turkish balcony writing a depressing ream to you in a flood of tears, and then sobbing again when my brother kissed my forehead and said, "I understand, sis," my desire to go on a psychotic rampage subsided.

Back home I tearfully dared to tell the Yorkshireman how scared I was that my kidneys were shot. His response of, "Stop crying, it's not attractive" jolted; here was a man who would deflect and joke and keep me out of the sorrowful depths of my feelings – but ultimately out of the peace that comes with being properly heard and having the chance to transform hard feelings. We soon agreed that we were too different and a relationship wasn't going to work – which was great; we both took the risk of being open and honest about how we felt and ended on friendly and mutually respectful terms.

A little later I met 'Blue Eyes,' an intense eco-warrior who I fell a bit in love with. But he wanted children. In days gone by I would have just shut down and immediately scuttled away in shame on getting a whiff of rejection but instead I lay on the sofa with Blue Eyes and cried as we talked. He sent me a beautiful text the next day thanking me for teaching him more about being 'real,' open and vulnerable. I was learning...

Despite my romantic disasters, I had my party celebrating my tenth year after being given ten hours to live. My house is great for parties; a relaxing front room for conversation, a middle room with a wooden floor for dancing, a big kitchen for eating and my 'shed' (a half open pine summer house) for the smokers if it rains. I had some lovely people here, many who love dancing as much as me and I'd had a blood transfusion the previous week which sorted out my anaemia enough for me to 'get on down' and dance with joy. I couldn't move from the sofa for the next few days – or speak much after all my screechy singing – but what a great night!

Then came another downer. I'd gone for the usual blood tests to the renal unit and happened to have a slight infection in my gut, which was still getting blocked occasionally. I asked the young, on-call doctor, a nervy, slender, clean-cut man I didn't know, for some antibiotics.

"You need to be admitted."

"But I feel better than I've felt all week, in fact I just managed a sandwich for lunch, the first thing I've eaten for days. I'm okay, really, I just think getting some antibiotics would be a wise precaution with the weekend coming up."

"We have no antibiotic we can prescribe you."

"But I've had shed-loads of oral antibiotics in the past."

"I really think you should come onto the ward."

"Look, I'm sorry, I really appreciate your concern but I know I'm getting better and I'd be grateful if you'd trust my judgement. I'm definitely nearly well again but covering myself, just in case."

"You need to come in."

"Yes, the doctor's right, Jayne," backed up a nurse with a patronizing smile.

I sighed. "I'm not coming in. I have a dog to look after and I refuse to take up an expensive hospital bed – and risk catching MRSA and being traumatised again – when I *know* I'm getting better."

"That's not a sensible attitude."

"Are you telling me that you know more about my body and how I feel than I do?"

At this point the doctor turned on his heels and bustled towards the door muttering, "Give her some Cipro." Luckily I was on the ball. "Do you mean Ciprofloxacin?" I called after him.

"Yes."

"I'm allergic to that."

"No you're not." *Oh my God!* shrieked my brain as a familiar pit opened in my belly.

"Why would I possibly tell you that I'm allergic to it if I'm not?"

"Well there's nothing else we can give you."

"What about Levofloxacin? I've had that loads of times for my gut."

"Tut. Fine!" said his ten-year-old sulk. Sure enough, my body rebalanced over the weekend where I rested peacefully on my sofa instead of on a nervous breakdown-inducing ward. A few days later I received a copy of a letter which the nurse had sent to all the other medics involved in my care explaining how I'd refused admission and made me out to be a stubborn, foolhardy pain in the arse. My soul wept. When I returned for my next appointment it turned out that the renal unit only had one of my seven or eight files. This time I had to argue with a consultant who was trying to give me *another* dodgy prescription (for weekly 'EPO' injections – the evil, stinging little number which I had to stick into my belly every week to boost my red blood cells.) The doctor's insisted dose was twice the dose that I needed – and could have clotted my blood. Luckily she believed me in the end. AAAAGGGGHHHH! To all you doctors out there, PLEASE LISTEN TO YOUR PATIENTS! And I wonder why I'm a nervous wreck!

'Right then' I decided in late 2008, 'With regard to this 'ere 'fistula', I can give myself up to the professional opinion of the 'experts' who see only the bit of my body they need to sort out – and have the operation. The wheels were put in motion at my last appointment. Or I can stand up for myself, be possibly viewed as a pain in the arse and tell them to get stuffed. The renal consultant I saw was really kind once we'd had our ten-minute argument about the correct dose of my 'EPO' and was sympathetic as she explained how the fistula operation could make my hand go a bit numb, my thumb a bit blue and require me to wear a permanent glove – but she is not living in my body and hasn't been full of blood clots. There may be a risk of infection if my kidneys deteriorate and I need a line fitted in my chest to have dialysis but the choice is mine and I'm going to take the risk. Only the other day my GP was commenting on how amazing I look considering my kidneys are so shot, I'm still working, getting Alfie out every day and managing the odd swim (though it's exhausting to be fair) – so I'm not having a fistula done yet. End of. Instead I've sent off for a new passport and am going to see my delightful friend Mary in Bahrain where we'll meditate in the sunshine together. Life is what happens whilst you're not busy worrying about shit that isn't happening yet!'

I checked out my cunning plan to postpone having a fistula operation with my haematologist who was respectful of my decision, given the risk of my clotting during an op, so I returned home and wrote 'WHEEEEE! No bloody death sentence hanging over me at the moment!' I then turned on the telly at the *exact* moment that a character on *Neighbours* was saying "I'm not having the operation and that's final and now I'm just going to get on with my life." Coincidence? A message from the universe? Who knows, but it made me smile a *lot*.

I also smiled a lot when I recently video-interviewed my mum and dad when they came down for a few days. It felt so lovely; I love them so much and now have them on film (well, chip) forever. And it was fun doing it; I'd heard many of their family stories, especially from my chatterbox mama, but some were new, like my dad recalling his grandmother coming to visit in her long, black Victorian lace dress, going for a drink to 'The Crimea' and then having to be wheeled home drunk in a wheelbarrow! It's even clearer where I get my refinement from!

And so the winter months of 2008 went by. I took the voting in of the first Black President of the USA, Barack Obama in January 2009 as a beautiful sign of a movement towards a better, more caring, *deeper* attitude in which we recognize we really are all in this together. If only Martin Luther King,

Rosa Parkes and all the other incredibly brave Civil Rights activists who each did their little bit towards our evolution, could have been here to see it. (I'm now editing in 2020 and wishing Obama, who turned grey during his challenging time in office, wasn't having to witness much of his hard work being undermined by the outrageous Mr Trump (even his name's insane! *The Simpsons* couldn't make him up.)

In terms of my own evolution, I was getting more and more spells of feeling that I was 'going with the flow.' In my twenties I can remember panicking about how it would be to get older and not have dancing as a focus; what would I do for fun? But now I was settling into a simple life. A weekend in my garden, planting, pruning and clearing leaves, with adorable Alfie helping by taking the weeds to the compost heap, felt both invigorating and relaxing. I *felt* a part of the bigger picture; I was just *being*...listening to the birds, feeling the earth in my hands (and apparently it's a natural antidepressant[46]), watching the flowers grow and change, seeing the constant process of death and rebirth and not worrying about anything – just being 'in the moment.' Being in the moment and accepting things *as they are*. I think my new 'flowing' followed a particularly poignant day of learning over the summer. I'd bought some bags of white 'Cotswold' stone to spread on my garden (aiming for a clean, Japanese feel.) The kind man in the shop had lifted them into my van for me and I *just* managed to drag them out onto my drive but no way could I move them the fifteen metres or so to the garden. I tried putting some into a bucket but, much to my dismay, it was still too heavy for me. In the end I started carrying the stones in a dustpan. Cross and frustrated at first, I caught my thoughts and told myself that I could curse and complain for the next two hours or I could listen to the birds, feel the sunshine on my skin and do some relaxing,

46. *See https://dailyhealthpost.com/antidepressant-microbes-soil/*

strengthening, mindful walking. I opted for the latter and had a beautiful afternoon of just pottering backwards and forwards and then feeling great satisfaction at my lovely new garden by the end of it. I realised that I had a great new tool for life; 'Zen and the art of just accepting things as they are and going with it.' 'Oh thank you universe' I wrote 'for helping me to accept my body as it is and for teaching me that there is no stress or pain in the moment, just being. And thank you that I'm not one of the five hundred people who have just been killed by hurricanes in Haiti, the *seven million* people who, living with drought, are facing starvation in Ethiopia, Kenya and Somaliland and the many women and girls who suffer rape on a daily basis in Liberia. (I've just read an *Action Aid* magazine.) Thank you that I feel at peace again. I guess this book is not as optimistic as I'd hoped but perhaps it's enough to be about coping with trauma and grief. And as far as I can make out, gnashing, thrashing, wailing, and being self-compassionate and grateful are the best ways to get through to the acceptance, serenity, hope and happiness on the other side. Oh how I'm learning!'

Chapter 18
Accepting my Shadow Self

"You do not have to be good. You do not have to walk on your knees for a hundred miles through the desert, repenting. You only have to let the soft animal of your body love what it loves."

Mary Oliver (Wild Geese)

'Wheee! It's January 2009 and I'm just flying over North Africa on my way to Bahrain to stay with Irish-colouring Mary (dark, curly-bobbed hair and eyebrows and huge blue eyes). I had a blood test on Monday and my kidney filtration rate was 17 percent. "Oh great," I chirped to the renal nurse, "Seventeen will get me to Bahrain."

"You *what*?"

"My friend lives in Bahrain and I'm going to visit her."

"You can't go to Bahrain!" she shrieked, her eyes bulging behind her glasses.

"Why not?"

"Why not? We just had a patient who came back from Cambodia with hepatitis!"

"Well that's not Bahrain. Blimey, I bet their hospitals are better than ours. Don't worry, my friend's husband works at an international school and they'll know the best hospitals if needs be."

"Can't you go to Tenerife?"

"Mary's in Bahrain."

"Look, I think you should talk to the doctor."

"I'm sorry but a doctor's not going to change my mind."

"Your insurance will be a fortune!"

"As if I'd get insurance with my list of crap. The last time I spoke to an insurance company they ran through a ten-minute list of bodily complaints and when I said yes to nearly every one they wouldn't touch me."

"You can't go without insurance!"

"It's only a week and what's the chances of a disaster that particular week? I'll just be sitting in the sun and chatting – there's more chance of my body collapsing under the stress of life here!"

"No chance of your friend meeting you in Tenerife?"

"No"

"But..."

"Please don't worry. I survived a trip to Kenya, six months in Asia and six weeks in Central America with Lupus and that was against doctors' orders but they were some of the best times of my life. I'm happy to confirm that you tried to talk me out of it if the shit hits the fan but what's the point of my being here if I don't live? And it may be my last chance. Ever." She slowly shook her head in resignation.

Mmm, despite my apparent bravado I'm having trouble keeping my eyes open given how little I've slept over the past week because of my anxiety about this insurance-less trip but I'm just christening my new baby lap-top as I write. A few weeks ago I bought myself a shiny blue 'notepad' for writing in cafés (and Bahrain) so I don't have to carry my heavy laptop. As I'm not good at spending money on myself unless it's imperative, it felt like a miracle when, the very next day, I received a refund from the tax office which covered my costs! It feels like a vote of confidence from the universe in my writing.

I'm now in Mary's enclosed, leafy garden and whilst it snows in England, it's twenty-plus degrees and I'm in my bikini lapping up vitamin D (poorly processed with defunct kidneys.) Oh God, I love being warm and despite my lack of insurance, I'm feeling safe. Mary is spirited, honest, deep, interesting, compassionate and funny, and we laugh a lot about the madness of being human. Her seven-year-old son is a bright, quite serious child with the bluest eyes I've ever seen and her four-year-old has possibly the cheekiest smile in the world. They're adorable. I was in my element last night, reading them a bedtime story, with all the silly voices. It was followed by the searing pain of my childlessness (and I'm in tears as I write) but that didn't take away the lovely time I had. It is getting easier not being able to have children – I can appreciate my easy, selfish life – but boy, when the tide of loss hits me I feel like just opening my lungs and drowning. I'm missing Alfie and have to keep texting Andrew the Yorkshireman, who kindly agreed to take care of him, to check he's okay.

Bahrain's an interesting place with its diverse population and pearl-diving and fruitful trading history, though because of my fragility and lack of insurance, an anxious Mary (fearful of having to re-mortgage her house!) is trying to keep me safe by only taking me to clean, modern areas. We're not seeing local cafes, lush allotments, swaying palm trees and average neighbourhoods so sadly my lasting impression will be huge sky-scraping office blocks, ex-pat, security-guarded complexes, rubbish-strewn beaches and sandy ground with garden-less buildings just plonked on the stark barrenness. Oh okay, there are birds too, I'm reminded; a seedy dropping has just landed on my brand new screen! There are also bright petunias and bougainvillea, and the camels we visited yesterday at the king's farm were gorgeous with their giant, lolloping feet, soft, hairy chops and big brown, heavily lashed eyes. The stick-legged babies were cute too; happily I didn't feel jealous of the mothers which I've done over the years when I've seen families of swans and ducks gliding together on lakes!

No doubt these olive-skinned people in their black burkas (the women) and chequered head-scarves held on by a ring of thick chord and long, white tunics – thawbs/thorbs – (the men) have the same fundamental feelings, needs and desires as people everywhere else in the world; we all just want to be safe and happy. I'm looking for differences which will tell me more about them and my own Eurocentric mentality but it's hard to see them as we walk round glittering shopping centres where people are necking Coke and McDonalds. We're going to the café-bar attached to a clean, private beach tomorrow; Mary has a pass which takes the cost down but it's normally fifty pounds a day to step on the sand. Yet again, the wealthy secure the best bits.

It's quite soothing to hear the sounds of regular calls for prayers emanating from the mosques; I imagine a spiritual unity that we don't have in Britain. But then again I also find it unnerving seeing images of martyrs and spiritual leaders all over the place; being a bit religion-phobic and all, I feel it smacks of indoctrination. Talking of which, I had a shock the other day when I saw a huge bill-board on the side of a main road of a scowling, bearded man holding a rifle. I asked Mary to stop the car so I could take a photo, at which point I realized that the man was not particularly gruff looking and was holding a *baby*, proving

the point that we see with our conditioned, media-warped brains, not our eyes! The 'War on Terror' propaganda since '9/11' had mashed up my sight. My experience so far is that most Bahraini seem to be chilled-out, family orientated people. Chilled people who walk *slowly* in the heat and make us Brits seem like road-runners!

I'm reading one of Mary's books whilst I'm here 'Getting the Love You Want' by Harville Hendrix who's an American couples therapist. His ideas reflect that of Gestalt's 'unfinished business' – the idea that we're often attracted to people who unconsciously remind us of our parents, carers or role models and give us the hope that we'll get the care, cuddles, safety and affirmation that we didn't get enough of as children. Except, sometimes it's the familiar negative traits of a person which unconsciously attract us; in my case men who can be critical, defensive and too hurt to acknowledge much of their own crap, for example. So, of course, once the 'honeymoon period' of mutual adoration is over, you realize that this wonderful person who you think is going to heal you, also has needs and wounds of his or her own and can't give you all the unconditional love that your 'inner child' is still craving and so you get disappointed, angry, hurt and afraid and you begin to withdraw or criticise and suddenly it all goes horribly pear-shaped...

On top of carrying the pressure to repair old emotional wounds, relationships, points out Mr Hendrix, can also be warped by other unconscious (or conscious) drives and motivations that say 'I want you because you're as attractive, educated, wealthy etc. as me so it's a fair deal' which means that if circumstances change those variables, things can fall apart and also the *real* person behind the list may be totally unsuitable. Then there's the issue of 'projection.' Often our unconscious may decide that 'I want you because you make me feel whole by bringing the personality traits I don't *think* I have...you're the angry, sad, intelligent, funny, in-secure, powerful or fun one – and so I can maintain the image of myself that's been wired into my hard-drive as I grew up when it wasn't okay for me to be angry, sad, insecure or even intelligent, funny, powerful or fun.' Mr Hendrix asks of us 'What do you see in your partner that you don't like to acknowledge in yourself?' More pear-shapes occur when one half of a couple wants to change or deviates from the other's expectations (the insecure wife gains confidence, the depressed husband becomes happy or the powerful partner breaks down) – one's disowned parts can no longer be comfortably projected away onto your partner. Similarly, if your partner sees through your self-image and points out to you that actually you can be angry, sad, mean or insecure, you immediately start to feel off-balance and want to run a mile!

Well at least it's clearer to me, post Mr Hendrix, why I picked the men in my life. I was repeating my history over and over and choosing men who were very like my dad or I was projecting my own 'stuff' (negative and positive traits) onto them. I could keep myself 'good' by sticking to the image of myself I'd developed in childhood in an attempt to stay close to my parents by being like them or getting their approval; I could pretend to be kind, strong, thoughtful, humble, selfless and sane and instead of me, my head could see my partners as the selfish, weak, mean, arrogant, vain and crazy one. They could also make me feel whole by being arty, intelligent, musical, funny and computer-literate, things I'd like to be but can't really own in myself. (I remember really falling for my chappie who was sectioned, when I saw a fantastic picture of a tiger he'd drawn and of course he was crazy, not me!) Mmm...interesting stuff.

Phew...what a painful process accepting the whole of me! I am at times selfish, weak, mean, arrogant, rude, greedy, vain, stupid, naïve and cruel...okay and crazy at times! I too am a demon goddess and growl round the temple door. Tibetan (and many other Buddhist) temples are adorned with grotesque demons. I puzzled over their grotesque faces in S.E Asia; were they meant to scare us and protect the temples? It turns out they represent *our normal*, *universal* human demons which we have to face in order to stop our blaming, raging, criticising, repressing and distorting. In facing the demons we have the chance of changing and being able to enter the temple, our natural state of happiness, open-heartedness and inner peace. La la…! So, I'm just a scaredy-cat human just like every other human and I do dumb bozo stuff. It doesn't make me unlovable or unworthy. I can also be funny, intelligent, creative, musical and attractive and not be rejected; it's not a fact (though my brain's been programmed with this) that other people will envy and hate me if I own my attributes. ('showing off' in any way was *not* acceptable in 1970's Yorkshire and my fragile parents' 'wounded inner children' didn't like to be outdone.) I'm just a human being with innate weaknesses, strengths and fears just like anybody else! We're all *just human* eh?

Phew, okay…maybe Mr Right can appear now! Now I'm feeling more self-compassionate – and therefore other-compassionate (instead of being self-berating and therefore critical of others in an attempt to feel less inadequate.) Oh God, I wonder if I will ever be able to let in a man who's human and knows it; a man who can be open, vulnerable, powerful, selfish, kind, intelligent, dizzy, hard-working, lazy, loving, withdrawn…a man who is honest and *real* – and will appreciate me being the same (as well as a physical wreck. Invitations for coffee on a postcard, please!)

Wow, despite being a critical, short-tempered meanie sometimes, I think I have finally rearranged my neurological wiring and actually like myself these days (mostly.) Let me write that again…I *like* myself!

Jayne, you can't write that!

Why not?

Everyone will think you're an arrogant narcissist!

Well that's their stuff.

That's as may be but still...

I've spent four decades giving myself a really *hard time, possibly making myself ill in the process and that's enough. Enough! If I was a flower or a dog I'd just be being a miracle of nature and revelling in the sunshine and my amazing body and senses, not berating myself for having a bent stalk or a capacity for biting people...*

I don't think it's only Mary's holding up of a loving mirror, reading the Hendrix book and having about ten grands worth of therapy that have led to my being more gentle on myself. It's also related to a scan of my arms last week to investigate where I have a good vein to make a fistula for dialysis. I was scanned by a gentle and handsome man about my age called Andrew. He was quietly respectful when the tears began to spill down my cheeks in response to him telling me that the veins in my forearms were so damaged it would be impossible to put a fistula in my wrist, the usual first port of call. *Ah that explains why my hands get so many chilblains and are freezing all the time and why my fingers sometimes go painfully rigid when I'm sewing or writing a lot...oh my God, what does that mean? Oh my God, have I done myself in?...*"How much of this damage is due to being an ex-smoker do you think?"

"Compared to a lot of needles, not a lot."

"Really? And warfarin fluff?"

"Have you been on it a long time?"

"Twenty-five years."

"Oh. Yes, both needles and warfarin are bad news for veins and renal trouble can mean your veins get a bit calcified. The good news," he continued with a weak smile, "is that it looks like..." *only looks like?* "...it will still be possible to put a fistula in the crook of your elbow." I just stared at him as my insides crumpled. I go rigid when I think about needles going into that part of my arm. When I give blood at the minute they take it from the back of my hand or a tiny vein near my wrist bone; both places really hurt but feel nowhere near as gross – or painful – as having blood taken from the deeply scarred cruxes of my arms. And so I feel distraught and yet my physically mashed-up state has helped me to *finally* override all that hard core Northern shit in my head about being 'soft' and self-pitying. Interestingly, over the years I've noticed in myself, and others, that being self-critical and harsh can actually be easier than being self-compassionate; being really loving towards ourselves can hurt like hell but I think I've now gone through enough of a pain barrier to allow in some gentleness. So, I have to find the middle ground here. I have to allow myself space to feel scared and process my fear but I also have to remember that I'm alive, today.

When I saw an unfamiliar renal consultant last week he looked so surprised when I walked into his consulting room that he felt a need to excuse his double take with, "Oh I'm sorry, I've just been reading your file and I didn't expect you to look so well!" You never know, in five years' time I could have had a kidney transplant and be running marathons...maybe stem cells will be growing new kidneys by then...I must remember the positive and the *now* and that here I am here in this alive moment with my body cosseted on a comfy sun-lounger, bees merrily buzzing over the pots of petunias and birds throwing happy whistles from a tree.

In a moment of feeling lonely I was called earlier by my eighteen year old nephew. He's on a trial period at a farrier's yard, loves it and finds out next week whether he's got an apprenticeship there. I worry for him working in a baking, sooty forge and shoeing grumpy racehorses but it's his life. We were just laughing about the phrase 'built like a brick shithouse' (which he is.) Like his supercool, backwards base-ball hat wearing brother, I adore him. He's a gentle, thoughtful but determined soul and I feel so lucky to have a nephew who will phone me because he wants to. Wheeee! Right then, I'm just off to Rache and Mark's (two members of 'The Amber Herd' – www.theamberherd.com – who create some of the most magnificent walls of sound I've ever heard) where, in a bid to be fed, a squirrel swings on the patio door handle looking into their kitchen! Kind, funny Kirsty and super-brain Matt will be sitting in the sunshine too. Today is today, and a good day.

'It's now October 2009. I've just been reading a book about Jewish Mysticism lent by my witty, moustached musician friend Steve. Just as I was feeling like I could wither away and die, I read a sentence about God sometimes destroying the bodies of the best souls – rather than those of the most terrible sinners (my default position) – so they come closer to the Divine. It made me smile. I like the idea of trying to do my bit towards promoting what the book calls a 'messianic consciousness' or a more loving way of being. Mmm, having said that I'm aware that I don't feel very loving in this particular moment after just hearing news of two friends having babies; for one friend it's her third. It's not fair. But who said life was fair? I've still got the choice of wallowing in self-pity or doing what I can do. I'm so grateful that I know that this despair will pass. And thank God that Alfie can come through the door with his bushy tail wagging and my heart will lighten in an instant. I think I'll give him a whistle...'

Chapter 19
My Final Year of Freedom

"The real voyage of discovery consists not in seeking out new landscapes but in having new eyes."

Marcel Proust

Making the most of my final year of freedom, Bahrain in January 2009 was followed by Lanzarote in April with Kirsty. Like Mary in Bahrain, she's a compassionate gem of a friend for whom I'm incredibly grateful. Kirsty's big brother, J. has a degenerative muscle disorder and she has grown up knowing how lucky she is; you very rarely hear her (or the arty, dry-humoured, mega-brained J.) moaning or bitching about anybody and she's an absolute delight, with a deep appreciation of life and its beauty.

Lanzarote was fabulous. We stayed in a four-star hotel and took full advantage of being cooked for. The lush breakfast fruit, with huge fresh figs and dates, was followed by a perfectly cooked English breakfast and a glass of chilled champagne on the two days we weren't driving. The choice of tasty buffet food in the evenings, with *fresh* seafood, was phenomenal and the puddings and cheese selection was something else. Talk about mindful eating and savouring every mouthful! We also decided to treat ourselves to an open-topped car so that we could feel the warm breeze on our faces. Bliss! The island is beautiful; random volcanoes scatter the peaceful, rusty landscape, flowers are abundant and César Manrique, a sadly deceased local artist, showered the island with soothing wind sculptures, an exquisite, palm-tree edged, turquoise-pooled garden and an amazing, artily whitewashed house made from natural, cave-sized lava bubbles. As we roamed the beauty I relaxed.

In the north of Lanzarote is Fire Mountain where geysers shoot steam thirty feet into the air and a tour bus drives you around the volcanic landscape which looks like something out of *Star Trek*, with incredible rock formations created by once-running lava. Its barrenness was like being at the beginning of time and reminded me of how incredibly lucky we are that the earth developed as it did, with the moon in exactly the right place, the earth tilting at the perfect angle, the stars spurting out the amazing chemical elements which built the vast myriad of life...I'd better stop, my brain's about to blow! I bet I could give Brian Cox a run for his money these days with my awe at the world.

Again, foolhardy though it may have been and not something I'd recommend, I'm so glad that I took the risk of a holiday without insurance and didn't allow myself to be overwhelmed by fear. I had a few freaky moments thinking *Oh my God I may never be able to come here again once I'm strapped to a dialysis machine* but those moments quickly passed, especially when I asked myself the classic Buddhist question 'Does everything have to be perfect for me to be happy *right now*?'

'It's November and life goes on. I'm in the middle of painting a basement scene for the pantomime, *Stand Up Cinders*, which, with the help of my hilarious, seriously cute, afro-bobbed friend Valerie, I'm putting on in my community work job. We're an interesting cast with issues including Parkinson's disease, alcoholism, autism, cancer, depression, learning difficulties, drug addiction, anxiety, dyspraxia and my renal failure. Some people with English as their second language don't feel confident speaking out, and the women who were playing Cinderella and a 'bling sister' (a modern take on the ugly sisters) had to pull out. However, we have a new, pink-haired, forty-ish-year-old Cinderella (Penny) who's fantastic and has learned half her lines already and the community centre vicar's daughter (we're attached to a church) wants to be a bling sister in her short skirt and spikey heels. Puppy-eyed Pete came up with the theme tune from *The Good, the Bad and the Ugly* (Cinderella, the step-mum and the sisters) as our opening gambit, the ex-vicar, Graham, who has Parkinson's, is using his shaking to his advantage by playing a spectacular drunken father and outrageous Geordie community worker, Linda, the wicked stepmother, has come up with a legend of a song to go with her tickling stick! My faith that all will be okay has just been bolstered by opening two tins of donated paint, a baby blue and a crazy bright pink; they were the *exact* colours that I needed for the basement scene's armchair and door which had been started in crayon by two of our panto mice.

Oh wow, I went to see a band in Birmingham last night with Kirsty and Matt, The Airborne Toxic Event, and they were fantastic! Musicians extraordinaire, their enthusiasm and energy was in*toxic*ating! A great moment for the memory box was the bass guitarist standing on a huge speaker, rocking like a maniac as Kirsty and I sang ourselves hoarse. I also have another load of memories to store from my perfect holiday with Sensational Susie; yesterday we were in Egypt! As usual my doctors weren't happy but I reckoned that, given this was possibly my last opportunity in my life to see Egypt, a kidney function rate of fifteen percent was enough to get me there and back. Again, we cast frugality to the wind and stayed in a five-star hotel in Sharm el-Sheikh where our pristine ground-floor room opened onto a blue, landscaped pool area and we had swan-shaped towels and pink petals sprinkled over our soft, Egyptian-cotton beds. Our gorgeous meals were eaten on a terrace overlooking the serene, turquoise Red Sea. In the morning there was a warm, fresh sea breeze and birds tweeting merrily from the sculptured bushes and at night, candlelight and a massive sky with Orion's Belt glistening right above us.

I haven't laughed so much for ages. Whilst on a day trip to Karnak Temple, Susie was taking a photo of a grand, pillar-lined thoroughfare and I stuck my head out horizontally from behind a distant column; not obvious when you first look at the photo – a 'wally.' From then on, totally sober, we 'wallied' in five-year-old hysterics whenever the opportunity arose. At Karnak we also lay down on my trusty orange sarong behind some columns, having got up at five and walked for miles. It was interesting when a group of tourists walked by; they reacted with puzzlement, wonder, disapproval and laughter...we had challenged the parameters of acceptable behaviour; two grown women *should not* snooze on the dusty ground of a historic wonder. Susie's truly spectacular code of conduct breaking came the next day when, as I was videoing, she started running up the towering steps of Queen Hatshepsut's sun-drenched, four thousand year-old temple singing the *Rocky* film tune. She got more smiles than frowns. Bless her free heart.

Another precious memory came from sailing down the wide, graceful Nile in a twenty-foot wooden boat. About fifteen of us lounged on the benched sides as random trinkets hanging from the wooden roof twinkled in the sunlight. The sound of the motor was drowned out by the Egyptian tunes being played on a battered radio by our rugged young captain and his delightful, eight-ish, tatty t-shirted and big-grinned son. As my nose took in the watery freshness, my eyes soaked up the magic of the myriad triangular-sailed and coloured boats breezing along (though I felt sad at a sombre fisherman rowing home with his young son and their meagre catch.) I was in awe of the riverbanks' duck-like creatures whose carved outlines had adorned the temples and the donkeys and camels grazing in the gentle evening light. I envied the farmers who chatted as they tended the river's green banks, just as they may have been envying me with my likely relative wealth and easy life. As the sky blazed orange, with rich wisps of pink and gold, I was at one with the beautiful moment and so appreciate that my memory can take me back to that mesmerising stillness any time. I wonder if I learned how precious memories could be from my Grandad as I grew up reading this poem...

Your Cottage

We all possess a cottage
and we all possess the key.
'Tis a cottage full of treasures
that belong to you and me.

One room is full of memories,
of golden days now gone,
yet from this fragrant room
you can recall them one by one.

There's another full of pictures
of things that might have been
when youth was in his castle,
king of all that could be seen.

Alas for all its treasures,
they're too oft locked under seal
these beautiful golden moments
no-one can ever steal.

So open wide your cottage
open wide its door,
let your heart browse all its treasures
browse for ever more.

Arthur Downs

It's a hard call but I think my absolute best Egyptian moment came when Susie and I were looking at Hatshepsut's carved temple; a wonder of engineering built into a vast, red mountainside. As I was being blown away by the creativity and pre-machine effort that had built the temple, I glanced up into a deep, vibrant sky, so blue it almost beamed me up. I looked back at the temple then back up to the sky and, as a few puffs of gentle, shining white cloud floated by, a huge grin spread across my face; *that temple's crap compared to the sky and I can see it from my back garden every day*! The dark dread I'd been feeling about being tied to a dialysis machine and no longer able to travel much just lifted from me. As tears of relief trickled down my face I sensed that whatever happened, the amazing natural world would sustain me.

Ah thank you for my lovely holidays, Mary, Kirsty and Susie, you wonderful women, you'.

Chapter 20
The Gold in Suffering

"Everything can be taken from man but one thing. The last of the human freedoms – to choose one's attitude to any given set of circumstances, to choose one's own way."

Victor Frankl

'It's now December 2009 and I've just been for a stroll round the park for the first time in five days, after what I presume was a massive Lupus attack; my inflamed joints were red and swollen and felt a mixture of crushed and burnt. I can only just straighten my left elbow again. Interestingly it followed an encounter at a party with a handsome rugby player who I knew vaguely through friends. Not wanting my joyful night (with lots of lovely dancing) to end I invited him home with me; he'd lost his wife to death several years earlier and I loved that he could connect with me in the 'grief and death zone.' I really enjoyed our long chat over my kitchen table and couldn't resist being cuddled by him (or stop my crazy brain's fantasy of becoming step-mum to his two children despite him just having moved miles away.) Now I'm wondering if my Lupus (or whatever it is) is related to my body's attachment system; maybe my flare was a physical manifestation of my despair from having being reminded of the closeness I'm missing in my life. Perhaps it was a stress reaction; I felt pretty stressed and ashamed when I caught my man's momentary look of horror as I told him that dialysis was pending and I was badly whacked with his 'Well thanks for a good night and goodbye' speech the next morning. There's also the chance, of course, that my Lupus flare was me getting in there before God for misbehaving.

With my body totally wrecked, Claire, Kirsty and Teresa have been driving me to the doctors and dressing me. I look like something out of the blue lagoon; my eyes and cheeks are massively swollen and my right eye's red and bruised. It's a good job I'm not as vain as I used to be and that I have faith that 'this too will pass.' I think I might be finally understanding the Buddhist notion of 'attachment,' that is, wanting things to be how you want them to be and suffering if they're not, rather than simply accepting how things actually are. I've been calmly lying here, just trying to simply 'observe' the horrendous pain and its changing quality without letting my mind go off into thinking, *Oh my God, I'm a wreck...my life's a disaster...I'm an idiot...another wasted day...* and adding to my pain with tension and panic – with the second dagger. Don't get me wrong, I took as many painkillers as I could but when they didn't work I just tried to relax into my pain and it seemed to reduce, just like it did when I observed and accepted it in hospital. Very interesting – and perhaps something that should be incorporated into our medical system to reduce our need for so many toxic and addictive painkillers.

Well, a week on and I still feel whacked but relatively great as I can fully open my eye, walk instead of crawling upstairs and stuff my face full of flapjack! Oh...I've just had a call from the hospital; my kidneys weren't happy with this Lupus flare and are now working on ten percent. I've finally agreed to my fistula operation (connecting a vein to an artery.) You might be thinking 'Good! Get your fistula quick, you foolhardy woman!'

I'm thinking *My God, in a month's time I'm going to have a stranger, possibly with a massive hangover or distracting worries, cut a vein and an artery in my arm. I don't know if I'll clot up or have a major bleed...* From somewhere I've then got to find the grace to walk forward into a buzzing room full of dialysis machines and have two big, fat needles rammed into my vein. Three times a week. The idea of rocking in the corner of a mental health unit somewhere (so long as there's a view of a garden, good food and Alf can come) feels very appealing today. Thank God for the glistening snow and sunshine twinkling through the trees.

It's now 2010! Where did that decade go? I was just on my way to bed but wanted to write whilst I was feeling good. It's been a full-on Christmas holiday with pantomime scenery nailed to my walls and paint and half-made panto costumes scattered all over the floor – but what a wonderful creative buzz! The panto stage is now secured care of a local school, the sound and lighting men are on top of things, twelve-year-old Zipper ('Buttons' in the original story) is finally talking a bit louder, the acts for the talent show are fabulous (we're having a talent show of local school kids and community members instead of the traditional Cinderella ball) and the mice are very cute. We've got nine days to finish the scenery, learn our lines (!) and get the prince, beautiful Johanna, who has a nightmare legal job, to finally make a rehearsal. So, not a done job yet but the process of this panto has been wonderful. We've come up with joint ideas and encouraged, supported, shared, laughed and panicked *together.* It's fantastic seeing this amazing creative end product emerging from a random moment when Valerie and I were sitting at my kitchen table a few months ago deciding to do it. It's like when I came back from travelling in Asia and Australia, felt a bit depressed and so knocked on my neighbours' doors and suggested a street party. Some people initially thought me mad but as a few of us met in the pub, shared ideas and each did our little bit (writing, copying and distributing minutes initially to engage more people) we ended up with most people involved and tables piled with food, games on the park, dancing on the street, a pair of stocks in which the local bobby (and half the street) got soaked with sponges, wheelchair races for the older residents and a wonderful display of fireworks. Again, a fabulous example of the potential of humanity when we all take some responsibility and use our cooperative natures to work *together*! I also got to know Kirsty and Matt who live at the far end of the street to me – what a bonus!

And so the panto went ahead and it was brilliant…I'll tell you about it later this week when hopefully I'll be lying on the sofa recovering from my fistula op. tomorrow. Blimey, in five hours, community-dynamo Linda (our eccentric panto stepmother) will be collecting me to take me to hospital where I'm going to have a hole sliced in my arm, a vein and an artery yanked out, cut and hopefully pasted, and all the while I'll be conscious and watching. Well I won't, actually, I'll be looking the other way and going a grim shade of green probably, but keeping my ears open to every word, especially given this week's appointment with my fistula surgeon, a man I didn't know and, interestingly, can't picture. Our conversation went something like this…

"Come in. Take a seat. I'm Dr Barnes."

"Hi."

"You look anxious."

"Yes, I am."

"Oh you don't need to worry; it's only a small operation. We'll be using local, not general anaesthetic."

"You're not worried about my veins being shot then?"

"What do you mean?"

"Have you seen my vein scans?"

"Well, no, but I'm sure they'll be fine."

"You know I've got a lot of needle damage?"

"Oh I'm sure it won't be a problem."

"And you know about my antiphospholipid syndrome?"

"Erm...yes, I think it was mentioned..."

"And that I've had a massive clotting history?"

"Yes, yes," he mumbled as he nervously peered at my notes.

"Dr D's team are sorting out my blood issues, I believe."

"Oh yes, yes. Don't worry, we're on top of things." *Yes, it fucking looks like it* cursed my terrified reptile brain. Luckily by this point, I'd spent enough time being kind to myself and building new connections to my calm front cortex that I managed to stop myself trying to choke the doctor with his tie.

I couldn't turn my lounge light off and go to bed just now (despite being exhausted) because my brain's whirring with *This may be the last time I do this, or the last time in a long time if it all goes horribly wrong again...* and I don't like it! I really, really need a cuddle. But you know, amazingly, it's still bearable – again, I'm only feeling *waves* of terror. The rest of the time my cardigan is still cosy, the flowers given to me by the panto cast are still beautiful and I still have the capacity for laughter. Kirsty popped by earlier and calmly allowed me the comfort, "just in case," of manically telling her the details of my bank account and funeral plans and her agreeing to organise a sale of my belongings, with proceeds going to my workplace. We laughed a lot too, especially about how the operation could become such an out of control bloodbath that I come away with one arm. How could she possibly think that was funny? In fact, how could *I* think that was funny!

So *bonne nuit*, farewell, *auf wiedersehen* and all that. If I die – which is very unlikely – I will have died relatively happy and hopeful that the human race is, albeit slowly and with a few backward steps, evolving towards a more peaceful and loving way of being. Let's smile more at each other, eh? Loads of love to you and wishing you peace, love, fulfilment and lots and lots of joy xxx

...Wheeeeee! No complications from my fistula operation and I was home by half past seven. It was pretty horrendous though. I went into shock as soon as I was asked to don my paper knickers and gown-sack; I started shaking with cold, my temperature shot up from the normal 37 degrees to 38.5 and tears began to stream down my face. Triggers to my trauma were everywhere; the signing of the pink consent form (it reminded me of when I could only manage a cross as a signature during my seven-month incarceration) the familiar square light fittings which went pink with my brain haemorrhage and being wheeled into a mini theatre which had the same antiseptic stench as the ERCP theatres. The staff on the admissions ward where I started off politely ignored the fact that I was falling apart but thankfully, the team in operating Room 6 were more compassionate, acknowledging my fear and passing me tissues for my tears.

Once I'd climbed onto a trolley-bed, my left arm was cleaned in freezing sterile fluid and then, thank goodness, hidden from my sight by a sheet of blue plastic. Whilst a sensitive theatre nurse stroked my silently screaming head (physically reducing my cortisol levels, increasing my oxytocin and keeping me connected to my grounded front cortex and therefore calm) two male surgeons painfully inserted local anaesthetic and then cut a two inch hole in the crux of my elbow. I could then feel them pulling on my veins; it was gross. I had to have a plastic pad attached to the back of my thigh to 'earth' me in case they had to cauterize any veins; without the pad I would have fried, apparently. It wasn't reassuring when I felt a flare of fire shoot down into my hand; did I squeeze down on that earthing pad!

I'm feeling very relieved that I'm out of hospital and okay despite my whole body aching from tensing my muscles so much yesterday, and my arm feeling bruised. My new fistula is very weird and cringe-worthy. When I woke up this morning I could hear the *wooosh* of high pressured arterial blood (which yesterday fed my hand) gushing through the poor vein it had been connected to. Gross. Blimey. Oh well, I'm sure I'll get used to it and it shouldn't hurt soon.... So. On with my life now...but I'm tired today...panto news tomorrow...

Mmm. It's tomorrow now – actually it's today – and I'm feeling a bit weird and just want to be alone. It feels like a time to take stock, shake myself down again and prepare for my life without the fistula operation hanging over me but with the circulation in my hand having been significantly reduced; as I sit here in front of my 'real' gas fire my hand looks corpse-blue and feels pretty dead. And again I remind myself that my suffering is relative; the other night I watched a TV programme about a man who, as a boy, had his arms blown off by a bomb in Iraq. God, it makes me feel so sick knowing that my taxes have paid for bombs which blew thousands of innocent Iraqi – and Syrian – people into bloody pieces and left thousands more mentally and physically broken for life. I can't believe that we Brits bang on about the horrors of the London Blitz yet can do the same thing to our fellow human beings!

Ah, this takes me back to the pantomime and my wonderful moment as Cinderella's fairy godmother when I was able to share my hope for humanity. I appear to Cinderella as she's been locked in the cellar by her terrible 'bling sisters' and stepmother to prevent her getting to the talent show organized by the King and Queen who want to find a bride for their dashing Prince. I'm wearing my bridesmaid's long, blue, Celtic satin dress, my beautiful blue and silver Venetian mask and have a big fairy wand in my (then warm) hand. I'm speaking in a broad, over-the-top Yorkshire accent and being as physically dramatic as I can without falling off the stage. The scene's interspersed with spontaneous songs, at which point the cast, sitting either side of the foot-high stage, get up to dance until I wave my wand to tell our fantastic sound man, Rob, to cut the music (oh the power!)...

Fairy Godmother:	Ey up me duck! What's the matter?
Cinders (shocked):	How did you get in here?
Fairy Godmother:	Magic happens when there's love in the air, my dear and it seems to me there's a lot of love in this 'ere community centre

(Song: *Love is in the air, every sight and every sound...*" – John Paul Young)

Cinders:	Who are you?
Fairy Godmother:	I'm the woman who can show you that miracles happen and lives can turn around; all you need, my love, is hope and faith.
Cinders:	Faith?

(Song: *Oh you gotta have faith...*" – George Michael)

Fairy Godmother:	God moves in mysterious ways, my dear.
Cinders:	Yes, it would have to be very mysterious for me to get a break!
Fairy Godmother:	Oh, Cinderella, I know that you're hurting, I know that it feels like your heart's *breaking in two* because you're being bullied by your own family but you know, you still have a freedom that they can't take away!
Cinders:	It doesn't feel like it!
Fairy Godmother:	No, but you see, your freedom's in the way you *react* to situations! You could become vengeful, bitter, twisted or *consumed* by rage, Cinderella, or you can choose to continue being your gorgeous kind-hearted and loving self ...now that's real freedom!

Cinders: But it still hurts.

Fairy Godmother: I know, lovely, but you know, that terrible, excruciating, mind-blowing pain can be the key to becoming a real, hundred percent authentic and loving human being! The pain at the heart of human evolution!

Cinders: What?

Fairy Godmother: Well you see, something magical can happen when you go down into the terrible depths of your hurt

(Song: *It's a kind of magic…*" – Queen)

Cinders: What? Magic in misery?

Fairy Godmother: Exactly, my dear! You see, pain makes you learn that you are a vulnerable, struggling, out of control human being spinning round on a random planet in the middle of a thoroughly incomprehensible universe!

Cinders: Is that good then?!

Fairy Godmother: It is indeed, my love, because it takes off your blinkers! It makes you realise that pretending to be a self-important big shot who needs a big house, car and job title to feel superior isn't the answer to happiness. You learn that we're all just little, scared people trying to master fears that are common to all of us!

Cinders: But everybody else seems so together!

Fairy Godmother: Oh, people say they're fine but we live in a culture where people are afraid to admit that their lives aren't as perfect as those portrayed on social media and the telly! The reality is that there's hurt and suffering all around; *everybody* hurts sometimes.

(Song: *Everybody hurts…*" – R.E.M)

Cinders: It's not nice to relish in other people's misery but I guess that means I'm not alone then?

Fairy Godmother: Exactly! That's it! You're *not* alone, you're part of the human condition all across the world! And this is the exciting bit! Once we realise that we're all vulnerable, scared little beings made up of the same feelings and space dust, we don't shy away from others' pain! We don't say "Oh I'm sorry I didn't come and visit when you were ill, but I didn't know what to *say*"…can you see where I'm going with this, can you see?!

Cinders: Mmm...not really…

Fairy Godmother: Audience, do you see? Do you get it?.... No? Oh...well you see, once we've stopped watching TV long enough to feel our own fear and pain, we can no longer turn away from other people who are hurting ….now do you see, do you see where I'm going…oh this is just so exciting! Once we can *feel*, it's just one small step to lovely, yummy, mutual caring for one another all across the world! You can't kill or hate someone if you can see that they feel just like you do! That they *are* just like you, wherever they were born in the world! That they just want to be happy and care for their loved ones in peace, just like you. Now do you see, Cinderella?

Cinders: So let me see if I get this straight...feeling pain makes you see other people's suffering which is just like yours really and so it makes people want to help each other?

Fairy Godmother: That's it! That's it! That's what makes you into a real, lovely, compassionate, connected human being who knows there's a whole world of love and yumminess beyond what money and status can buy! The joy! Being an integral part of the beautiful whole, the miracle and wonder of being alive! Ah, what a gift life is...

(Song: *Imagine* "You may say I'm a dreamer, but I'm not the only one..." – John Lennon)

Fairy Godmother: Now, I presume you want to get to that talent show.....

So there you go. That's what sense I've made of suffering and it makes me smile. If you're hurting, I hope you know what I mean.

We did two performances of the panto, the afternoon one being, unbelievably, our first full run-through with all the cast and costumes present – but it worked! The audiences, of about a hundred and fifty people, got well into their "Oh no it isn't!" and "They're" (the dastardly mice) "behind you!" and there was a lot of laughter. Their voluntary contributions made nearly a thousand pounds. Valerie's directive and improvisation skills were brilliant and the cast had a ball. It will go down as one of the absolute best moments of my life as I stood looking up at the wounded cast taking their bows at the end; many of them had absolutely flourished over the life of the panto, taking centre stage when they never imagined they could, and their beaming smiles and looks of pride sent tears pouring down my face. Ah, connection.

Right – must go; I have the panto cast arriving in a bit for a 'bring and share' and to watch the panto video. I bet there will be a lot more laughter...'

OK
Scandal

Chapter 21
Feeling the Fear but Living Anyway

"What sunshine is to flowers, smiles are to humanity. These are but trifles...but scattered along life's pathways the good they do is inconceivable."

Joseph Addison

As 2010 progressed and dialysis approached, I was very grateful for having an 'enquiring mind' which could take me away from my overwhelming feelings of dread. My microbiology, molecular biology and analytical biochemist friends, Dr's Matt, Kirsty and Marie, regularly blow my brain at the miniscule wonders of life and I grinned a lot when they told me that genes have certain messages but it's their *relationship* with proteins, enzymes, hormones, neurotransmitters etcetera – and one's experiences – that make them express their information or not; biology is about *connections*. I then went to a free lecture with Kirsty at our local university about the relationships between galaxies and how they have internal reactions due to their *interactions* with other galaxies; even they're not isolated entities! Another lecture was a call for biologists, physicists and chemists to come together and look at the *relational* totality of things, rather than working in isolation and reducing everything to separate microscopic investigations. It seems that science across the board is acknowledging that we're parts of a moving, changing, interdependent whole. Even medicine, I'm told by many of the doctors I chat to these days, is moving towards a more holistic way of looking at illness; my very rational renal consultant goes so far as to acknowledge the physical impacts of stress. Yeah! Maybe my feeling of connectedness when I was dying really *was*, just as Eastern spirituality and quantum physics maintain, an intuitive sense of what's at the heart of things.

Talking of connection, I'm still curious about 'coincidences.' Like the day I decided that my book was a ridiculous ramble and looked through some old e-mails instead of writing. The first one I opened was about a book written by a woman whose opening paragraphs spoke about her fears of looking stupid, but she was doing it anyway. Then the next day I got a random letter from a writers' magazine, offering a free, three-month subscription. Who knows, maybe we really are little cells on the earth's living 'body' (as NASA's James Lovelock's 'Gaia' hypothesis maintains[47]) and just like the antibodies and platelets from all over our body presumably know where to go when we get an injury, we perhaps also get help from the whole, especially if it's in the interests of the whole...

I don't know if it was another weird coincidence but just when I was feeling particularly lonely and going through massive regret about my defunct love-life, a client asked me to take a look at a book she'd been reading – 'Women Who Love Too Much' by Robin Norwood[48] – an old but poignant best-seller. Again it's about the interpersonal patterns that I know from my psychotherapy training but Ms Norwood's straightforward

---

47. See bibliography p. 435
48. See bibliography p. 437

style and clear case-studies brought home that *I* was clearly a woman who 'loved too much.' The basic theory is again that of us 'creatively adjusting' to our childhood situations in order to maximise the level of love we get and minimize the amount of criticism or rejection by being 'good,' quiet, unemotional or hard-working for example and then continuing those adaptive attachment patterns into adult life and relationships without being aware of them and forever functioning in this unconscious, programmed, 'automatic pilot' mode. Having been brought up with parental conflict and trauma, my 'adaptive pattern' became to constantly attend to my parents' emotional states, moods and needs instead of my own; what was happening with them? Was my mum ready for flipping? Was she upset? What TV programme did my dad want to watch? Was I being quiet enough? I tried hard to be 'good' (i.e. to sit quietly and draw or read) 'strong' (i.e. to keep my hurt to myself) and, later, attentive (i.e. listen to my mum's grief) in attempts to avoid my parents' irritation and worry or make them happy. And so the patterns I learned followed me into adulthood. Forgetting my own needs, I have often chosen men I could 'rescue' and care for, in some sub-conscious hope that I'd be secure in my 'recuing' role - like my creative genius who I knew had been sectioned and boyfriends who had been adopted or lost their fathers as children and were vulnerable and far from macho – like my dad; I was drawn to look after them like I tried to look after my dad. My other 'type' was men who I had to work far too hard with; the confident, disinterested 'wide-boy' like charming, denim-clad Nick throughout school, gorgeous, hilarious, sailor-boy 'Bird' throughout poly, emotion-resistant 'Yorkshire' and my whirlwind husband. Here was another familiar pattern; being 'missed' and feeling fear and self-doubt. I presumed, as kids often do, that it was my fault when my mum lost it and my dad was in his little bubble ignoring me and as an adult, with the self-fulfilling prophesy hurtling me forward, I chose to be with or pursue men with whom I could keep feeling 'not enough.' I could also keep a safe emotional distance and not risk the shame of feeling vulnerable or the awkwardness of approaching real intimacy. I'd never seen what intimacy between adults was; my parents, terrified of being vulnerable themselves, squabbled instead of touching and talking. So, I've had a few weeks of more in-my-face hard-hitting reality checking, in which I've had to fully take on board that it's absolutely no coincidence that at forty-three (at this point in the book) I am without a partner because of the choices *I* have made. Which is depressing but at least gives me some hope that with this awareness and *if* I can get beyond my fear of being rejected perhaps I can make different choices. If you find yourself drooling over Mr or Ms Unavailable, trying to please your partner all the time, asking 'how can I make him or her happy?' instead of 'is this relationship making *me* happy?' and being totally focused on someone who isn't giving you what you need, then please read Ms Norwood's fabulous book – because you're worth it!

Despite my regret at having made such a mess of my love life (whilst appreciating all that I've learned in different relationships) I decided that being alone wasn't going to hold me back when I had my summer break and set off, with an excited Alfie on the passenger seat, for a campervan writing holiday in Wales. My sense of direction is appalling (apparently trauma can affect the brain's hypothalamus which is involved in finding your way about) but our drive down was smooth, with blue sky, sunshine and good tunes on the drawling old tape player; "I'm Free to do what I want any old ti-ime..." by the Soup Dragons brought on my strangled singing particularly well. I got Alf's totally unimpressed sideways glance but for once I didn't let him dominate me and positively howled at James's "If you find yourself ridiculous, sit down next to me!"

Pembrokeshire and the Gower Peninsula were beautiful; big

blue skies, *fresh* sea air, white sand, wild, grassy dunes, gentle waves, few people and a very cute rabbit sitting outside the van looking at me as I pulled up a blind one morning. Another morning I felt so wrecked that I had to stay in bed and when I eventually did get up, editing was challenging. *My God, did that really happen to me? Gosh I'd forgotten my second belly op. Blimey how did I not just kill myself? Ouch…oh shit, what if this all happens again?…* Alf and I also had fantastic walks along undisturbed, sunlit sand. Do you find it slightly thrilling to walk on 'virgin' sand or snow and have your mark so clearly imprinted or is it just narcissistic me who gets a lovely sense of my own existence? What strange creatures we are; we're so desperate to fit in and belong, to be the same as others, yet seem to love having a clearly delineated separate 'me' too. The 'me' who we constantly compare to others and feel either great or crap in that process. Gestalt theory (again in line with Buddhist thought) maintains that there is no 'me' and so you can't say I *am* X, Y or Z because that 'me' is in constant interaction with everything around it and changing as a result. This gives us a less rigid 'self' to defend with blame, arrogance and anger; you know that your opinions ebb and flow and that everything is relative. I would say I'm a pacifist, for example, but if I could go back in time and shoot Hitler, Stalin or Pol Pot, I maybe would. So next time I feel like verbally attacking someone for having a different opinion, I'll take a breath instead…

I made it through my Welsh holiday without going stir crazy though by day five, when the cheery young farmer came to collect the night's rent for parking on his field, I was so missing human contact that I nearly grabbed him by his lapels and kissed him. Being at my best in at least thirty degrees I was left a bit freaked out at the prospect of not being able to jump on a plane to the sun very easily on dialysis (I can currently get free dialysis in Europe but this will no doubt change with Brexit) but I was pleased to learn that I can go away in my camper in the

UK and have a good time. It wasn't *fun* like it was on holiday with my friends last year – Alfie doesn't appreciate 'Wallies' in quite the same way as Susie – but his appreciation of the wild beauty matched mine, I felt safe and his quiet company warmed my soul.

As well as feeling pleased about my independent British holiday, I was happy to discover that I could come home to find that the ceiling above my front room's bay window had fallen down and not even flinch! Kirsty, my next-door neighbour, Barbara and her laid-back granddaughter Rachel had cleaned up the mess for me (how lovely's that?) but I still had a very unattractive, crumbling, three-foot hole. So that's one great thing about my life; nothing material bothers me much. It was like the time I was reversing out of my drive, caught my iron gate and pulled my garden wall down; I just calmly watched it collapse onto the pavement before driving straight off to work. *Mmm, I'll sort that out later.* Liberation!

On not such a great note, as my kidneys struggled through 2010 and early 2011, life also brought two or three (or was it four?) hospitalizations with intense gut-pains, dodgy liver tests and random, undiagnosed infections. I sobbed with a hysterical resistance to being admitted – and often needed Claire's calm, head-stroking encouragement to get me there – but I soon experienced the soul-crushing moments which reminded me why I'd been so scared. Whilst waiting in the Accident and Emergency department I'd not eaten for a few days, was feeling sick with hunger and asked a nurse where I could go to buy a sandwich. "You don't come to hospital to get fed, you know" was her brutal reply. Then came the casual, off the cuff, totally unsubstantiated possible diagnoses by robotic doctors. The first, in the middle of A and E, was, "You may have a PE."

"A what?"

"A pulmonary embolism; a blood clot on your lung."

"Oh my God, what makes you think that?"

"Well you have Antiphospholipid Syndrome."

"Well yes, but you haven't done any tests yet and my breathing's fine!"

"Well you need to be admitted so we can do some tests." When the doctor whisked away and my trauma erupted in hyperventilating and streaming tears I suspect that I became invisible because not one of the doctors, nurses or ambulance crew around me so much as passed me a tissue. That old 'Diffusion of Responsibility' from social science research which I learnt about at poly; we often ignore people needing help if we're in a crowd but are more likely to give assistance if there's just ourselves there. I had a similar experience when I walked onto a renal ward, literally half collapsed, and there were about six people sitting at the nurses' station. Somebody asked me if I was okay and when I said, "I'm really struggling actually," every one of them, obviously very busy, returned to their paperwork, leaving me two feet away, collapsed over a metal trolley in an attempt to stay on my feet. Eventually one nurse decided she'd treat me like a human being and began to lead me towards a bed – but she walked so fast that she totally lost me and I ended up crumpling onto a random chair. A few minutes later, as I sat in shocked disbelief, a cleaner came along buffing the floor. She picked up on my distress, turned off her machine and gave me a hug. At that I bawled; she bawled too and then we laughed. What a beautiful moment; thank you so much, Yvonne.

A second wild diagnosis, presented by a young female doctor with the tact of a Nazi, came when I was trying to point out that I was having a panic attack; "You may be having a heart attack." She then immediately walked off, leaving me alone on a strange ward in the middle of the night and so freaked out that I nearly had a heart attack! Then there was the agency nurse who was giving me an anti-sickness injection into a cannula in my hand. I asked her to stop because it was burning. She carried on. Again I asked her to stop because it was seriously burning! She carried on. My hand was burnt to shit for days.

Another traumatic moment entailed having a drip machine, weighing about five kilos, knocked off the side of the bed by a clumsy nurse and onto my head! A small lump evidenced another *very* lucky escape. I really should have complained about that one. Then there was the usual score of, like a child, having my daily tablets locked away from me but then being dosed the wrong medication and being half-delirious and throwing up all over myself and my bedside table but having no help at all in cleaning myself up because there were simply not enough staff. Luckily for me, Susie's visit was timely and she kindly helped to sort me out, gross though I felt.

During one stay, when I reached saturation point with disempowerment and the cacophony of noise, I limped off in my dressing gown for a wander down hospital corridors, crying as I went. Whenever someone approached, I wiped away my tears and attempted a bit of eye contact, a smile or a greeting. With each person who ignored my desperate 'Hiya's my heart sank more but with each smile or greeting, it rose a bit. By the time I got back to the ward my heart was out of my leaden feet and back in my chest where it belonged. The power of a random stranger's smile!

The smilers on the corridors weren't the only angels I encountered. Having been sent for a scan of my burning abdomen one day (which, as usual, concluded nothing) my wheelchair was parked up next to a young woman's and when I limped to the pile of magazines in the corner I picked up two and offered her one. This got us chatting and it turned out that she also had Lupus and resultant kidney failure and we each knew exactly what the other meant as we talked about aching joints, exhaustion, childlessness, pain and fear. The main difference was that E. had been on dialysis since she was a teenager and was still only twenty-four. I've thought about gutsy, blue-eyed E. many times since that day and all the travelling she hasn't done and the partying she's not had the energy for and her young friends who are too frightened by her condition to call her. Thank you, E., for helping me to recognise how lucky I am for having got to my forties in relatively good shape and inspiring me to walk forward with courage, gratitude and grace.

Another angel in the midst of the chaos was the gentle Muslim registrar, Hudda, who was extremely humane. As she made her assessment of me after my 'possible heart-attack' diagnosis, she sat on the floor at the side of my bed (I was curled over my convulsing belly) so that she could look up into my face. She patiently listened to my health story, trusting that I had the capacity to tell it correctly. I can't tell you how much her compassion – and her trust in my knowledge of my own medical history – meant to me. There were of course other angels, from doctors and nurses to auxiliary nurses and cleaners, who worked like ants. As I watched them running about I felt so gutted that our present government didn't appear to be appreciating or supporting them but was instead wearing them down with underfunding, ridiculous hours, too much responsibility and in most cases, poor pay.

When I wasn't in hospital I had the energy of a sloth and decided I'd have to give up my community work job; running round with boxes of craft stuff and trays of tea, lugging play-group equipment about and chasing manic toddlers had become too much. Amazingly, in a moment of panic (and grief) about my potentially lonely and financially tight future, I got a random call from my friend James, asking me if I would be interested in a morning's work offering counselling to teenage girls in the school where he worked. Two days later I'd been for an interview with the deputy head and had secured the post, earning in a morning what I earned in four in my current job. I did earn my money, mind you; counselling teenagers who were so distraught that they were cutting holes in themselves was deeply upsetting. If only our society and education system encouraged and supported our young people to express their feelings instead of them having to resort to such self-annihilating measures in an attempt to cope with overwhelming emotions or, sometimes, trauma induced numbness. I have a friend who has an assessment job with CAMHS (the NHS Children and Adolescents Mental Health Services) and they have to turn away self-harming and depressed kids because resources simply won't meet more than dire emergency needs. Some young people interviewed on a Radio 4 programme about their mental health struggles, talked about the huge stress which comes from the non-stop tests and exams at school (British schools apparently have more tests than any other country), social media comparisons and the immense pressure to buy designer gear and look like an air-brushed model. In other words, our insane society is literally sending our young people mad!

Talking of going bonkers, as my weird, *wooshy* fistula 'bedded in' it started to grow and what had started as a two-inch cut became a frightening, swollen 'mouse' as the massive pressure of arterial blood pumped up my poor vein. At the same time I began to look like a puffer fish, with my left cheek, arm and boob swelling up; I'd always wanted breasts that I'm not ashamed of but I didn't bank on just having one! I was also getting increasingly breathless. On the very bad days – like the day I was told by a kidney transplant surgeon that, because of my clotting history, I may not, depending on what conclusion a multi-disciplinary team and various tests came to, be able to go on the transplant waiting list – the thought of ending my life again crossed my mind. Mostly, however, I was out of bed as soon as I woke up, intent on making the most of my day, and one look from the beautiful Alfie made any self-destructive thoughts impossible.

When I had a clanging, claustrophobic, tunnel-shaped MRI scan to explore why my left side was swelling up, it transpired that the main vein going from my arm back to my heart is constricted – as a result of being damaged by having a line in my neck back in 1998/9. The gentle doctor who scanned me told me I'd have to have an 'angioplasty' or 'fistulaplasti.' "A fine tube will be inserted into your vein via your groin or fistula and the damaged vein will be expanded with the help of a little balloon. It's only a small procedure with local anaesthetic... but I'm sorry things are so tough for you." His sympathy was soothing but I still wanted to howl like a wounded wolf. I was partly glad that the reason for my swelling left side and increasingly protruding veins had been found but kept flashing back to the 'ERCP' nightmares when a balloon stretched my bile duct but caused me immense pain and ended up with my belly operations. *Oh God, oh God...but moment by moment... and as much cake as I can fit in...*

Trying to live in the moment, one of my favourite things became 'mindful walking' in an expansive local park. With Alfie (whose tinkling collar tags I could hear) doing a fine job of protecting me, I'd walk with my eyes closed and try to turn my racing mind off by focusing on the minute detail of each slow step; foot lifting, moving forward, planting down, flattening, other foot lifting...Or I'd imagine, with each out-breath, my stress sinking down my body and out through my feet into the ground. I was also deeply soothed by focusing on the singing birds. Alfie got his turn at bliss by splashing about in the glistening lake. I'd often notice the families and the couples as we walked through the park and, imagining them feeling loved and secure (which could have been way off the mark, of course) it jarred a bit, but I also knew that some of them were missing the magnificence of the moment.

In October 2010 I survived my first 'fistulaplasti.' A slightly wide-eyed Kirsty came with me and we spent six hours doing crosswords and drinking tea in an admissions ward's waiting room but because 'plastis' are done with the guidance of radioactive X-rays, she couldn't come down for my actual procedure. As the doctor in Room 6 explained that there was about a one in a hundred chance of bursting my vein I literally squeaked. Looking at the metal-armed X-ray machine, a four-foot monitor screen and the trolley full of scalpels and needles, I shook. The six members of the team were wearing lead-lined tabards, making me acutely aware that I was the only one to be zapped by radiation. As I was invited to 'jump up' onto the bed-cum-operating table, the tears that I'd been grinding back began to spill. After their initial looks of awkwardness, I explained to the staff that I just had a touch of Post-Traumatic Stress Disorder and a history of nasty ERCPs and was then given tissues and soothing words of reassurance, though, when I asked, none of them had been on any training in trauma.

The local anaesthetic stung but stopped me feeling my arm being cut. I could however, feel the inserted wire travelling up my arm and getting stuck by my shoulder. As the doctor viciously prodded and poked he explained it was, "Just the wire hitting a valve in your vein." My attempts to distract myself by imagining swinging in a hammock in Thailand failed badly when I got another nerve-crunching tug in my chest and opened my eyes to see a huge, ghostly picture on the X-ray screen of my ribs and the deadly wire worming its way towards a curvy, dense mass. "What's that?" I managed.

"That's your vein; can you see how it's narrowed? Can I have a six gauge sheath please..."

"Can you get in there?" I pleaded, my eyes streaming.

"It's a bit tough but we'll do it...please hold your breath and don't move!" I tried to stay still but it felt like my heart was bouncing me off the bed. Finally, the doc's cheery, "We're in!" reached my ears but my relief was short-lived. "Okay, an eight gauge balloon please...now this may hurt a bit..." The bit was in fact a *lot*; when the balloon on the end of the wire was distended it felt like an elephant was sitting on my chest and creating such pressure that I feared it may burst my brain or blow off my nose (the pressure was real, of course, as the balloon caused a pressurised back flow of blood.) Luckily the intense pain only lasted about twenty seconds and the balloon was only distended three times. My arm needed a few stitches but wasn't mega sore afterwards. Being told I may need further 'plastis' felt bloody sore though.

I've just had a birthday and managed to avoid going along with what I thought I *should* do, which was to go out for a meal and have a hoot with friends, as arranged. Instead I asked them at the last minute (when I faced the fact that I really didn't have the energy to go upstairs and get ready) to come round to mine for a take-away and I let them know how shit I felt. Initially I felt that I was risking depressing or annoying my friends but we ended up having a lovely evening. My open vulnerability encouraged Kazza to talk about her grief at losing her dad, Kirsty, her father-in-law having open-heart surgery and her cat (and pseudo baby) being seriously poorly, for Sally, her dream of communal living was fading fast and Carol had learned that her once-in-a lifetime holiday to the Maldives was going to be plagued with clouds and hurricanes. Only Claire felt okay. Yet we weren't miserable or 'victimy' as we shared our feelings; each of us accepted that that was just how things were for us at the moment and as we felt the genuine care and love from each other we were able to champagne toast ourselves and laugh heartily at the motley crew that we were. That old paradoxical theory of change again; going *into* our grief and despair and then having it witnessed by another human being made it magically lighten.

Chapter 22
The Downhill Slope

"Owning our story is hard, but not nearly as difficult as spending our lives running from it."

Brené Brown

As 2010 drew to a close I worried that my constant aching and fear about impending dialysis would make me bitter and twisted. With what felt like a monstrous hangover (renal failure toxicity) I was woken early one Sunday morning to the sounds of a running engine and blasting dance music. I told myself to stay calm, turned over, went to the loo and then stuck my head under the pillow but my mounting rage finally enveloped me. I grabbed my dressing gown, stormed outside in bare feet, nearly ripped the offending car door off and told the shocked, scrawny youth, who was reclining with closed eyes, that he was a selfish little shit and could he have a bit of respect for myself, my neighbours and the elderly residents in the nursing home next to him before I poured a tin of paint over his car!

My mood wasn't helped by needing another fistulaplasti within eight weeks. I was also being haunted by a novel which had suggested that disabled people made others feel a mixture of pity and repulsion. It convinced me that I wasn't imagining things; I *was* a walking reminder of sickness and death, others who saw me as different to their healthy selves *did* pity me (as opposed to feeling genuine compassion) or feel disgusted or awkward. That wasn't good. Neither was finally building up enough courage to 'Google' 'kidney dialysis.' I was mortified to discover that though it can take away toxins and fluid, there are lots of things that your kidneys do that dialysis can't sort out – like regulating salt, blood pressure and acidity in the body, producing red blood cells and balancing our metabolism, oxygen, calcium, potassium, vitamin D, phosphates and all sorts of enzymes and hormones which have an impact throughout our bodies. Our kidneys control everything from our moods, stress levels, sleep patterns, sex drive, body temperature, mineral balance and heart function. (*Fucking hell!*) I also researched kidney transplants and the immune-suppression medication which you have to take for the life of the kidney; they all have side-effects like anxiety, depression, acne, weight gain, puffy face and hands, poor circulation, aggression and then there's the increased risks of infection and skin cancer if you go in the sun. Needless to say, I wasn't sleeping well.

As ever though, I still had great moments, like going with 'Rocky' Susie to see the dance band Faithless. I was dreading it. Feeling exhausted, I was worried that I may not find somewhere on the floor to sit down without being stomped on but we ended up with a whole row of seats to ourselves and a perfect, straight-on view of the stage. It took about three seconds of being blasted by a massive wall of sound to zap my weary body into dance mode. As the amazing lyrics came thick and fast about respect, connectedness, love and caring for each other and the thousands of people pumped one finger in the air, symbolizing our unity, I was catapulted into beautiful, *alive* human ecstasy! It was totally inspiring. The world *is* changing! There ARE tons of people who know that love, compassion and connection are much more likely to make you happy than money, Botox and power!

Faithless sang another song about not giving up until the sun goes down which sent tears streaming down my face with that strange mixture of pain and optimism. Thank you, Susie, Faithless and all the people who were there on 3rd December 2010, for restoring my hope and allowing me to cry, holler, sing my heart out, laugh my head off *and* confirm my belief that the whole is definitely more than the sum of the parts. My wrecked body danced – if mostly with my arms – for two hours. I wonder; given that we're basically balls of energy, is there's something in the energy of a crowd and music which literally enhances ours? Certainly it would seem that 'health' is definitely physical, psychological *and* environmental.

My cortisol levels had only just come down from a *third* horrible fistulaplasti when my renal consultant announced that because of the stenosis (narrowed vein) in my chest, my fistula wasn't looking good. I was being sent for scans of my legs to see if there was a vein suitable for a fistula in my thigh. Apparently, it would be a big, swollen vein about four inches from the top of my leg. My arm may or may not go back to normal if my current fistula's 'tied off'. *Oh God, this is too much. If I need dialysis before the fistula's sorted in my leg I'll have to have a 'line' which damaged my chest vein in the first place! Bloody hell. I can't take this in; dialysis has actually become my secondary problem!*

In the depths of despair I listened to a talk by Eckhart Tolle. He'd been planning to retire from teaching when he was invited by Oprah Winfrey to appear on her show. His book *The Power of Now* then sold millions of copies and spurred him on to keep sharing his wisdom. I cried at the fact that, even though he sounded like he had a virus, Eckhart was still doing what he could to try and make this world a better place. He talked about the Hindi notion that there are four basic states of human consciousness; awake, dreaming, having dreamless sleep and being in the 'now' where there is a wonderful sense of stillness when you just tune in to your breathing or sensory input, and your incessant chattering thoughts – and any problems – ease up for a while. So, my life's a disaster but yet here I am, in this moment, experiencing the snugness of my sofa and there's no suffering, just *being*.

It wasn't easy just 'being' as I clocked the worried faces of my family over Christmas. I stayed in my brother's lovely new home; it was fantastic to see him and his partner, Di, in a house he deserves after twenty-five years' hard slog on the shop floor of an engineering works. I'd always felt bad that I've had more opportunities than him; four years as a partying student, lots of travel and meaningful work which I love, but now he was happy and settled as my life went down the toilet, it felt kind of fair. Christmas day brought a fine feast – Di is a very skilled Jamie Oliver fan – and even teenage Pan took a break from her new smartphone to make a superb chocolate cheesecake. We had fun playing games but I caught my parents looking at me at different times throughout the day and imagined them thinking 'Can she really be that poorly...will this be our last Christmas with our daughter? Why can't we help her? What's dialysis and will it kill her?' Similarly, when I left, my brother's

goodbye was intense and he looked gutted. Again, it's one thing being ill myself but quite another making the people I love suffer. I need to go and watch some crap TV before my heart breaks or I finally go insane...

The end of 2010 saw me shopping for a dress for the 'glam' New Year's Eve party of Susie and her equally life-loving husband Nic. I was looking forward to guzzling champagne and getting as wrecked as I possibly could without going into a renal-failure-induced coma (although that was also quite appealing!) Whilst trying on dresses I was heart-broken; I'd been very blessed for over forty years with lean arms and had often worn vest-type dresses and tops – partly to distract from my tiny boobs. Now my left arm was like a sack of potatoes; half the size again of my right arm and the fistula vein had grown to an incredible four by two centimetres. All across my shoulder, throat and chest, vibrant blue veins stuck out, alongside masses of red, 'threadbare' veins in my chest and face; I looked as if I had the Lupus wolf rash I thought I'd got away with. I had to remind myself that I still had choices; *I can think Oh my God, I'm a freak or I can think I've been lucky not being too self-conscious about my body (apart from having no boobs, one fat leg and blue ankles) for most of my life...and so what I have an ugly arm? I'm still me!* How tragic that millions of us have trauma when we look in mirrors because we're comparing ourselves to the beautiful people chosen for TV (who often have stand-ins for shots of 'imperfect' body parts so they aren't even real) instead of valuing ourselves from the *inside*, where just a warm breeze can make us feel divine. To all of us who are mortified when we look in a mirror, let's say "Fuck it!" We're much more than what we look like. And see where my good looks got me – I often attracted vain, narcissistic men who wanted me as a trophy and now I'm on my own. If I'd had a fistula in my twenties I might have settled down with a good man who wasn't just interested in my looks.

2011 began well with Susie and Nic's party; I had great company with mischievous, blue beret and tights-clad Kazza, there was amazing fire-eating, jamming, singing, drumming and Susie, looking like a silver-spangled film star, played some fabulous tunes. Happily, I got to move my body a bit but my desire to get into a paralytic escape ended in my throwing up into the gutter after half a glass of champagne and I paid the price for a bit of dancing with days of exhaustion. I had to miss my planned sales shop with Maria but she brought me the electric blanket which had been on the top of my shopping list and we spent five minutes in disbelieving hysteria about preferring to get into a warm, cosy bed with a book than go out to have fun!

By mid-January my kidney function had dwindled to six percent. I had legs like jelly and a mind which struggled to formulate articulate sentences. I called the hospital to ask if I could have a planned renal appointment over the phone as I felt so ill but that "wasn't protocol and I had to be seen." I dragged myself from the sofa, donned my dressing gown and a furry blanket, and was taken to the bug-ravaged hospital by saucer-eyed rock goddess, Anne-Marie, who fired questions at my consultant and clarified points like a 'good 'un.' It was fabulous to have an articulate advocate on my side looking out for me and I'm smiling as I think about that day. It was such a gift to the usually self-sufficient me; I hope Anne-Marie felt equally bonded and not freaked out!

A few days later I was back at the hospital for scans of my limbs and to see the 'access team,' the specialist nurse, anaesthetist and surgeon who would be deciding where to try and make me another fistula. Maria drove for four hours to come with me; allowing her to do that was really hard but I'm so glad she did (ah, tears of gratitude are trickling again) because to get to the scan room meant us walking through the dialysis unit. It was nine-o-clock so maybe the thirty or so people strapped to the dialysis machines had got up really early and were just half asleep – but it was like a blooming mortuary. A few people were reading but most were sleeping, hanging their heads or staring into space. The atmosphere was *grim*. I was so overwhelmed that my legs literally buckled and as Maria led me out, I went into hyperventilation mode, gasping for breath. Maria just sat quietly with her arm round me until I got through the shock.

The scan showed my right side to have no line-damage and so, despite my terror of my writing and drawing hand going blue and numb, my right arm was to be chopped up. At the last minute, however, I asked the scanning doctor to check my left side again and on doing so, his view was that it didn't look too bad and we could still attempt dialysis on that side. This plan of action – to leave my right arm alone for now – was confirmed in an eight-o-clock phone call from the overworked but empathic vascular surgeon, Ms Knight. I was over the moon; my right hand was safe. I'm so grateful to Sergeant Major Ben-John, whose voice in the war and then as a tram driver got clearly heard, Sarah-Anne, who was brave enough to confront the woman in the village who kept her abortion needles up her chimney and was about to 'treat' my great-aunt, argumentative Arthur who spoke his truth in his thick Yorkshire tones and my parents for teaching me to stand up for myself. This could have been an even worse story if I hadn't asked for my left side to be scanned.

Feeling sad, I ran the last event of my community work job; a fund-raising cabaret. Public speaking terrifies me and I was grateful that down-to-earth Yorkshireman, puppy-eyed Pete, who was our joking town crier in the pantomime, co-hosted with me. We had fantastic acts from the community; Stylish Sarah, a parent from the toddler group, and her friend Helen harmonised like angels, 'the DJ girls' Alisha and Iqra danced their self-choreographed bhangra, warm grandad

Ron recited heartfelt poems, young man of colour, giant-sized G., who struggled with the school system, sang his heart out like the star that he is, Pete, Graham and Dee did a hilarious 'Two Ronnies' sketch about the English class system, George, with his guitar and Scottish tones, reduced me to tears with 'Redemption Song' and 'Tears of Heaven,' and university law students performed a funny, satirical sketch about a drunken judge and a legal system made by the rich to serve the rich. Kathy engaged the audience with sing-alongs and my friend Jude's husband, Martin the magician[49], travelled all the way from York to perform his amazing stunts of disbelief. The community centre's two ageing Celtic superstars, cleaner, Irene and reception volunteer, Mary, brought the ladies from the church on board and they put together a fantastic buffet. Like the street party and pantomime, I was overwhelmed by the beautiful result of individuals coming together and creating something so much bigger than the individual parts. Needless to say, I bawled my eyes out as I was thanked and presented with lovely leaving gifts at the end of the show. I was particularly gutted because I knew such jobs would be increasingly hard to come by as our government's 'austerity' policies slammed our communities.

The end of January brought another fistulaplasti. The nurse who admitted me said she'd "not been warned about me" simply because I told her that I didn't need my blood testing, having just established my INR (blood thickness) on my machine at home and, having washed my usual sleeveless red top, declined a traumatising, flap-open hospital gown. I refused both very politely but that was enough to get myself labelled as trouble. AAAGGGHHH!! Another nurse referred to the woman who was sharing my room – and dying of cancer – as "this one" as if she were an inanimate object. Luckily the gang who did

49. *www.martinwaring.co.uk*

my plasti, including a couple of really kind and gentle nurses and a mesmerizingly beautiful Anglo-Jamaican doctor, were compassionate and understood my apprehension. My doctor even engaged with me about the 'mind-body connection' and maintained that most doctors are now aware that stress and ways of thinking have a profound effect on the body.

In February 2011 I went for my renal appointment with the kind, spirited Dr Byrne so she could finally book me in for dialysis. Having learned to trust her, I was upset to learn that I'd be transferred to an unknown renal consultant once I started dialysis. Maybe that was part of the reason I bottled it. Completely. Despite knowing that I was desperate for dialysis, I scuttled out of her consulting room saying I'd be back in a fortnight! I then felt really scared; I hadn't realized that I really *couldn't* face starting dialysis and I poured my heart out to an understanding but worried nurse Claire and an anxious Maria. As usual, their empathic responses strengthened me and Maria persuaded me to arrange my first dialysis for when she was here at half term and could come with me. I wrote 'It's now a week until I start dialysis. My nerves are shredded and my angry outbursts are on the increase. All these years of 'awareness' later and I'm still covering my terror with rage. I've just lost it with a young nurse who phoned from the dialysis unit. She explained that I can't book my times to go on dialysis, which means I can't work it round my therapy clients as I'd hoped. I can't have a parking permit so it will cost me a fortune to park at the hospital (where a private company fleeces the patients, visitors and staff) and disability benefits for people on dialysis aren't guaranteed, despite how draining it is and the amount of time it takes up. In order to get trained up for having a machine at home I have to go for my dialysis in the evenings (when I'm often still working) which means I won't get home 'till about midnight. So much for my hope of having the energy, once I start dialysis, to resume a social life; three evenings per week at the hospital isn't what I had in mind!

On a different note, I had a strange but hopeful experience the other day. Last week, after fifteen years of no contact, I decided to write to Gerly, the beautiful Austrian I should possibly have married when I was twenty-one. I'm not sure what prompted me other than feeling like I had nothing to lose – I couldn't feel any worse than I did – or maybe wanting to find out how his life was going before I died. I'd written most of it and was planning to send it to his parents' house when I turned on my computer and there was an e-mail from him! "Long time no see. But now it's time." He'd quoted snippets from my website, including "Recovery is not a solitary journey; just because you can do it alone it doesn't mean you deserve to" and then another one about my work assessment process – "when you contact me I generally invite you for an appointment where you assess me as well as me assessing you…" Now how weird is that? I wrote back and told him a bit about my life – including some of my health stuff. I've not heard back yet and presume he's run a mile but the coincidence of him contacting me the same week as I write to him is so unbelievable that I've not yet given up on life and its amazing little twirls.

Which is just as well because I watched a pretty depressing video on YouTube today by Native American elders who are trying to share their wisdom in conferences across America. Did you know that there were about eight million Native Americans when we marauding Europeans stuck our greedy beaks in and annihilated seven million of them? If only we'd respected them and learned from their deep ecological wisdom, mutual care of one another and wise rituals (talking circles, rites of passage and the like) for processing hard emotions together! The elders were talking about their grave fears for the planet because of our incessant disregard for the environment. One soulful character was talking about the fact that profit-seeking corporations are now the major international decision-makers with 'puppet politicians' and called for a new paradigm based on a moral rather than economic code. Oh if only we'd each take responsibility – and appreciate that power, as the 'demand' part of the economic 'supply and demand model' lies with us! If only we'd face the reality of our wilting world rather than blocking it out with our hyperactivity, screens and mindless shopping (I include myself in this; I still have a way to go in my use of the TV as an escapist drug and selfish habits of consumption.)

I wonder if our popular denial of death is tied to our rampant disregard for the future of our planet and we just can't face the reality and pain of it without more emotional support from one another. We'd better get hugging more! And, I guess, seeking out people of a like mind who we can connect and share ideas and emotional support with.

The BBC news today reported on UK banks scamming their corporation tax (despite their *massive* £850 billion tax-payer bail-out in 2008/9) and demonstrations in the UK against the demolition of our public sector, pensions and welfare system. I used to worry that I was a bit of a naïve, overly dramatic conspiracy theorist but now the 'neoliberal elite's' disgusting self-interest is no longer disguised. There's talk of our government trying to restrict human rights, demonstrations and union activity; it seems that our UK democracy's under some threat. Well, we're living in very interesting times, eh? It feels to me like we're in the middle of *The Lord of the Rings*; the power and money-obsessed orks are banging the boardroom tables and trampling down the earth as they scream for more and more profit. But the elves are getting wise and, knowing that endless consuming is the road to extinction are, all across the world, calling for a halt to the madness.

Sending you a hopeful smile. xxx

Chapter 23
Torture

"Having courage does not mean that we are unafraid. Having courage and showing courage means we face our fears. We are able to say "I have fallen but I will get up."

Maya Angelou

On the 19th February 2011 I wrote 'I started kidney dialysis today. The dialysis unit is a big, busy, open-plan room with lots of sinks, bins and trolleys holding 'kit' such as blood bottles, syringes, saline and swabs. A square nurses' station decked with computers and files – and housing a cramped receptionist – sits in the centre. The patients, aged from eighteen, sit about ten feet apart in wipe-able recliner chairs. They're attached via needles in their arms (mostly) or legs (some) or lines sticking out of their chests (a few) to a system of plastic tubing which is wound round the front of a four feet tall and two feet wide dialysis machine and connected to either ends of a foot-long glass tube (the 'kidney') which is clipped to the machine. The gentle whirring of the machines made me think of giant washing machines but I had no thoughts to sum up the sight of blood being sucked out of people' bodies and sent round the see-through tubing – there was just a sick feeling deep in my gut. I was about to spend three times a week, possibly for the rest of my life, in a torture chamber.

As I looked around in silent horror, I was greeted by a cheery, middle-aged nurse with a crew-cut and quickly directed to my chair. As he attempted to humour me out of my catatonic grimace (it failed) his female colleague assured me that he was their best 'needler' and not to worry. There was no time for worry; before I knew it I was having a nail-sized needle rammed into my arm, closely followed by a second. The pain was acute despite the surreal distraction of being told about the routine hepatitis, MRSA and HIV blood tests that I'd need to have "Though the risk of being infected by a machine is only minimal." Just as the blood began to leave my body and snake its way up the plastic lines, the machine started screaming, Mr skin-head started cursing and my bicep started feeling like it was going to explode. It transpired that I'd had 'a blow;' a needle had gone straight through my vein and caused a huge bleed in my arm. Given the level of agony I was in, I couldn't believe that the only painkillers they could give me were Paracetamol; anything stronger had to be prescribed by a doctor but there were none on the unit. Now, despite my massively toxic blood, I have to wait a week to try dialysis again. I think part of me's so used to things going wrong that this feels almost normal – but the other part's frozen stiff.

Bloody hell....

Not too successfully, I'm trying not to feel sorry for myself because I'm only one of about four hundred adults – plus the poor children on a separate unit – who go for dialysis in my city alone. Many are vulnerable older people who have to be ready to be picked up by hospital transport *two hours* before their dialysis time and then afterwards have to wait for what can be hours in the draughty, mind-numbing waiting room. I saw many of their weary, drawn faces today. I also saw, only briefly because I didn't want to gawp, a fragile, scrawny scrap of a frightened-eyed man with learning difficulties having dialysis – ah, there was my pathway to my pain; now I'm crying like a baby. (I can still cry for others easier than for myself.) Depressingly, a bubbly, blonde, motherly nurse, Tina, who gave me a *much* appreciated hug as I left the unit, told me that the funding for research into kidney failure doesn't come anywhere near the money put into devising new slimming pills and 'beauty products.' Also, despite one in ten people suffering from some renal failure at some point in their lives, because the client group's largely older or vulnerable, there isn't the high profile charitable status of illnesses such as cancer. And of course both kidney and cancer research is minimal compared to military and space research which employs a large chunk of our most skilled scientists and engineers. Mmm. I don't know what else to say. I think I need to read another of Grandad's poems...'

Faith and Hope

Sometimes there's a path we've to travel
that leads from the valley of doom,
when your only companions are faith and hope
to lead you out of the gloom.

For the hand that was there to help you
when you stumbled on life's road,
on this path cannot help you
nor yet carry part of your load.

It's a path that's rough but well-trodden
there's no fear of losing your way;
if you keep your companions beside you
they'll lead you to the light of day.

Sometimes you'll think hope has left you
and feel that you've got to give in
but faith will be there helping you on,
giving you courage to win.

And then when you reach the end,
out to the blue sky and sun,
you'll know that without these companions,
without them you couldn't have won.

Arthur Downs

A week later I'd perked up a bit: 'Well I've just had a week off my therapy work and stared at walls, pottered around my garden (one-armed digging is possible) had a massage, a hair trim, a few hot, sob-filled baths, some soothing meditations and a few seriously weepy movies. I feel so lucky that I've had the time to just 'be' and work through some of my fear and grief. I cannot do a thing about my situation except take care of myself and allow myself to feel what I feel in order to come through it. Also, to take note of the good moments, like when I opened a letter from Dr Byrne, who'd taken the time to let me know that a recent 'treadmill test' (which involved jogging whilst wired up and was blooming exhausting) showed my heart to be well enough for her to request that I go on the transplant list. The ultimate decision will be made by a multidisciplinary team, some who I don't know or know me. My life's in the hands a bunch of strangers again.

My second 'pick-me-up' came from a meeting with a new group of people. Anne-Marie, cheery, deep as the ocean, rock goddess who'd been a great advocate when she accompanied me to a renal appointment, knew a bunch of us from our various community work jobs and brought us together with a view to seeing if we could do something positive. I took an immediate liking to giant body and brained Darran, beautiful, meditating Mandy, anarchistic, funny, doting father of two adopted lads with learning difficulties, Jeff, fiery and deeply spiritual community grants allocator Nina, witty, big-grinned, marathon-running Andy and energetic, elfish, Woodlands Trust manager Kaye. We called ourselves 'In Kind,' developed the strapline 'Celebrating Human Kindness' and, following much discussion, focused on Darran's information about the International Charter for Compassion. With the intention of trying to make the 'golden rule' of 'treating others how you'd like to be treated' central to policy-making, Sydney, Lahore, Louisville, Los Angeles and about eighty other cities around the world had signed up to the Charter. Botswana had signed up the whole country and Cornwall and California the county and state. I've been on the internet today researching compassion, acts of kindness, wellbeing and happiness in preparation for writing to the leader of our local council to propose that we make our city into a 'City of Compassion'. There is so much *scientific* evidence out there now which, backing up the 'real' Darwin, shows that though we can be competitive and hostile, especially when we feel under attack and are on the defensive, we're also deeply empathic and cooperative by nature.

I was very excited when I heard a TED talk by Ramachadran[50] about neuroscience's revelation that we have 'mirror neurons' in our brains which allow us to *feel* what other people are experiencing. As we watch somebody doing something, say painting, our own mirror neurons are activated (as evidenced by brain scans) as if *we* were painting. Physiotherapists are now getting people who have had strokes but can't lift their limbs to simply watch other people lifting theirs and they're finding this helps to repair people's damaged brains as if they were lifting their own arms. As we watch people on TV being hurt, we cringe, our hearts start pounding, our blood pressure

---

50. See https://brainobserver.com/mirror-neurons/

goes up, muscles tense, guts weaken etc as we're flooded with cortisol and adrenaline – be careful what you're watching! When someone's looking sad we often feel sad, we yawn when others yawn and often feel elated – or cry – when we see acts of kindness and connection. We're *biologically* connected!

I also beamed with excitement when I read that in the same way that being touched and performing, witnessing or being the recipient of kindness releases oxytocin (the fabulous happiness, compassion and good health promoting hormone) simply *thinking* loving thoughts also releases it. On the insides of our blood vessels are oxytocin receptors and when the oxytocin connects here we release nitric acid. Nitric acid dilates our blood vessels, lowering blood pressure and *physically* protecting our hearts.[51] In other words, *we're hard-wired for kindness, communal living and co-operation, not competing and killing!* We're generally happy when others are happy! We're sad and no doubt inviting cardiovascular disease and a weakened immune system when we see our vulnerable and abused youngsters and traumatised soldiers living on our streets. Apparently a big proportion of our homeless people are ex-servicemen with issues such as Post-Traumatic Stress Disorder and *many* troops have killed themselves. In his fantastic book "Human Kind: A Hopeful History," Rutger Bregman[52] notes that ninety percent of the 27,574 muskets found after the Battle of Gettysburg in the American Civil War were still loaded and that half the veterans of the Second World War had not killed anybody (just like many trench soldiers fired over enemy heads) and most fighter pilots had not shot down any planes – or even tried to! He talks about the 1914 Christmas armistice in the trenches when thousands of German and Allied troops sang carols together then met on no-man's land to swap gifts and addresses,

---

51. David R Hamilton's I Heart Me book is very informative on the subject of oxytocin

52. See bibliography p. 436. I seriously recommend buying this book

take photos and play football – and in doing so realised that the enemy weren't the ruthless tyrants of their media's propaganda but just like them. The war may have ended at this point if distant commanders hadn't ordered more horrific bloodshed (at gunpoint). Another interesting fact discovered in the Second World War was that the Germans – like most troops – fought to the death to support their peers, not because of their leaders' ideology. (German commanders actually held battered groups of soldiers back from the front lines until new friendships had been established.) We're most strongly motivated by love, not hate and much prefer using drones to drop bombs than see our 'targets' directly. We're not designed to hurt each other!

Psychology in the last century tended to focus on what makes us dysfunctional ('neuropathology') such as Stanley Milgram's famous Electric Shock Experiment at Yale (where volunteers electrocuted peers with an experimenter's encouragement) and Philip Zimbardo's grim Stanford Prison Experiment (which had to be stopped because the pretend guards were so violent). The media – and the public – pounced on these (and other alleged confirmations of our dastardly natures) – as I did at poly – but it turns out that both experiments were deeply flawed (many of the 'shockers' guessed the shocks weren't real, for example, and just wanted to help the experimenter rather than feeling coerced and the 'guards' were told the experiment needed them to be abusive)[53]. It's taken us a while to stop believing in William Golding's *Lord of the Flies* but there's now a massive amount of research being done ('positive psychology') about how cooperative we – and children – actually are (Bregman tells us about a group of boys marooned on a Pacific island for over a year who got along brilliantly) and what makes us happy. Most research concludes that happiness is found in having a strong sense of belonging, giving to others,

53. Bregman 2020

having a connection to nature, having a purpose and meaning in our lives and experiencing love and connection with others (including pets.) Happiness hasn't been found in having loads of money, power, plastic surgery or the latest phone.[54] I've just heard on Radio 4 of a recent study of young people who were asked what they'd prefer to give up, their i-Pads, smartphones or sense of taste...yup...they'd prefer to give up their taste-buds! How sad is that? But I guess such is their need for connection!'

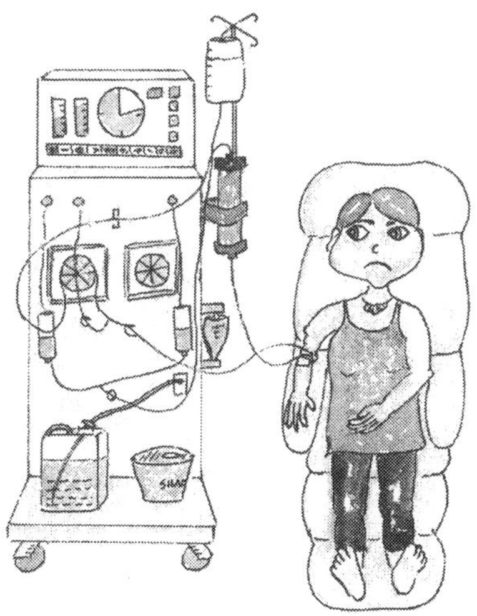

On the 14th March 2011, with my arm still deeply bruised from my 'blow,' I had my first successful kidney dialysis. I wrote 'I should be grateful that my fistula worked and I'm heading in the right direction but I still feel in shock six hours later. I was painfully connected to the machine by a kind and empathic nurse who told me she had nightmares about being on dialysis but then I was given a book about renal failure and just left to it. I could see that the nurses were busy but couldn't believe

54 Typical articles can be found at https://psychcentral.com/lib/what-makes-us-happy/, https://medium.com/@MaxWeigand/the-science-of-happiness-what-actually-makes-us-happy-78edcc9bdd58

that I received no more emotional support even though my heart was screaming for more human contact and reassurance. When I was freed from the machine (which hurt nearly as much as having the needles put in) after an introductory two hours, I had a banging heart, wobbly legs and felt slightly breathless, shaky and blurry-eyed. Following a snooze in my new but not so lovely hammock I still feel unsteady and now understand why half the people on the dialysis unit – who usually have *four* hours of dialysis – look like slumped waxworks.

My shaking may be partly due to what I read in that damned book. Apparently dialysis only does *five* percent of what your kidneys do! There I was thinking that I might be going to play tennis again but it turns out that I have to go through all this pain (I still can't fully straighten my needled arm) trauma and life-restriction just to maintain a not quite fatal state of being! I was aware that, with defunct kidneys, you have to avoid salt (because it makes you thirsty) and acidic foods and I knew your kidneys affected the body's stress response; I can't ignore my whooshes of adrenalin and cortisol which can take a while to get balanced by the seemingly struggling 'parasympathetic' part of my nervous system. I knew that our kidneys cleanse us of the thousands of toxins (poisons) that we accumulate on a daily basis but learned that it isn't clear which of the tens of thousands of different substances in the blood are toxic to us. Urea and creatinine are used as general indicators of toxicity levels. Used up protein (amino acids) is processed by the liver and made into urea. This then moves on to the kidneys (along with toxins and excess fluid) to be eliminated (via the bladder) in urine, usually about two litres a day. Creatinine is produced in the muscles when they're used and isn't actually poisonous in itself but once normal levels rise above 70 to 120 micromoles (whatever *they* are) per litre, you know you're in a lot of renal trouble. Mine are currently 720 and the urea in my blood is over 30 mill moles (I think that was the term) per litre and should be between 3.3 and 3.7.

My kidney book informed me that fluid generally makes up about 60 percent of men's bodies and 55 percent of women's, so the kidney's fluid balance role is crucial. Too much fluid leads to bloating, high blood pressure and strain on the heart and, if it goes to your lungs, potentially fatal 'pulmonary oedema' – basically drowning (as I experienced when I was 'being sick' from my lungs in 1999.) Once you start dialysis, your remaining kidney function often grinds to a halt so you may stop peeing altogether and have to restrict your fluid intake to a maximum of a litre a day – which includes gravy, ice-cream, custard and the like. Dialysis is designed to take off the excess fluid you're carrying but it's hard to get the balance right; you weigh yourself to estimate how much fluid you have to take off but of course your weight can fluctuate massively with what you eat and sweat and you can easily get dehydrated on dialysis – which lowers blood pressure and results in weakness and even keeling over – or not take enough fluid off and remain breathless, exhausted and at risk of heart failure.

High blood pressure, which is a third side-effect of renal failure, irrespective of fluid issues (though it's not clear what causes it to rise) can mash up the kidneys still further and put huge strain on your heart, increasing the risk of strokes and heart attacks. *Fuck!*

A fourth mega impact of renal failure, which I knew all about, is anaemia. The kidneys send off a chemical to your bone marrow telling it how many blood cells to produce but in renal failure this system fails and your red blood cells plummet. Red blood cells contain haemoglobin which not only carry oxygen around the body but also combine with nutrients to give you energy so without enough haemoglobin you can get exhausted, short of breath, off your food, irritable and unable to think clearly. Your haemoglobin (HB) should be 11.5 to 17 grams per decilitre. Mine is currently 8.5. I reckon that's some justification for falling asleep whenever I sit down!

Fifthly (yes, the list goes on), your kidneys produce bicarbonates which maintain a healthy PH balance in your blood. Without this your body can get too acidic which has a knock-on effect on a catalogue of metabolic processes including the regulation of chemicals such as calcium, phosphates and potassium. Too little calcium and you can get bone disease or osteoporosis; too much calcium and your arteries can get calcified and blocked. A build-up of phosphates results in horrendous itching (which currently drives me crazy.) Potassium's integral to maintaining nerve and muscle health; too much and the electrical impulses to your heart can be affected, resulting in heart attacks! Low potassium levels can also be fatal. *Fuck, fuck and more fuck!*

And that's what I've learned so far and I'm only on page twenty-six of the book 'Kidney Failure explained.'[55] I also read that when you have stage five renal failure death can be imminent within weeks without dialysis, so I literally have been at death's door for months. Phew... and I can't even eat chocolate to fill up my gaping void inside as it's full of potentially lethal phosphates!

Okay, one more moan and I might feel better... I had an e-mail from Gerly yesterday. He talked about how much turmoil our contact has brought up for him and asked if he could come and visit me. It turns out however that he's been with somebody for fifteen years and has two children and they all live in the middle of nowhere in their new home. He said he wanted to see me without talking on the phone or e-mailing, which makes me conclude that his partner doesn't know about his desire to meet up. So much for the mega coincidence of Gerly and me contacting one another within a week and my faint hope that maybe I was going to get a heart-warming break! There's no way I want to see him if he's got a family, not just because that's not right (the golden rule and all that) but because I

55. See bibliography p.437

don't want to face the possibility that he really *is* the love of my life and then have to wave him off back to them. Mmm... what meaning can I glean from this coincidence? Maybe that it's time for me to wipe my entire slate clean, stop dreaming about the past, making Gerly into 'the one that got away' and get on with finding myself a decent bloke who doesn't look like a Greek god, like Gerly, but has a good heart. Or at the very least getting on with my life without regret now I know Gerly's not perfect; I'm not impressed by his initial portrayal of being single or apparent willingness to betray his partner. Not marrying him has always been a regret, which goes to show that it's the things we *don't* do that can haunt us the most, but maybe I made the right call. Or maybe our exchange was about him needing to know I was a wreck so he could stop thinking about the one that got away and get over my awful rejection of him. It felt kind of good to be able to tell him he'd had a lucky escape!

Well then. That's that. I'm on kidney dialysis – alongside the other sixty thousand or so people in the UK who are on dialysis and the twenty people who get diagnosed with degrees of kidney failure every day. And today millions of people will die from heart disease, cancer, car accidents, racist attacks, starvation, dirty water poisoning and a thousand other horrendous deaths. Thousands of people are lying dead or sitting in shock in Japan following a devastating earthquake and tsunami which has damaged a nuclear reactor. What's dialysis compared to seeing your family crushed to death, looking at piles of rubble which used to be your home or waiting to be slowly killed by leaking radiation? *Get a grip, Jaynie, get a grip...who said life was easy?*

Just as a little aside whilst we're on the subject; did you know that we've had many (Fritjov Capra suggests about thirty) near-catastrophic nuclear accidents since the 1950's? It was 'classified information' until recently of course and a typical example of what our 'democracy' keeps quiet. I recently saw one such incident from 1951 (declassified after fifty years) reported in the Independent newspaper. I was agog that the report covered a few inches on the inside pages rather than it being headline news; an H-bomb had fallen from a B52 bomber over farmland in the USA and four out of five safety procedures had failed. Luckily (and that's an understatement) two wires didn't connect. If the Hiroshima bomb's power measured 0.01, this baby was 3.8! Let us be grateful we're alive and well!' Go, CND,[56] go!

A week after starting dialysis I found out that I'd been approved for the transplant list. I wasn't over-excited, given the slim chance of a transplant because of all the antibodies I've collected from blood transfusions, but I was pleased that my body was in good enough shape to get on the list and at least there was a glimmer of hope. Life expectancy – especially with a transplant from a 'live donor'- is much better than being on dialysis. Then I went to one of the hospital's 'Introduction to Kidney Transplants' evenings.

56. *The Campaign for Nuclear Disarmament*

Thankfully Kirsty came with me, which cut my trauma down by at least half, but it was still pretty bad. From what I remember a fifth of transplants fail, some within days, some after months or a few years. Several patients who'd had successful transplants were there and talked about their new leases of life but they also threw in a few little side-lines. For example, the anti-rejection drugs you have to take not only suppress your immune system, often make you look like a chipmunk and leave you vulnerable to infections, lymphomas and the like, they can also cause eye cataracts and skin cancer, so you can't go in the sun. A lean, wide-eyed man told us about his six bouts of skin cancer whilst his big, cheery mate told us about his gums growing over his teeth and having to have them burnt off with liquid nitrogen! A third, slightly manic chap brought home the reality of potential phosphate damage with his "I had to have fourteen X-rays because my calcium was so depleted they could hardly see my bones." A pretty, red-haired woman about my age talked about being on her third transplant...and these were *success* stories! *Mmm. Where's my teddy?*

I needed a *collection* of teddies after my first evening session on dialysis. I told the nurses who connected me up (chatting to each other over my head) how traumatized I was feeling and they called me 'darling' and acknowledged that it was a scary thing to have to do and how they'd hate it – and then left me completely alone for the next four hours. I appreciate that they were busy, but, despite walking straight past me not one of them asked how I was doing. My faith in them wasn't improved when I was almost given somebody else's medication (which I'm allergic to) but not given the blood results I asked for. I wrote 'I'm absolutely bloody terrified. They can stick their patronizing 'darlings' that are said without real feeling. I don't know if I've ever felt more lonely and despairing in my life than I did tonight as I watched the second hand on the clock take an hour to move five minutes. Again, I was absolutely screaming internally for just a bit of *human contact!* Instead, towards the end of my session, two young nurses bounced over to ask me for money towards some collection or other. I told them "No you can stick your bloody pound when none of you can even be arsed to speak to me!" They quickly scuttled away, spreading the word that I was a scary nutter, no doubt.

I did have a bit of, albeit voice-challenging contact (we were competing with the whirring sound of the machines) with the young, blonde, flowy-haired mermaid woman, D, who was in the chair nearest to me. She'd had kidney failure since being a child and had been given two transplants but both had failed; she was waiting for a third. When a nurse came over, the mermaid told her that the previous week she'd been an inpatient, "And it was horrible on the ward because I was with a load of women who had all just had babies." The nurse, who would have known that Ms Mermaid will struggle to have children, attempted to make her feel better by saying "Oh what would you want one of them for?" She then looked up at me and her first words to me in four hours were, "You wouldn't want one of them would you?" I doubt the nurse knew my history but as you can imagine I wasn't impressed and when she came to take me off the machine I didn't hold back on pointing out her insensitivity. She said she'd been having a joke. I told her she wasn't funny. My anger then waned and I cried like a baby as I told her how terrible it was being left alone all night. She apologized. I acknowledged her stress and we ended up having a reasonable chat about our mutual burdens. I tend not to hold grudges once I've said my bit. I hope she doesn't either, given how totally dependent I am on her and her peers.

The young mermaid, a beautiful woman with big blue eyes, smooth, tanned skin and big floppy, untied boots, was absolutely inspiring; she was 'trained up' and went through the clinical process of doing all her own dialysis, including plugging herself in, taking herself off and cleaning the machine. It was amazing – and I felt like I was about ninety-three million miles away (like the sun – thanks for that random fact, space-mad dad) from being able to do that myself.

I'm sitting here now, at nearly midnight, with my heart pounding and my arm, head and belly hurting, wondering if this is worth it; I'm not sure I want to live with this level of fear and pain. I feel absolutely overwhelmed and out of control. I'm very grateful that I'm not as young as the mermaid going through this, but it's bloody crap all the same. I'm even scared of eating anything but bread sticks because I don't want to suck the calcium out of my bones or give myself a heart attack! If I can't even eat good food (phosphates and potassium are abundant in most healthy foods) and am too knackered to exercise, then what can I do? AAAGGGHHH! Alongside my little doggie's faithful companionship, my friends, family and clients, a big thing that's keeping me from opening my tablet drawer and eating the lot is the thought of finishing this book and doing the little bit that I can to let you and others know about dialysis and maybe make things easier for young women like the mermaid. God, please help me to make this nightmare into a positive thing. Right; I need an Alfie cuddle…night night xx'

My next dialysis session was a bit better, despite the fact that I learned from 'Mr best needler,' Richard, that each session is "so aggressive on your body, especially your heart, that it's like running a marathon." That explains why I'm starving but collapse into a sleepy heap the minute I get home, why I can, three hours post-machine, still feel my heart banging and why many older patients end up in wheelchairs within a couple of years; their hearts are knackered. Apparently it's the speed with which you're dialysed and the fluid sucked out of your blood, which has to be quickly replaced by tissue fluid, that does the damage; "Ideally you'd dialyse over a much longer period but we don't have the resources for that." The improved session was, of course, due to some human contact. Richard made it clear that he understood my fear and we chatted about growing vegetables, so I have a great new advisor for my veg patch! I also spent half an hour with Bruno, a sparkly, Italian dietician (with kind brown eyes like my grandad) who gave me good news about my new diet. "A bit of what you fancy" is fine occasionally, even if it's on the potassium and phosphate-heavy 'restricted' list (especially if I'm about to dialyse) but I'll still have to mostly avoid crisps, chocolate, bananas, tomatoes, mushrooms, avocados, seafood, yoghurt, fruit (apart from apples and pears), fruit juice, un-boiled potatoes (no more jacket potatoes or curry and chips!) vegetables (which have to be boiled to death) nuts, dried fruit and salted crackers..... (frigging hell.) I've got to remember that there's still a lot I can eat and Bruno used to be a cook so I can pick his brain and develop my new enthusiasm for cooking which came from buying a renal diet cookbook last week.

As the weeks went by, life went on, despite some *massively* painful, post-dialysis 'whole torso and kidney cum bottom – pulsating' reactions (which prompted scary heart tests but got me no *much* needed pain killers or a diagnosis), being cold or freaked out by others' suffering on the unit and having nightmares about being lost or attacked. Some friends went quiet and as usual my default setting told me it was because I was so flawed, but I was able to notice what my critical mind was saying and remind myself that they had busy lives and were probably feeling overwhelm, powerlessness and existential angst. Thankfully those friends who did phone and visit kept me afloat – as did crying when I needed to. Thoughtful Kirsty bought me a beautiful bamboo table to put across my lap whilst on the machine; it fits perfectly into the unit's chairs and has set me up for my 'new career' in writing. I met Andy, the gentle ex-RAF home dialysis trainer, who seemed kind, sensitive and competent and I met with the perky, swinging haired renal counsellor, Emma. She reassured me that not everybody goes downhill on dialysis and if I take good care of myself I may be okay for years. She also explained how there are dialysis units all over Europe (including Tenerife for winter sun) and generally you just book in a few months ahead (if they have spaces). She even recommended a company that will insure dialysis patients so I may be able to go on holiday with insurance! I also met a bright and bubbly woman on the unit who worked as a teaching assistant, had been on dialysis for twenty years and reassured me that, "You just get used to it."

By about my tenth dialysis I started to feel a bit better, managing to get up the hill at my local park again and my headaches and phosphate itching eased off. My post-dialysis banging heart concerned me but I was assured by Andy that when I got round to dialysing at home (which still seemed a distant dream) this would put less pressure on my heart. In the meantime, for the first time in my life (apart from when I was in hospital) I began to learn to relax and not push myself to 'do.' I didn't take on any new clients and enjoyed having space for *me* without feeling guilty. I didn't worry too much about money; my frugal roots kept me in check and I already had everything I needed; a gorgeous dog, campervan, stereo, boots and Birkenstocks, sarongs and jumpers, a phone, SLE camera, laptop, piano, paints, a good spade, a selection of seeds, lots of books, an electric blanket and a recliner settee. What else did I need?

In my new, more leisurely routine, I read *The Turning Point*, Fritjof Capra's third book. It's about the Western scientific paradigm which is, in his and my opinion, the root of our cultural madness; the obsession with 'development' and continuous growth which has contributed to profit-seeking greed, raging inequality, ecological devastation, detached, biomedical medicine and the threat of nuclear annihilation. Fritjof argues that we need to develop a bit more 'yin;' the feminine, the intuitive, the caring side of our natures rather than being ruled by the 'yang' values of aggressive domination, power and competition. Fritjof's conclusion was that if we don't rethink our fundamental values we're done for. Go Fritjof!

I'm holding on to a shred of optimism for us humans, partly because of my lived experience. I used to be totally ruled by my fragile ego and did all that I could to appear attractive, cool, 'successful' and pleasing to others. I used to live in fear and paranoia; *Should I have said that? I need a new car and more money in the bank. Do they like me? Am I stupid, bad, ugly, selfish, sinful?* I used to give others an equally hard time, judging them by my own critical standards so I didn't feel so bad about myself. As I've learned to be more gentle on myself, my critical self is much quieter and I mostly feel tolerant and kind-hearted. Things *can* change. The world *can* change! Don't get me wrong, I still have my moments of being bitter and judgemental but more and more I'm recognizing that I only get venomous when I feel scared or upset and I absolutely believe that's a process at the core of all of us – fear pushing us into our highly cautious, 'negatively biased,' defensive, attacking 'reptile brains.' This fear is, of course, intensified by a lack of connection. Let's connect more!

A few months into dialysis, I went on a therapy training day with Richard Bowlby, son of John, the original 'Attachment Theory' researcher. He said it's estimated from recent research that nearly half of us don't experience very secure early attachments and have a frightened, wounded kid 'inside,' especially those of us whose parents and grandparents were massively scarred by two World Wars and received ridiculous advice about 'sparing the rod and spoiling the child,' not having too much eye contact with babies ('back in the day' it was seen as them trying to be manipulative) and leaving children to cry alone at the bottom of the garden! The workshop increased my self-compassion and also my compassion for my stressed out dialysis nurses. *Oh how I feel that I'm growing despite my aggressive 'reptile' moments when my tongue can lash out or my scared brain think bad thoughts about people. Oh thank you, universe that I'm understanding how damaging poor early attachments are and how most of us struggle with just being human and that I'm learning to give myself – and others – a break and chill out a bit!'*

Chapter 24
Can Anybody Hear Me?

"Character cannot be developed in ease and quiet. Only through experience of trial and suffering can the soul be strengthened, ambition inspired, and success achieved."

Helen Keller

Well I wrote a lot to you after starting dialysis in 2011, sharing the despair with you that I didn't want to upset my friends and family with (mostly about being so battered by it) but I'm having to massively edit or this book will be longer than 'War and Peace'! Though I was feeling generally stronger after about three months on dialysis, I remained anaemic (partly because the machine lines and 'kidney' keep some of your blood after each dialysis) and I kept getting temperatures on the machine. I thought my fevers were stress-related but the medics insisted on taking away more of my blood to test it for bugs. They never found any. Having got my 'phosphate itching' down it was very frustrating that I often itched in response to the machines' chemicals, sometimes well into the night, as if my ability to sleep wasn't bad enough! Then I got a headache. It started with me getting up one day and being blinded by the sunlight. I felt exhausted and sick, drew my curtains, cancelled my therapy clients and curled into a ball on my new, well timed, recliner sofa. I'd not had a migraine before but presumed that's what it must be. As the days passed my headache got no better and I had to ask friends to take Alfie for walks and get taxis to dialysis, wearing my pyjamas mostly because I felt too weak to get dressed. I kept asking the nurses on the unit if they'd bleep a doctor because my head was *really* killing me. Eventually I got to see a junior doctor but despite my tearful protestations, he didn't seem overly concerned that my HB had plummeted down to 8.9 (12 and over is normal) and I had the energy of a dying sloth. When he recommended Paracetemol, my feeling that I was in a totally powerless nightmare intensified.

By this time my new renal consultant, Dr T. had gone on maternity leave so nobody had personal responsibility for me and I was plummeting 'through the cracks.' After *two weeks* of agony and unsuccessful pleas with unfamiliar junior doctors, I was called into hospital with a "life-threateningly low" platelet count of sixteen. You can easily start to bleed to death when your count drops below twenty. I wailed out loud as I packed my bags, glad that someone was finally taking some action but terrified that this was the beginning of another nightmare. Thankfully, Claire was free and, understanding my semi-hysteria, calmly helped me from the sofa, gave me a long, soothing hug and drove me to the hospital. Unbelievably, the random doctor who examined me, though compassionate, still didn't investigate my headache. Because I'd stopped being sick and my platelet count had gone up a little by the next day, he sent me home. Feeling a bit better, I was grateful to be out of hospital but within two days I was back in migraine agony, unable to open my eyes, stay upright or keep down food or fluid. I felt so ill that I actually asked my mum to come and stay with me. My brother drove her down and I have lovely memories of him tenderly rubbing my back in an attempt to ease my gut pain (a stress blockage no doubt) and my mum tenderly rubbing my massively sore neck; it turns out she's a natural masseur.

When my brother came to collect my mum a few days later I was lucky that Maria came to my rescue again. All five foot two of her virtually carried me into the hospital for dialysis, demanded that I see a doctor as "this headache just wasn't normal" (she was fobbed off) and then stayed the night with me. At four in the morning she cleaned up my sick, held my glass as I sipped water and then sat in bed with me as we both cried with worry that my luck may've finally run out; another grim, but on reflection, beautiful and memorable moment.

When Maria had to go home to her children my parents, in their seventies, came once more to look after their sickly daughter. I felt so bad that it should have been me looking after them at this point in our lives and couldn't bear it when they looked at me through fearful eyes. As usual they showed their love by being practical; my dad fixed my gate and pulled up every weed from my patio and my mum manically dusted and made me cups of soup - but little stayed down. A few days later I was bed-bound, sick every time I tried to lift my head from the pillow and feeling so close to death that this fear finally outweighed my terror of going back into hospital – and abandoning Alfie again. I asked my mum to call an ambulance. My legs were useless by now and I had to be carried downstairs in a wheelchair by the poor paramedics. In the Accident and Emergency department I was given a CAT scan which revealed that I'd had a bleed in my head.

Fortunately, I was given a quiet side room on a renal ward with a friendly staff team, led by the hyper but warm, funny and competent sister, Sharon, whose creatively tied-up hair and gorgeous, friendly face I recalled from previous admissions. She helped to soothe my profound tachycardia (my heart was ready for bursting) and by the next day I wrote 'What a difference a day can make! I'm sitting in the sunshine in a secluded courtyard next to the ward with some iced juice and have the lovely feeling of peace which is becoming more and more familiar to me. Me and this blackbird hopping alongside me are one. I'm upset that I've had to ask my fellow therapist, Jez, to finally tell my therapy clients (who I've been cancelling week by week for the last month) that I don't know when I'll be back to work. Scarily I've given them the numbers of other therapists should they feel the need...that was hard. I want to be there for my clients, not worrying them! I don't know if my livelihood's down the drain or whether I'll make it to a planned festival next weekend with petite, big-booted, black and white bobbed Marie but I'm flooded with gratitude that I'm still here. I'm also angry (and scared) that I wasn't heard by the medics when I really needed it, after being given so many pills, x-rays and needles over the years when I didn't want them.'

I lost my lovely side-room after a few days but was moved to a relatively quiet ward where, in the bed opposite was the beautiful, blonde 'mermaid' who I'd met on dialysis. As we chatted I learnt that she was twenty-eight, feisty, and absolutely covered in fistula and line scars. She currently had a blocked line and couldn't dialyse, was full of painful fluid and toxins *and* had been to a 'Take That' concert in Manchester the night before! When she was taken down into the dark bowels of the hospital to have another hole cut in her young body I cried at the immensity of her suffering and spirit.

I was very grateful that familiar Dr Byrne (whose giant brain understood all my haematological complications) was around when I took another massive nose-dive; the familiar 'can't lift my head from the pillow' feeling was back. After another scan Dr Byrne, looking into my eyes and rubbing my hand from my bedside, gently told me the good news; the swelling around the original bleed in the back of my head had gone down. The bad news was that I had another small bleed in the top of my head, possibly because the clotting power of the blood can reduce with kidney failure – or maybe due to an infection or a possible flare of my antiphospholipid syndrome. I wondered if there was any relation to being whacked on my head by the drip machine; that was much more comfortable a thought than *yet* another 'reason unknown.'

Dr Byrne's care and sensitivity made it possible for me to ask her if I was likely to die. Looking into my eyes she reassured me that my bleeds were 'subdural' which meant they weren't in my brain but in the lining between my brain and skull and treatable by neurosurgery if necessary. The small agreement that Dr Byrne would tell me if things were heading in a fatal direction meant the world to me; she understood my need for a good death surrounded by my loved ones, should it come to that.

When my friends came to the hospital, it was as usual both beautiful and difficult; the worry on their faces was hard to see. Trisha went flying off to buy sunglasses to keep out the blinding light, Jez held my hand in my scan, Claire rubbed my feet, Carol brought Jelly Babies and stroked my sore head 'till I went to sleep and Kirsty and Matt brought their usual love, positivity and Alfie-visits. How blessed? I also felt blessed when, after another post-dialysis, agonizing, 'pulsating body' episode I'd shouted at a nurse, Amy, for the delay in getting me painkillers but her compassion brought her back to my bedside. She spent time reassuring me that people on dialysis can live normal lives, going to work and even the gym.

As the days passed, my trusted haematologist, giant-brained Dr D. appeared to try and sort out a way of controlling any further random bleeding without leaving me open to clotting to death. He gave me a big dose of steroids which seemed to reduce the swelling in my head but turned me into a giant hamster with disconcerting convulsions in my legs. As my temperature, sickness and gut pain reduced and young D., the mermaid, kept smiling and showing me the way, my despair subsided and life began to seep back.

After a week I managed to escape the usual head-mashing noise on the ward by limping (avoiding the curbs which I couldn't step up) to a bench outside. As I was laying down and taking in the fact that, despite everything, my wrecked body could still give me pleasure by simply feeling the sun on my face, my phone rang (we had mobiles by this point!) and Carol asked me if I was having a nice time. I looked around for her curvy shape and shiny, long hair but to no avail and wondered for a second or two whether she, reflexologist extraordinaire who diagnosed my ovary issue before my doctors in 1998, really was a white witch. She laughed at my confusion and explained that she'd just gone by on the bus on her way to work (she's an amazing, gruesome-tolerant theatre nurse) and had recognised my skinny legs (and baby blue dressing gown) hanging over the side of the bench.

It took me two weeks to get out of hospital, what with more blood complications, fevers and a horribly painful fistulaplasti during which a piece of metal snapped off the end of the 'wire' used to open my vein! "Oh don't worry," said the doctor, "You'll only beep a bit when you go through customs" (!) Another bad moment came when the mermaid tearfully explained that she had one vein left which they were going to try and fit with a 'graft.' Like a fistula, a high-pressured artery's connected to a vein but a bit of plastic tubing's involved – which increases the risk of infection and vein collapse. "And if that doesn't work I'm done for." I cried with her, not being able to understand how she didn't just jump out of our fourth floor window. I would come to understand.

In contrast, a good moment in hospital came when I was waiting for a blood transfusion and wrote 'The blood I'm going to get today will be from the specialist blood bank in Sheffield, given all my additional antibodies; gentle, blond-bobbed Nurse Pip says it will take two and a half hours to get here. How incredible is it that, as I sit here writing, a whole network of people will be liaising, sifting through fridges of blood, walking it down corridors and driving it down the M1? My blood donor will be totally oblivious to my thinking about him or her taking the time, effort and needle pain to go and give their blood. Now I have yet more tears of gratitude trickling down my face. Thank you so much if you give blood; maybe it's you who will save my life today.'

As usual, it was blissful when I got home to my beautiful, ecstatic Alfie-dog; I knew my friends took good care of him but I'd missed him terribly. Just standing in my bleep-free garden with him clinging to my leg and listening to nothing but birdsong, was glorious, as was having a long bath, going to bed and getting up when I wanted and not having to worry anybody. My mum and dad came down again to help me for a few days, tidying up my vegetable patch (I was over the moon that, like me, my lettuce had survived) and taking me shopping. Being in the supermarket I spun round in wonder. It was like all my Christmases had come at once! Shelves and shelves of lush fruit, biscuits, pies, yoghurts, thick vanilla slices, tins, packets, jars, boxes...pure abundance! How lucky are we in the UK to have such a *massive* variety of wonderful food from all over the world? That's most of us; sadly food banks are on the rise big-time here in the UK as working families' crap, zero hour contracts, low wages and benefit stoppages send more and more people into desperation. And of course we really should 'buy local' or we and our supermarkets may soon be underwater.

Talking of annihilation, whilst my parents were caring for me, I had a great talk with them about our potential deaths and funerals and I updated all my 'personal affairs' for my mum. It didn't feel morbid, it just felt sensible. Having said that, we didn't exactly reach our conclusions; my dad wanted cremating so that his atoms could disperse and become something else quickly but my romantic mum wanted 'Faithful to the end' written on their mutual headstone. I'm opting for space-saving cremation and debating between 'Life's for *living*,' 'Seize the moment' and 'Kindness Rocks' for my plaque.

Chapter 25
A Chance for Redemption

"The wound is the place where the Light enters you."

Rumi

A trip to a hospital isn't something you'd imagine would be much fun but I really enjoyed the day I spent with my brother seeking out different departments where he had tests to see if he was a potential kidney donor match for me. I can't remember the last time we had quality time together on our own and I've never had anybody offer me such an amazing 'gift.' It felt pretty surreal, mind you, as I couldn't *really* imagine being able to accept him being chopped up on my behalf if, by a long-shot, he was a match for me.

Apparently we only need one of our kidneys to lead a full and totally healthy life; some people are born with only one. A dialysis nurse told me that kidney donors actually often live longer than average – maybe that's partly the magic of kindness!

The operation to take out a kidney is relatively safe keyhole surgery. Some people, which I do actually find hard to get my head round, donate kidneys to random strangers. The cheery, bouncy-pony-tailed transplant nurse told my brother and I that she had a patient whose transplanted kidney lasted for thirty years and she'd seen a patient just that day who'd had one for fifteen. She reassured us that 'live donor' transplants were the most successful and that nobody had died donating a kidney in my hospital. The risks of complications were about one in three thousand.

When I got home I wrote 'In three weeks' time I will know whether or not I have my best chance of a transplant. My brother's no doubt got the closest tissue match there is. This is really weird shit. I have tiny glimmers of imagining my evenings with friends instead of being strapped to a scary machine and having a life of tennis, travel and even love but I daren't build my hopes up. I daren't think about a potentially blood-clotting, or bleeding, transplant operation either and I just can't imagine saying "Okay thanks Bro, see you when you come out of surgery, if there are no complications and the surgery doesn't kill you, leaving your boys without a dad – or having lost the possibility of having a kidney from you should they ever need one." Mmm...a one in three thousand risk? I don't think I could do it even if there was only a one in three million risk...I think I'll read my novel for a bit, 'The Girl With the Dragon Tattoo' by Stieg Larson. His trilogy has become massively successful and made into a film, but sadly, Stieg died before that happened. Gulp.'

A month after the bleeds in my head, my voice was still a bit weak but I saw my first client, a wonderful man who I'd been seeing on and off for nearly two years and was finally realizing how fantastic he is and how much he deserves from life, having not quite believed that because his mother had left him with his grandmother when she began a new relationship. Only two clients didn't return and my school kept my counselling job open; I was over the moon. I was also excited about a planned 'In Kind' event; our wee group had arranged to meet in the middle of town with a gazebo, a trestle table and a pile of buns, flowers, balloons, chocolates and paper windmills made by local schoolchildren, to carry out twelve hours' 'Random Acts of Kindness.' We'd give out things to people, including hugs (we'd had 'Free Hugs' banners made) and invite passing shoppers and their children to get arty; we had cushions and a roll of wallpaper for people to sit and draw and write what their ideas of kindness were. We'd also invite people to sign a petition to support our plea to the local council to make us a 'City of Compassion.'

My platelets continued to bob up and down at this time and I had a terrible moment on dialysis when joking nurse Jody took out a dialysis needle and it was followed by a long string of disgusting blood clot; it was like a sick magic trick as she pulled and it just kept coming – until it got to the end and blood spurted all over the place! Obviously I was worried that my blood was going crazy again but wrote 'I must remember that I seem fine. Tomorrow I may be dead but today my little miracle of a body's still walking me round our amazing planet and having delightful moments – like in the petrol station where I bought some 'Werther's Originals' and offered one to the depressed-looking cashier. He was initially a bit shocked saying 'Nobody's ever done that before' before beaming a massive grin. Such a simple, easy and beautiful moment. I hope you're having a good day with some magic moments.'

A week later I wrote 'Well I've tidied the house, weeded the garden, messed about on the internet and walked and brushed Alfie; I'm very aware that I don't want to write today and am feeling pretty numb. My brother isn't a kidney donor match for me; my best hope of a successful transplant is gone. This is so weird I just can't get my head round it. I'm partly gutted that my brother's not a match but I also feel relieved that I don't have to wrestle with the immense decision about putting him at risk or face another mind-blowing operation myself. Thank goodness the sun's out. I don't know what else to say. Last night Claire, Kirsty and Matt were their usual fantastic selves when I told them about the non-match, acknowledging how crap it was and just calmly sitting with me in my grief. Actually, Claire was partly relieved; having nursed me through my operations and subsequent clotting in 1998/9, she was terrified about my having a transplant operation. I'm so grateful that I know my grief won't last and that my human spirit will perk itself up and I'll feel happy again soon. Even today I know there'll be beautiful moments, especially as Floydie Frankie (we once spent a fantastic day 'colour washing' my middle room as we sang along to 'The Wall' album) will be here any minute and we're going out for lunch so I'd better go and brush my mop-head.'

In July I had loads of beautiful moments during our 'Random Acts of Kindness Day.' Wearing new t-shirts printed with our logo and supported by George making a film of the event, Claire offering free massages and Reiki, Elaine, Valerie and Sarah giving out goodies and hugs with us, 'Pulp Friction' making free smoothies using pedal-power and 'The Major Oak' barbershop choir singing, it was absolutely fantastic. As we started giving out free flowers and buns there were a few suspicious looks, with disbelief that an ulterior motive wasn't involved, but on the whole, people responded with delight. I must admit I was a bit surprised myself when a steady stream of people, from teenagers to older people, came up for hugs rather than regarding us as a bunch of weirdos. As we hugged, one older woman told me, "This is my first hug since my husband died four years ago." It was a beautiful moment as we teared up then beamed together. A constant flow of people passed through our gazebo wanting to sign our petition and the enthusiasm people had for the idea of being a City of

Compassion was *so* heart-warming; "What a great antidote to greed and selfishness"... "It's about time"... "Yes! Let's do it!" You may say I'm a dreamer (along with John Lennon) but I'm certainly not the only one! I think my best moment (perhaps on a par with when I donned my big-headed teddy-bear costume and got my skinny legs dancing to the wonderful sounds of the Major Oak singers) was when I had a conversation with a tie-and-jacketed Mr Colin Fischer, aged about 70. He told me that he'd been sitting in McDonalds where it was "like a death sentence" with everybody being very sombre and quiet until Andy and Darran went in with the offer of hugs. "I can't find words to describe what happened; it was like the whole place lit up! It just came to life and everybody started laughing and I mean proper belly laughs; they loved it. It was brilliant, absolutely brilliant. Thank you. You've just made my day!" Thank you, Mr Fischer, you made mine. Several people made a point of popping back to our gazebo to tell us that our actions had inspired them to be kinder... "I'm thirty-six and I bought a *Big Issue* for the first time and it felt great; thank you"... "I saw a woman struggling with her pushchair and helped her; I would normally have just walked past but it felt so much better not doing!"... "I've been smiling at everybody I've passed today and it feels so good! Thank you." I saw so many beaming smiles yesterday that I'll be buzzing for weeks. Ah, connections! As a growing number of scientific experiments support our experience that kindness is contagious, again I have hope for humanity.[57]

Talking of connections, I received a lovely letter from my Uncle Kenny today. As usual he wrote 'Our Jayne' on the envelope, which makes me smile every time. Growing up we didn't socialise much with my dad's big family, insular as my

---

57. See for e.g. the video at www.youtube.com/user/GoodVirusOrg/ or the article https://www.huffingtonpost.co.uk/entry/kindness-contagious-psych_n_7292862

dad is, but I organised a get-together a few years ago with my mum and dad, Uncle Kenny, his partner, bubbly foster-mum Barbara, my Auntie Christine, Auntie Mavis and her bright, creative, French polishing husband, David. It was fascinating to hear my dad's siblings talking about their childhood. A live chicken was dropped down the chimney to sweep it, their staple diet was 'jam-bread' and they got one toy and a tangerine at Christmas. My dad was fourteen, Mavis ten, Kenny seven and Christine a baby when their mum died; nobody bothered telling Kenny the terrible news. When their dad died a year later and their married sister, who still lived in the family home with her "idle" husband, took responsibility for them, Mavis often had to clean instead of going to school, hiding under the table when the school inspector came. She became an expert at 'crocodile tears' as she begged for credit at the local shop. Kenny left school unable to read or write because he was kept off so often to do housework and be company for his elder sister who didn't like being alone. Christine used to have to brush her big sister's hair for an hour to earn one of the chocolate biscuits locked in the wardrobe.

It depressed me to hear their tales but I also felt proud that I had a family that had gone through so much pain and yet come out of it such kind, warm-hearted and spirited people; my comedian uncle's an ex-social worker and now gardens for some older folks and my hilarious, dry-humoured aunts both cared for the elderly. Sadly, in the spirit of my mum and I (though I'm getting better), they find it easier to give more to others than themselves. Like my uncle, my aunties write to me and I really love it; they all say the loving things that my dad can't. I'm so pleased that I made the effort to organise our gathering, for both me, my brother and my mum who feels she has siblings now, after being a resentful 'only one' for most of her life.

My two nephews remain total superstars; the elder one passed his farrier apprenticeship after a hard graft and is now raking in the cash, determined to have a house and stables of his own (I keep reminding him to try and enjoy the present too…) My younger, super-cool nephew plans to train alongside his brother – which will be weird; it just means I'll have to head south more often. They're ace. Like my bro they're big, bright, kind, resilient and just a bit mischievous. I may not have a partner and kids but I feel love and loved. La la!

Still on the theme of connections, dialysis got a bit easier as I came out of my suspicious, fearful 'reptile brain' and got to know and therefore trust the staff more; V. whose daughter-in-law had just lost her baby, smiley J. from the Philippines who patted my knee with understanding as he walked by, gentle P. whose mum was ill, R. who had ducks on his allotment, sporty C. from Australia, B. who liked to shop with her sister, R. who loved her horse and pretended to be mean but was far from it, K. who fascinated me with stories about his upbringing in Kenya, black and blond-haired C. who was going with 'the girls' to Skegness, Big A. who raised sheep, J. who sang karaoke, D. who joked flippantly over her obvious deep compassion, H. from Zimbabwe who sang as she worked, A. whose petite frame never stopped moving, young L. whose no-nonsense encouragement made me smile (mostly) and the gentle, humble, senior nurses from the Philippines and India who modelled warm, competent nursing – and womanhood – at its best. (I wish I could write about every one of the seventy-five strong staff team as each deserve a mention as well as a medal.)

At home I continued to have moments of loneliness which felt like I was floating in space and I remained worried that no man would come near me in my state but I continued to pour my affection onto Alfie-dog and my therapy clients, enjoying the lovely relationships with these people without a need for being too vulnerable or disclosing that I was ill. I could be 'normal' in my work and I still got immense satisfaction from helping people out of the dark forest.

Talking of darkness, I was deeply impacted in August 2011 by an interesting turn of events in the UK. Some of our young people went on a rampage, breaking into shops and helping themselves to designer clothes, trainers and phones. Some people lost their homes and businesses to fires and three young men were mowed down on the pavement as they tried to protect a petrol station. Our holidaying government, away for their long summer break, came together for an emergency sitting. There was lots of talk of punishment and retribution but I didn't hear any members of the government ask why our young people had gone berserk. None of them acknowledged how hard it must be for bored, hopeless young people, with little chance of a job (twenty-five percent of school-leavers at the time) being constantly fed images of the 'right' clothes, phones and lifestyle on their screens. There was just heavy talk about not putting up with their "insane violence" and "gang culture" and the courts "processed" offenders throughout the night, giving many of them custodial sentences. Custody, where any glimmers of self-esteem they had would likely be decimated, where they'd learn to become more skilled criminals and where their chances of ever getting work and buying their own designer trainers would plummet; not the best way to get a load of angry and disillusioned teenagers on-side, I would argue! I read about a young woman who was given three months in prison for receiving a pair of stolen shorts from her mate and another young man got two years for stealing a t-shirt! And yet major tax evaders, politicians who scammed their expenses and bankers who carried out appalling deceptions, lost the country billions and nearly destroyed the economy with their greedy, irresponsible and immoral ways just went home – with their bonuses. AAAGGGHHH!

Surely appealing to the better natures of our young people, showing them the harm that they did, giving them purpose (like repairing their damage or volunteering in the community) teaching them how to deal with difficult feelings and encouraging them to feel like worthy members of society -without the need for flash trainers and the latest smart-phones – would have a better result than scaring the crap out of them and making them even angrier! Oh God, the self-serving powers that be are lording it just like they did when the starving poor were sent to Australia for stealing a loaf of bread! There seems to be no compassion or understanding, just the same idiotic brutality as some of the rioters exhibited. I read an article recently where, amongst a 'primitive' jungle tribe, if somebody does something out of order, the entire tribe surrounds him or her for two days, pointing out the good things they've done in their life and encouraging them back onto a straight road. I would bet Alfie on that being a whole lot more successful than a humiliating prison sentence! Today I despair.

Chapter 26
Please, please, Hear Me!

"When we get caught up in the busyness of the world, we lose connection with one another – and ourselves."

Jack Kornfield

Unbelievably, September 2011 brought yet another living nightmare. Catching my leg on my picnic table, I superficially grazed my right calf but instead of healing it seemed to be turning into some sort of ulcer and felt like a burning coal was burrowing into my leg. My renal doctor was still off and I saw three on-call doctors on the dialysis unit before I was finally referred to the 'leg assessment clinic.' There was a depressing suggestion that the steroids I'd taken for my head bleeds could have thinned my skin. By this time I was literally screaming when I got out of bed and put weight onto my leg. Then a random graze appeared on my left leg. I felt like I was disintegrating!

Oh come on, Jaynie, pull yourself together.

But my leg bloody kills! I can't stand it! The painkillers aren't touching it!

Don't worry, the doctors will sort it out.

Oh right! Just like they are doing every time I go for dialysis and tell them I'm in agony!

Well they've referred you to the clinic, don't worry.

Yes two bloody weeks ago and I haven't heard owt yet!

It'll be okay...

Oh fuck off. I've had enough! Dialysis, Lupus flares and fistulaplastis are bad enough. This is just too much. I can't do it.

Well you have to. Remember the young Mermaid...and Alfie-dog...

Well yes but I really don't know if I can cope with this level of pain!

Moment by moment, flower...

Despite my pain I somehow managed to limp to a small music festival with Kirsty which I'd been looking forward to. At one point we passed the 'Chill Tent' just as a long-skirted, middle-aged hippy was giving an enthusiastic talk about connectedness, feeling the energy of trees and opening your heart. She sounded like a fruit-cake – and was largely saying what I'm trying to say in my book! Mmm... that's it then. I'm a voice in the wilderness crying out for open-hearted yumminess when all around me people want to tie me to a stake and watch me burn...or lock me in a psychiatric hospital where I can't bang on about scary feelings and change. Except I know really that I'm not a voice in the wilderness. Most of the festival bands were thrashing their guitars at the craziness of life, howling from their hearts about the anguishes of life and beaming from their souls as they celebrated the joys of life. I do really believe the tide's swelling; there are a hell of a lot of compassionate 'elves' out there, talking, planning, writing, painting, making films and singing (which is perhaps partly why the arts have such a low priority in our schools' national curriculum in the UK; they threaten the powers that be who don't want the balance of power or wealth to change!)

As the wound on my right leg grew, surrounded by a sore, red mass of blood spots, so did the pain; it was the worst I'd ever experienced, with no painkillers touching it. I kept fantasising about grabbing a knife and sawing off my leg. A month after the referral, I had my appointment with a district nurse, Margaret, at the leg assessment clinic. Just like the doctors, my kind lady couldn't explain it and the scans she was intending to do went to pot because there was no sign of a pulse in my ankle. She called the specialist hospital team but was told that I shouldn't worry about calling it a leg ulcer yet and just keep dressing it myself!

At least I was getting on with my book as sitting down was my only option. As I was writing on the dialysis unit one evening, Mr Veg patch nurse invited me to add "And at that moment Richard, a young Burt Reynolds, swaggered onto the ward and poised handsomely as his debonair smile revealed the brightest glimmer of twinkling gnashers..." Beautiful (but completely unaware of it because nobody ever told her she was) twenty-something Nurse Jodie came up with the lightening response of "Twinkling from your bloomin' bald head, mate." The unit isn't the easiest place to be funny but sometimes humour, if there's enough affection, can be a way of counteracting the horror. The nurses run round like manic squirrels, their feet and bodies sore and brains whirring, giving out kind words even though they're exhausted, mostly for twelve hours at a time. (Maybe it was my scowling face and steaming ears that made them avoid me in my early days.)

With my usually calm nurse friend Claire freaking out at the state of my leg, I continued to show my bloody, pussy leg to a myriad of nurses and doctors on the dialysis unit but with my consultant still off, I again 'fell between the cracks' and began to lose the will to lift up my trousers.

My drawer full of tablets had begun to call me again when my blood's 'infection indicators' began to rise and Sister Helen, a beautiful cheeky blonde with a hard-core façade but a lot of compassion, wheel-chaired me to see renal doctor Jeremy, two colleagues and a registrar from 'plastics.' (Yet another classic example of 'the medical model' needing 'scientific evidence' of something being amiss rather listening to what I was saying about my pain levels.) Following much discussion they eventually concluded that I had a rare and complicated condition called calciphylaxis, in which imbalanced calcium (due to my kidney failure) was getting stuck in my blood vessels and stopping blood getting into my leg tissue, causing it to wither and die! I was reassured that there was medication for it, though they'd perhaps have to get it from abroad, it may not work and my legs may get worse before they get better! I really didn't need to know that when I was already beyond a manageable pain threshold. *What the f'k?! I really am disintegrating!*

Talking with bubbly Sister Helen during my next dialysis session she said that she'd only come across calciphylaxis three times in her career and it took over two months for one patient, who was being given the 'Sodium Thiosulphate' medication, to improve. "Oh my God, you're telling me I could be in this level of pain 'till Christmas?"

"I'm sorry, Jayne. We'll make sure you have good painkillers."

"But even morphine hardly touches it, it just makes me sick."

"I'll speak to the doctor about anti-sickness tablets."

"I'm already on them. They don't work."

"We'll try some different ones."

"Thanks. Mmm. Look. I don't want to be dramatic but what would happen if I gave up and came off dialysis?"

"Is it that bad?"

"About half an inch away," I squeaked. Helen, usually

a flippant comedienne, nodded gravely. "Well you'd have palliative McMillan support and they're really good."

"How long to die?"

"Maybe only two weeks. You'd slowly slip into a coma. You'd be pretty sick but with good pain relief..."

"Just grind to a bit of a sickly halt?"

"Pretty much. It's not the best, but not the worst way to go."

"Okay thanks. It's sort of a relief to know I have that option if I really can't stand it anymore."

"I understand."

"Thank you." We both teared up and then hugged. Another terrible yet beautiful moment.

I went home and wrote 'Little Alfie's looking at me with his big brown eyes and I cannot imagine being able to say goodbye to him, no matter how bad my pain is. And I really can't imagine telling my family, friends or clients that I'm throwing in the towel either. Fuck. Oh fuck.'

My wound soon became a gaping, bloody mass about four inches across and I could literally smell my leg rotting. Changing my dressings was excruciating. I had to keep telling myself that when it was better (or, in the worst – or possibly best – case scenario, had been cut off) the lack of pain would be magnificent and a normal walk – or hop – round the park would be blissful. 'Living in the moment' is the best thing I've ever learned but sometimes tomorrow helps, as Arthur learned in the war no doubt...

Tomorrow

However hard the parting, or dark the clouds
    may seem,
there always comes tomorrow,
with its friendly gleam.

We oft forget tomorrow when skies are dark
and grey,
forget that tomorrow's sunbeam
will always lead the way.

For however hard the parting, there are joys
we've yet to meet
and when tomorrow brings them,
the meeting is doubly sweet.

So keep tomorrow in your heart, though dark
the path you roam
then when the grey dawn turns to gold,
your joys will all come home.

Arthur Downs

Coping with my leg pain also meant I had to cry a lot. Being grateful helped too; Alfie was well whilst Peta's Billy, her beautiful, big-eared German Shepherd had to be put down because his legs went and Kazza's dribbling, squeaking cat, Alice, died. I was reminded of how lucky I was when I phoned June, the artistic mother of my brother's partner, who was dying of cancer and restricted to a bedroom in her house. If I'm honest, despite my deep conviction that we should all be more open about death, I wasn't looking forward to calling June. I'd only met her twice, though I liked her joyful energy. In the end, I just bit the bullet, picked up the phone and went for it, asking her how she really was (relatively calm) whether she was in pain (she wasn't) and whether she was afraid of death (not really.) I told her about my blissful feelings when I nearly died. We talked about 'capturing the moment' even in the face of death – she was still able to use her watercolours to capture the moment at times – and we joked about meeting up for a drink on the 'other side.' It was lovely. Oh how I wish she – and we – didn't have to die. But then, what would it be like without Dr Death? We'd all be fighting even more for land and food for starters! And would we bother to get out of bed and do anything if we knew we could do it tomorrow? Would we really appreciate anything if it wasn't all fragile and finite?

The pain and worry about my little body, as usual, came out in my dreams. I've had a repetitive dream for years about losing my clothes one way or another whilst going on, or coming back from, holiday; it's symbolic of my not having the adequate body for my journey I presume. In the thick of my pain my entire house was crumbling. I again wrote reams to you in an attempt to overcome my despair, saying twice that I'd really had enough and viewing Death as a welcome friend with open arms – and again I found that just voicing my despair and going right to the darkest edge was enough to bring me back to wanting to live. That old paradox again.

One day an old friend, part of the old 'poly crowd' turned up at my door. His face said it all; he looked mortified. "Are you on steroids?" he asked, noting my fluid-swollen face. "No," was as far as my weary explanation went, at which point he headed for the kitchen where he washed up, emptied my bin and kept all conversation to a minimum before being saved by the early arrival of my dialysis transport. A close friend actually acknowledged how hard it was to love me when I was "so ill" and said she avoided me at times because it was so hard to see me suffering. She also suggested that I have a whip-round so I could talk to my therapist more, instead of talking to friends, about "the heavy stuff." I appreciated her honesty and my reality check; I knew I wasn't imagining things when I sensed that some friends were afraid of me – and of my dying- and called me less. I didn't blame them and suspected that I might've been the same in their shoes but I did feel terribly sad. Not just for me, but for all the people, old and young, who are side-lined because they're not always fun and remind those around them of their own vulnerability and mortality. A friend was telling me recently that when her friend's son died, someone she knew actually crossed the road to avoid her. How crap's that? Again there are no words to express my gratitude for my friends who have stayed close over the past thirteen years; just the big lump in my throat.

As well as friends keeping me going, so did my fellow dialysis patients who understood my suffering; blind, cheery C. who adores her grandchildren, beautiful, vibrant farm-worker R. with her determination to cycle everywhere, frightened, fed-up C. with her learning difficulties and booming Caribbean shrieks, DJ J. with his tattooed neck, pumped up muscles and bum-flashing jeans, shuffling, gold-decked, stick-like J. who dragged herself around in her tailored clothes, silent M. who slumped in her wheelchair but lit up like an angel when she smiled, scared, timid R. who had to try hard to smile and chatty B. the big ex-soldier who, like many of us, had dwindling strength and growing fear.

In mid-November 2011 I finally wrote 'I have some amazing news! My leg's definitely healing! It still hurts like hell but it's definitely improving; the dead, black flesh has come off (too much information?) and I've only cried out in pain a couple of times this week. I keep sobbing with relief as my weary mind toys with the possibility that it may not yet be all over for me, as it was for June who lost her fight with cancer. Her daughter, husband and grandchildren are gutted. Bless you for the light – and my beautiful painting of Alfie – you've left behind, June.'

Another week on and I wrote 'I'm anaemic and knackered again but I've had no morphine for a week and it's fabulous to not feel sick and spaced out. Yesterday I went to buy some modelling clay with a view to getting my kiln in action, took Alf to the park and made it to the supermarket! All on my own skinny legs. I can't tell you how fantastic it felt just having a normal day. I'm alive and determined to make the most of it!

I've been contacting friends and arranging nights out again. I saw my new renal consultant on Monday (thankfully now back from maternity leave) who re-emphasized how serious my dodgy leg condition is, and, chatting with Claire this morning, who's seen several body parts fall or be taken off during her twenty-five-year nursing career, I took in fully that if my leg had got worse or badly infected – and there was a good chance of that – I could've easily ended up with it being amputated. God, I love my little mashed-up leg!'

By the end of 2011 I was basking in normal, almost pain-free life and I had a smile on my face again. My leg was improving by the day and my sense of safety growing as I developed more trust in my renal consultant. I'd started struggling to breathe on dialysis (which naturally brought up all sorts of nightmares) but clever Dr T. suggested that maybe I was having an adverse reaction to the type of glass 'kidney' which my blood gets 'sieved' through. My brand was changed and that sorted out the problem. With life getting steadier again, I began to think about dialysing at home; going to the hospital three times a week felt relentless and it depressed me seeing other broken patients like beautiful T. who was about my age and totally with it but slumped in her wheelchair looking about twenty years older than her husband, or cheery G whose veins were shot and was dead if her last possible line clogged up. Sometimes patients squirted blood all over the place (all over their partner's face on one grim occasion!), I had to watch doctors' faces drop as they read depressing blood results, hear manic nurses shouting "Can I have assistance here" as a beeping dialysis machine pierced the air, somebody slumped behind closed eyes, the curtains got whooshed across and the rest of us sat holding our breath, wondering whether they'd just fainted because they'd had too much fluid taken off or something worse. Sometimes I loved my fellow patients. Sometimes their vulnerability and pain made me want to run away, like G's when he'd sat in his wheelchair with no legs waiting five hours for his hospital transport to take him home, by which time he'd missed the carers who helped him to bed. Having accepted the patient rep. role for the unit I regularly phoned the private transport company to complain but nothing changed; profits came first.

I kept trying to put my dialysis needles in myself but usually only managed to get them in half-way before going sickly white and asking the nurses to complete the process whilst I turned away and filled my head with whatever distracting tune sprang to mind. On a positive note, I stopped having my crazy, post-dialysis pulsating body pain and I started seeing someone. Again I already knew him so felt there was some safety in that, I found him pretty wise and liked that he sang for the hell of it. It was lovely to be hugged and feel comfort in my body. I was scared of getting close to him and kept flashing back to my traumatic marriage, but I had to give it a go.

By March 2012 my red blood cells were the highest they'd been for years and my platelets were doing well. I hadn't had a lupus flare for about six months and the beautiful lyrics of Noah and the Whale's "Day by day...joy's coming back to me" resonated with me. Tears of relief and optimism came when I managed to dance at my friend Nic's fantastic 60th birthday party where a cover band blasted out Prince tunes. My legs didn't move much, it was more 'arm dancing' but still; it felt wonderful. I also met a man at the party; attractive, bright, deep (a therapist) and a whole human being. He was still attractive, bright, deep and a whole human being when I discovered that he had renal failure. He'd been on dialysis for two and a half years then got a transplant three years ago. I had that tiny glimmer of hope again that maybe one day I may be free and not so close to Death's door.

As the weeks went by, kind dialysis nurse Andy and bright, chatty and excited bride–to-be, nurse Lorna continued to encourage me to put in my own dialysis needles. "Come on, you can do it...just one good push...you've done it before; it'll be okay."

"Oh God, I feel sick, Lorna."

"Take your time, it's okay...just breathe and then when you're ready, one big steady push..."

"Shit, I'm shaking."

"I know, it's alright, I've got a close eye on you."

"Okay...right! Oww!" and whoosh! In slides needle one and it doesn't hurt too much and there hasn't been a bloodbath. "Wehey! You did it!" sang Lorna, her big bunch of blonde hair bouncing in excitement. "Okay, needle two. Just there, between these two puncture marks...go on, you can do it."

"But what if it goes through the vein? You sure that's the right direction? How deep do I do it?"

"That's it, this angle, not too deep..."

"Ouch! It's not going in...here, will you do it?"

"Aw go on, you can do it, just one firm push; you're at the right angle, it's okay..."

"Eeeow!" and whoosh! Number two needle slides in and Lorna and I both beam. I can't tell you how pleased I felt that I was a step closer to dialysing at home; no more watching people suffer and die, less intense battering of my heart, no more being frozen to the marrow, cold drives home at midnight or being surrounded by people coughing out killer bugs.

Unfortunately I wasn't so chuffed with the new bloke. I felt that I should be grateful that he was 'taking me on' with all my problems and he could be fun and cooked me healthy meals but I wasn't convinced he had a good heart. He told me things he'd done which he thought were funny but made my toes curl and cancelled on me twice, after I'd re-arranged my dialysis slots, because he 'accidentally' had four pints. It was actually his bouncy, twelve-year old daughter having a tearful rant about him and voicing all I was worried about that clarified that he wasn't the man for me and that I had more value than eight pints. Saved by connections again!

'Writing on dialysis I've just checked with nurse Lorna that what I wrote about her was okay and Andrew, a young patient in the opposite chair, asked if I've written about him, "The idiot in the corner who keeps speaking to Lorna in a mad Irish accent."

"Not yet, but I wouldn't write that," I replied, smiling.

"What would you write?"

"I'd write Andrew is an inspiration. He's twenty-four, handsome, humble, has an amazing right arm covered in self-designed tattoos and likes Tintin" (he lent me his box-set last week when I'd brought my portable DVD player but forgot my DVD's.) "He's been on dialysis since he was a child and I've never heard him complain or be snappy with the staff; he just gets down to watching his DVD's. He's courageous enough to be preparing for home dialysis and if he can cope with this shit in good spirits at his age, then I can do it too. Thanks for being you, and an inspiration, Andrew." His hazel eyes glowed as he beamed a beautiful grin.'

Chapter 27
Having Unknowingly Found Mindfulness

"Mindfulness is about love and loving life. When you cultivate this love, it gives you clarity and compassion for life and your actions happen in accordance with that."

Jon Kabat-Zinn

2012 continued with lots of editing and many hours of re-traumatising and doubting myself. Why on earth do I want to keep going over this shit and bare my innermost thoughts to the world? And then I'd think about the twenty-something twin lads on the dialysis unit, J. and A. Neither had the bulk to fit their six foot frames (protein loss and muscle wastage is a symptom of kidney failure and an egg's worth of protein is lost with each dialysis session) but they had a lean, handsome gorgeousness. Sadly neither of them could see how attractive they were, feeling 'less than' because of their kidney failure. The plan had been for their mum to donate a kidney to A. and their dad one to J. but then their mum wasn't a match for A. so J. let his brother, who has a weaker heart, have their dad's kidney.

A's transplant went well and he's now going out with his mates on Saturday nights but J's still unable to drink and is having to make the two-hour journey for dialysis on his own. When I was feeling shame about telling you about my disastrous love life I'd also bring to mind petite, feisty, chuckling, white blond Sharon, whose scarred, scabby body was a mass of pain and horror but she kept dragging it around for the sake of her two children – until a few weeks ago when she finally ground to a complete halt.

Fortunate as I felt when Sharon died, my own challenges kept coming. Just as my leg had stopped hurting, I saw my renal consultant who threw in another cheery little number. "Your parathyroid hormones are a bit high. You're on Cinacalcet for it aren't you?

"Yes, thirty milligrams."

"It's very important that we try to control your parathyroid as we don't want another calciphylaxis incident."

"Is my parathyroid marker really high?"

"No, but we need to keep an eye on it. If we can't control it with medication we'll have to take it out."

"What?"

"It's only a small operation."

"You mean cutting my blooming throat!"

"Well, yes, I'm afraid so."

"Oh my God," I managed, before going into a vacant haze. I breathed deeply and focused on a tree outside the window to bring myself back. "And how likely do you think that is?" my brain managed.

"I don't know."

"So I may not need it?"

"No, we may be able to control it with medication. I wouldn't worry about it." My fight-triggered brain conjured up a fleeting image of grabbing her pen to stab her throat to see how worried she felt about *that* but thankfully I let the insane thought just float by. If only it had been as easy, in the middle of the night, to let images of my throat being cut just drift away; again, I wish I'd not been told about this thing that I couldn't influence and might – but might not – happen.

A few weeks later my platelets and HB had dropped again, my gut was sore and I was feeling pretty grim so when I came across an online advert for a training day called 'Hope and Suffering,' I decided that I had to go, despite it being seventy miles away. I definitely needed more hope and wondered if it would throw more light on my weird belief that my seven-month incarceration had been a good thing. Within twenty minutes the trainer, Carolyn Spring[58] had totally blown me away. She talked about her suicide attempt whilst studying at Cambridge University, having massive waves of terror in her early twenties which made her do 'crazy' things like hide under the table, and finally experiencing a major nervous breakdown – without having a clue as to why she'd fallen apart. Gradually the memories of horrific, ritualistic sexual abuse started coming back to her and she developed 'Dissociative Identity Disorder' (formerly 'multiple personality disorder') as a way of trying to cope. Psychologically she had 'split off' the most horrendous symptoms of her childhood abuse, such as her intolerable powerlessness and rage, and ascribed them to different 'parts' of herself, not her 'real' self. Now here she was, standing in front of a room full of counsellors and therapists, sharing her vulnerability in a very articulate, professional, humorous and 'real' way. I choked back tears as she talked about her gradual recovery through facing her immense pain in therapy and being supported by her husband and friends.

A few months later I attended another of Carolyn's workshops, 'Trauma and the Body.' Given my ongoing attempts to relax more, it was useful to be reminded of what "Killer

58. See bibliography p. 430

Cortisol" can do, from scrambling our brains to damaging our nervous, immune, cardiovascular, reproduction and digestive systems. I then became all ears as Carolyn explored cortisol's possible connection with auto-immune conditions like M.E, Fibromyalgia and Lupus. I'd spent years trying to understand my health nightmare and wondering if it was related to my family's traumatic past and 'retroflection' (the denial and numbing of feelings.) It made such sense that a ton of cortisol had been whooshing round my body when my brother was chasing me up to my bedroom (which was fortunately small and I could often wedge myself between my drawers and door to keep out his violence) and Mum was losing the plot because of the huge amounts of cortisol which had been passed down to her care of a poorly mothered mother, two World Wars, a broken attachment with her dad, terrifying bomb sirens, having her horrendous burnt neck trauma and also being bullied at school.

Luckily Carolyn had an antidote to the stress (*and* poor early attachments *and* death anxiety); mindfulness, the simple practices that had been part of spiritual traditions (Buddhism, Hinduism, Sufism, Judaism and even early Christianity) for over 2,500 years and for decades brave Eastern Buddhists and travelling westerners had shared them with us. Following the great success in 1989 of Jon Kabat-Zinn's eight-week 'Mindfulness-Based Stress Reduction' programme with chronically ill patients in a Massachusetts hospital, mindfulness had spread like wildfire, soon reaching most hospitals in the USA and some in the UK. It had been adopted for its capacity to manage stress and enhance concentration, creativity and innovation in huge companies like Google (I heard it's their biggest in-house training) the public sector and charities, universities, schools and colleges, police forces, counselling centres, pain clinics, government agencies and even the Army (presumably to enhance focus and try and combat stress and

Post-Traumatic Stress Disorder.) As Carolyn talked about mindfulness – deliberately focusing your attention, in the present moment, without any sort of self-judgement of what you observe in yourself but with lots of self-compassion (as you notice your vulnerability, pain and also envy, malice, tendencies to criticise etc) – she described the science behind it, backed up by over ten thousand research papers, and how it works on the parasympathetic part of our autonomic nervous system, balancing the cortisol boosting, sympathetic part. Brain scans and blood tests have shown that regular mindfulness practice can soothe 'fight-flight' reactions, literally shrink the brain's manic, danger-alert amygdala and grow the rational, grounded, creative, clever, compassionate grey matter of our frontal cortex! It has been shown to help with all sorts of difficulties, from anxiety, depression, sleeplessness and addictions to pain management and a range of physical illnesses. It appears that it can even keep us younger – and possibly extend our lives – by protecting the telomeres at the ends of our chromosomes, stopping them, as the plastic ends of shoe laces do, unravelling so much as we age. By this point I was hooked! *My God, when people learn that mindfulness practice and being kind can keep us looking young we'll have the world sorted!*

Carolyn explained that mindfulness can be 'formal,' with meditations focusing attention on our breath, an object like a candle, passing sounds or being open to whatever emerges in that moment. It's about turning *inward*, simply *experiencing* our feelings, sensory input and other bodily sensations and just sitting with them, both the pleasant and unpleasant. Daily practice is encouraged in mindfulness so that, bit by bit, we can learn to spot our loving inner core, acknowledge our not so kind parts and also recognise and tolerate difficult sensations and emotions and grow to accept life *as it is* rather than being hell-bent on trying to make it how we *want it to be* (and how we want other people to behave) often paying the price of chasing only happiness with hangovers, exhaustion, conflict, debt and anxiety. Mindfulness, like therapy, is about facing and learning to tolerate and accept our sadness and fear in order to reach the natural happiness and peace on the other side. *Ah, this is so Gestalt, I get it!*

Also like the process of therapy, mindfulness is about developing awareness by 'standing back' and noticing our thoughts; the gratitude and wonder that can make us happy – and healthy – or the negative stuff that so often whirls round our egocentric and danger-obsessed minds (self-criticism, comparing, worrying, catastrophizing…) and can make us miserable as well as flooding us with cortisol. I liked Carolyn's notion that mindfulness is like body-building for the mind; consciously training it to be compassionate and focused – or quiet – rather than it just going over and over automatic – and often destructive or delusional 'programmed thoughts.' The brilliant Eckhart Tolle put it something like this: 'If you think you are your mind, the machine has taken over' – in other words mindfulness is about curious observation and enhanced awareness of what's going on with ourselves – and others – and not believing all that our crazy, critical minds are thinking!

Mindfulness has a myriad different practices (there are hundreds on phone apps and the internet) but an important one is called 'Metta' or the 'loving kindness meditation' which is designed to enhance compassion for yourself and others; the main key to inner and global peace and happiness. *Yeah! This is great stuff!*

With its focus on what is happening in the present moment, mindfulness can stop us regurgitating the past or worrying about the future and instead experience the depth and aliveness of now. *Oh yes, like Zen and the art of moving stones with a dustpan or the bliss of walking round the park with my eyes closed...* Reflecting on how much I'd noticed my pain and moods change when I had the space to just observe them in hospital, I got it when Carolyn explained that with regular practice, we can come to see the subtle, changing nature of our experiences, reflecting the fluid reality of life and overriding our fear of change and tendency to try and cling to what's familiar in order to feel some semblance of predictability and control. It helps us to capture the good bits of life and accept and flow with the difficult. Ah...this is about the Paradoxical Theory of Change again! You simply have to take the time to sit and simply notice and accept what's happening without aiming to change anything and then transformation naturally happens! *Yeah! I don't have to be anything other than what I am!*

Carolyn went on to explain that on top of structured meditation, mindfulness could be 'informal,' where you focus your attention on things in everyday life; the lovely warm water and smell of your soap during a shower (rather than missing the joy by getting lost in thinking) or the colour, smell, texture and taste of food (instead of just wolfing it down as you're focused on something else or concentrating on your next forkful instead of the one in your mouth.) Being mindful included being really present with others; open, honest and willing to be emotionally impacted rather than not *really* listening or just talking *at* people. It also included an awareness of our natural world and mindfully trying to care for it. 'Mindful walking' is experiencing the subtle movement of your legs and the feel of your feet on the ground, mindful housework could be tuning into your bodily sensations, breathing and noticing unhelpful thoughts whilst washing up, ironing, drilling or sanding...Zen and the art of patiently, willingly hoovering!

As Carolyn talked, I turned into a jubilant, wide-mouthed frog. I saw that all the years of shit I'd been through had made me into a little mindful 'observer' without even knowing it! My experiences had taught me the secret of 'living in the moment' with self-compassion and an acceptance of 'what is.' *Ah, I was practising mindfulness in hospital when I was being curious about how my needle pain felt, whilst eating my food on the Nutrition Unit, when my body was totally shot but I could still experience pleasure from the feel of the breeze on my body. All those hours alone in side-rooms gave me the opportunity to become more mindful of the crazy and peevish stuff that was going round in my head and how I treated people. Mindfulness must be what I experienced when Dr H. said the chemotherapy might kill me and I felt so happy! Not knowing if I had a future, I was totally in the moment, and, being possibly close to losing it, I was tuned into the awesomeness of life. Oh my God, having my ego and my fixed ideas about who I was and how I wanted my life to be smashed to pieces and learning to give up control and accept whatever happened really was a gift! And re-entering my body and its beautiful sensory feelings, just 'being,' really WAS the best thing that's ever happened to me! It really did do me good to stop 'doing' and be catapulted into my inner world of just 'being.' Mmm...happiness is an inside job!*

I grinned (and cried with gratitude) a lot after Carolyn's workshops, knowing that I wasn't crazy to have thought that my seven months in hospital was partly positive, and feeling that my life was on the right path to happiness and inner peace.

I finally felt ready for the ego-taming practices which Jiddu Krishnamurti and Thich Naht Hanh had told me about in my early twenties. I'd been resistant to meditation and spiritual practice for years, given how much I already felt 'out there' as a psychotherapist; at parties people sometimes looked horrified when I told them what I did (I can't actually mind-read by the way) so I didn't want to be even 'weirder' by also being 'spiritual.' But now I thought *fuck it! So what I may be regarded as a space cadet if I meditate and it may be hard facing myself full-on, but if brave, amazing Carolyn is on this path, then I'm definitely going to join her!*

Throughout 2012 I continued with the present moment-focused mindfulness that Alfie was such an expert at and started to regularly practise 'body scans' and sitting and walking meditations. They weren't easy; it was pretty freaky, to be honest, slowly scanning my body and facing the twinges and 'implicit,' unconscious body memories. For example, one of the first times I did the body scan (where you go up from your toes, focusing on the sensations in each part of your body for a few moments at a time) when I got to my left calf, where I had my second DVT, I just burst into a spontaneous flood of tears; the tears that I hadn't had the privacy to shed in the Austrian hospital, I presume. In the same way, Carolyn had felt tremors and terrible pains from implicit memories held in her body as a result of the terror and abuse she'd experienced. She explained that the key to ousting implicit memories is to just (I say 'just' but of course it takes great courage) 'sit with' the feeling that emerges until it passes, rather than going into denial, getting annihilated with alcohol or drugs, keeping mega busy or 'acting it out' with rage or self-pitying dramas and much stabbing of the second dagger.

Interestingly, as I increasingly practised mindfulness, I had a relatively healthy time. No stinking wounds anywhere, no sickening headaches, platelet crisis or mega Lupus attacks. I was less anaemic and dialysis was steady. My confidence grew a bit and I checked out a few dating sites. I had lots of responses to my ad, mostly about my 'lovely hair' and 'beautiful face' which my daft ego smiled wanly at but which depressed the hell out of my lonely soul, which was desperate to be met. My enthusiasm soon waned and I resigned myself to a continuing partnership with a sheepdog. At least with Alfie my heart was safe.

Still struggling with my relentless evening trips to the hospital, I kept practising putting my own needles in, much as I hated it and late 2012 brought intense dialysis training. I watched young, amazing Andrew, calm, grandmother Jackie and supercool builder Denis thread up their machines, connect the lines to their needles and confidently press their beeping screens but I'm a technophobe at the best of times (like my parents, I wasn't allowed to touch anything for fear of breaking it) so the idea of pressing anything on my blood-eating monster mortified me.

Setting up the machine entails (after a sterile hand wash) methodically threading three long rubber 'lines' (thin tubes) round a cog-type pump, twisting them onto three pressure gauges and then screwing them to both ends of the foot-long, artificial glass 'kidney' (which is full of minute strands and uses osmosis to suck the toxins out of your blood.) The lines incorporate two plastic 'air chambers' which catch any air bubbles which may kill you in minutes if they got into your body. Then you add a bicarbonate cylinder to the machine which rebalances your body's PH as renal failure and dialysis mash it up and you put a probe into a big bottle of 'acetate' which gives you back some of your essential minerals which the machine sucks out of your blood alongside the toxins. Next you programme the foot-square touch screen on the top of the machine... 'haemodialysis', check...'four hours', check...

taking off '1600 millilitres' of fluid...check, temperature '36', check...The machine's pump then starts to whir and circulates a bag of saline which 'primes' the lines, getting rid of the air in them. More saline 'recirculates' or pushes the blood in the lines back into your body at the end of dialysis (well, most of it.)

In February 2013 I had a call to say that my dialysis machine was coming soon and that a plumber would be round the following week to get my water system ready (all the water going into the machine has to be purified through tubular filters attached to the wall and also by a couple of two by two foot 'box' filters which sit next to the machine.) I'd decided, after much deliberation and a major clean-out of my bedroom with the strict help of my efficient, kind friends Sally and Maria (I wasn't good at letting things go), to have my dialysis machine in my bedroom, with a view to perhaps progressing onto overnight dialysis which is done over eight hours and is much gentler on your body. When my young, beefy plumber arrived and began to survey my house, he said that if I had the machine in my bedroom I'd have to have a very loud pump to get the water up through the ceiling from the bathroom.

"You're joking!"

"No. It really is pretty loud too."

"Oh shit. Sorry, oh dear. What about my middle room downstairs? My bathroom was in there when I moved here so there must be some plumbing possibilities."

"No, I'm afraid I can't put it there without digging all the floor up and then there's no guarantee and you may still need the loud pump."

"Oh crap. It's gonna have to be my therapy room upstairs next to the bathroom then!"

"What, your work room?"

"Yes, I'll just have to make a therapy room in my middle room downstairs." This meant clients would go through my front room and I'd lose the privacy which currently came with them going straight up the stairs from the front porch. I was disappointed, especially as my therapy room, with its futon, was also my guest bedroom.

"Shall I go for it upstairs, then?"

"Phew…yes please." *Oh crap.*

The following weekend I nearly killed myself trying to clear out my junk-packed middle room to create a new therapy room but, again, in the spirit of Zen, moment by moment and step by step, I made ready for my new life. Sort of.

Chapter 28
Alone with Big Bertha. And a Death Sentence

"What saves a man is to take a step. Then another step."

C.S. Lewis

Right let me think...what's the hardest thing I've ever done? Climbing Mount Tryfan in Snowdonia and jumping the terrifying gap between the 'Adam' and 'Eve' stones on the top? Going for therapy? Swimming with sharks and sting-rays in Belize?...No, absolutely no comparison to starting kidney dialysis at home! Once the plumber had finished, a pair of quiet, burly men heaved my dialysis machine upstairs (battering my wooden stairs and red paint-work) and placed it on a four feet square plastic tray alongside the water filters. Next they wrestled in a big, cream (wipe-able) recliner chair. My spare bedroom cum therapy room was now a packed dialysis room. I kept poking my face round the door to have a look. After a few days I managed to actually walk into the room and test out the chair; *okay, reasonably comfortable though this cream's gonna show any blood stains up terribly. My God; I've got to come up here four or five times a week and stick two massive needles into my arm then plug myself into that machine…oh my God; I wonder if I'll have a major bloodbath, heart attack or get a massive air bubble in my blood stream and die in this chair? Oh my God… I'm probably going to die right here…*

Though my plan had been to spend my dialysis time reading and writing, I treated myself to an all singing and dancing 'smart' TV which could switch off my brain. My next job was to clear out the fitted cupboard in my bedroom which was to be the storeroom for all the dialysis equipment; litre bags of saline, cartridges of bicarbonate and big, two litre bottles of acetate, 'giving sets' (packs of the lines) needles, syringes, swabs, tape (to secure the needles) sterile fluid (to prepare the needling site) sterile hand-washes, sterile cleaning cloths, tissues, gloves…. When I had my first delivery of kit and the boxes were piled up in my front room I nearly had a fit but like a miracle, as I emptied boxes and packed things into the two bookcases in my dialysis room, it eventually blended in. I was ready physically, if not psychologically.

Nurse Andy was with me the first few times I dialysed and there were no major bloodbaths or problems. It was a bit weird though, him sitting there in my bedroom and us trying to make conversation for four hours; the next time he just came at the start and the end. The in-between hours were a nerve-frazzling nightmare. I felt sick as my blood circulated through the lines and I watched the pressure gauges like a hawk. *Oh shit, what did Andy say? Below 200 for the venous line? That's the blue gauge…or is it the red one? Oh my God…oh, yes it's the blue one with the V next to it…oh okay; 143, that's fine; oh okay… oh my God I can't believe I'm doing this. What was I thinking? This is insane!*

When Andy let himself back in I babbled, "I don't think I can do this; it's madness, I'm going to kill myself!"

"You're doing really well! You're bound to be scared but you'll get used to it, honestly."

"If I don't blow myself up."

"It's okay, really. These machines are hypersensitive and if anything's not right it will alarm and tell you."

"It won't know if I'm having a heart attack."

"No. But that's pretty unlikely."

"Mmm; you try telling my banging heart that..."

"You can always come back to the unit if you're not happy; you don't have to do this."

"Mmm. I'm not sure I can stand that either; if I hear about one more amputation or death I may have a heart attack anyway" (a lot of kidney failure comes with limb-threatening diabetes.)

"I know you can do this; you know what you're doing"

"We bloody hope I know what I'm doing!"

Andy suggested that I have a 'dummy run' over the weekend and set up the machine without actually plugging myself in. It wasn't my best ever Saturday night entertainment but, supported by a wary-looking Alfie and the detailed instructions written out on big sheets of paper stuck to the wall, I managed to wire everything up, open and shut the right clamps, add the 'kidney,' bicarbonate cylinder and bottle of acetate at the right time and finally got myself a shiny green light and the message that I could 'connect the patient.' "Fuck you, I'm not connecting anything! I hate you Big Bertha" (so christened by 'Rocky' Susie) "but it looks like we're gonna have to hang out anyway....Yes I know you're just trying to keep me alive and I appreciate that, really I do, it's just that you're one scary beast..."

A few sessions later, with me feeling guilty for Andy having to chaperone me when he was a very busy man, I suggested (like an idiot) that I could do the next one on my own. *You'll be okay if you concentrate, you can do this, Jaynie...* I was literally shaking as I set up the machine, primed my needles with saline and took my blood pressure which, funnily enough, was through the roof. The two needles are attached to rubber lines about ten inches long so that, when I'm finished, I can bend over my wrist and pull out my needles with my left hand, as my right hand gets ready to stop the blood with a folded pad of gauze. If I time pulling out the needle and pressing down the gauze wrongly, there's a bloodbath squirted across the room (or, annoyingly, down the cream voile curtain I'd hung to protect the sterile equipment in a bookcase.) If I press hard on the needle site it hurts like hell. If I don't press hard enough, the gauze gets flooded, blood pours out over my arm, soaks the pillow that my arm's resting on and sends me into a sickening panic; if I don't manage to stem the bleeding, bearing in mind my fistula has high pressure arterial blood flowing through it, I'm again apparently dead in minutes... And so, with my heart pounding, I treble-checked that I had everything I needed before I was pinned down for four hours; TV remote, laptop, phone, food and drink, dog treats, Jaynie treats (lots of them) and my EPO injection (which I could now needle into specially designed circular pads on the dialysis lines instead of having to sting my belly three times a week; one silver lining!) Claire and Kirsty had spare keys if it all went pear-shaped and Andy and the dialysis unit staff were at the end of the phone. I could do this...

I sat down with clumsy fingers but managed to fumble my needles in. There was the usual scream-level, searing pain but a 'good blood flow' going into the plastic syringes initially connected to the ends of the needles to check for that. Acknowledging my pretty cool one-handed skill, I taped my needles on very securely. *Check. Okay, press 'haemo' on the screen... check...add bicarb...check...oh my God...unclamp saline, check...this is crazy...add acetate, check...I'm gonna die in a massive bloodbath and Claire or Kirsty's going to have to find me like this...prime lines, check...okay...oh shit... oh shit...* I eventually took a massive breath and pressed the little green man for 'go' and 'Connect patient' flashed onto the screen. Fuck, that'll be me... I closed the saline, clamped 'little red,' 'big red' and 'big blue' then, through bated breath, removed the syringes and screwed my needles to the lines on the machine. *Okay, unclamp needles and big red and blue...and press start...*and with a beep my blood *wooshed* out of my arm, scurried down the rubber line, slowly wound round the pump and up towards the white kidney which began to seep pink...I then had to turn away because I felt my usual gut squeezing horror. A minute later the alarm started its furious screaming, my heart jolted into my throat and I froze with numb panic before remembering that I just needed to press 'alarm' twice then 'start' and the 'kidney' symbol...and then, glory be, the wonderful green 'all's well' light came on and the screen flashed with 'haemodialysis in progress.' I turned up the pump speed to three hundred, checked that the pressure levels in the lines weren't exceeding two hundred and then started to breathe again. After a minute of no bleeps or flashing lights, just the steady, deep whirring of the machine and the annoyingly loud chugging of the water filters, my tears of relief (or trauma, or both) poured. *Oh thank God, thank God! PLEASE don't go wrong, please, please...* With a desperate desire to block out my banging heart and swirling blood, I turned on the TV and stared. *I'm having dialysis in my bedroom. My blood's running round a machine. This is surreal. And I may have to do it for the rest of my life. Oh my God...*

This traumatic Monday blends into other nerve-wracking days; I can't remember the details but the striking image I have of the first few weeks is the machine beeping wildly and flashing various yellow danger warnings about blockages, air in the lines and dodgy pressures – which I didn't understand – and me screaming "Shut up! Shut the fuck up!" like a maniac whilst Alfie cowered under the table with just his nose peering out. I'd call Andy or the dialysis unit in a state of semi-hysteria and sometimes they'd manage to talk me through problems but at other times I'd be in such a panic that I'd have total reptile brain take-over and just couldn't take information in; I'd then often get shirty, much to my shame. I lost three 'circuits' of blood in two weeks when it went so pear-shaped that I had to just clamp off my needles and lose all the blood going round the machine, making myself anaemic again. Once I saw a load of air in the line coming straight towards my body but managed to clamp the needle just in time.

I was desperate for support from family or friends but when brave Claire came round one evening to help me, I found that her presence made it harder to concentrate. It was grim to realize that my ongoing debate about whether or not I wanted people with me on dialysis had just been concluded; I needed to be alone and focused. Which is just as well, given that most of my friends were again pretty quiet at this time and my family too overwhelmed to face what dialysis involved. It was another excruciatingly lonely time.

Luckily, after things had gone smoothly for a couple of months, I began to relax a bit and my HB returned to normal; walking without panting felt great! I did miss the staff and patients on the dialysis unit with their understanding of what I meant by "Groundhog day" and I was a bit sad to give up my role as the patient representative; I'd enjoyed my sense of purpose, emotionally supporting other patients, liaising with the transport company, organising free reflexology for patients and instigating a fund-raising cabaret. I didn't miss my complete reliance on others though, lovely as they were. *Ah, Jaynie…you still hate being vulnerable, eh? Yes! But now I'm in control – well sort of!*

After about six months I was, amazingly, still alive. The beeping, screaming, blood-eating sessions only happened occasionally and I tried to view dialysis as my relaxing TV time. Sometimes I'd look through e-mails or write but even a slight movement of my needled arm could affect the pressure and make the machine alarm and also, with some of my blood missing, I often felt cold and needed to burrow under my fluffy, heated blanket. Not only alive, I began to feel physically better; I remember having a stretch in my kitchen one day and realizing that my general level of aching had decreased. It was a bloody pain trying to get my dialysis hours in though; I couldn't possibly face the ideal of three hours five times a week as it was just too painful to needle my arm so much but on twelve or sixteen hours a week, doing it alternate days for four hours, I seemed to be doing okay despite the ongoing battering of my heart. Once again, I'm astounded at the human spirit and what we can do if we have to. And I'm so grateful for my little dog who lies on 'his' futon next to my chair, staring at me and then subtly glancing over at his treats on the shelf which he's trained me to throw him at regular intervals. God, I love that dog.

Well, as seems to be the story of my life, just as I began to relax a little and get into the swing of home dialysis, I had another bit of bad news. Well, a bloody massive bit actually. My plasti doctors had started to worry about the levels of scan radiation I was receiving by having such regular fistulaplastis to blow up my dodgy chest vein and keep my fistula working. My renal consultant proposed that I go for a scan of my arms and legs to see where they could put another fistula. I went into immediate fight mode. "Look, I know my veins are shot; I don't need a scan to tell us that!"

"Oh, I'm sure we can find something."

"Well I'm not. The last few times I was in hospital they weren't able to get any blood from me, never mind get a cannula in; they had to take blood from my feet!"

"Well, we really need to get a scan done."

"But I really don't *want* one. My toes can feel a bit numb, my right hand goes dead and I have constant chilblains in winter; I can feel that my veins are shot and I'd really rather not have that confirmed."

"Well if we don't look for options for a new fistula and

yours stops working, or they can't do any more 'plastis, you'll have to have a line."

"Look I realise that but I think I need to go with more radiation and the risk of cancer for a bit; I really don't think my nerves can cope with any more stress at the moment."

"Jayne, I'm not sure that's a great idea and you know there's the huge risk of infection with a line – it may also damage the veins in your right side too. Chances are there will be a vein we can use...."

"Okay, okay! I'll go for a scan but be prepared for me going insane when we get the results."

Three jittery weeks later came scan day. Supercool theatre nurse Witchypoo Carol kindly came with me. As my right leg was ultra-sounded in a little room off West Corridor, the radiographer, a quiet, beautiful, hair-braided woman who looked about thirty, asked me if I'd had blood clots in that leg. "Yes. A DVT when I was eighteen."

"Oh well, not to worry; let's look at your other leg." As she silently ultra-sounded my jellied left leg she kept her head down and asked if I'd clots in that. "Yes, a DVT when I was twenty-one." As I glanced across the room at Carol, she looked as gutted as I felt but attempted a reassuring nod. My innards were disintegrating. "Mmm. Shall we look at your arm?... Okay, here we go...oh...urm, well, urm...have you had a lot of needles?" Her dilated pupils said it all.

"Yes. A lot. It's not looking good, is it?" I managed, choking back my tears.

"I'm sorry, but you'll need to speak to the doctor."

Carol helped me to get my body dressed whilst I went into a stupefied bubble. *Oh my God. I knew it, I knew it! I really am fucked! I am D, the vein-mashed mermaid. I am G who was on her last vein. Then died. Oh my God. Oh my God! This is for real...* Holding onto a sombre Carol for support, I shuffled out of the hospital and we sat side by side on a low wall. She rubbed my back as I sobbed and gulped for breath and, clutching at disintegrating straws said, "You need to see what the doctor says."

"Yes. I know. Did you see her face though?"

"Let's just see."

"Can I have a hug please?"

"Course." My nerves soothed a bit as I clung to Carol like a baby monkey. "Ta, luv." We took a deep breath and turned back towards to glass doors...

The middle-aged, softly spoken doctor of South-Asian origin explained that he was sorry to tell me but the veins in my legs were shot (he may've said "damaged") the veins in my arm were shot and I had nowhere to put another fistula. *Fuck. Fuck. Fuck*. I did have a vein in my right shoulder that they could try and make a graft from though (if you remember, a graft's like a fistula except it involves using plastic to attach your artery and vein, so stands more chance of clotting up or causing infection).

"Shit. Sorry," I mumbled as tears streamed down my face.

"It's okay. It's bad news. I understand. But you know we all have to die; I may get run over by a truck on my way home. It's how it is."

"Yes."

"But you have been dealt some very challenging cards..."

As my brain came back from gaga land where I'd heard myself whimper like a wounded dog, I managed to croak, "What's the average lifespan of a graft?"

"Three to five years."

"Oh."

I spent the next few weeks in a dazed panic. *My God. If they say I can't have any more plastis cos of the radiation I might be dead in three years. Three years. Three years? Maybe five. That's if they can make a graft. Three years! Oh my God, what shall I do? Focus on my book? Move back to be with Mum and Dad? Go and strap myself to Nelson's Column or ride into Westminster on a horse, naked, in protest at the growing inequality and environmental destruction? Do a load of fundraising? Blog like a maniac?* A part of me felt quite liberated and energised; I could do and say anything! I'd nothing to lose. What was shame compared to death? There was also a part of me that just wanted to get *massively* off my face.

This was another biggie to share with my friends and I debated what to do. If I told them, there was a risk they'd freak and even do a runner. I couldn't bear to tell my parents. I eventually told my brother but tried to look on the bright side and did the "Oh well, I'll just have to risk getting bloody cancer; there's no way I can have this graft done, and with the size of my boobs there's not a huge risk of breast cancer! It'll be okay, this current fistula could last for years..." A couple of friends I was more real with.

"How did your scan go?"

"Are you ready, Maz?"

"Shit."

"A bit, yeah."

"Go on..."

"They can do a graft in my right shoulder."

"What, not a fistula?"

"Nowhere to put one apparently. My veins are shot."

"Oh my God!"

"I know."

"Shit!"

"I know. But I'm still here and by the time the graft packs up they may've developed better access techniques or grown kidneys. I might've even had a transplant."

"I hope so."

"Me too."

"Shit though!"

"I know." Maria had a wee cry with me and we talked about days out and holidays and other lovely things we'd do. Quickly. Interestingly, we had a bit of a fallout the next time we met up, something we very rarely have but it was easily resolved, both of us aware that Death had been warping our reality. Poor Claire, who knew the exact implications of what I was telling her, went pale. God, I hate being the bearer of bad news.

I remained in shock until I went for another appointment with my renal consultant. She still wasn't my favourite doctor but today I'd resolved to be less judgemental and more open-hearted and sure enough, as is the way when we change our inner world, the outer world changes too and she seemed much warmer. I told her what the scan doctor had said but she was quick to reassure me that I wouldn't be dead in three years' time because of access trouble; they could try lines from my chest or groin if the graft didn't work or stopped working and, "people can be on lines for years if they're well looked after – and you're good at taking care of yourself so don't worry, just keep living your life, you'll be fine. There's still a chance you may get a transplant..." I gobbled up her words and began to feel my life-force seeping back into my toes. Its soothing warmth began to snake up my legs and by the time I left Dr T's room (having been very close to grabbing and kissing her) my life-force had reached my heart.

I was back.

Determined again to make the most of every single moment, I was pretty floored by my next cortisol explosion a month later when one of my favourite plasti doctors, pretty, gentle Dr W., told me she'd been doing research and had decided, after my always having been told that the damage to my chest vein was too close to my heart to put a stent in, that they *could* safely get a newly designed stent in after all. In other words, I presume, the risk of trying a stent outweighed the risk of a load more radiation. Another month of dread and planning a new will was followed by a long, hard 'plasti' which was close to being aborted when Dr W. and her colleague couldn't open my totally closed vein. Finally, however, with me close to feinting, they managed to get the stent in. I then had a load more radioactive radar-ing to check it wasn't on its way to my heart. I was initially pleased that my left-side swelling seemed to reduce a bit but then gutted a few days later when it began to puff up again and it became apparent that the stent had made little difference, though I had to have less frequent fistulaplastis; only a three-monthly nightmare. Apparently my antibodies regard the stent as a foreign body and tend to block it up. I've now had over twenty of the damned plastis. Interestingly I haven't written about the most traumatic one; I guess I blocked it out. I was resting on my bed in the recovery area after the plasti and put my hand up to scratch my neck...*what the fuck?* I had a massive swelling. "Hello!" I shouted through to the docs, "I think I need a bit of help here!" My plasti doctor came bounding through and looked pretty mortified but soothed. "Oh don't worry, it's just a little bleed, it'll be okay."

"What, my vein's popped!"

"Ah a little, but it'll be fine..." Fortunately I had enough platelets that day to clot my blood quickly and I survived to tell the tale. I have to regularly remind myself that I'm not on a front line in some crazy war or watching my child die of starvation or malaria.

To end 2013 on a good note, I had a lovely week's holiday in Sussex with a chap I'd met just before I went on my six months travels and had contacted me on Facebook. With a spontaneous plan for us to go and see the band 'The Waterboys' perform, I called my new dialysis nurse, the friendly, warm and on-the-ball Sharon who I knew from being a sister on the renal ward. She needed the details of my holiday two months before departure in order to complete all the relevant blood tests and paperwork to send to the hospital where I'd booked my dialysis. I was nervous about dialysing on a strange unit but, dialysing at home before I left and as soon as I got back, I only had to go twice. It was scary, awkward and almost an hour's drive from our holiday home but it gave me the reassurance that I can go away on holiday without *too much* stress. Our cottage was great; in the middle of nowhere, cosy, clean, toasty and part of a smallholding with two mud-caked, hairy black and white pigs, a huge, chestnut, apparently un-rideable horse, chickens, goats and three young alpacas with fluffy flat-tops and long-lashed, bottomless brown eyes. My idea of Heaven, especially alongside seeing The Waterboys on Saturday night, 'The Whole of the Moon' being one of my favourite dancing tunes from my student days. Little did I realize back then that it would be Death who got me to see the whole of the moon!

Again it didn't work out with me and the bloke, sadly. Amazingly, I did it again in terms of him being very like my dad; insular, sporty, bandy-legged, easily shamed and classed as 'weird' by his own family. Which I guess was why it felt so easy being with him to start with; his complete reluctance to talk, emotional distance and apparent indifference felt normal to me and when he was kind, buying me a bun, for example, I felt like he'd given me the world! And the 'kid' part of him was so appealing too; so wounded and in need of my love and care! I just got fed up of being wounded by that same critical, un-empathic and hugely defensive kid. At least my pattern, my 'repetition-compulsion' became starkly clear and each time he rebuffed me, I had the opportunity to sob through more of the pain – the 'unfinished business' – that came with having a distant, traumatized dada. As I tapped into the old yearnings for a closer connection to my dad, my self-compassion grew. *If it's this painful as an adult being blanked by my bloke, imagine how devastated I must've felt as a child when I needed a cuddle from my dad!* By the time I'm seventy I may yet have processed enough of my pain and mustered enough self-compassion, self-esteem and courage for a great relationship!

Chapter 29
The Party's Not Over Yet!

*"Although the physicality of death destroys us,
the idea of death saves us."*

Irvin D. Yalom

Okay, nearly twenty years in the writing, this book *must* end! Shame's still goading; "You're a narcissistic nut-case, a pathetic show-off, a loony liberal..." and a part of me remains sick to the stomach at the thought of 'putting my head above the parapet' but as I look at some of the crazy and ruthless leaders who have powerful voices in the world at the moment I feel strengthened; if *they* can have a voice, why not me? I'm also determined to fulfil my grandad's dream of getting his poems into print. It's been interesting focusing on his poems again and seeing where so much of my thinking patterns came from. I feel indebted to him and also the brave 'whistleblowers,' artists, writers, poets, film, TV programme and internet video makers etc who have showing me the way in speaking my truth.

So, how to conclude? Well, I'm now fifty-three, which I find both shocking because it's come so quickly and amazing because I never dreamed I'd make this age. My face is looking like a raisin and, with my sticky limbs, I slightly resemble a Teletubby but, luckily, I'm increasingly able to smile and say 'Fuck it'; I know that when I was young, toned and gorgeous it got me absolutely nowhere and if I do have a moment of panic I find comfort in Roald Dahl's quote "If you have good thoughts they will shine out of your face like sunbeams and you'll always look lovely." (Not that I always have good thoughts!) I guess my looks feel pretty irrelevant given my health issues anyhow, what with our cultural obsession with perfect bodies; in that respect I still don't have much hope for a loving relationship though I did recently, in a moment of heart-strangling loneliness, join a dating site and even had a date but we agreed that a certain chemistry was lacking between us. I miss the small things like pointing out some pretty flowers in the garden or a picture I've just spent five hours drawing as well as the bigger things like intimacy and holidays and I find it hard maintaining my home and garden on my own – not to mention dialysing. I can also appreciate that nobody's snoring next to me at night and I don't have the inevitable stress and compromise that relationships can bring. I'm so grateful that I'm finally able to support and love myself.

My loneliness isn't helped by still feeling my childlessness keenly. I'm lucky to have friends without children so I don't feel too freaky but when I visit friends with children, go out with a bunch of mums or walk past families in the park, I'm often slammed by the familiar pain; the emptiness feels like a black hole I could jump into. I hate that I've deprived my parents of a set of grandchildren too; my mum especially feels this loss deeply. There are also moments when I watch parents struggling with their children and appreciate that I can just do what I want and don't have to worry about any little people or partying teenagers at four in the morning. During bad moments, I remind myself that though I may not be connected to my children or other parents, I can connect to the one in about five women who don't have children in the UK, the millions of people across the world who are also feeling grief and loneliness in any given moment and the whole of humanity through our common feelings, mirror neurons, DNA and atoms.

My feelings of loss about children are particularly rough at the moment because just over a year ago, I'm gutted to say, I lost the love of my life, little Alfie (ouch, ouch...) He was an old boy with arthritis and I was finding it hard lifting him into the car and carrying him up and down the stairs pre and post dialysis but I couldn't imagine ever being selfless enough to have him put to sleep. It was therefore a kind of relief when he was diagnosed with cancer and stopped eating, and I managed to call in the vet before he suffered too much. I'm glad that he died before me but it was devastating – especially as he made a terrible, anguished howl whilst he was dying. I've only recently been able to put up photos of him, look at his beautiful face and smile at the fact that I lived with the most amazing door-shutting, weed-sorting, paw-waving, leg-hugging sheepdog for fourteen whole years. I'm sure Alfie saved my life, taking me on so many walks, making me laugh so much and giving me blasts of life-enhancing oxytocin when I stroked him or looked into his eyes. He also gave me complete unconditional love – well, apart from the odd moment when he was sulking because he wanted to go out or threatening me with a curled lip if I stroked him on his bed (I don't think I ever really got top dog position!) Talking kindly to Alfie also helped to teach me a compassionate vocabulary and since he died I seem to have transferred the kindness I used to give him to myself – "Come on, Jaynie, it's time for bed lovvy..." Alf also taught me to live in the moment and really sniff the flowers. Thank you *so* much, beautiful Alfie-dog. My Grandad had a dog, a black spaniel, Bess, who he apparently loved dearly. When it was kicked by the milkman's horse and killed, Grandad presumably tried to ease his despair by writing this poem.

Only a Dog

The best friend I had, I've laid him to rest;
his love was a wonderful thing,
he never failed me, whatever the test
and looked upon me like a king.

He had no beauty if beauty be breed
no forbears of distinguished name;
he didn't choose friends by colour or creed,
nor to fame did he ever lay claim.

I remember his welcome as I opened the gate,
saw the love in his eyes just for me;
never reproachful, how e're long his wait
– it was there for the whole world to see.

Now wherever he's gone, I know in my heart
he's just waiting to hear my feet;
though in this world we've had to part
our next meeting'll be doubly sweet.

Arthur Downs

I don't bank on meeting Alfie again but it would be marvellous! I really miss him sitting with me whilst I'm on dialysis and, nine years on (nine years!) I *still* hate it with a passion; the horror of it, the time and organisation it takes, the frequently wrong equipment orders, the two floods from the water filters which ruined my downstairs ceiling, the restricted food and drink, the protein loss, my inability to travel widely or easily, the fear of further calcified veins and the damage it's doing to my heart. It's a bummer - but what can I do other than just get on with it?

Interestingly, as I worked towards finishing my book, after being so careful about not subconsciously sabotaging myself by accidentally deleting it or blowing up my house and lap-top at the last minute, my left hand, robbed of blood by my fistula, became increasingly blue, stiff and sore. Two small grazes from gardening over last summer began to spread and deepen until they were so sore I struggled to get dressed, could no longer put my hair up, cook much or drive. After seeing several doctors I was finally informed that I had 'arterial gangrene' and needed to have my precious fistula 'tied off.' I had more scans of my legs to see if there was anywhere I could have another fistula or graft; there was no chance in my right leg but further investigations of my left one are planned. I've asked that my right arm be left alone (not that it's a great option anyway – my chilblains are sore this year and my right hand's as stiff as a board) – no way can I risk my right hand becoming as numb as my left one did. I wrote in late December 2019 'The plan is for me to have a line fitted (it will go into my neck and then pop out of my chest) on the 14th January and my fistula tied off, under a general anaesthetic on the 15th. I'm dreading having to stay in hospital. The surgeon I saw, Mr Yates, was bright, sensitive and remarkably handsome, not that that's relevant other than it gave Kirsty (who kindly came to my appointment) and me a slight distraction from his hard-hitting words; "We *hope* the blood will come back into your hand and I *hope* I'll be able to take the lumps off your arm when I operate but if there's too much bleeding I won't – and it will mean bigger scars. I'm afraid until we do it we can't guarantee an outcome. Mmm…and I do wonder if there's some auto-immune activity going on given how stiff your hands are and I'm referring you to rheumatology. I'm sorry to say this but you'll have to prepare for some serious pain when the blood starts to re-enter your hand again; we may have to give you Ketamine…" Needless to say, I felt extremely anxious and quite grateful for the panic-soothing morphine I was already taking for the scream-level pain in my hand. I clung like mad to a conversation I'd had with my dialysis nurse, dynamo Sharon, a few months previously when she'd been to a conference where a doctor was advocating that using lines for dialysis were actually less problematic than fistulas.

"Really?"

"Really."

"So, I don't have to worry about dropping dead in the foreseeable then, even if I have no other veins for a fistula?"

"NO! I have another patient who's had a line for over twenty years and is fine."

"Still, I wouldn't be able to have a bath or go swimming with a line sticking out of my chest and there's a high risk of infection?"

"Yes, but things are managed well these days so stop worrying!"

"Okay, okay…"

Having a line – if all goes well – means I'll have to stay in hospital for three days and then go back to the unit for my dialysis until I can be trained in how to use my line at home. When Alfie died I bought myself an electronic bed and I like climbing into it when I'm knackered and know that I'll be comfortable and toasty for my four hours of dialysis. I'm dreading those long, uncomfortable and chilly evenings on the dialysis unit without my TV or wi-fi. (I can't believe there's no wi-fi in this day and age when patients, many who work, have to spend so long on dialysis.) I'm also dreading the late, cold drives home, the bugs and the horror. There will be perks with a line though; I shouldn't need the dreaded, radioactive fistulaplastis any more, I'll be free of dialysis needles (the dialysis tubing just screws onto the line) and hopefully I won't have the fistula's side-effects of a jittery heart, a swollen left side, pumped up veins and the occasional popping of small blood vessels in my eyes which make me look like a vampire for a week. I actually feel massively relieved (underneath my worry about the operations) that I'll no longer be home alone with needles and the scary blood-baths which come when I take my needles out; I'm absolutely sick of the sight of blood. If anybody mentions a bloody incident I generally heave and feel feint and gruesome films are out of the question.

Phew...what else can I say about my situation? I am the mermaid at the last chance saloon. Fuck. My amazing, pink-haired friend Ged offered to donate me a kidney about a year ago, as did her mum who I'd only met once at the shop (but she's over seventy so too old.) I was touched to my core but dismissed Ged's offer straight away because she has three children. I wish I were more selfish. I'm very aware I've not written about this but I do sometimes struggle with the thought "If my friends loved me they'd offer me a kidney; how can they see me in this state and not do something..." But of course 'doing something' is a massive, massive ask and I'm not sure I'd donate a kidney - or ever be able to accept the offer even if someone magically turned out to be a match. I see my friends' awkwardness and guilt sometimes that they aren't offering to donate me a kidney; kidney failure is so brain-frazzling and traumatic all round.

On a more pleasant note, my gynaecologist and I have finally agreed, after many years of us both being too scared, to stop my 'Zoladex,' the monthly hormone capsule that I had rammed into my belly every month to stop ovulation and the risk of further bleeding. My poor belly had its last painful assault in August 2019 and I presume I'm safely into my natural menopause as I've had no dodgy gut pains so far...

In general I still ache and am tired virtually all the time and when I have 'a lot of fluid on' can struggle to lift my legs. I can feel embarrassed using my 'Blue Badge' which gives me flexible parking but I greatly appreciate it as just walking through town can feel like climbing Everest. When I went swimming (frustratingly I haven't felt up to it for months) I wore a bandage over my fistula and was sometimes asked what I'd done to my arm; the looks of horror and quick, awkward retreats when I told them made me sad or amused, depending on my mood. I'd rather they asked than not, mind you, since a nurse once tried to comfort me by saying, "Oh don't worry, people will just think you're on heroin" (!) I can go to gentle yoga and pilates classes without feeling freaky and manage to stay awake through many of them! Ironically the red, threadbare veins on my face look like the classic Lupus 'red wolf' butterfly rash which I thought I'd got away with; I imagine people think I'm a rosy-cheeked alcoholic even though I rarely drink.

My leg's still got a significant dent and beer-mat sized scar, along with a brown, mottled tint below my knees which is apparently dead blood cells getting stuck due to the valves in my legs being damaged from my DVT's; they're not pretty. I get a few burning twinges near my scar sometimes which makes my blood run cold. When I'd got over my calciphylaxis, a young nurse gleefully let me know that I was the only person she knew who had survived it; not that reassuring when there's always the risk that I could get it again. Headaches also freak me out, but so far so good...

My gut was getting blocked near my operation site a lot last year (and bloody killed when it did) sending my liver results off the scale. I think it was at least partly related to my grief over Alfie and not feeling safe in the house without him. Following an MRI scan of my gut I got a brief letter out of the blue saying that they didn't *think* a dodgy shadow on my liver was malignant but I needed further tests – and had to come off the kidney donor register in the meantime. I then had a two months' nerve-sparking wait to check whether or not I had cancer with a 'trans-jugular liver biopsy.' The internet said that there was only a 0.09 percent mortality rate with this procedure but I kept having flashbacks to the time I had a line fitted and my squirting blood hit the wall. At an appointment just before my biopsy a cheery young registrar who I didn't know casually reassured me that if my liver was shot I'd be able to have a transplant...more cortisol!

In the end the biopsy wasn't half as traumatic as I'd imagined; it was done in the familiar Room 6 by some kind nurses and the friendly, Indian god look-a-like doctor I knew and trusted from doing some of my fistulaplastis. Only a tiny hole was cut in my neck and the wire wiggled easily down to my liver where a few small nicks of tissue were taken without too much pain (interestingly, I felt it in my shoulder, not my gut; 'referred pain.') After a month of chasing up my results, I finally got a letter saying that I didn't have liver cancer or cirrhosis but scarring of my liver ducts from all the gut infections I've had. Who knows how that will pan out; in recent months I've been eating like a horse with little pain.

One of my biggest frustrations in life continues to be doctors speculating about scary things which haven't been verified, like maybe having cancer or needing a liver transplant. Twice in the last few months I've had urgent calls from hospital reception staff telling me that my bed was ready and I should come in immediately – but being unable to tell me why! Half-day, panicked phone calls established that some random doctors had seen my terrible renal blood results but not the fact that I'm on dialysis. I appreciate being kept a close eye on but hate the cortisol explosions! I also had a carpel tunnel nightmare recently. Following tests I was told that I needed an operation which meant I wouldn't be able to use my right hand for six weeks (and if I was unlucky might sustain permanent damage.) I had to book onto the dialysis unit but wouldn't be able to drive myself there. When I initially asked what the operation would involve, the doctor said, "Nobody else has asked me that in fifteen years," implying that I was a freak for wanting to know what was going to happen to my own hand! Funnily enough his explanation was crap – how typically human is that, blaming others to cover our own perceived inadequacies. After weeks of cooking and filling my freezer – and having a ton of sleepless nights and nightmares – I was at the hospital and ready to go in my flap-open gown when my surgeon came to get my signed consent. "You know my hand doesn't feel too bad, are you sure I need this operation?" I asked.

"Well does it tingle like electric shocks?"

"No, it's just a bit weak and I keep dropping things."

"Does it go dead in the night?"

"No, it's more just stiff."

"Do your fingers curl up?"

"No."

"Well it's not carpel tunnel then and there's no point doing this operation. You probably need to see a rheumatologist. We'll see you in clinic in six weeks." I didn't know whether to kiss him for putting away his knife or smack him for giving me months of unnecessary stress. I didn't hear from the department again; too awkward perhaps. I didn't get my rheumatology appointment either. I *try* not to worry about my hands grinding to a halt; they do now tingle, go dead and curl up...

About a week after the liver doctors gave me the okay to go back on the transplant list I had my annual transplant list-related 'ECHO' or heart scan. It showed 'mild to moderate' impairment of my left ventricle and pressure in my heart. This meant yet another claustrophobic 'tunnel' MRI scan and then the month's wait for *another* random stranger to decide my fate. Luckily I was approved to go back on the transplant list by my cardiologist (the pressure was coming from my fistula) and apparently I'm now a 'priority case' because I've been on the waiting list for so long and my veins are shot though that doesn't mean my chances of finding a donor match have increased.

You'd think I'd be used to pain and bad news by now, but not really. I'm not sleeping well, partly because my hand hurts so much – even morphine doesn't really ease it – but also because I'm getting frequent flashes of Death's dark, blank eye sockets; during long nights I'm shaken to my core by his thunderous bellows and can feel his electric fury zapping my nerves. Interestingly, I feel absolutely overwhelmed by our climate crisis at the moment and the wipe-out of so many creatures; I find myself literally howling at David Attenborough's bad news – if I can face watching his programmes. I guess there's some projection of my own fear of extinction in there, terrifying though our climate emergency is in its own right. Australia is currently on fire, having temperatures of forty plus degrees centigrade when the norm is twenty-four. I've recently updated all my 'personal affairs' for my brother and given him my funeral and 'party' (wake) funds. Some days, when I'm on my knees with pain or exhaustion and feel like I've reached my limit of suffering, I toy with whispering a plea to Death to gently carry me away but I don't because I know that all things pass and that I'm blessed in a thousand different ways.

I don't think about it often or with real hope but I'm aware that stem-cell research is still working on growing kidneys (with an estimated twenty years until success is thought to be likely) and there's talk in the USA of one day implanting renal patients with super-sleek, mechanical kidneys. The UK's just joined Wales and Scotland with its organ donor 'opting out' scheme (i.e. we're automatically donors unless we take our names off the register) but it's not thought that will make a huge amount of difference. I'm not holding my breath for a dialysis-free future, especially as renal failure research funding is so crap and there aren't enough organ transplant surgeons at present, never mind with more organs becoming available, but you never know, I've certainly experienced miracles before! Talking of miracles, I heard the other day that the inspirational, vein-shot 'mermaid' has had another transplant and is doing well. I'm gutted to say that many of the other patients I've mentioned, including Stuart, the 'whole' man I met at Nic's birthday party, didn't make it.

I'm not sure if I still have post-traumatic stress disorder or just pretty shot nerves. I still jump (or shriek) at sudden noises; the toaster popping, the doorbell ringing, scary cinema scenes or someone suddenly appearing behind me. I noticed recently that I always sit at the back or far corner in public spaces so I can scan the whole room and I generally ask friends to meet me in the same café-bar, where it's open-plan, there are familiar faces and I feel safe. I can easily get overwhelmed and lose my clarity of thought if I have too many things to do (lists are an imperative) and whooshes of adrenal come easily. Claire's recently been studying to be a reflexologist and to build up her practice hours has been giving me the most sublime treatments; she always notices that my adrenal glands are screaming. Thankfully I can smile at myself when I attempt to gain some sense of safety and control by, in the spirit of my mama and Grandma, moving my kettle back into its rightful place or giving a garden bush a short back and sides.

I'm so glad that my own trauma (and psychotherapy training) has helped me to understand my younger mum's sometimes hysterical need for control. Interestingly, she had a huge stroke three years ago and has had a few smaller ones since and each time she's been in hospital she's regressed to her terrified, wounded six-year-old self, having hallucinations related to being left alone and actually looking like a wide-eyed, shaky-lipped child. It was horrendous seeing my mum so ill but also sort of good to be able to comfort that terrified child and be part of what seems to have been healing experiences for her; as is often the case with stroke survivors she cries a lot now but is much less spikey and critical. Thankfully my mama's recovered amazingly well physically (we must have good repair genes or her God really is taking care of us) though I do worry about her, especially as my never very helpful dad has a degree of dementia and does little in the house. After her big stroke, which left her left side very weak, my mum said "We'll be fine; we have one head and one body between us; your dad can push me up the stairs and I'll come down on my bum" and she and Dad have carried on living at home with just a bit of cleaning and care support. I'm so appreciative of my parents' dogged and stoic determination and I feel *so* lucky that, despite being over eighty and painfully fragile, my mum and dad are still here – and have each other – especially when I've put them through so much worry for so many years.

As with Alfie, I'm so relieved that I've not died on my parents and may yet save them from the nightmare of losing their daughter. It would be bloody grim losing them though! After working through a lot of our family trauma in therapy and having had many frank conversations with my mum, which included my being able to explain to her why she had fried nerves and her being brave enough to acknowledge her mistakes, I feel closer to my parents than I've ever done. I think they did a cracking job of bringing up my brother (who's a good man) and I considering the trauma passed down to them, the horrors they went through as children and their generation's wartime emotional shut-down. I know they love me dearly; my mum because she tells me all the time and nearly squashes me when she hugs me these days and my dad in the slightly upbeat way he says "Hiya" when he answers the phone and then carries on talking instead of passing the phone to my mum as he usually does. He often goes over the same familiar 'loops' during our conversations but I feel so grateful that his dementia is only taking him away slowly and I'm still able to connect – as much as I ever could – with him. And my parents are learning and softening all the time; they've had central heating put in (only downstairs, mind you) and bought two recliner sofas! My therapy has helped to heal us all; it was worth every penny. At Christmas when my brother and I were having our traditional argument about the rules of the game our dad just stood up and casually announced "I'm just going to go and kill myself" which immediately cut through our crap; his one-liners can be hilarious. My mum also makes me laugh when she comes out with her Yorkshire phrases; just yesterday she spoke of only being "knee-high to a grasshopper" (i.e. a child). She laughs a lot too; I love it when we laugh together. Mum knows most people in the village and is loving her new life outside The Chapel, which ground to a halt; her weekly exercise class, the fire station's dementia group fun Friday morning sessions and lunches out with new friends. She talks with surprise at noticing that people seem to like her; over seventy years on she's still scarred by her childhood experiences which is such a tragedy given how sociable, friendly and kind she actually is.

As I've learned to understand my parents' pain and behaviour, I'm pleased that I can also understand my brother's, so when we disagree about politics and the nature of humanity I can still love him dearly (he sometimes views me as a dreaming idealist - a fair comment I suppose!) I have great admiration for him. I know that he can't afford to be a 'space cadet' in his very down-to-earth place of work but, to his courageous credit, he has been brave enough to go for some therapy when many of his work colleagues and co-football obsessed Town fans would have considered that a weakness. I'm over the moon that my brother's increasingly self-reflective and open to a deeper way of looking at things – and connecting with me in that place. He initiated a great chat about consciousness recently and then sent me a video by Joe Dispenza about how thoughts affect the body (interesting stuff.) His eldest son is a lovely, gentle man, doing well as a brave farrier and he and his boyfriend have just bought their first home and my other cool as a cucumber nephew, who dared to leave his idiotic, wild animal-shooting boss and secured another apprenticeship up north, is almost qualified. I'm still hoping that neither of them gets hurt; they've both been kicked by horses already and the job's a hard physical graft. How do you parents cope with the worry for your kids?

Despite my concerns for my nephews, my parents and my own health, I generally feel pretty chilled and open-hearted these days. Having trained so much (through therapy and meditation) in 'mindfully observing' my thoughts, I've been able to see how much crap my mind came up with – the self-criticism, comparing, judging and worrying – and I am increasingly letting it go; "Yes Mind, thank you for that creative way of trying to make me feel superior but now can we please just focus on that beautiful sky…" I don't always manage to stay in my place of serenity of course; road rage especially can ensnare me if I've been cut up and flipped into 'fight' mode (I'm an expert in 'wanker' sign-language) and recently a council worker got the brunt of my foul-mouthed 'reptile brain take-over' when he and a probation team annihilated my local park, destroying birds' nests, loads of animal habitats and every single flower on the place. I wear a bracelet which I swap to my other wrist when I notice I'm getting cross or thinking unkind thoughts about somebody (including myself) and I ask myself what I'm feeling; normally the answer is sad or scared so I try to make space to 'turn towards' my sadness in meditation - guided by a good, solid teacher (generally Suryacitta, Tara Brach, Jon Kabat-Zinn, Eckhart Tolle, Jack Kornfield or Pema Chödrön) if I feel particularly vulnerable and need a sense of support.

So, amazingly, I'm doing okay, especially when I'm in a place of connection with myself, others and nature. I call death 'Doctor Death' these days because he's taught me how to live with such gratitude at simply being alive – and in such good shape, considering. The more I edit my book, the more blown away I am about everything that's happened, but, as mindfulness pioneer Jon Kabat-Zinn would say, there's still more right with me than wrong.

As most of my friends work full-time I can't actually believe my luck that I only need to work part-time and have lots of opportunity to do what I want. Over the summer I took great delight in pottering in my garden between clients, listening to the birds (I rate recent research which maintains that birdsong improves our mental health) and feeling the miracle of nature. I get immense joy from going outside and picking fresh, organic salad and vegetables for my tea. Though I can't run, play a serious tennis match or climb mountains, I recently got the train up Mount Snowdon with kind Kirsty and Marie (who would've chosen to walk up) and we strolled down. It was absolutely stunning and I'm learning that life can still be amazing even if I can't do all I'd like to.

Wonderfully, I haven't had to stay in hospital for about five years and about a year ago my parathyroid markers returned to normal and, unusually, I was able to stop taking my medication. I'm over the moon at being miles away from a knife coming anywhere near my throat! Also a bone density scan in 2018 revealed that my hips and spine had moved out of the 'at risk of osteoporosis' band on the graph to 'almost back to normal'. "Oh what have you been doing?" asked the impressed radiologist.

"I walk my dog a lot and do a fair bit of gardening."

"You must have been drinking a lot of milk."

"Actually just the opposite, I'm on a low calcium, renal failure diet."

"Wow...that's amazing; normally at your age your bones would be getting worse, not better!"

"Yes, well my friend Carol calls me Mrs Invincible; maybe she's right, eh?" My internal smile beamed.

I had two great holidays over the summer of 2015. The first was in Kent with Alfie, playful Pixie Julie (she's petite and pointy-chinned, with short, tussled hair) and her old, teddy-bear dog, Charlie, a cute but food-obsessed Bichon Frise; I took a while to forgive him for eating my whole bag of expensive, delicious fudge! Our mobile home was right next to the sea and a beautiful, peaceful bird sanctuary and we had a pool which was *thirty-six* degrees; floating in that, with foam strips under our feet and necks and sunshine beating down was probably the best my body's ever felt in my life! We'd gone to Kent because it was the only place I could find a dialysis unit with spaces; apparently a lot of notice is required for the summer months, a year ahead in Brighton hospital for example and many units don't have 'holiday spaces.'

Alf and I's second holiday was with Mike, a giant-brained old meditation group buddy who'd just moved to Devon. Our laughter-packed days out at the seaside and strolling and napping on coastal paths in the sun were beautifully freeing. The sea was so *blue!* In contrast, both visits to strange dialysis centres were scary and in Kent I had a small bloodbath because a connection hadn't been secured properly. Despite this, the kindness I received gave me enough confidence in 2016 to go to Tenerife with laid-back, Witchypoo Carol, and Málaga with bionic Susie. It was a pain having to get up for dialysis at half past six on three mornings out of seven and a bit unnerving that most of the Spanish staff couldn't speak English (and my Spanish extends to ordering two beers) but it all went smoothly. Listening to the sea, beach-combing for shells, swimming in the pool and lying reading in the winter sun was *glorious*. As was being cooked delicious food; the huge buffet nature of the hotels meals meant that again I could freely choose one date, a fig, a few cashews or strawberries and a couple of chips from my 'restricted' high potassium or phosphates list. Blissful! I really hope that Brexit doesn't result in my having to pay a grand for private dialysis during any weeks' holiday abroad.

Just as I feel high when I eat tasty food, I love the days I don't have to dialyse and really appreciate being able to see friends, garden, paint (I'm loving water-colours after an introductory class last year) write, play my piano or watch TV without painful needles embedded. My favourite evening is having friends round, including the joyful singer-guitarist Sharon (aka the singer Anya) gentle fiddler extraordinaire Ruth, cheeky, multi-instrumented music teacher Noah, laid-back, incredible improviser Jonny, haunting flautist Nic and fun-loving, dance-mad Susie, and we jam and sing to our heart's content.

Talking of friends, I was reading a renal patient Facebook page the other day and many patients were talking about friends falling by the wayside since they became ill. A couple of mine have too - my oldest friend, for example, said, "I knew you'd want to talk about things I didn't want to talk about" when I was going in for my big belly operation in 2007 and hasn't called me since but most of my friends are still around and new ones have emerged. Some are therapists, so can generally cope with me and others have challenging health issues themselves (including an ex-social worker and two nurses who gave too much) and they really get it when I talk about dragging myself about. Sadly the friend I could most relate to died two years ago. I met joyful, humble, sparkly eyed Sharon on a therapy training course and she called me, once we'd compared medical notes, the white version of her (her parents were Jamaican). Her crippling auto-immune problem was kicked off by the injections she was given when she was sent out to the war in Iraq as a military nurse (fucking war!) I was absolutely gutted when, just as she was about to be released from hospital after a torturous *year* of battling yet another nightmare, leukemia, the blood cancer reared up again and finally killed her. The world has lost a woman with a beautiful heart – as well as face – and I remain gutted and have felt much more alone since she died. I can feel pretty alone too when I meet friends who are fit and healthy and see their struggle with my constant, walking reminder of death and ill-health; my impulse can be to hide away in shame. Thankfully I understand their culturally encouraged fear but I'm aware that I try and keep 'plenty of eggs in my basket', partly in fear of rejection. I'm incredibly grateful for my brave friends as it seems Arthur was...

True Friendship

True friendships are made in heaven,
cast from a very rare mould
for though time turns your hair into silver,
this friendship it turns into gold.
Tis a beautiful thing, this gift from god
that lasts until life's end
out-shining the most precious jewel,
the hand of a proven friend.
Over life's hill though the paths become rough,
its beauty never grows cold
for as time turns your hair into silver,
this friendship it turns into gold.

Arthur Downs

Despite the odd issue which does my nut in, generally around feeling disempowered, being scared to death unnecessarily and never being advised on holistic aspects of health, like healing foods, exercise or stress management, I'm also *massively* grateful for my amazing, committed, empathic doctors and nurses who are under increasingly insane pressure as their workloads grow but staff numbers tumble. I'm particularly appreciative of my beautiful, chirpy and conscientious dialysis nurse, Sharon, who visits me at home once a month to take bloods, check the flow of my fistula (now line) give me intravenous iron, listen to my latest moans and reassure me (when she can) that all's well. She always gets back to me when I call; I trust that she does her best for me, and I *so* appreciate the feeling of safety she gives me. Sadly my trusted haematologist, Dr D., who had been my calming rock for nearly twenty years, moved to London. He sent me a card saying I could contact him if I needed advice and thanked me for what he'd learned from me! I was astounded and deeply touched (I cried a bucket) having presumed that he saw my manic ramblings about mind-body connections and the like as crazy. It's so good just knowing he's there if any local doctors unknowingly try to kill me, though he passed me on to Dr G, the giant-brained 'blonde half of the kind Abba duo' from E17 and I really rate and like her, as I do her colleague, Dr Swallow, who I've only met once but is an Antiphospholipid specialist and appears kind and 'on it.' Dr D. and Dr G. have my *absolute* gratitude for always having recognised that I'm a vulnerable human being as well as a sick body – just as my GP, Dr Liau, who retired last month, did. He always listened and responded sensitively and authentically, giving me a hug on bad days. There was a real security in knowing that he knew my 'whole story' – and had become a speedy expert in whacking my Zoladex implants into my belly. I'm pretty gutted that he's left but there are other kind GPs at my surgery. I'm very thankful that I now trust and like my petite, giant-brained renal consultant; she's really committed and thorough and more emotional and empathic than I first thought (even though she doesn't like to show it) – again a big lesson for me in the folly of seeing things through a scared brain (and my jealousy of her pregnancy) rather than realistic eyes.

I still think our NHS is one of the most incredible institutions ever established and something for the UK to be proud of. I can't tell you how blessed I feel for the mostly wonderful care I've received over the years and I'm scared – and disgusted – that our current government still appears to be running it down and moving towards privatisation; billions of pounds worth of NHS contracts are in the hands of private firms, nurses' training bursaries have been stopped, doctors are fleeing abroad where pay and conditions are much better and we're incredibly short of GPs, doctors, nurses and surgeons. I would be so gutted if a potential kidney finally became available from the organ donor register but there were no surgeons to transplant it! But that's not something I need to worry about today. Today I'll just be grateful. Grateful for our NHS and all the staff who are hanging on in there despite their exhaustion – and in many cases, appalling pay. Grateful that I live in a relatively rich, peaceful and democratic country (well, kind of – lying, self-serving MP's, a biased media owned by billionaires who have to be pampered by any party who wants to win an election, 'classified information,' a restriction on peaceful protesting, institutional racism, unequal opportunities and a half-cocked voting system hardly constitutes a real democracy but it could be much worse.) I'm also grateful that I have kind neighbours, a lovely home (including a roof, running water and a fridge – luxuries that *billions* of people just like me don't have) and a tree-bottomed, big-skied garden. I often feel that I'm literally one of the luckiest people in the history of humanity; my birth date and place gave me mostly peace time (other than the UK's scuffles with the IRA, Argentina, Kuwait, Iraq, Afghanistan and Syria) good food, a childhood playing out (I wonder if that's why I'm still here) free schooling which wasn't stressful by today's test-obsessed standards, quality, non means-tested school dinners, a student grant, great opportunities to travel, fantastic healthcare, a home bought in 1994 (when they were cheap), interesting jobs and the ability to live as a single woman without destitution or ridicule. I'm so appreciative too of the fact that my mind enjoys being blown away by the wonder of our amazing universe – from DNA and the sub-atomic world popping in and out of existence to infinite space; I can feel high just planting seeds or looking at a furry creature and each spring is getting more beautiful as my capacity for being mindful increases.

Mahatma Gandhi apparently said "Happiness is when what we think, what we say and what we do are in harmony" which makes me *constantly* grateful that I'm in a position to 'walk my talk.' I love my therapy work; it can be challenging, exhausting and painful but the reward of connecting with hurting people and figuring out the reasons for their pain and difficulties *together* feels like an almost sacred process. And, of course, the gift of them feeling better is absolutely immeasurable. In line with my therapy work, with self-compassion, acceptance of things as they are and 'being in the moment' at its heart, I'm also now teaching mindfulness; as with my confidence building and stress management, I'm teaching what I need to learn. It began in 2013, with a day's nerve-wracking workshop for fifteen counsellors. Luckily for me I ran it with my bright and efficient physiotherapist friend, Sally, who delivered the neuroscience behind stress and saved me the headache of trying to remember HPA axis, manic amygdalas and the like whilst in a state of major anxiety. We did okay; from building new neurons and being kind to ourselves to living happily despite grief and death in six hours!

I then began to deliver day trainings in my therapy space and facilitating a monthly 'Mindfulness Evening' with Sarah, a beautiful, deep, gentle yet sparkly and funny woman who I met on an eight-week mindfulness training, and then studied with on a week's fantastic mindfulness teacher training in 2014 (with the chuckly, wise Dr Patrizia Collard and the giant-brained and deeply compassionate and musical Liverpudlian, Dr Karen

Neil.) It's so refreshing running the evenings with Sarah rather than alone and a lovely, open-hearted group of men and women have been coming along. I facilitate a second group and again feel honoured and over the moon to be spending evenings with a bunch of courageous women who dare to risk being open, honest and real. Sitting meditating, sharing our thoughts and feelings and recognising our common humanity (including our envy, anger, criticalness *and* vulnerability) is so beautiful; we're all just human!

I've delivered mindfulness trainings to a myriad of community groups, charities, counsellors, care managers, teachers, school children and young people and I *love* it. I recently asked a class of six- and seven-year-olds what they could take away from our two forty-minute sessions; "That kindness is good for you!"..."That it's good to cry"... "That it's okay to feel angry so long as you don't hit anybody" (the mouse regretted hitting 'Little Frog' in the face with her tail in the story I'd written and illustrated for them.) I had to choke back my tears of joy at how much these little people had taken on board. I was equally moved as I encouraged about seven hundred teenagers (on a six week 'citizenship' project over last summer) to reflect on their self-care and why most of them felt the need to use filters before posting their photos on social media. (How sad's that?) As in my women's confidence building groups we looked at the 'programming' which makes us feel bad about ourselves; comparisons on social media, aspiring to look like beautiful film-stars (and their stand-in body parts) only being rewarded for the ability to write essays and pass exams at school, the pressures of homework and exams, needing the 'right' gear to wear, having popular hairstyles etc. I tried to show them how mindfulness can help us to live and love life from the *inside!*

If it was up to me I'd hold weekly 'get real' gatherings in our town centres. We could have a communal howl or cry at the madness, share our latest reptile brain blunders, what we struggle with and what joyous and lovely things have happened. Imagine just turning up in the town square and hearing that, like you, other people have had road rage this week, hated their kids or spouses or felt terrible shame. Imagine listening to a lovely old man telling you about his loneliness and then seeing how much better he feels, or you sharing with a stranger how worried you feel and then your anxiety magically lifting. Imagine sharing hugs and what you're grateful for with strangers and realising how similar you are to others, whatever their struggles, class, skin colour or cultural background – and then laughing at our craziness and going off to do your shopping on a high. I was actually joking but the more I think about it, the more this seems like a good idea! Normalising our universal human shadow, shame, vulnerability and pain; connecting and being compassionate and sharing the love and our joy!

On that feeling alive note, I have to tell you about my lovely moment as I delivered a mindfulness training day at home recently. As people were relaxing to a body scan on my turquoise velvet sofa and new, plush green rug (like my parents I'm no longer just 'making do') I suddenly realized that my dream of having my cosy therapeutic community where people could come to 'just be' and feel safe had arrived! My place isn't the converted barn in the country with a loving husband which I'd imagined but I have warmth, cosiness, a slightly wild, insect-friendly garden and my 'Shed,' a beautiful, eighteen foot pine cabin built by my clever neighbour, Roger, recently insulated and lined in fresh pine (it smells divine) by the creative Martin and Kieran and then fitted with electricity by my big, Greek god look-a-like neighbour, Simon. And the 'commune' I've often dreamed of is made up of all my lovely neighbours who keep an eye out for me as well as any husband would; I can't have closed curtains for long without a call to check I'm okay. We're having another street party on Saturday, having connected with some Muslim women, Zhanara and Sana from the next street when they kindly brought food gifts round during Eid. I've now got a beaming smile on my face as I'm recalling my "Make me a channel of your peace" moment during my wedding and feeling so grateful that I'm on that path and mostly well enough to walk it.

I find it *so* interesting that I've had no major Lupus flares (the latest medical opinion was that I *do* have Lupus, as well as Antiphospholipid Syndrome) or hospital admissions since making mindfulness (the great cortisol and inflammation soother) an integral part of my life. In becoming calmer and more self-compassionate instead of viciously self-berating and more in touch with my emotions (and able to cry) it seems that my auto-immune self-destruction has eased. I remain curious about whether my auto-immune 'self-destructive saboteur' is linked to my family's survivor guilt from my grandads surviving World Wars, my dad's National Service (when a peer was blown up three weeks before his discharge and he had to guard and chat with two men in Cyprus who were being executed the next day) my grandma living whilst her two brothers died and my mum and I seeing fellow patients die. I'm so pleased that medics are finally acknowledging the physical impact of stress and that neuroscience is proving how different behaviours and thoughts release different bodily chemicals, such as kindness releasing happy, healing oxytocin, whilst stress, anger and aggression produce killer cortisol. Research is now telling us, by the way, that we can increase our oxytocin by caring for wild birds and animals (seeing hedgehogs in my garden munching on food I've put out certainly boosts my oxytocin) and also plants as well as pets and fellow humans, being massaged (magical touch), inspired by music, art or anything else that makes our 'heart sing' and also expressing our emotions; it seems that a problem shared is indeed a problem halved.

And so, whilst I believe that stress, my ruthless inner critic and having to ignore my fear fuelled my auto-immune self-destruction, I also appreciate that cutting off my fear got me to the tops of trees and ropes as a kid and all over the world as an adult and that my family's stoic spirit of 'just getting on with it' has been a part of what's kept me going all these years. As has slowing down, taking care of myself (with mindfulness, gardening, yoga, walking in nature, sleep, rest and nutritious food), doing what *I* want to do, learning to 'be' as well as 'do,' feeling properly heard by my therapist and friends, becoming aware of and changing my negative thinking patterns, re-engaging with my wise body, its intuition and landscape of feelings and capturing – and being grateful for – the good bits of life whilst trying to accept the hard bits as normal and inevitable. With regard to feeling sad, I don't relish it but I know that if I feel appalling I'm learning about myself and what I need to change and also widening my 'window of tolerance' (a useful term from the fabulous relational neuroscientist, Daniel Siegel[59]) for difficult feelings so they become less overwhelming and debilitating. I'm so grateful that I've learned that my tears release sadness and stress hormones and carry me to a better place – the old paradoxical theory of change – and that, ultimately, sadness is just a bunch of physical sensations such as waves of tightness or sickness in our gut, stinging behind our eyes and maybe feeling a bit feint or achey if we feel really crap - but all stuff that we can just be curious about. If I'm crying for people or animals who are suffering or am sobbing at a beautiful scene of care or connection on TV I feel very *human*. Having said all that, my ability to stay with my feelings is of course not constant and I can still add to my unhappiness by attaching those dastardly stories (the 'second arrow') to my life; *OMG my life's a nightmare, I can't stand being on dialysis a moment longer... I'm probably going to die soon...I'm so lonely but who on earth's going to want to be with me in this state?*

---

59. See bibliography p. 430

Look, do you really think you're going to lie on your death-bed thinking 'Oh great I kept myself safe from heart-ache' just like you did with Gerly?

Well, maybe not. That is a regret in my life…more so than my disastrous marriage, I guess…it's what we don't *do… Mmm…okay, okay, I'll try to get out more but what if I really am un-dateable…*

You are *lovable, Jaynie…*

Mmm…Okay, next time I see a kind-looking man I'll try not to just automatically put my head down and look away like Alfie did what he saw another dog…

Absolutely! Come on, Jaynie; muster the courage to take down that wall and be vulnerable, flower! Just you keep telling your nervous system that you're safe now.

Okay!….

Well, my book doesn't have the romantic happy ending that I'd secretly hoped for but I realise that it possibly has an even happier one; the last decade's been about me forming a positive relationship with *myself* and transforming my vicious self-berating into gentle self-compassion – and much of my unkindness into compassion. If I make a mistake I remind myself that I'm just a normal, imperfect human. If I'm hurting I remember that, in that moment, so are millions of other people – with many of them in much worse pain – and if I feel vulnerable I know that therein lies strength, empathy, compassion and an open heart. Now I want to reach out to fragile women crumpled into their pillows instead of pulling on my curtains to avoid them – and that puts a smile on my face. I am so glad that I've been softened by my life experiences; I much prefer this Jaynie to the self-important, defensive and easily angered princess who first went into hospital. I totally accept that I can't feel deep happiness without the illumination and softening of sadness and vulnerability, and more than ever I find our popular culture's notion that wealth and so-called 'success' can buy you a constant state of happiness, a sad, sick joke. For me, success is an open heart.

Just as I struggle to see people working themselves stupid in order to appear 'successful,' I feel puzzled when people say they're bored. Mindfulness has taught me that if there's little going on, I have the space to tune into the wonder of the moment – the beautiful sky, birdsong, my cup of tea or the patterns on a rug – and if it's a crap time, well it's just a crap time and it will change. I can also turn inward, with curiosity and self-compassion, and there's a whole world to observe – a plethora of fascinating sensations, feelings and monkey mind thoughts; thoughts which can delight me or put me and others down and have such an impact on my health, brain structure, genes, hormones, protein levels, enzymes, neuropeptides, chemical receptors and the rest.

Despite being able to soothe my fearful monkey mind easier these days, I've still got a way to go with asking for help but I'm working on it. I have a gardener, Nick, and though I have to pay him well so I don't feel exploitative, it's a step on for me and I recently managed to ask my brother and his partner to help with some DIY and friends to help me dig a new pond for the frogs – and other wild creatures – as irises had taken over my old one. We had a lovely morning and once again I was blown away by a bit of communal effort; one minute a flat patch of ground, an hour later a beautiful pond!

Despite my amazing Near-death Experience I don't know what I believe about an afterlife; maybe there's something after death, maybe not. How do I know? I no longer wrestle with whether or not we're all part of 'god,' I just accept we're all part of the amazing life-force, *here, now* (with the 'natural intelligence' – thanks for that useful term Suryacitta – of nature built into us and guiding us towards wellbeing). I'm not sure about anything really; I have no solid ground beneath my feet – apart from knowing that my life's a miraculous and precious gift and that really connecting with nature, music, our amazing variety of tasty foods, each other and *ourselves* feels great!

I suspect this is a bid to feel a sense of control, but I sometimes imagine having a chat with God (despite not believing in Him) before I was born. "Well, Jayne, I have a choice of two lives for you."

"Go on..."

"This one, where you get married at twenty-six, have a great husband, two lovely children and live a fairly uneventful but happy life..."

"Oh okay, that sounds good."

"...Or this one, where you have traumatised parents, get Lupus, have a tough job in social work, become really ill, can't have kids and live with death constantly. You have some disastrous relationships, face enormous pain and loneliness but it softens, strengthens and moulds you into an open-hearted person; you get to travel, learn shed-loads, help a lot of people along the way and feel happy most of the time with just the simple things in life..."

"Mmm...it sounds great – not!"

"I'm offering you this because your spirit can do it, Jayne... you even get to write a book, trying to do your bit towards human evolution..."

"Oh...what's it about?"

"Being human."

"Mmm...are you *sure* I'm strong enough?"

"You will be...you'll have some good, resilient family and friends behind you..."

"Tut...go on then, I guess if it's for the greater good..."

And some moments, usually when I'm in a lot of physical or emotional pain, I shout, "Not on your nelly! No, no! Give me the blinkers, husband and children!"

In mostly accepting my life as it is, I'm also still on a roll accepting myself as I am. I no longer care much that I have mottled, odd-sized legs and scarred arm (though I do miss my freeing strappy tops and swishing knee-length skirts in the summer.) I don't worry that I'm seen as the 'crazy' woman who's had years of therapy and writes in the corner of the café, beaming one minute and wiping tears the next. The 'loser' who chooses to work part-time and gives concessions to clients when she could be making a fortune. The 'nutcase' who strikes up random conversations with strangers, laughs raucously, swears profusely, and loves dance classes where people are encouraged to go wild. The 'outrageous delver' who asks people how they are when I know they're hurting. The 'loony' who ranted about suffering in a community pantomime and stands in the town centre giving away home-made buns and random hugs. The 'dreamer' who believes that hatred and conflict could be minimised by wealth and land sharing, empowerment and connection. The 'spinster' whose life's love was a sheepdog. The 'morbid nutter' whose favourite subject is death...

In my so-called craziness, I feel pretty free!

Ironically, after being criticised over the years (mostly by people who are trying hard not to feel) for 'naval gazing,' I've discovered that what makes me most happy is not an insular or selfish thing but rather, being kind. My latest project was fundraising (we had a great gig night with the fabulous bands, The Amber Herd and The New Apostles playing for free) and collecting clothes and provisions in my flowered campervan (which I sold when my co-traveller, Alfie, died) for a Refugee Action group. It hurt to see thousands of bombed-out, traumatised Syrian people being barricaded behind European fences and trying to bring up their children in muddy, rat-infested camps but that hurt and compassion inspired me to action. Yeah! Feelings rock!

I recently read a great article by the brilliant Jack Kornfield[60] about the world needing us to work on our own capacity for peace and sitting quietly until a path of action to do what we can to help others, in our own unique way, emerges. That seems about right to me.

So, though I'm sick of pain – like at the moment with my vein and dialysis 'access' plight – and sometimes feel completely overwhelmed, life goes on. I don't always get it right and have a way to go in terms of self-awareness, ego-centred thinking and behaviour (it's all about me, me, me), ethical shopping, eco-action, non-judgement, intimate relationship courage etc but I accept that I'm imperfect and just keep trying to live by my good intentions in each new moment. Despite my flaws and challenging circumstances, if I take life a moment at a time, trying to live from the 'inside,' from my miraculous body and senses, consciously noticing the beauty and remembering how lucky I am, most moments feel pretty good, in fact many feel wonderful. As for my relationship with Dr Death, I once wrote a poem about death (on a spirituality weekend facilitated by my ex-husband actually, bless him) and it still pretty much sums things up for me…

---

60. *www.lionsroar.com/Buddhism's Call to Action*

An Ode to Dr Death

Oh fearful Death, you haunt me so.
Each waking hour, each dreamful sleep
there you are, prowling behind me
with your huge, glistening knife,
teasing, testing, torturing me
as you silently debate whether or not
to cut my string to life.
I hate you, I HATE YOU!!
You're a foul, sadistic beast!
...And yet I wonder...
Without you would I really live?
Would I feel the fullness of a misty morning?
Would I really see the dandelion's clock of
    perfect stars?
Without darkness is there light?
Without fear would I know what it is to be
    human?
Would I bother to reach out
to the others whose strings you also threaten?
Would I be alone?
Ha, ha, Dr Death!
Prowl as much as you like.
Go on, snarl! Growl! Brandish your knife.
All you're gonna do is wake me from sleep
and remind me
to dance with the miracle of life!'

Jayne Pigford

PS: It's now the end of January 2020 and I'm back on my sofa, post operation, with *both* my lovely hands, after what turned out to be a challenging week in hospital. Back in a place of terror, it was interesting to stand back and clearly watch myself going through the full range of fight-flight-freeze reactions. When I was admitted, knew few of the staff and felt scared stiff, I immediately went into fight mode, disliking everybody, including the poor woman shaking with Parkinson's in the opposite bed when she was moaning and shouting in the night. The plan, if you recall, meticulously negotiated by my haematologists and renal team to minimise any blood clotting or bleeding issues, was to put the line in my chest the day before my life-sustaining fistula was tied off but because my blood was too thin on 'line day,' the fistula operation came first, leaving me, potentially, with no dialysis access. At this point I went into flight (and illogical but total control) mode thinking, *that's it, I give up, I'm gonna sign myself out and go home; I don't care if I die...* then my insides collapsed and I had a pretty embarrassing ward round with four doctors and surgeons when I just couldn't stop crying.

A day later, despite having been told that my fistula operation had gone well and clever Mr Yates had managed to cut off the horrendous fistula bumps on my arm without a bloodbath (Yeah!), you should have seen my spectacular return to 'fight' when I was wheeled down to Room 6 for my line. I'd already been freaked out with the news that my blood-clotting platelets were low, and being given (via a drip) an emergency bag of platelets as I was being wheeled down hospital corridors for my line (by the gracious, lithe, black-English porter, John and a kind, chatty nurse) didn't help one jot. Then I really lost it when a doctor who I hadn't been introduced to stood behind me in Room 6, prepped me up (a good clean with sterile fluid, being covered in a sterile sheet and then injected with local anaesthetic) and then started cutting a hole in my neck... "Excuse me, but who are you?"

"I'm Doctor X."

"Well I just signed the consent form with Dr M.!" (I knew and trusted him from doing some of my fistulaplastis) "Where's he gone?"

"Oh he's keeping an eye on things, don't worry." When I broke down into hysterical sobs the nurse who, I presume, was supposed to be my emotional support threw in "What's wrong with you? You just signed the consent form!"

"What's wrong with me? This is my last chance at staying alive, what the hell do you think's wrong with me? And I didn't sign for a complete stranger to be doing this!"

"Please calm down."

"Calm down? Bloody hell, I'm guessing you haven't done any trauma training by the way you're using that tone and standing there with your hands on your hips?"

"No."

"Well can I suggest that you do some!"

The doctor came round and stuck his green-hatted head under the X-ray machine to introduce himself, and seeing his face helped a little, but when he resumed the procedure and Dr M. came in and started telling him that his lines were too short and to do it like so and so, I freaked again. "Christ, how many lines have you actually done?"

"Oh about ten."

"Ten!" At that point I again collapsed into complete powerlessness and froze; now only my quiet, steady flow of tears revealed the extent of my trauma. I felt about five years old.

At the end of the – thankfully successful I think – nightmare, I was able to stop crying and express my gratitude to the slightly disturbed crew of Room 6 (I owe them a big hamper of goodies.) Dr X came through to the recovery area to apologise and assure me that he did know how important the procedure had been for me, having been a renal transplant surgeon for many years. I apologised too. Looking up into his face I told him that he looked kind and that it would all have been so much easier if there'd been that human connection first. I'm not proud of my behaviour but maybe it will save another terrified patient from a similar fate, though to be fair, the staff of Room

6 have usually been good at introducing themselves when I've had fistulaplastis.

Safely back on the renal ward I managed to glance briefly at the new line sticking out of my chest; hanging from a bloody hole about three inches above my right breast were two, three inch rubber lines with a plastic clamp on each and a screwed on end-piece. Two weeks on and I've only once managed to have a proper look at it in the mirror, and it freaks me out that there are only two clamps and bits of plastic between a line going straight to my heart and a million airborne bugs. The good news, however, is that the line tucks pretty inconspicuously into my bra (one advantage to having mini breasts) and I've had dialysis through my line about four times now and it works fine; it's actually *great* not having to face needles – or bloodbaths – when I have dialysis! I feel released from regular torture and realise just how stressful my dialysis was. As I predicted, it's not fun being back on the dialysis unit sitting in an uncomfortable chair with my nose like an ice-cube and surrounded by suffering people – and bugs and radios, beeping machines, a hundred voices, tellies, coughing and shrieking– for four hours. But the staff team is stable (a sign of a good unit) and it was really nice to see some kind, familiar faces. I can train up to dialyse at home through my line – as long as I keep everything absolutely sterile. It may take me a while to psyche myself up for that but I'll get there...my warm, comfy dialysis bed and TV are calling!

I'm feeling extremely grateful that my operations went smoothly and that my two, three-inch-long arm scars are healing well, as is my left hand. When I came round from my fistula operation, which was under general anaesthetic, I felt my right hand holding a warm hand and looked to my left for the person it belonged to but there was nobody there. Looking down I saw that the hand was mine and for the first time in years was toasty warm – just numb from the 'nerve block' they'd given me in an attempt to give me twenty-four hours before the predicted mega-pain of the blood running back into it. When I lifted my arm, my limp hand just swung toward me and hit me in the face and I nearly fell off my bed when I went to get on it and forgot that my left arm wouldn't work! Magically, when the pain block wore off the pain in my hand was not too terrible and manageable with morphine – a huge relief!

I've mentioned in previous chapters how the suffering of other patients in hospital is hard to cope with and again, this really struck me during this admission. Interestingly it took me days to remember the names of the three other woman on my ward and make them into 'real' people. Seeing Jackie, my age, shaking and in agony because she was unable to take her Parkinson's medication as it had affected her liver and kidneys, was terrible, as was, on my second day, seeing a tall, booted, female doctor stride over to Linda in the next bed to me, pull round her curtain and then proceed – with me hearing every word – to tell her that she didn't think further dialysis was going to benefit her given how weak her heart was; in other words, she gave her a death sentence. I cried quietly when her two teenage daughters, with what seemed to be a degree of learning difficulty, came to visit later, looking awkward and upset at the sight of their tiny mother's fragile bones. Actually a week on, Linda and I had twice laid side by side having dialysis on the ward and there was talk of her being well enough to go home. Not for long I imagine.

I felt very fortunate that just outside my ward was a long, quiet corridor where I could take myself off for a break from the usual head-mashing noise, a leg-stretch and a whimper. I didn't feel dramatic or sorry for myself as I doubled over in tears, crying for me, my worried parents up in Yorkshire, Jackie, Linda and our ward's fourth patient, Sandra, with her missing front teeth and an inability to keep down food or tablets. Again, I feel *so* lucky that I've learned to cry and know it's simply nature's way of releasing stress and trauma. When I got home (oh the peace!) I was perturbed to find that I still couldn't sleep (as in hospital with all the noise and being woken up for the required blood pressure readings and the like at 4.00am.) I guess I was processing what had happened and I'd also been violently struck by my loneliness when I got home; there was no Alfie-dog waiting to cling to my leg this time. But, as ever, the more I've bawled my eyes out, the easier it's got. Last night I was dreaming that I was sobbing and woke up drenched in tears with my heart banging; my subsequent waking wails gave way to such peace that I spent the rest of the night sleeping like a baby and woke up feeling great.

Although my hospital stay was hard it was also beautiful; again I felt that I was basking in the best of humanity. My brother and friends were stars and kept me going with visits – Claire and Kirsty with a delicious take-away one evening – and Maria went to my house and washed my bedding so it'd be clean for my new line (how thoughtful is that?) whilst kind Carol brought me her usual Jelly Baby treat and then filled my fridge. Susie was away but had sent me flowers and a book, and some lovely cards and a beautiful indoor fern from In Kind's Kaye welcomed me home. I felt very blessed.

On top of the goodness of friends there were again staff members from all over the world working together in the service of strangers, no matter how scared they were of making mistakes (the anxious, litigation-fear back-covering was clear) how pissed off they were at us patients being irritable, demanding and rude or how tired and undervalued they felt. I had moments of great sadness as I watched them flying about and knackering themselves out during twelve-hour shifts, especially when there weren't enough staff and I felt waves of rage that most of them weren't being given anywhere near the financial rewards they deserved whilst ruthless gits working in finance and cut-throat businessmen were raking in the cash. As I observed from my bed, it appeared that the staff demands and stress levels were higher than when I was in hospital twenty years ago and that the NHS really is in trouble. I had an interesting conversation with a 'registrar' (doctor) about this. When I asked him if he thought the NHS was being deliberately underfunded so that the government could justify privatising it he said, "I can't talk to you about that."

"My God, do you mean you're gagged and may lose your job if you do?"

"Exactly."

"So our NHS is falling apart but nobody's allowed to talk about it?"

"What can I say?" My admiration for our frustrated, overworked NHS staff only increased with his comments. We are SO lucky that there are so many people willing to undertake such self-sacrifice in order to care for those of us who are sick and I'm even more convinced that we humans have good hearts and are wired to connect.

There were a few more platelet scares before I managed to fight my way out of hospital; they'd gone down to twenty-one (if you remember, severe bleeding can start below twenty) and I was stuck on a big dose of steroids, despite trying to tell my doctors that over the years my platelets have tended to drop when I'm scared stiff and losing the will to live but perk up again when my mood does. So I have steroid edginess going on and look like a giant hamster again but at least now my fistula's gone I no longer have a swollen left side; my breasts and the two sides of my face nearly match again!

And so life still goes on, vulnerability, fear and all and despite my trauma, being home alone and having a wrecked body, life's generally good. I wake up every morning with gratitude that I have another day in my miraculous body on our beautiful earth and I'm determined to enjoy this life, aim to be kind and 'evolve' as much as I can whilst I'm still here.

Chapter 30
My hope for humanity

"Another world is not only possible, she is on her way. On a quiet day, I can hear her breathing."

Arundhati Roy

So then, maybe my seven months in hospital and inadvertently discovering mindfulness and the resilience and joy that's come with it really was the best thing that ever happened to me and I'm not as mad as a badger after all! And maybe I'm not crazy to think that at the heart of us we're kind and designed to connect, as exemplified by the UK's amazing National Health Service. I really believe that my 'chemotherapy bliss time' was a glimpse of our natural human state when our fear, egos and crazy, conditioned and 'negatively biased' minds get out of the way. My positive view of humanity means that I try (and don't always succeed) to go round in the world being open and sociable and my experience is that most people are receptive and friendly in return. I'm convinced that we could create a much more peaceful and loving world if we really took on board that we're biologically and psychologically wired to connect – and all just want to love and be loved – instead of gobbling up society's notion (currently embedded in the neoliberal economic model) that it's 'natural' to compete, accumulate more than we need and lord it over others!

Interestingly, as I come to the end of my book in late 2019 (before the Corona virus, though I have added a 'Corona chapter') the news is painting a picture of a world which appears to be pretty disconnected with many world and corporate leaders doing all they can to grab as much power as possible and epitomising divisive, oppressive, unethical and earth-plundering attitudes. The shift to the extreme right of politics in many places has been exacerbated by the old 'divide and rule' tactic where, when the going gets tough, the media (generally government-backed) blames minority groups. At the moment it's interesting to see how people who are so desperate that they've trekked for hundreds of miles and are risking their lives in rubber boats on the sea, often from places like Iraq and Syria where the UK was partly responsible for annihilating their country, are being portrayed on the news as slightly less then human - they're pesky 'migrants' trying to take advantage of the UK, not human beings just like us.

Morality seems to be going out of the window as many politicians and their billionaire friends, who own most of the (phone tapping, police bribing) media, lie their socks off. We no longer know what is real or 'fake news.' In December 2019 Boris Johnson's right-wing Tory party won a landslide victory in the UK's parliamentary election, with support from many traditional left-wing voters (and the media and possibly Russia's covert flooding of social media); it appears that many people, after three and a half years of 'the unknown' since the UK European Referendum, just wanted to "Get Brexit Done." I don't want to upset those of you who like Boris but I can't personally trust a Prime Minister who has a habitual pattern of lying – as a widely philandering husband, twice-sacked journalist, dismissed Shadow Cabinet minister *and*

Prime Minister. I'm scared by the many predictions that our economy – and workforce, including well-trained NHS staff from Europe – will be whacked badly by Brexit, that we'll lose a lot of workers' rights and environmental and food hygiene protections and, increasing trade with countries outside Europe, our carbon footprint will go through the roof (and add to the ten thousand or so containers apparently dropped into the sea every year).[61] I'd much prefer us to be 'buying local,' connecting with our neighbours in order to pool defensive, crime-busting and life-enhancing resources, learn the best ways of doing things from each other and having a voice at the 'European table,' than being an isolated island.

Whatever the outcome of Brexit is (and nobody knows what it will be) I just hope our current government follows through with its promises of investing well in our public services given their decimation of them over the past decade with their 'austerity' policies. The United Nations felt so concerned by our social policy that it felt the need to investigate the UK and, in 2019, reported that our welfare state had been "deliberately removed and replaced by a harsh and uncaring ethos" which was likened to the Victorian workhouse mentality![62] It found *fourteen million* people living in relative poverty, including *thirty percent* of our children – despite Britain being the fifth richest country in the world! *Thousands* of our children are regularly hungry and developing health problems from poor diets. Britain was also found to be one of the worst in Europe regarding its treatment of disabled people[63], with about *twenty thousand* people dying as they waited for their applications for

---

61. See this very conservative article by the World Shipping Industry: http://www.worldshipping.org/industry-issues/safety/Containers_Lost_at_Sea_-_2017_Update_FINAL_July_10.pdf

62. See for e.g. https://www.independent.co.uk/news/uk/home-news/un-poverty-austerity-uk-universal-credit-report-philip-alston-a8924576.html

63. See for e.g. https://www.independent.co.uk/news/uk/uk-disability-rights-un-report-government-treatment-disabled-people-a7616101.html

financial assistance to be processed.[64] Only a few months ago a man in Nottingham who had mental health problems died of *starvation* because his benefits were stopped when he didn't attend a 'back to work' interview with the DWP (Department for Work and Pensions) – this was despite his GP *and* family members letting the DWP know how much he was struggling. According to a BBC2 'Victoria Derbyshire' news programme in November 2019, three quarters of people dependent on food banks are ill or disabled though an increasing number of working families are also reliant on the growing number of food banks – bloody food banks in the world's 5th richest country! Our Welfare State's punitive measures appears to be the norm; I heard of one father having his family's benefits stopped when he couldn't attend a DWP interview because he was in court. It's shocking, as is the fact that many people have killed themselves as a result of having their benefits withdrawn[65].It's been estimated by doctors that a *hundred and twenty thousand* deaths have occurred in the UK as a result of our government's austerity policies[66]. And we call ourselves civilised!

Meanwhile the rich in the UK – and across the globe – are getting richer by the minute; it's said that about a hundred people now own nearly the same as the rest of the entire world.[67] the so-called 'trickle-down effect' of Neo-liberalism clearly hasn't worked! The Neo-liberal economic model maintains that the state should back off and let us all just get on with it because we're all equal and have the same opportunities to 'succeed' (i.e. make a ton of money) under a capitalist 'free market system' – and if we don't succeed, well, that's our *own* stupid fault. And

64. *https://www.parliament.uk/business/publications/written-questions-answers-statements/written-question/Commons/2018-12-19/203812/*
65. *https://www.theguardian.com/society/2020/feb/07/three-cases-of-suicides-linked-to-dwps-handling-of-benefits*
66. *https://www.bmj.com/company/newsroom/health-and-social-care-spending-cuts-linked-to-120000-excess-deaths-in-england/*
67. *See for e.g. https://wwwh.bbc.co.uk/news/business-35339475;*

yet I'll bet very few of the country's CEOs, earning an average of about £4.5 *million* pounds a year – a hundred and forty-nine times that of the average employee – came from council estates. Some earn nearly thirty million. With institutional racism and sexism, the 'who you know' connections amongst the upper echelons (with lucrative government contracts and subsidies often being dished out to their party funders), 'cycles of deprivation,' the impacts of poverty, self-fulfilling prophesies, children in poor areas only being seen by their teachers as 'factory fodder,' a two-tier education system which only rewards certain types of academic brains and excludes children who can't cope with the pressure, it's hardly a system which offers equal opportunities!

Despite profits of millions and *billions*, corporate tax evasion is rampant, with big companies employing expensive lawyers to find dodgy tax loopholes and 'laundering' their money in works of art, empty buildings and offshore bank accounts (where *trillions* are stashed away doing nothing.) It's been suggested that up to a third of taxes owed by the rich aren't paid.[68] In the UK many of our top politicians are millionaires yet have been scamming their expenses (and apparently 'losing' dodgy accounts on occasions) as well as their taxes no doubt, and using public funds for their lives of luxury and to subsidise their friends' grouse estates.[69]

And yet this obsession with accumulating wealth – no matter who or what you crush on the way – flies in the face of research that suggests that whilst the GDP has risen in the UK and America since the fifties, our happiness levels haven't, just like it's been evidenced that you don't get any happier with more money, once you have a decent standard of living. So the

---

68. Cited in Richard Swift's fascinating book 'S.O S Alternatives to Capitalism'

69. See https://fullfact.org/environment/does-government-subsidise-grouse-shooting/.

top hundred FTSE company bosses may be earning millions but are perhaps selling their souls for nothing – except perhaps a lot of envy, a massive, isolated house, a huge risk of heart failure and constant worry about losing their wealth and power. I once read that a global study in search of the happiest man found him to be a rickshaw driver living in a three-walled house in India. He felt happy because he knew how rampant infant death was but his two girls were healthy, he loved and appreciated his wife, they had enough to eat and when they didn't, their neighbours, also living partly out on the street with their front walls missing, would help them out. There was love, kindness, gratitude and a strong sense of belonging in his life. I wonder whether he had a spiritual connection too and perhaps a belief that he'd be reincarnated.

Whilst our rickshaw driver presumably felt connected, many of us in the West are struggling with all sorts of disconnection. Millions of us are lonely as we tend to interact little within our neighbourhoods and focus more on our smart phones than each other (it does my head in seeing so many parents ignoring their children as they stare at their phones). Many of us are so stressed out that we actually lose the capacity to be open and able to properly connect with each other. Our schools are increasingly excluding (disconnecting) pupils who struggle to sit quietly or don't perform well academically.[70] Internet porn is giving our young people some very non-intimate ideas about sex and relationships, and rape is on a dramatic increase in the UK.[71] Prolific child porn, some involving animals and torture (even murder, it's said) is showing the extent of our depravity, as is the increasing exposure of paedophiles, many of whom were trusted public figures. Just this week it was reported by the BBC that the police are currently making four hundred and

---

70. See this scary article at https://www.theguardian.com/education/2018/aug/31/dozens-of-secondary-schools-exclude-at-least-20-of-pupils#img-1
71. See for e.g. https://rapecrisis.org.uk/news/latest-news/latest-crime-figures-show-14-increase-in-sexual-offences-reported-to-police/

fifty arrests per month in the UK for online child abuse but can't get on top of the problem. The UK is harbouring many of the estimated *twenty-six million* people who are currently enslaved, possibly many more[72] (millions of whom are 'sex slaves'). I heard on BBC Radio 4 that whilst some men die at the hands of their partners, at least two women a week (and figures are apparently rising) are being killed by their partners in Britain – with millions more around the world experiencing excruciating injuries or death at the hands of their 'loved ones.' Female oppression is still rife globally and women continue to be paid less than men for doing the same job, even in 'liberal democracies' like the UK.

Alongside women and disabled people, people of colour remain under-represented in politics, the whole of the media, the legal system, the arts, finance, education, science, management, the police and army, the top echelons of the corporate world[73] – in fact all influential spheres of society – but yet remain massively overrepresented in stop-and-search instances (in fact nine times more likely to be stopped), the criminal justice system (where you are three times more likely to be arrested and twice as likely to be *killed* in police custody – yes, in the UK) and mental health services.[74] Can you imagine, if you're white, walking down the street knowing that people are judging, hating or feeling wary of you or wanting to hurt or *kill* you just because of the colour of your skin? Imagine people wanting to 'send you home' to Scandinavia or Italy (where you've never been and know nothing of the culture or language) because of your Viking or Roman ancestry. Imagine the lives and achievements of *your* ancestors being largely wiped out of the history books but the people who enslaved, tortured, massacred and stole your land, gold, diamonds – and the rest – being held up as heroes, with

72. *see https://www.endslaverynow.org/learn/slavery-today*
73. *See https://www.theguardian.com/world/2017/oct/07/ethnic-minorities-jobs-gap-bame-degrees*
74. *See further Race Relations statistics & information at www.irr.org.uk*

their statues still standing even though the terrible reality of what they did is now clear! Imagine your grandad, who was invited to 'the Mother Country' to support its economy (he or his dad may have even fought in the British Army along with ten thousand or so Afro-Caribbean men, two and a half million Indian (and Pakistani Bangladeshi and Nepalese) men and the *many* thousands more men from other Commonwealth countries) suddenly being told – in 2012 – that he had no rights to remain in the UK because the documentation proving his legal right to be here had been destroyed by the Home Office! I find it absolutely gutting that according to the BBC news, racist attacks have increased in line with some of the Brexit propaganda (such as Nigel Farage's posters of long rows of alleged migrants who were actually nothing to do with the UK) and racist comments from some of our leaders. Racist and homophobic chanting is to be heard at football matches across Europe (even though so many of the team's players and managers are black.) Not one of the six thousand League footballers in the UK has dared to acknowledge he's gay for fear of persecution. How sad's that?

This year's been very interesting (actually terrifying) ecologically; as the ice-shelves crash and 'feedback loops' intensify (like the decreasing reflection of the sun's heat as the polar ice-caps shrink and the release of warming methane from the melting tundra) we've had unusual flooding in the UK; in January 2020 distraught peoples' homes could be seen underwater and the BBC news announced that there were ninety flood warnings in place. There were fires – instead of snow – on the moors of Yorkshire last February, forest fires in Siberia and Alaska and huge swathes of Australia are still on fire burning alive masses of wildlife as well as people. Highest recorded temperatures have been reported all over the globe, and hurricanes and mega-storms are raging.

Inspired by the teenage, ass-kicking Greta Thunberg, young people (bless their beautiful but frightened hearts) have been 'striking' and demonstrating across the world, calling for our governments to act *now* to fend off a global catastrophe and the international environmental protection group 'Extinction Rebellion'[75] have in the past year been bravely – and peacefully – blocking off roads and the like to push our governments to declare a 'climate emergency' and take radical action. This 'eco-action' has made many people sit up and listen to the climate scientists to the extent that most of the political parties who have just fought the UK election were prioritising climate action. Sadly, the Tories didn't and, whilst Boris Johnson was rudely calling Extiction Rebellion activists "a bunch of crusties," his cronies were lying about subsidising fossil fuel companies[76]; no doubt many of them and their friends have fingers in the massive fossil fuel pie so I can't see a green revolution in the UK just yet...which is so scary when we can see with our own eyes that the climate's going crazy. Even cheery David Attenborough's been very clear in his recent TV documentaries that we need to act on a massive scale NOW if we don't want a very grim future with mass flooding, droughts, fires, starvation, migration and wars over dry land and water.

The NHS continues to be strangled by underfunding and our government's still allowing the pharmaceutical industry to fleece our hospitals (reported on Radio 4, a drugs company recently upped its annual fee for some epilepsy medication from £2.3 million to *£40* million overnight) and the private sector is snaking its way into the most profitable parts of the NHS.[77] Braun supply all my dialysis equipment (and frequently get my life-maintaining orders wrong) and I have to pay a fortune to

---

75. www.rebellion.earth

76. See this depressing article at https://www.theguardian.com/environment/2019/jan/23/uk-has-biggest-fossil-fuel-subsidies-in-the-eu-finds-commission

77. See this great article at http://www.patients4nhs.org.uk/how-is-the-nhs-being-privatised/.

park on the hospital grounds' privatised car parks and for food in the private cafés there.

Northerners and working-class people are now dying up to twelve years sooner than their more privileged southern and middle-class counterparts and in the past month Professor Sir Michael Marmot's report has revealed that life expectancy for women in the North East has just gone down instead of up for the first year in decades.[78] About forty thousand people per year are dying from pollution in the UK[79], with many more dying from stress-related diseases.[80] Up to a sixth of British adults are still popping antidepressants, men are still killing themselves in droves and we have increasing numbers of depressed and self-harming children. Head-teachers (who can't generally afford counsellors in their schools) are screaming about the fact that children are literally being sent crazy with exam pressures, negative self-comparisons and bullying on social media; millions of our children have eating disorders and other self-harming habits.

It feels like things are imploding!

...And yet, given my own experiences of going to suicidal, self-destructive edges in order to be flipped back into balance again, I'm hanging on to the fact that 'crisis' is the same word as 'opportunity' in Chinese and that historically, times of crisis have often led to positive change. The thirties' depression brought unemployment benefits, the Second World War the Welfare State, extreme racism the Civil Rights Movement, female oppression the Women's Movement and terrible homophobia, enhanced by the AIDS epidemic, eased in the Gay Rights revolution. Facts that were almost exclusive to

---

78. See https://www.bbc.co.uk/news/health-51619608

79. Some articles maintain the figure is higher but see this article at https://www.nhs.uk/news/heart-and-lungs/air-pollution-kills-40000-a-year-in-the-uk-says-report/

80. See this scary article https://www.mentalhealth.org.uk/news/stressed-nation-74-uk-overwhelmed-or-unable-cope-some-point-past-year

social studies students like myself twenty years ago are now common knowledge as journalists discover truths *together* and the internet often reveals what the traditional media doesn't. It seems that, for the first time in history, it's abundantly clear what we humans are dealing with and what we need to change.

And change is happening. There's less extreme poverty, victims of war, child mortality, crime, famine, child labour and deaths in natural disasters than there's been for decades.[81] In 1972 Bhutan replaced their GDP measurement with GDH; Gross Domestic Happiness and in 2011 the United Nations General Assembly adopted Bhutan's resolution calling for other nations to make happiness a central feature of their development. Other countries are starting to look at this notion and even Westminster is exploring the notion of 'wellbeing'[82]. Universities across the globe are conducting happiness research which is revealing that addressing trauma, creating equality, valuing everybody, protecting nature and developing rituals and practices which support our well-being are steps toward sustainable happiness. Universities are also researching mindfulness and how we can develop practices to enhance our awareness, happiness and compassion.

When you think about it, we seem to have evolved loads in just the past twenty years. 'Emotional intelligence' is no longer viewed as a weird concept and it seems that many men, like the strong yet gentle Nepalese I met, are softening. The other night I went to a band's brilliant sing-and-dance-along gig and was totally heartened to see a load of young men belting out 'uncool' songs like Dolly Parton and Kenny Rogers' 'Islands in the Stream.' British men are hugging, crying in public, talking about their sexual abuse and being 'hands on' dads, playing with and attuning to their children. We've evolved enough to understand that emotional stability in adulthood is linked to the

81. *Bregman 2020,* Human Kind: A hopeful history *page 13*
82. *See https://www.ons.gov.uk/peoplepopulationandcommunity/wellbeing*

care and love we receive as children and that mental ill-health is generally related to tough circumstances (including isolation) and poor attachments (connections) in childhood rather than individual weaknesses. Rather than simply labelling people with a mental disorder, many psychiatrists are now looking for the circumstances in people's lives with which they've struggled or are struggling and have sent them 'over the edge.' We've also evolved enough in the UK to have developed a fairly stable – if, crazily, still racist and unequal – multi-racial society; people from all over the world *can* live together! Brave men and women 'coming out' also means that we're starting to embrace every sexual orientation – or not, as in 'non binary' – and individual expression. Disabled athletes, Prince Harry's Help for Heroes and 'Invictus Games' and an increasing presence of disabled people on TV are normalising different bodies. We seem to becoming more accepting of our differences and vulnerabilities.

At the same time, as we're being woken up by our young eco-warriors, Extinction Rebellion and no-longer 'radical' groups like Greenpeace and Friends of The Earth, increasing numbers of people are taking 'climate action' such as the eight brave Extinction 'rebels' who were recently arrested in Brighton for sitting in the road to block traffic; four of them were in their eighties and nineties. Happily more leaders across the globe seem to be being judged on their capacity for developing green agendas and there are *millions* of people involved in grass-roots, non-partisan, anti-growth movements fighting for social justice and the protection of vulnerable people, animals and the earth; they just don't make the news very often. Renewable energy sources are booming all over the world.[83] Business people and scientists are setting up green, spiritual and ethically sound conferences and organisations and many rich people have learnt

83. See https://en.wikipedia.org/wiki/List_of_countries_by_electricity_production_from_renewable_sources for a table of countries with percentages of renewable energy

that giving away their cash can feel better than clinging to it; they've experienced the 'helper's high,' the happiness from the endorphins, oxytocin and dopamine which are released when we're kind and giving.

I was very pleased to read recently that the new field of 'ecological economics,'[84] like positive psychology, is supporting the view that we're not the selfish, competitive humans of the traditional neo-liberal, free market economic model but rather, altruistic by nature. Similarly, 'neuro-economics'[85] is showing that if we trust more, we invest more and can increase profits without needing to be cut-throat and immoral. Within 'conscious' business models and 'negotiation science'[86] the 'self-first' model is also crumbling and leadership models are becoming more pro-social; the best leaders are being shown to be those who are self-aware, listen properly, self-disclose, share decisions, take innovative risks, promote caring and eco-friendly environments and seek 'win-win,' mutually beneficial solutions. They allow themselves to be vulnerable and know the importance of *connection*.[87] Universities have brought science out of theoretical lecture theatres and into our communities to create technologies which serve our environment and the poor. The International Monetary Fund has recognised that diverse communities across the globe need to be empowered to do things their *own* way, not the Western way. Individuals across the globe are volunteering in their millions, giving billions to charity, planting forests of trees, setting up food banks and soup kitchens, buying coffees and meals for strangers, recycling and upcycling and no longer just giving blood but painfully donating bone marrow – and kidneys – to random strangers.

---

84. For an explanation of ecological economics see https://www.wisegeek.com/what-is-ecological-economics.htm
85. See https://en.wikipedia.org/wiki/Neuroeconomics
86. Some insight into this can be found at https://www.inc.com/neil-patel/the-science-of-successful-negotiation.html
87. See for e.g. https://blog.taskque.com/characteristics-good-leaders or Macloud and Clark 2012.

It seems that another sign of our evolving consciousness is that we're now able to see things systemically; we can see, for example, the connections in our world-wide ecosystems and climate. We've learned that meddling with nature isn't a bright idea, having realised that overusing soil, chopping down trees and straightening our rivers has led to desertification, increased carbon dioxide in the atmosphere and flooding. (Not to mention killing so many animals by destroying their habitats and moving them between continents where they mess up natural ecosystems – and possibly lead to global pandemics!) We're finally learning some humility and that we can't control and abuse nature! We're also more aware these days about the systemic quality of trauma – such as that passed down to many of us from colonialism and last century's wars, or the West's backing and sacking of various oil-producers since the 1950's (that's another very interesting issue which we rarely hear about in the West) and our bombing of thousands of innocent families in the Middle East and how we now seem to be facing the repercussions, with increasing 'terrorist' attacks. We're learning!

Maybe, just maybe, if we supported each other (via our friendship groups, families, communities, workplaces, educational establishments and the media) to really understand ourselves, with our fundamental need and capacity for love and connection, our 'negatively biased' monkey minds, our normal human 'shadow' and our deep, existential fears, then we could work through our emotional wounds, fear and pain *together* and allow our naturally caring hearts, inner wisdom, courage and compassion to mobilise us into positive action. Maybe then we'd no longer have to numb ourselves, consume like hoovers or act like sheep and power-crazed lunatics, and we may yet overcome our indoctrination into racist, elitist cut-throat, neo-liberal capitalism and fuel a creative paradigm shift and further human evolution instead of insanity, massive injustice and potential extinction!

Which brings me back to Jiddu Krishnamurti and Thich Naht Hanh who told me in my twenties that the way to universal peace and happiness is for us all to really connect with *ourselves*, take full responsibility for our own feelings, thoughts and actions and consciously use education, the arts, the media, conscientious business models, mindfulness, yoga, counselling and the like to enhance our self-awareness and compassion. We could ask how we make ourselves and others miserable; how do we personally add to the world's pollution and aggression? What fear and pain are we covering up with disgust, hate, criticism, defensiveness, blame and rage? What is our programmed mind banging on about? Are we being indoctrinated by a biased media? Are we standing up to destruction and immorality, or leaving it to others to sort out? Are we properly listening to our patients, colleagues, neighbours, the homeless and our loved ones? Are we 'loving too much' and caring too little for ourselves – then getting burnt out or resentful? Do we allow ourselves to get the love and support (including the many online talks and meditations) we need to stay open-hearted? Are we trying to walk with grace and remembering we're not alone when we're hurting? Are we making the most of the fact that this is *our* time, *now*, and living the life *we* want to live? Are we recognising that we're walking, connected miracles of nature with hundreds of people behind us in all that we do? Are we able to 'be more dog?'[88] i.e just 'be' and love life with our amazing bodies and senses without constantly thinking we need to be better and achieve and accumulate *more*.

I feel so grateful to my mum for teaching me to chat easily and it's been such a gift to have sat, all these years, with so many social work and psychotherapy colleagues and clients, FE students, mindfulness students, hospital staff and patients, friends, family and random people across the world, from

88. My thanks to The Happy Buddha, Suryacitta for that wonderful term!

Thai monks, Belizean fishermen, Guatemalan housewives and Balinese teachers to magistrates, armed robbers and paedophiles. It's also been something of a gift to observe myself going through my own trauma. I've come to the firm conclusion (along with many others) that we little, vulnerable humans are not made happy with outer *things* or power or good looks but, rather, by feeling safe, like we have purpose in life and feeling *connected* to ourselves and others. So to be happy we need to keep in mind 'survival of the empathic and connected,' like Darwin said, not survival of the fittest, richest, busiest or most powerful!

Just as I believe that my chemo-bliss was what's at the heart of us, I'm now convinced that the sense of interconnectedness I had at death's door was what's at the heart of 'reality.' I smile when I come across the increasing number of articles from economics, chemistry, physics, biology, sociology, psychology, neurology, anthropology and cosmology which stress the interconnected, systemic nature of everything. With our empathic hearts, mirror neurons and happiness chemicals being stimulated by emotional connection and touch, it's so clear that we're *wired* to respond compassionately to each other. We've had some terrible incidents of late in the UK; the Grenfell Tower fire (a massacre seemingly fuelled by cheap, substandard cladding) bombings, stabbings and people being mowed down in the street but for each act of irresponsibility or aggression by a few, many more people have gone well out of their way to help strangers with incredible acts of bravery and kindness. I often reflect on the miners and soldiers I've spoken with who look back at the great time they had; their circumstances were *horrendous* but they recall the solidarity, mutual support and *connection* that they felt. Like the euphoria in football and music gig crowds. It's so clear that connection is the thing that makes us feel the most safe, relaxed, happy and focused and I totally believe that when we feel safe enough to allow ourselves to connect to that real, open, honest, vulnerable, compassionate part of ourselves, we're basically 'good.' All the evidence I've seen is that we're only mistrustful, blaming, cruel and aggressive when we've experienced disconnection or feel afraid, isolated, insecure and are in fight or flight, self-protective 'reptile' mode.

So, in accepting that people are basically 'good,' I'm convinced that it's just our current Western paradigm which is bringing out the worst in us; our profit and competition-driven mentality demands us to play roles and cut off our feelings, vulnerability and sense of personal responsibility. It's hard with our current 'gagging order' madness stopping employees telling the truth about immoral and unethical practices but can we afford to hide behind "I'm just doing my job" and be hardened with "I'm knackered and unhappy but I need to pay my mortgage, buy a better car and secure my pension pot," forgetting our deeper values and to enjoy life *now*.

"It's just the way it is" can feel so overwhelming but in any given moment we each have the choice of adding to our paradigm's madness or working for connection; even if we feel stuck or overwhelmed we still have choices – just like Victor Frankl who gave away bread whilst starving in a Nazi concentration camp.[89] In simple daily life we can blank, criticise and bully others or engage, smile and act kindly (it's been estimated that one smile can produce as much happiness as two hundred bars of chocolate and genuine smiles activate our parasympathetic nervous system, cleaning up killer cortisol and the associated bad tempers and poor health.) We can hoard or share, pollute or be responsible, focus on our differences (and fail to challenge institutionalised racism, sexism, prejudice and homophobia) or look for our similarities, be judgemental or compassionate, blame and get angry or take responsibility for our painful feelings and our fears. I'm reminded of a

---

89. See his 'Man's Search for Meaning' in my bibliography p. 436

Cherokee notion that we humans have two wolves inside. One is loving, peaceful, hopeful, humble, compassionate, kind and courageous, the other angry, fearful, competitive, bitter, envious, greedy and arrogant. *Everything depends on which wolf we choose to feed.* Last century, with our two horrific World Wars (and our negative view of ourselves) we closed down our feelings and fed the divisive, angry wolf. Maybe in this century we'll see through the media, the self-serving powers that be and our social conditioning and feed our kind wolf, consciously trying to open our hearts so we can care for *all* our human – and animal-shaped – brethren!

A good ward like E17 seems to me to be a great example of how the world could be. There are inevitably different roles and jobs but the doctors don't lord it over the nurses and physio's; they *listen* to them and value them for their essential role. The nurses don't lord it over the auxiliaries, phlebotomists or porters; they respect and *value* them as equal human beings and for performing their crucial work. Everybody's grateful to the vital cleaners, the people who empty the bins and wash the bedding for keeping infection and chaos at bay (maybe the most important jobs) and to the cooks for feeding patients well and aiding their recovery. Everybody respects the patients, are humble enough to know they don't know all the answers and are grounded and self-aware enough to see the person they're interacting with as a whole, feeling human being, just like them. E17 exuded love and respect, presumably because the staff felt safe, respected and supported and death anxiety was acknowledged, talked about and normalised. The staff were connected to one another and were getting regular boosts of oxytocin from their acts of kindness toward patients and the appreciative responses given back to them. They were giving care because they *wanted* to, because it was meaningful to them and made them *happy!*

Despite only really knowing that I don't know anything for

sure, I can see a world – get me, sounding like Martin Luther King – where we each dig deep and courageously challenge prescribed roles if our actions *feel* wrong. Where we each take responsibility, get properly informed, push for fair institutions and systems and support each other to think of new ways of doing things on a grass-roots level rather than waiting for the 'leaders' to sort it all out. I was over the moon when I read that in 2016 there were 1500 cities with 'participatory budgeting'; ordinary citizens having a say in how their local taxes were spent, making a real positive difference and in some places wanting to raise their own taxes![90] I was also happy when I heard on BBC Radio 4 that Harvard University, which feeds the highest echelons of the legal and corporate worlds in the USA, added to its intake criteria a capacity for kindness! I felt similar hope when Prince William and Kate sent their children to a school where the focus is on kindness. I was also pleased to read that more women – who it was said were found, in over thirty independent studies, to act more ethically in business – are increasingly represented on corporate boards and, happily, in politics. Women were, until recently, the leaders of three out of four of our countries here in the UK despite their online abuse and death threats. What brave women!

I've been positively beaming since Jez bought me Rutger Bregman's *Human Kind* for my recent birthday. Delving historically, he gives good evidence to support the notion that our nomadic ancestors (up to only 10,000 years ago) were mainly peaceful and that we've only gone crazy since claiming land and possessions (getting greedy, scared and army-supported leader-led). He notes that both capitalism and communism took on the view that the daft masses needed controlling (by managers and strict rules). Citing many convincing examples, he shows how we're (children included) more motivated by our internal

---

90. *Bregman 2020,* Human Kind: A hopeful history

creativity, passions and need for connection than external bonuses and orders and he states that for centuries we believed that "civilisation is a flimsy veneer that will crack at the merest provocation. Now we know this view of humankind, and this perspective of our history, is utterly unrealistic."[91]

I can see a world – and again this is already happening – where we no longer allow ourselves to be lazy, or brain-washed by advertisements – and our false view of ourselves – but choose to buy ethically and locally, to recycle, swap and exchange goods (instead of putting an approximate ten thousand items of clothing into landfill sites and thousands of plastic bottles into the sea every five minutes.) I can see us grinning happily as we grow more stuff (according to Radio 4 the demand for allotments is the highest it's ever been and about one in four of us already grows some food) instead of amassing outrageous carbon footprints from so much imported food. *We are 'the demand' which determines 'the supply' of goods and services and we need to own and use our power!* Let me say that again, given how easy is for us to feel powerless, *we are 'the demand' which determines 'the supply' of goods and services!* We're already influencing so much – look how many fuel and car companies are 'turning green' and even 'McDonalds' is claiming to use free-range eggs and British beef (instead of bulldozing more South American rainforest for grazing land) because it knows that's what we want. We have an internet; we're connected and it only takes a hundred thousand of our sixty-seven million in the UK to sign a petition which then obliges our government to discuss an issue. If a hundred thousand of us told a bank to stuff their mortgage and overdraft rates they'd soon come down. We are the demand! We're also the tree-planters, litter-clearers, inventors of organic packaging and cutlery, solar walkways and roof tiles, solar powered machines which suck

91 *Bregman 2020,* Human Kind: A hopeful history, *page 281*

the plastic debris out of waterways, humane farming and fishing techniques, biodegradable 'cling-film' and plastic, etc. Good stuff is happening! I know it's hard – I still despair at the plastic in my shopping trolley but if we all tried that bit harder, that amounts to a lot of change and if each of us wrote an e-mail to our supermarkets saying we'll no longer shop there, they'd soon use ethical packaging.

We've now got automated factories where only a couple of people oversee the whole thing; 'artificial intelligence,' especially if more rich people get the endorphin buzz of sharing their wealth or the state 'intervenes' more, gives us the potential to cut down the working week. Radio 4 reported recently that the UK's creative industry (fixing and making things) is currently worth about eighty-four billion and is the fastest growing sector in the UK economy and over Christmas 2019 we apparently spent less on useless 'tat.' We appear to be waking up to our hearts' voices! Alternative therapies are also expanding; maybe we're slowly creating a place where the dwindling high streets become less about accumulating 'stuff' and more about embracing our sensual bodies and our creative selves by buying and selling second-hand stuff and providing or teaching skills such as DIY, massage, art and crafts, yoga, upcycling, painting, counselling, sewing, woodwork, gardening and cooking.

I can see a criminal justice system (and schools) where we sort out our terrible racism and our focus on locking up our poor, recognise that many of our offenders (and disruptive pupils) had awful early attachments and give them safety, respect and compassion – and a reminder of the good hearts and potential they were born with, like the 'primitive' jungle tribe. They need gentleness, genuine care and support in order to come out of prison in a better state than they went in! A recent TV programme was about a UK project which invited law students to help offenders set up their own businesses and they claimed a zero re-offending rate rate and comfortable, humane (but maximum security) prisons in Norway (Halden and Bastøn), where guards without uniforms talk to and eat with the prisoners, have reoffending rates of 16% compared to 60% in punishing, degrading American prisons and also better economic outcomes. When the hard-core director of the Dakota Department of Correction visited Halden she sobbed, saying "How did we think it was okay to put human beings in cage like settings?" and the three to four violent or tragic 'incidents' per week in her prisons petered out once they adopted more humane methods.[92] Where did we get this idea of punishment and retribution and how can we possibly think it could have a good outcome? Of course people need showing the error of their ways but they also need to be shown how they can change – and have the hope of a decent life if they do. It's not rocket science that love heals and cruelty, poverty, oppression and hopelessness warps people and leads to more aggression! This view seems to have been held by the millions of UK citizens who opposed the invasion of Iraq in 2003 (and is no doubt the reason for our government's recent lack of openness about bombing Syria) – most of us can see that war is not only evil, insane and generally of benefit to the rich at the expense of mostly poor troops and innocent civilians, but really, really *stupid*.

Can you imagine if we came together and demanded that our schools didn't just prepare our precious kids for the gaping jaws of the capitalist machine (simply accepting that many kids who can't do exams will fail) but instead tried to nurture well-rounded, happy human beings! I see schools where teachers aren't leaving in droves (a head-master recently told me that a quarter of teachers qualified since 2011 have quit already) because of overwork due to financial cuts and rigid curriculums, but get to use their individual skills and creativity

92. *Bregman 2020,* Human Kind: A hopeful history

to pass on useful knowledge. Schools where kids aren't pegging out in the heat because they aren't allowed to take off their preparing-for-work ties and blazers, as, shockingly, my young neighbour claimed on a *really* hot day last year. Schools where there's less brain-freezing, body-battering, cortisol-producing competition, exams and targets, which send children (especially disadvantaged, stressed ones) into their unthinking 'reptile' brains and contribute much to poor mental health, bullying, drug use and illiteracy. Instead, imagine if kids were allowed to play and have more fun, were learning to be more creative, innovative and co-operative (skills they most need for work, especially in an A.I. world) and were properly rewarded for different capabilities and skills and thinking outside the box - and not tied to uncomfortable desks all day long! Imagine also if schools taught self-care, self-responsibility, compassion for self and others, necessary life skills like how to get a mortgage, pay bills and run a business (as I bet Eton does) communication skills and positive parenting – the NHS, social care, benefits agency, police and prison budgets would plummet and people may not feel so powerless or be so easily manipulated by the media and the elite. Schools in Scandinavia where children are allowed to play till they're eight have had some of the best results in the world. My new hero, Rutger Bregman, describes a fantastic Norwegian school where rows of desks have been ditched and children are allowed to pursue (with the help of guides) what they want to learn; motivation, enthusiasm and achievement run high! 'Forest schools,' where children learn outside in the natural world, appear to be showing promise too.

Optimistically, in the autumn of 2015, a British All Party Parliamentary Group (APPG) on Wellbeing Economics (with a goal of trying to reduce the UK's *nine billion pound* mental health bill)[93] reported that children are holistic beings who need

---

93. See https://wellbeingeconomics.co.uk/

to be in a good, calm head-space in order to learn well at school and recommended that all teachers are trained in mindfulness. Happily, the APPG recommendations also included "addressing the root causes of poor health and low wellbeing, including the structure of the economy."

I also think it would be great if we taught children – and each other – to normalise Death, recognising 'him' as a friend, not a taboo subject which leaves the suffering, ill and dying in miserable isolation and the rest of us cut off from our feelings – and half asleep. We look with bewilderment and superiority at 'primitive' cultures where rituals and practices flag up death and unite communities in their communal fear but maybe that's exactly where we're going wrong. *We're ignoring the best life enhancer there is!* If only we could all muster the courage and connection to face death; as I raved in the pantomime, if we faced our vulnerability and fear, I can see us melting into mutual care with an *awesome* appreciation of life.

Talking of death, I can see a health-care system which isn't just about doctors battling germs and chopping people up (amazing – and in my case, much appreciated – though these skills are) but which encourages us to take responsibility for our *own* health and unites the mind and body, both of which have an immense capacity to heal naturally with connection, a good diet, movement, awareness of self-critical and cortisol-fuelling thinking and plenty of oxytocin boosts. We also need a health-care system (and work-places) where the grass-roots staff are trusted to inform policy decisions rather than having distant, paper-work producing managers who just reduce morale (Just as patients need to be trusted to know what they're taking about!). In addition, we need a mental health system which fully recognises that society's demands – and traumatic experiences – are sending people crazy, rather than labelling and blaming the individual. Happily the Economics and Wellbeing APPG from 2015 stated that patients are 'holistic beings' who need a 'biopsychosocial' model of health care, which takes into account the social and emotional aspects of illness and health, not just the physical. The APPG proposed that, as part of 'better integrating mental and physical health' and providing 'whole person care,' mindfulness training be a part of doctors' education. (Yes, come on!) I have friends who are physiotherapists and are already using a biopsychosocial model of healthcare and mindfulness is being taught within the NHS...we are evolving! Yeah! It would also help of course, if our nurses got back their training bursaries and the government stopped crucifying our hospital staff with impossible demands!

Chris Ruane, a Welsh MP since 1997 (and trustee of the Oxford Mindfulness Centre)[94] co-established the APPG and, some time ago, had already given free mindfulness training to over a hundred and fifty Members of Parliament and Peers and over two hundred and fifty of their staff. He's currently working with leaders in many countries who want to take mindfulness into their legislatures. The UK is becoming a pretty cool place...a leading light in mindfulness, largely peaceful multi-culturally and hugely generous in terms of charitable giving and volunteering. I cringe when I think about our marauding British Empire but carry a hope that we may yet learn from our mistakes and become truly 'Great Britain' by being a beautiful, open-minded, accepting, wealth-balanced, non-racist, eco-friendly, kind, compassionate and deeply connected nation.

And so, after three decades of battling with head-mashing ideas, my simple conclusion is that I really believe, if we confront the madness together, that we have the capacity to create a wonderful world. A world where we stop pretending we can control everything, ground ourselves in 'the moment,' listen to our empathic mirror neurons and our naturally loving hearts and face the unknown, disappointments and difficulties

94. *See www.oxfordmindfulness.org*

with grace. I'm always astounded by what went into 'the war. effort' with everybody working so hard and sacrificing so much; how amazing would it be if we supported each other to put that amount of effort into compassionate action, giving us and our recipients more happiness, better mental and physical health, less wrinkles and a potentially longer life!

Imagine if we looked for the good in everybody. I try to smile at random people who, with my judgemental head on or being in a bad mood, I take an instant dislike to and mostly we end up having lovely exchanges. Imagine if we all upped the ante in chatting with strangers, driving kindly, taking flowers or meals to lonely neighbours, planting bee-friendly areas, asking shops to be more ethical and environmentally sound (I ask the manager in my local supermarket to reduce plastic and stop selling only crappy right-wing papers whenever I see him), 'being real' on social media, speaking our truth in art, blogs, letters and articles, signing and devising petitions, volunteering, getting political, standing up to bullies and liars, supporting green energy, helping to protect our creatures, creating community events and talking more about 'real stuff,' even when we're afraid of being seen as 'too serious' or 'crazy.' In the words of Margaret Mead, "Never doubt that a small group of people can change the world. Indeed it is the only thing that ever has."

You may think Margaret and I are space cadets but research has suggested that we only need about ten or twenty percent of us (some people argue only three percent) to create a 'tipping point' or radical change;[95] maybe an evolutionary place where kindness, connection, creativity and happiness, not profit, looks, busyness and 'stuff' could become our principle driving forces, where we tune into our miraculous, connected bodies and amazing, resilient, human spirit and feel what's the right thing – not the sheep thing – to do. I can see a world where,

95. See bibliography: Malcolm Gladwell's 'The Tipping Point' p. 436

after the decimation of most historic civilisations through greed and over-expansion, we finally leave the bloody forbidden apple on the tree and save ourselves a whole load of anguish by remembering that there's nowhere we need to go; we're in the miraculous Garden of Eden already!

Imagine if we all got up in a morning and, bursting with gratitude at simply being alive, pictured a big conch shell beaming love out of our hearts to everyone. And then we'd beam out love to every elephant and they'd stop, in the middle of the Savannah to wave their trunks in glee, every tiger, whose glorious roar would echo through the mountains, every chuckling squirrel, every furry bear and every little whistling bird. And we'd all feel ecstatically happy! Just imagine if you knew that over *seven billion* people were sending you love every morning! And of course, we're half way there already because the animals are *already* doing their trunk-waving, roaring and joyful whistling because they can *feel* the miracle of life (when we're not threatening them) and aren't being shut down by scared, selfish, programmed thoughts.

Yes, yes, I know, I'm out there, but really, can you imagine how it could be if we did kick 'it's just the way it is' right up the backside – including the false, grim view that we (and those others just like us) need to be kept in check by the wise powers that be – and allowed our hearts and our feelings to define 'success'? Step by step, I think if we *really* worked for connection we could make a bloody great Heaven, for *all of us*, on our beautiful Earth. Yeehaa!

Thank you so much for reading (wow, book written, woo ooo!) and may the love be with you! xxx

P.S. Chapter 31
All Change with Corona!

"The world is indeed full of peril, and in it there are many dark places; but still there is much that is fair, and though in all lands love is now mingled with grief, it grows perhaps the greater."

J.R.R. Tolkien

Gosh (and that's an understatement) just as I'm about to finally send my book off for publication my concluding 'Chapter 30' seems strangely out of date as humanity's just been hit by the terrifying 'Coronavirus' (COVID-19) pandemic. If you recall, I vaguely thought that a pandemic might 'wake us up' to what's important when I was reading about the transformative effects of a close brush with death but I never actually imagined I'd live through one! So, Dr Death has just hit the main stage in a big way and may be about to radically change our world, right from the gated mansions to the ghettos. I guess most people will now know what I mean by 'death anxiety!' (A lot of people know already of course; apparently whilst a recorded 52,805 people across the world died from the Coronavirus in the past three months, it's been calculated that 2,523,690 people died from hunger.[96] Equally depressing was the fact that 272,398 people were recorded as killing themselves.)

In the UK we've been emptying supermarkets with our panic-buying and, like many countries, gone into 'lock-down,' closing our schools (other than for the children of 'key workers'), pubs, restaurants and non-essential shops, cancelling all types of gatherings and domestic flights and only travelling on the roads if it's vital. Older people and people with underlying health conditions like myself have to 'self-isolate' for three months and the rest of the population must "stay at home" other than for essential work, food shopping and daily exercise, staying two metres away from people they're not living with; 'social distancing'.

It's strange how quickly a whole new vocabulary has arisen but it gives me hope about how easily and quickly we could write a new story about ourselves and our societies!

The UK has gone very quiet; most people seem to be accepting the government's plea for us to see that we're 'in this together.' As ever, however, some people are not following the rules, perhaps being so scared or arrogant that they're in denial about the severity of the virus or because they're being forced to keep working (such as, unbelievably, people being employed by the government to build the HS2 rail link, a decades-long project – and arms production continues). Thankfully, like many governments across the world, ours (which, being Tory, is generally opposed to state intervention) has just made a massive public investment by covering the bulk of many (far from all) lost incomes. God knows what that, on top of the lock-down, will do to our national and global economies.

I last went food shopping two months ago (it's 10th May 2020 today) trying to breathe very shallowly! Most of the mass of people standing in the queues were anxiously staring ahead

---

96. Sourced by www.worldometres.info

and one small, older man was clinging to his two packs of nine-roll toilet paper for grim death. I saw nobody interacting, just a tall, spacey student doing a non-stop monologue to her mate as she twizzled her hair. It was *weird*; a nation in shock. Having already 'bought in' a few essentials from abroad for a potential Brexit catastrophe, my cupboards are now full. Thankfully I got a place on the dialysis unit for training in how to use my new chest line at home just as my hospital began to admit Corona patients; I'm now dialysing at home again. I'm not yet confident in knowing what I'm doing but I have good written instructions and, despite my line being freaky and leaving me susceptible to serious infection, it's wonderful that my dialysis is no longer painful or a blood-bath nightmare (so far...though one missed clamp on my line and it could be!) That's me home alone now for goodness knows how long and with no chance of a transplant as all transplant operations have been cancelled due to the virus. I was lucky to get in and out of hospital for my arm operation and line fitting when I did.

Selfishly, I'm glad I've been instructed via a letter from the government to stay at home as it stops me feeling guilty for not being out there trying to help; Corona affects the lungs and I really don't want to be in a position where I can't breathe and need to be on a respirator again. I feel so upset for the people who have died - and are dying - such a painful and traumatic death, in many cases without their loved ones being able to be present. Thousands of people have died in care homes where no visiting has been allowed. Having said I'm glad to be staying in, the weight of death all around and the barrenness of isolation is already making me feel slightly strange and in desperation I'm talking to the cats, birds and squirrels who come into my garden and the vegetable plants I'm growing in the house (they seem to like it and are doing well!) I so wish Alfie was here. I'm grateful that I'm good at keeping myself occupied; I'm on to illustrated mindfulness books for children after this...

I feel almost guilty now for flippantly thinking we needed a pandemic to wake us up from our earth-plundering madness and extreme injustices as it's absolutely *terrible* with many thousands of people, all across the world suffering, dying, grieving and worrying about their livelihoods. Perhaps due to not 'locking down' quickly enough (it seems that money came before lives as usual) the UK has the second highest Corona death toll in the world, currently over thirty thousand people, but thankfully we're not yet having to bury people in mass graves as they are in New York. We still don't know much about the virus other than it seems to weirdly turn our immune system against itself a bit like Lupus and we have no treatments in the UK other than Paracetamol and ventilation, no vaccination and no idea how this will pan out. Some countries have been giving Corona patients 'Hydroxychloroquine' which I took for many years to treat my Lupus, and on BBC Radio 4 I heard haematologists and rheumatologists recommending it but apparently in the UK we've not had enough research about it; I wonder if my life-savers Dr H. and Dr D. are involved in discussions. Interestingly – and depressingly – some people of colour are dying at a rate twice to four times the national average (I've heard both figures reported on the BBC news), just as more black women get Lupus; I do wonder, on top of generally poorer living conditions, whether there's any relationship to trauma, stress and self-criticism which, given historic and institutionalised racism, may weigh more heavily on some people of colour.

Whilst I feel uncomfortable for almost wishing for a pandemic, a part of me is holding onto the hope that it *may* actually wake us up! As I understand it, what transformed me for the better in hospital was being forced into isolation and stillness and having to face myself and my vulnerability – and here we have most of us in quiet 'isolation' and all of us having to face our vulnerability, the 'elite' and Prime Ministers included (Boris Johnson has just come out of hospital having been seriously ill with the virus.) What my vulnerability brought out in me was more compassion and care for myself, my loved ones, strangers near and far, our animals and the Earth. My total lack of control – something we're all experiencing to a degree – taught me to stop being such a hyperactive, self-centred princess, wanting things how I wanted them to be and gave me more patience, acceptance and consideration of others.

Chaos equals opportunity...

So, what was I saying about us needing a 'war effort' to change things? Some car plants are making respirators to keep people with the virus alive, clothing firms – and many members of the public – are making protective clothing for front line workers, with private companies and the army being drafted in to help distribute them. 'Techies' are making face masks with 3D printers and temporary 'Nightingale hospitals' have been quickly assembled in huge arenas across Britain by dedicated workmen beavering through the night. Nearly a million people have volunteered to support the vulnerable members of our society and are basically risking their lives, along with thousands of retired doctors and nurses who are going back into the NHS.

It's absolutely shocking that many hospital, social care staff and teachers are dying because they've not got the right protective equipment (which the government was advised by virologists, predicting a pandemic, to stock five years ago) and I'm in awe of those, like my NHS friends Carol and Sally, who are still working as they see colleagues get ill or die in front of them. My God, they have such courage and compassion! And little choice. My parents' carer, feisty Fiona, works privately but is choosing to carry on, having to do scary, close-up personal care for some of her clients and also doing lots of shopping. Fiona goes to the supermarket once a week for my mum and dad and I feel terrible that she's risking her life when it should really be me taking care of them. I hate not being able to visit them (a 'non-essential journey'), especially given that they're over eighty, vulnerable and maybe won't be around for many more years.

The 'war against Corona effort' is also being seen in supermarkets where staff on low wages have been toiling like crazy, alongside poorly paid farmers, crop pickers, factory workers and drivers in the supply chains, the postmen and women, bus-drivers (at least fifteen of whom, unprotected, have died so far, including a man in Nottingham who drove the bus for hospital staff to get to work), delivery people, energy, phone and I.T. workers, teachers, teaching assistants, litter pickers, refuse collectors etc. These brave people are showing us who the most important members of society are; where are the rich CEO's, footballers, bankers, lawyers and accountants now? I *so* hope this all leads to massive pay reviews in our society. I also hope the situation reduces racism post the pretty racist 'Brexit frenzy'; we're hearing about many people of colour who are dying as they try to save the lives of others in hospitals and care homes and we're recognising how our NHS and social care sector are totally reliant on employees from abroad (who are grossly under-paid).

And what was I saying about us needing more connection? I'm over the moon that a beautiful community spirit seems to be emerging because of the virus; people are getting to know their neighbours, looking after the vulnerable and elderly and sharing food and resources. If my street is anything to go by following our street party, people's sense of safety, belonging and happiness will be increasing at a tremendous rate. My mum's chuffed to bits that many of her neighbours have been to the house to see if she and my dad need anything and are chatting (at a distance) when she has her daily walk on the street. I know it's not all good as domestic violence figures are going through the roof with families stuck at home together but also this will be the first time that some working parents who are isolating have had the chance to spend quality time with their children – and partners – without the usual manic activity that breaks from work usually bring; more valuable connection! My brother noted yesterday that on Facebook people are no longer posting all the great places they've been to or things they've bought, bringing down our tendency to compare ourselves and feel less (or more) than others. Instead we're seeing more funny, creative, uplifting and mutually encouraging posts. And talking of internet connection, many people working from home (including myself) have had to learn to use new software which connects us for meetings and the general public have been going wild for online exercise, yoga and cooking classes, meditations etc. (Twenty-five thousand people were watching Jon Kabat Zinn's mindfulness session the other day.) I'm hoping that this increase in online connecting will lead to more 'people power' where we share more about ethical shopping and wellbeing and come together to save nature or bring fuel or bank charges down (we, 'the demand' and all that.)

More connection's also been seen within the NHS as staff are being redeployed to cope with the virus and different departments interact and support each other; Carol and Sally tell me that the atmosphere is quite beautiful with a great sense of solidarity and mutual support. And we, the general public are doing our best to connect with and show our appreciation of the NHS staff by displaying rainbows in our windows and having a nationwide clap and cheer each Thursday evening at eight-o-clock. I hope our respect for the NHS continues when this is over; the staff of the NHS have been heroes since it was established in 1948 and it feels slightly weird that we're only appreciating them so much at the moment because we're scared - but then that was the case with me I guess; I didn't give the NHS much thought until I needed it. I do hope when things calm down that we take some massive, nationwide action to persuade the government to improve the working conditions and raise the wages of our absolutely indispensable and amazing NHS staff.

This is an interesting time in terms of trying to hold in mind the horrific *and* wonderful things that are happening at the same time; maybe that will help us all evolve a bit more as being able to hold conflicting realities instead of trying to gain security with rigid 'black or white' thinking seems to be a sign of maturity, as does being able to sit calmly with the 'unknown' and there's certainly plenty of that about!

I'm wondering if Corona (possibly caused by us meddling with wildlife instead of just leaving these creatures alone in their natural habitats) is Mother Nature's bid to stop us in our earth-poisoning, disconnected tracks. We've already seen the positive impact of us slowing down and reducing travel; the birds and insects sound like they're using megaphones, the canals in Venice are clearing, turtles are laying eggs again on previously abandoned beaches, people in China used to smog-thick cities can see blue sky again and stunning views of the Himalayas can be seen again in India. Here in the UK the cloud-less blue skies have been vivid and unusual for April. According to my friend Sally, who's a children's physiotherapist, the incidents of asthma-related admissions in our city have plummeted (partly because people are scared of going to hospital I guess, but interesting nonetheless.) These examples of how quickly things can start to heal (including children) will perhaps give us the impetus to clean up the planet, rather than just feeling overwhelmed by global-warming and pollution as many of us did before the pandemic. I'm hoping that when this is over – or vaguely manageable – the norm becomes working at home more so the roads remain cleaner and safer (over three hundred thousand people died on the roads whilst fifty-two died with Corona[97]) and the manufacturing industry focuses on making ethical and ecological stuff that we actually need!

As my publisher, Sarah, and I make the final amendments to my book, it's now August 2020. I've been 'in isolation' at home for six months now and, whilst previously not relishing it, am dying to go to the supermarket! I miss meals out, cooking for friends, my gym's yoga and pilates classes and writing in my favourite cafés over a good cappuccino. I'm feeling very frustrated that, after much hard work, my garden's looking lovely and my meditation cabin now has its matching loo - with running hot water - but I can't have anybody in it! Thankfully I've been able to visit my parents ('twas so good to be hugged!) and I have lovely local parks where I've been meeting friends but it's tough not being able to touch them and my home feels like a lonely, barren place. Radio 4 reported this morning that depression rates in the UK are up by fifty percent and I can understand that; I'm not feeling particularly chipper! I'm also aware that my nervous system is sparking a bit. My saving grace is all the meditation and online mindfulness courses and

---

97. *www.worldometres.info*

retreats that I've been doing, reminding me to just calmly stay with 'what is', capture the beauty, nurture loving feelings, remain grateful and learn more about myself (I've been quite surprised to learn, for example, that I'm quite tidy even when others aren't coming into my house!) Life's peaceful at least!

I'm grateful for so much, including the fact that I'm fascinated with what's happening as I look out at the world, even though it seems to be getting crazier by the week! In May, Black American George Floyd was murdered – in front of protesting pedestrians – by a *policeman* kneeling on his neck. He cried out for his mum as he suffocated. His was yet another brutal, senseless death in a long line of killings which re-fuelled the massive 2013 Black Lives Matter, global, non-violent, civil disobedience movement. It's brilliant to see institutionalised racism and violence against people of colour being challenged here in the UK, from enlightening TV programmes and racists being sacked to statues of slave-traders being thrown into the river and sports-people 'Taking the Knee' at big events in support of Black Lives Matter. It's not so great hearing about President Trump's brutal, military attacks on demonstrators and the alleged 'agitation' by unidentifiable cops in Black Mariah's (ah that same old tactic to justify violent oppression). Neither is it good to see many appalling statues of slave-traders and vicious colonialists still standing in the UK. We have a long way to go with our deep, institutionalised racism and facing the reality of our colonial past (and, in different ways, present) but I live in hope. If we can come together, with all our skin tones, histories and trauma and really hear – and feel – one another, processing the horror, rage, pain and guilt together, I think we stand the chance of creating that beautiful world.

That beautiful world may take a while though. It's now October and our current Coronavirus directives from the government appear extremely confusing and contradictory; you can pile into pubs, planes, casino's and shops now but not visit friends or relatives if they're not in your restricted 'bubble.' It also appears that corruption's going off the scale; whilst small companies in the UK were offering to make urgent protective equipment for NHS and care home staff, for example, the government gave lucrative contracts to their mates instead – many of whom had no experience of buying medical equipment and wasted millions of our hard-earned taxes on the wrong – and massively inflated – stuff! The 'Track and Trace' system, run by another incompetent friend of the top ministers, has allegedly wasted about £12 billion[98] and done little to get on top of the virus and it's her husband who's *supposed* to be investigating such misuse of public money. It's looking like securing party funding – and maintaining power – is more important to some of our government representatives than the people of this country. It's very interesting to see Corona rates across the globe; it appears that the least corrupt and narcissistic (or sociopathic) leaders have the lower figures; interestingly many of them are female. It's also interesting that more communally-minded countries in the East seem to have lower figures than individualistic, self-focused Western nations like the UK.

Our sense of madness was added to when many of our teenagers had their futures annihilated when the government devised A-level assessments (given Corona's wipe-out of exams) which disproportionately benefitted those pupils in the wealthier areas and prevented many bright working class young people getting their university places (whilst less bright, privately educated and affluent kids took them). A public outcry amended the process to make it fairer (people power!) but it was already too late for some young people.

So, as a great ending to my book we're seeing a world in which brutality, racism, inequality and the self-serving actions of some power-holders are being exposed more and more. I find it really hard to take the hard facts on the chin – it's much

98. *George Monbiot in the Guardian/Twitter*

easier to think I'm a dramatic conspiracy theorist – but what is seen can be challenged! And, interestingly, 'on the ground' the NHS and Social Care are currently being inundated with job applications, as are medical training places at universities; many people do want to help their vulnerable fellow humans! Which is just as well as our poor, exhausted and traumatised NHS staff are crashing and burning as a second Corona wave builds. Many people are also reassessing their lives and want to continue working at home; pollution really may be on the decrease...

Wow, this feels like a *massive* 'grey or white wolf moment' in human history; is this our global opportunity for radical change? Will we learn that we're all equal, no matter what our skin colour, gender or bank balance, and that cronyism in a supposedly democratic country isn't acceptable? Will we learn from seemingly having put financial considerations before lives and wellbeing? From allowing our NHS to be grossly underfunded and semi-privatised? From having smelled clean air and learned to value our natural world? From the joy of connecting with neighbours, helping each other and recognising who society's heroes actually are? Has Dr Death shaken us up enough to create the space for us to be creative and ease in a new – and happier – world? Will our terrible state of disconnection as we social distance and hide behind masks make us realise just how imperative to our happiness – and survival – connection is?

I have moments of feeling shocked, devastated and scared out of my wits (especially with the Brexit pandemonium pending too) but before I start stabbing myself with the second dagger I pause and remind myself that 'In this moment all's okay.' I cannot do a thing about the future but in this moment my jumper's soft and the quiet stillness and 'amplified' birdsong is beautiful.

Well, this is it, I really am done now. Sorry for going on a bit! I so appreciate you reading and really hope you've got something good out of it.

May the love be with you and, in the memory and spirit of Alfie, may we up the sniffing of flowers, joyfully try to help out where we can and be more *dog* in our beautiful Garden of Eden.

I'll let Arthur, my inspirational grandad, have the final word...

The Clarion Call

A trumpet is sounding a call to mankind,
it echoes o'er mountain and plain
calling the weary, the halt and the blind -
can it be it is calling in vain?

Hark to its sound now and what does it say?
What is the message it brings?
Again as the dawn breaks and welcomes the day
it soars like a bird on the wing.

"Heed me" it sounds, "ere it gets far too late
ere death's reaper starts counting his tally,
cast out the tyrants, stifle the hate,
to my standard, come free men, rally!

Build a new world, a world without fear
with no room for evil or greed,
a world where a friend is always near
whatever his colour or creed.

Build a new world, for you and for me
till then my call shall not cease,
fight for the blind, that they may see,
in a world of eternal peace.

Arthur Downs

Bibliography

The great books which informed my writing

Trauma

Bessel Van de Kolk MD (2014) 'The Body Keeps the Score': Penguin, UK

Peter A. Levine (1997) 'Waking the Tiger': North Atlantic Books, USA

Babette Rothschild (2000) 'The Body Remembers': & (2010) '8 Keys to Safe Trauma Recovery' WW Norton & Co, London

Judith Herman MD (1992) 'Trauma and Recovery': Pandora London, 1st Pub'd by Bantam Books, USA

Carolyn Spring (2016) 'Recovery is My Best Revenge' & (2019) 'Unshame': Carolyn Spring Publishing, UK

Daniel Siegel (2003) 'Healing Trauma; Attachment, Mind, Body and Brain': Norton

Gershen Kaufman (1992) 'Shame: The Power of Caring': Schenkman Books

See also Thomas Hübl online and in print November 2020 on Communal Trauma

Neuroscience & Mindfulness

The Happy Buddha (2001) 'Happiness & How it Happens' & (2015) 'Mindfulness and Compassion': The Leaping Hare Press, UK & (2017) 'A Mindful Life' & (2019) 'A Mindfulness Teacher's Handbook': Suryacitta, UK

Sarah McLean (2017) 'The Power of Attention': Hay House USA Canada, UK, India, S. Africa, Australia

David R. Hamilton PhD (2015) 'I Heart Me, The Science of Self-Love': Hay House UK Ltd

Sue Gerhardt (2004) 'Why Love Matters': Routledge, UK, New York

Daniel Goleman & Richard J. Davidson (2017) 'The Science of Meditation': Penguin Life, UK

Jiddu Krishnamurti (1978) 'The Impossible Question': Penguin (and another 74 books!)

Daniel J. Siegel MD (2010) 'Mindsight': Oneworld Publications, UK (and plenty more by him)

David Brazier (1997) 'The Feeling Buddha: A Buddhist Psychology of Character, Adversity and Passion': Constable, London

Jon Kabat Zinn (1990) 'Full Catastrophe Living': Random House USA. (2005) 'Wherever You Go, There You Are' Little Brown Book Group, UK. (2018) 'Falling Awake' Piatkus

Patricia Collard (2014) 'The Little Book of Mindfulness' Octopus Publishing Group, UK. (2013) 'MBCT for Dummies': John Wiley and Sons Ltd, UK. (2015) 'The Mindfulness Bible': Godsfield Press

Dr's Mark Williams and Danny Penman (2011) 'Finding Peace in a Hectic World': Piatkus, UK

Vidyamala Birch and Danny Penman (2013) 'Mindfulness for Health': Little Brown Books, UK

Eckhart Tolle (2001) 'The Power of Now': Hodder & Stoughton, UK. (2005) 'A New Earth' Penguin, UK

I'd recommend anything by the prolific Thich Naht Hanh, Pema Chödrön and Charlotte Joko Beck who, like the fabulous Jack Kornfield, help us understand Buddhism as westerners.

Brené Brown is great on shame and vulnerability, Sharon Saltzberg, Kristin Neff, Paul Glibert and Tara Brach on self-compassion & compassion. As well as books, these beautiful human beings have many box sets, on-line teachings and meditations, as do Suryacitta/The Happy Buddha, David Hamilton, Daniel Siegel, Jon Kabat Zinn & Eckhart Tolle. They muster wisdom, resilience, courage, compassionate action & how to be happy!

Louis Cozolini and Alan Schore are also good on neuroscience.

Attachment Theory

Dr John Bowlby (1952) 'Maternal Care and Mental Health'/ 'Children and the Growth of Love' (reporting to the World Health Organisation) & (1998) 'A Secure Base' 'The Making and Breaking of affectional Bonds': Routledge USA, Canada

Daniel A. Hughes, Kim S. Golding & Julie Hudson (2019) 'Healing Relational Trauma with Attachment- based Interventions': Norton, New York (and other books by Dan Hughes.)

Susan Goldberg, Roy Muir & John Kerr (2013) 'Attachment Theory: Social, Developmental & Clinical Perspectives': Routledge, London, NY

Omri Gillath, Gery C. Karantzas and R. Chris Fraley (2016) 'Adult Attachment: A Concise Introduction to Theory and Research': Elsevier

Near-death Experiences

Ernest Becker (1973) 'The Denial of Death': Free Press, New York (Good overview of death anxiety).

Stanislav and Christina Grof (1991) 'Understanding and Living with Spiritual Emergency': Thorsons UK

Raymond A Moody (1975) 'Life After Life': Mockingbird Press, (2001) Harper-Collins, USA

Paul Perry & Melvin Morse (1990) 'Learning From Children's Near-death Experiences': Villiard Bks NY & (1991) Souvenir Press, London & (1992) 'Transformed by the Light': Piatkus P's Ltd, London

Kenneth Ring (1980) 'Life at Death: An Exploration of the Near-death Experience': Will. Morrow NY

Michael Sabom (1998) 'Light and Death': Zondervan, USA

Michael Sabom & Sharon Cooper (1999) 'Mindsight: Near-death and Out-of Body Experiences of the Blind.' Ed. Charles

Tart, The William James Centre for Consciousness Studies, USA

Susan J. Blackmore (1993) 'Dying to Live': Prometheus Books, UK

Peter Fenwick (1997) 'The Truth in the Light': Berkeley, New York

Robert W. Firestone (1994) 'Psychological Defences Against Death' In Neimeyer (1994) Ed. 'The Death Anxiety Handbook' Taylor and Frances, USA

Bruce Greyson (1996) 'The NDE as a Transpersonal Crisis'. In Sutton et al, 1996, 'The Textbook of Transpersonal Psychiatry and Psychology': Basic Books, New York

George G Ritchie (1998) 'Ordered to Return: My Life After Dying': Hampton Books, USA

Otto Rank (1936/45) 'Will Therapy': Knopf, USA

Existentialism

Irving D. Yalom (1991) 'Love's Executioner - and other Tales of Psychotherapy': Penguin UK & (1999) 'Momma and the Meaning of Life' Piatkus & (2008) 'Staring at the Sun': Piatkus, UK

Soren Kierkegaard (1844) 'The Concept of Dread': Tr. Walter Lowrie (1957) Princeton University Press, USA

David E. Cooper (1999) 'Existentialism': 2nd Edition

The Connectedness of Nature/Quantum Physics

Fritjof Capra (1975) 'The Tao of Physics': Shambala. (1982) 'The Turning Point,' (1996) 'The Web of Life,' (2003) 'The Hidden Connections': Flamingo, London

James Lovelock (1979) 'Gaia': Oxford University Press, UK

Rupert Sheldrake (1983) 'A New Science of Life': Paladin, London (& many more books)

Deepak Chopra (1989) 'Quantum Healing': Bantum Books, USA & Canada (& lots more).

Gestalt Therapy

Fredrick S. Perls (1969) 'Gestalt Therapy Verbatim': Bantam Books, USA

Margaret Selwyn (1994) 'The Awakening Year: An Exploration of Gestalt Therapy' Tudor, London

Arnold .R Beisser (1970) 'The Paradoxical Theory of Change' In J. Fagan I. Shepherd 'Gestalt Therapy Now' Science & Behaviour Books, USA

Petruska Clarkson (1989) 'Gestalt Counselling in Action': Sage, London, California, New Delhi

Richard Hycner (1991) 'Between Person and Person': Gestalt Journal Press, New York

Jennifer Mackewn (1997) 'Developing Gestalt Counselling': Sage, London

Gary M Yontef (1993) 'Awareness Dialogue and Process': Gestalt Journal Press Inc. USA

Joseph Zinker (1978) 'Creative Process in Gestalt Therapy' Vintage Books, USA

Random

Rutger Bregman (2020) 'Human Kind: A Hopeful History': Bloomsbury, London (first pub. Netherlands 2019)

Rosenthal, R. & Jacobson, L. (1992) 'Pygmalion in the classroom' : Expanded edition Irvington, New York

Robin Diangelo (2018) 'White Fragility; why it's so hard for white people to talk about racism': Penguin, Random House

Oriah Mountain Dreamer (1999) 'The Invitation': Thorsons, London

Stephen Levine (1984) 'Meetings at the Edge' & (1988) 'Who Dies? An Investigation of Conscious Living and Dying': Gateway Books, Bath, USA

Mary Oliver (2017) 'Devotions: The selected Poems of Mary Oliver': Penguin

Malcolm Gladwell (2000) 'The Tipping Point': Abacus, UK

Victor Frankl (2004) 'Man's Search for Meaning'; Rider

Richard Wilkinson & Kate Pickett (2009) 'The Spirit Level: Why Equality is Better for Everyone" Penguin

Martin Buber (1937/70) 'I and Thou': Tr. Walter Kaufman, Charles Scribner and Sons, New York

Andy Stein & Janet Wild (1999) 'Kidney failure Explained': Class Publishing, London

Robin Norwood (1985) 'Women Who Love Too Much': Arrow Books

James Hawes (2020) 'The Secret Lives of Men': Hug Publishing, UK

Richard Swift (2016) 'S.O.S Alternatives to Capitalism': New Internationalist Publications Ltd, UK

Naomi Klein (2007) 'The Shock Doctrine: The Rise of Disaster Capitalism': Knopf, Canada

Gary Zukav and Linda Francis (2002) 'The Heart of the Soul: Emotions and Awareness': Simon and Schuster Ltd UK

Dr Wendy Dryden & Daniel Constantinue (2004) 'Awareness Step by Step': Sheldon, London

Nancy Good 'Slay Your Own Dragons' (1990): Sheldon, London (re. self-fulfilling prophesy)

Neale Donald Walsch (1995) 'Conversations with God': Hodder and Stoughton, London

Alberto Villoldo (2000) 'Shaman Healer and Sage': Bantam Books

Richard Lawrence (2002) 'Little Book of Yin and Yang': Thorsons, London

Eric Fromm (1941) 'Escape from Freedom': Holt, Rinehart and Winston, New York

Elisabeth Kübler Ross (1970/93) 'On Death and Dying': Routledge, London & New York

Bronwen and Frans Stiene (2003) 'The Reiki Sourcebook': O-Books, USA, 2003

Abraham Maslow (1971) 'The Farthest Reaches of Human Nature': Penguin UK Canada USA Oz, NZ

Thomas Kühn (1970) 'The Structure of Scientific Revolutions': University of Chicago Press, USA

Sogyal Rinpoche (1992) 'The Tibetan Book of Living and Dying': Rider, London

Dorothy Rowe (1994) 'The Courage to Live': Harper-Collins, London

About Arthur Downs

Arthur Downs, one of five children, with Florie, Charlie, Hilda and Edith, was born in 1904 and grew up in a village on the edge of the moors in West Yorkshire. He left school at fourteen and went into the textile mills to learn the craft of weaving. He became the first aid man, dealing with horrific machine accidents etc.

A straight-talking man, Arthur would make his views heard directly but he didn't bear grudges and was an honest and trusted member of his community; the man who was called when somebody in the village got hurt. As an adult, after marrying Annie Sykes in 1941, he lived in a secluded house on a track running through a wood, where family lore has it that he saw a ghost. They then moved to a small terraced house in another mill-strewn village on the canal; they had a baby girl, my mum, in 1940.

Having to leave his toddler daughter, Arthur served in the Second World War as a sick-berth attendant in the Royal Navy, where he qualified as a State Registered Nurse. He often talked about his traumatic time working on Navy rescue ships where, if they also came under fire, they would have to abandon the men in the water being ripped apart by both sharks and, on retreating, their ship's own propeller. He decided to return to the mill when the war was over.

Arthur was never wealthy or famous but he was rich because he was able to value life. I was rich too because, according to my mum, he adored me but sadly died the day before my fifth birthday, aged 67.

Acknowledgements

First of all, my love and gratitude go to my mum, Betty, dad, William and brother, Jonathan for loving me for thirty years despite the high risk of being heart-broken. I'm very thankful to Mum and Dad for giving me a love of the outdoors, a fascination with people, a passion for drawing and reading, an interest in politics, space and spirituality and also great resilience and an ability to laugh out loud. They were brave in encouraging me to write my authentic story despite it revealing their vulnerabilities. I have a huge appreciation of my Big Bro' for talking for me and holding my hand as a toddler, teaching me to play football as a youngster, stand up for myself as a teenager and for walking alongside me through our family trauma as an adult. My thanks also go to my Auntie Mavis, Auntie Christine, Uncle Kenny and 'Auntie' Barbara for their love and encouragement and to my beautiful nephews for always keeping my heart warm. Dianne, Pan, Jaymes and Austyn, my brother's second family, keep me warm too, especially at Christmas.

As is clear from his poems, my loving Grandad, Arthur Downs gave me many of my values and perspectives on life. Growing up knowing that he wanted to have his poems published and write a book, that such a feat was possible in our world, sowed the seeds of this book. I'm so pleased it's a collaborative effort with him.

Despite what came later, I'm indebted to 'Sam' who was my rock through my initial hospital nightmare. He was my voice on occasions when I couldn't speak and his love, fabulous massages and hope for the future helped to keep me alive and sane.

Alfie-dog needs my next huge thanks for also helping to keep me alive by giving me fourteen years of laughter, comfort, safety, exercise, beautiful, uncomplicated companionship and great patience when I was writing and he wanted a walk!

I'm so grateful for the companionship of my amazing friends too, who have stuck by me and given me so much love, support, real conversation and laughter, again despite the existential fear which surrounds me. They also encouraged me to keep writing when shame was getting the better of me. I could go on for ages about them because they're amazing but let me just say I'm indebted to Kirsty Kay Kindness Jewell, Claire Patience Turner, Maria Determination Kelk, Carol Supercool Smith, Marie Music Queen Limb, Susie Tornado Turner, Frankie Floydie Musgrove, Gilly Comrade Brearley, Sarah Sparkly White, Jolly Jane Kirtley, Julie Canny Katsoris and Doreen Ocean-deep Farooq.

I'm very grateful to Kirsty, Maria, Claire, Marie and Gilly for reading early drafts of my book and coaxing me onward and to Julie for the many hours she spent critiquing with her giant brain and helping to get me down from "fifteen books in one" to about five! I have a beaming grin for Kirsty and Matt Super-brain Edge who helped me to come up with the title as we sat on their garden bench one sunny afternoon.

More fantastic women who have walked alongside me and kept me upright and happy for many years are Karen Downward Dog Jarvis, Sally Supersonic Hawes, Ged Outrageous Ransford-Kilpatrick, Mary Meditation Sherry and Lovely Lizzy Cross,

Trish Scrabble O'Shea, Valerie Hilarity Kirlew, Julie Pixie Davies, Jeanette Super-brain Caw, Judith Che Guevara Waring, Sharon Creativity Pollitt, Wendy Intuition Gabboto, Susanna Mega-brain Williams, Rachel Cocktail Hopkins, Sally Lucien Freud Smith, Tina Kitchen Sink Phillips, Jenny Chopin Carlisle, Johanna Earthy Branham, Charlotte Inspirational Thorpe and Judi Vibrancy, Second Mum Thorpe.

I'm very thankful too to Kay, Claire, Karen and also Jeremy Buddha Tatman and Matt for caring for Alfie when I couldn't and bringing us both great joy. I'm also grateful to Claire, alongside fellow nurse Teresa Whirlwind Whitlam, for giving me sound medical advice over the years and encouraging me into hospital when needs be! My Brothers in Arms, or more accurately Alms, include Jeremy (Jez), Matt and Jonny Wildman White, Dan The Man Pitt, Iain Viking Dimmock, Russel Observation Dicks, Simon Revolution Cross and Steve Improvisation Lewis. My thanks too to Cheryl On It Gretton for her many years of uplifting letters and her faith in my writing, my neighbour, Barbara Colton, for looking out for me and the generous, inspiring 'In Kind' gang – Anne-Marie, Kaye Brennan, Jeff Buck, Darran and Mandy Trute and Nina Dauben for our beautiful, uplifting 'Random Acts of Kindness' days. My deep thanks too to my talented friends Valerie and Linda Grenville – and the rest of the crew and cast – for working with me to put on our heart-warming pantomime and making me laugh till I cried many times. Both projects furthered my belief in our inner goodness and motivated me to keep writing.

My therapist, Peter Orlando-Fantini, has been my solid ground for two decades. Knowing that even my bloodiest, most heart-wrenching tales wouldn't floor him, was absolutely invaluable. His loving presence helped to calm and rewire my brain; he no longer jokes about buying me a rubber hammer to hit myself with because I'm no longer so self-berating. I'd never have written this book without him.

I'm very grateful too to my inspiring therapy and mindfulness supervisors, Sarah Mann Shaw and Karen Neil, two strong, assertive women with big hearts and an abundance of wisdom which has informed both my work and my life. Karen and the bubbly Patrizia Collard were my first mindfulness teachers and set me off on a wonderful journey. 'The Happy Buddha' (the pen name for Suryacitta), his wife Gaynor Quilter and their two sheep-dogs Jaya and Bankei all receive my deep gratitude for being such beautiful beings, excellent teachers and facilitators of brilliant, nurturing retreats.

I have appreciation and deep warmth for the lovely men and women who are a part of my monthly mindfulness groups and have the courage to reveal who they really are and also for every client I've seen over the years; all have taught me something and given my life deep meaning and joy.

My appreciation also goes to Jacqui Turrell who walked alongside my broken self through art school and to my MSc training and supervision groups, including Frank, my ex-husband. Frank's wise teaching and my second training group's acceptance of my existential torment and capacity for deep connection brought me through as maybe nothing else could.

Next I need, of course, to thank our amazing NHS, in particular my excellent, friendly dependable GP's Dr Liau, Dr Kaur, Dr Lonsdale, bubbly practice nurse, Patricia Jones and the hundreds of staff at Queen's Medical Centre and Nottingham City Hospital, whose incredibly hard work and emotional care have kept me alive and sane enough to have written this. I'm indebted to my medics and their teams; my haematologists Dr H, Dr Gerry Dolan, Dr Charlotte Grimley and Dr Gillian Swallow, my liver surgeons Professor Steven Ryder, Mr Adam Brooks, Mr Ian Beckingham, my fistula reversal surgeon Mr James Yates and all the fabulous staff of 'Room 6' for carrying out my many fistulaplastis. I'm also indebted to my gynaecologists Mr Lawrence Mascarenhas and Dr James Hopkisson and my renal doctors, the gentle, deceased Dr Cassidy, spirited Dr Catherine Byrne, giant-brained Dr T. and access specialist (and surgeon) Ms A. Knight. I've yet to get to know my new cardiologist, Dr Mathew but his sensitivity looks promising.

I'm also extremely grateful to the kind and hard-working doctors and nurses of the Intensive Care and High Dependency Units (from 1998-9 and 2006-7) in particular Karen, Lesley, Brian and David. What can I say about the precious ward of E17, 1998-9? The committed, sensitive staff were my adopted family for half a year and their open-hearted professionalism – from doctors and nurses to auxiliary and admin. staff definitely kept me alive and sane. I can't remember the names of my gynie wards or where I was cared for at the City Hospital back in 1999 – but thank you!

My great thanks go too to all the physiotherapists, phlebotomists, radiographers, porters, lab technicians, cooks, cleaners, laundry-workers, water-testers, maintenance workers, technicians, waste managers, tea and toast-makers, the volunteers and the hundreds of others involved in my amazing care.

My indebted thanks also go to the brilliant, humane staff of the City Hospital's Dialysis Unit (since 2011) and the City Hospitals' two fabulous renal wards. I have a huge grin for my kind, thorough, 'dialysis at home' nurse, Sharon Superwoman Caunt, who keeps me feeling safe and well.

I've never been there but I'd like to send my appreciation to the specialist blood bank in Sheffield which has provided me with gallons of antibody-matching blood and platelets and for the ambulance driver who blue-lighted some blood down the M1 for me in 1999. Words aren't really enough to express my immense gratitude to my blood donors; I wish I could personally thank and hug every one.

I'm thankful to Nottingham Adult Education for my first writing classes and to my first writing critique group, Jane, Linda and Raif. They normalised my pain and gave me friendship, positivity and gentleness when I'd just come out of hospital and felt extremely vulnerable. I'd also like to thank the fantastic authors Megan Taylor, Giselle Lieb, Ian Douglas and Ian Collinson, my second critique group from Nottingham Writing Studio; they also, over several years, gave sensitive feedback and taught me much about the art of laying down words.

I'd like to acknowledge the brave director Tom Shadyac; when Kirsty bought me his brilliant film-documentary 'I Am,' having recognised that it was saying much of what I was trying to, this encouraged me on, as has the courage of The Guardian journalist George Monbiot and comedian and social commentator Russell Brand who've had their heads above the parapet for years, daring to challenge the status quo. My gratitude too to all the teachers and writers who make up my bibliography and had the strength to speak their truth and, in many cases, show me 'the mindful way.'

I've been working with Georgie Hunter for the past two years in an attempt to get over my fear of releasing this book; her gentle wisdom was just what I needed. I'll always be grateful for the encouragement she gave me by reading my manuscript in a weekend. Positive encouragement has also flowed from Sue Cooper of MOMM (Moments of Mass Mindfulness – www.mommworld.org), the beautiful women of the MOMM Community and Shaun and Jamie Glossop of the Nottingham Mindfulness Group (www.nottinghammindfulnessgroup.co.uk). I've also been encouraged by Mark Curwood in the Broadway Cinema's café-bar; jokes about whether I'd ever finish my book spurred me on!

Finally I need to thank Sarah Houldcroft of Goldcrest books. When we first met and she talked about her three rescued dogs, only one of them with four legs, I knew she was the publisher for me! Her professionalism, skill, humour, support and patience (I made a lot of 'tweaks'!) have been lovely to experience.

About the author

Jayne is an ex-social worker, FE tutor, school counsellor and community worker. She's had a psychotherapy practice for twenty years and teaches mindfulness. This is her first book but she is in the process of publishing an illustrated mindfulness book for children and has more therapeutic animal stories up her sleeve...

Contact Jayne here:

Websites: www.mindfulnessnottingham.co.uk
www.creativeleaps.co.uk

Facebook: Jayne Pigford
Mindfulness Nottingham

Twitter: @PJaynie

Printed in Great Britain
by Amazon

54195477R00253